D0801547

A NEW LOOK AT ELEMENTARY MATHEMATICS

PRENTICE-HALL INTERNATIONAL, INC., *London*
PRENTICE-HALL OF AUSTRALIA, PTY., LTD., *Sydney*
PRENTICE-HALL OF CANADA, LTD., *Toronto*
PRENTICE-HALL OF INDIA (PRIVATE) LTD., *New Delhi*
PRENTICE-HALL OF JAPAN, INC., *Tokyo*

A NEW LOOK AT
ELEMENTARY MATHEMATICS

Benjamin E. Mitchell and Haskell Cohen

Department of Mathematics, Louisiana State University

500
MI

Prentice-Hall, Inc., Englewood Cliffs, N.J.

Current printing (last digit):
12   11   10   9   8   7   6   5   4   3

Library of Congress Catalog Card Number 65-12877

Printed in the United States of America
C-61506

This book is designed to furnish a subject matter course for prospective elementary school teachers of mathematics. At the same time we feel it provides a most suitable course for terminal students of mathematics, as well as an opportunity for current elementary teachers and others to review or learn modern trends in elementary mathematics.

While much of the material and the method of its presentation included in the book has been used prior to the organization of CUPM (The Committee on the Undergraduate Program in Mathematics) in 1959, there is substantial agreement here with the recommendations of CUPM.

The present volume is an outgrowth of the authors' experiences in teaching mathematics to prospective elementary school teachers as well as in designing and conducting courses for In-Service, Summer and Academic Year Institutes sponsored by the National Science Foundation.

The central theme of the text is the development of the number system and applications thereof. Starting with the most primitive notions, the student is shown the "whys" and "hows" up through chapters on statistics, probability, and linear programming. Sets and set notation are gradually introduced and *used* throughout the book. A chapter on geometry and one on the history of mathematics are included to help broaden the student in areas which are often neglected.

We have used a multilith edition of this text and find there is ample material for nine semester hours of work. We strongly recommend that the reader (or

preface

teacher) proceed at a leisurely pace insofar as the number of pages that are covered. The idea is to delve with some depth into each topic—to re-prove theorems, to invent and then work additional exercises, etc.—not to skim rather hurriedly over a large number of pages.

The term "modern mathematics" is used (and misused) in a variety of ways, but perhaps it is best used to refer to those items which tend to make school mathematics more mathematical in the sense that mathematicians use the word "mathematical." We are concerned with modern mathematics in this sense. In this connection it is interesting to note that along with many topics usually thought of as "new" mathematics we have included exercises from a text published before 1900!

Selected exercises are from *An Advanced Arithmetic* by J. W. Nicholson copyrighted in 1889 by F. F. Hansell & Brothers, New Orleans. Most of these are marked with a dagger. Certain problems seem to be ageless and continue to interest through the years. The wording of some of these in this book has been taken from *Number Stories of Long Ago* by David Eugene Smith, 1919, Ginn & Company, Boston. This is now printed by the National Council of Teachers of Mathematics.

We are indebted to Professor L. I. Wade, Chairman of the Department of Mathematics at Louisiana State University for suggesting the preparation of the book, encouragement, and numerous ideas. We also appreciate suggestions for improvement made by various colleagues and students.

contents

A NEW LOOK AT ELEMENTARY MATHEMATICS

I

I.I. NUMBER SYSTEMS

The origin of number systems is clouded in the dim mists of antiquity; we can never be certain as to how they actually developed. However, since the development of some number system was essential for the progress of civilization, many number systems have evolved through the ages. We will draw on the accumulated knowledge of the past to give an imaginative version of how our present number system might have evolved. It will be a heuristic presentation and will endeavor to make certain formal rules and processes reasonable—at least from an intuitive viewpoint. Historically, the notion of counting as a formal procedure was probably mankind's first experience with numbers. Hence, we will consider counting first.

One must distinguish between the terms "number" and "numeral." A *number* is an abstract concept which we will define later. A *numeral* is a symbol which represents a number, i.e., a numeral is the name of a number. No one has ever seen a number, and no one ever will. However, nearly everyone has seen a numeral.

Numbers exist only in that wonderful domain called the mind of man; hence, one cannot exhibit a number but can only refer to numbers by means of symbols. In general, these symbols will be numerals. Hence, a numeral in one case will refer to a number and in another case will not. In this book single quotes will be used with a numeral when it does not refer to a number. For example (although here we are using notation that we have not yet

the cardinal numbers

developed), we would say that *12 is an even integer but '12' contains two digits.* Logicians customarily use this clarifying notation in their work. Thus, *Smith is a student in this class,* or *'Smith' contains five letters.* In the first sentence "Smith" refers to a person; in the second sentence "Smith" refers to a word.

1.2. COUNTING

Long ago some thoughtful forebear of ours whose flock (of sheep perhaps) had grown rather large wondered how he could be certain that the herdsmen returned all of his flock each night. He decided on a mark or token for each member of the flock so that he would have a mark for each sheep and a sheep for each mark. He might have used a short, straight line for each sheep (as is sometimes used today in "tallying" the votes for a given candidate); he might have carved a notch for each sheep on a long stick (as some western gunmen reputedly did on their pistol butts); or he might have formed a pile of stones by putting down one stone for each sheep.

Each of these methods illustrates the simple but important notion of a one-to-one (usually written 1–1) correspondence between two sets of objects. For example, we can pair the sheep with the stones so that there is one (and only one) sheep for each stone and one (and only one) stone for each sheep. This "pairing" constitutes a 1–1 correspondence between the set of sheep and the set of stones.

For the purpose of oral and written language it is desirable to have words and symbols for the number of sheep in the different flocks. Possible symbols for the number of sheep in a flock consisting of a ram, ewe, and lamb might be ///, ⌒⌒⌒, and $\circ^\circ_\circ$. These symbols (and probably all of the other early symbols also) have a 1–1 correspondence between portions of the symbols and the sheep in the flock. This latter symbol (with the addition of connecting lines $\circ\!\!-\!\!\circ_\circ$) was used by the Chinese over 4000 years ago. The meaning of the symbol $\circ\!\!-\!\!\circ_\circ$ is as clear to us as it was to the Chinese of olden times because of the 1–1 correspondence involved. We will utilize this symbol in the next section.

Let us consider the tally mark ///. Our thoughtful forebear might have tallied on his fingers until he ran out of fingers. Then he would make a mark in the sand /. Then he would tally on his fingers once more. When he ran out of fingers again, he would make another mark in the sand which would now look like //. If our thoughtful forebear had a large flock (and who among us does not want rich ancestors?) the marks in the sand might look like /////////////.

Eventually our thoughtful forebear, who besides being loaded with sheep could be clever when he had to, hit upon the following ingenious scheme.

Since each mark in the sand represented a double handful of sheep, he could carry on this idea by replacing each double handful of tally marks by a "kingsized" tally mark. Thus instead of the marks above we would have $/||||$. This idea can be generalized so that we can have super king-sized tallies and even the large, economy model, viz.

$$/|/|/|/|||$$

Our thoughtful forebear now has a "magic rule" to apply: Each double handful of symbols is replaced by a single, new symbol. It doesn't even matter whether we go from left to right or from right to left or both ways; however, it is easier to read if we go in one direction as in the example.

Notice that this system resembles the system we use today with our money. One starts to count pennies. When he reaches 10 pennies, he replaces them with a dime; when he reaches 10 dimes, he replaces them with a dollar. Instead of lines in the sand we make marks on paper, and a bill from the gas company for $3.57 is a request for seven pennies, five double handfuls of pennies, and three double handfuls of double handfuls of pennies. Note that the gas company goes from right to left.

For simple applications, arithmetic without numbers or numerals is possible. For instance housewife Mary, with husband Bill, and children Susie, Dick, and John might check the plates on the dinner table by "naming" them "Bill," "Susie," "Dick," "John," and "me." Then she would know when she had enough, but not too many plates to serve the family although she has not counted them, nor has she used any numbers.

EXERCISES

1. How does one determine whether a sweater is completely buttoned without counting?

2. How could one determine whether a carton of eggs contains a dozen eggs without counting the eggs?

3. How can you say that there are twice as many girls as boys in the room without using numbers?

4. How can you say there is *one* more person in the room than chairs without using numbers? (The word "a" is frequently used as an equivalent to "one" and so could not be used here in this sense.)

Discuss the meaning of the word "Joe" in the following two sentences.

5. Joe is married to Jane.

6. Joe has an O in the middle.

Show why the following sentences are ambiguous.

7. Joe saw a deer fly.

8. Joe saw a high school building.

9. Joe saw an old cow hide.

10. The telephone company does not need telephone poles any longer.

1.3. CARDINAL NUMBERS

The notion of counting that we have introduced in the last section needs a more careful, logical development. In Section 1.2 we assumed too much without justification and we did not state our assumptions. Our thoughtful forebear, although an ingenious individual, was probably too busy counting sheep to worry about a logical development of the number system, but modern mathematicians have managed to take care of most of the difficulties.

For a written language it is desirable, as stated earlier, to have symbols for the number of sheep in the different flocks. We saw that possible symbols for a flock of sheep consisting of a ram, a ewe, and a lamb, would be $///$, ᷍, and $\begin{smallmatrix} & O & \\ O & & O \end{smallmatrix}$. Let us focus our attention on the symbol $\begin{smallmatrix} & O & \\ O & & O \end{smallmatrix}$. In addition to the previously mentioned flock of sheep this symbol could also stand for any of the following sets

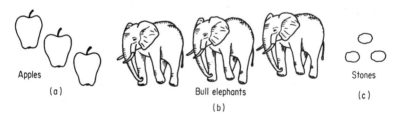

Apples   Bull elephants   Stones
(a)   (b)   (c)

At first we might think that apples, stones, and bull elephants have no common property, but in fact apples and bull elephants are composed of cells and each has grown to its present size through the process of cellular division. But stones, you might say, are inanimate objects. True, but stones, apples, and bull elephants are built up of atoms and molecules with protons and neutrons and all other "tons" and "trons" whizzing around. Thus these sets have a common property. The symbol $\begin{smallmatrix} & O & \\ O & & O \end{smallmatrix}$ could also stand for a set (d) consisting of the notion of love, the notion of beauty, and the notion of devotion.[1] Or we might have $_o{}^o{}_o$ standing for the set (e) whose members are the English language, the French language, and the German language. Sets (a), (b), (c), (d), and (e) no longer have the common property of their elements being material objects, but they still have a common property—i.e., each can be put into a 1–1 correspondence with the circles in the symbol $_o{}^o{}_o$. This common property also implies that each of these sets can be put into a 1–1 correspondence with any of the other sets. We are using here the fact that two sets each of which may be put into 1–1 correspondence with a third set may be put into 1–1 correspondence with each other. The following diagram illustrates this

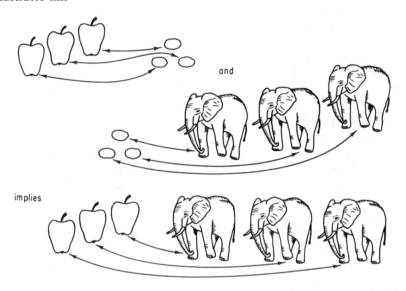

and

implies

Let us consider the collection which we temporarily name A and which consists of all the sets that can be put into a 1–1 correspondence with the circles in the symbol $_o{}^o{}_o$. Then, since any set in A can be put into a 1–1 correspondence with any other set in A, any set in A can be used to define A. For example, if we look at the collection of all sets which can be put into a 1–1 correspondence with the set (b) above, we get A again. This is because any set which can be put into 1–1 correspondence with (b) can be put into a 1–1 correspondence with $_o{}^o{}_o$ and conversely, any set which can be put into a 1–1 correspondence with $_o{}^o{}_o$ can be put into a 1–1 correspondence with (b). This common property of all elements of A is what we define to be the cardinal number "three." The notion of "threeness" should be clearer now. When we count on our fingers, "one, two, three," we are pointing out a 1–1 correspondence between a set of fingers and the circles in the symbol $_o{}^o{}_o$.

[1] It might be difficult to define these concepts carefully, since, e.g., each of us has his own idea of what constitutes beauty.

At one stage in the development of mankind the "three" in the phrase "three cats" was regarded as different from the "three" in "three sheep." This is something that does not concern us because we are accustomed to thinking of the cardinal number "three" as merely the "quantity" of elements in a set, and not dependent on the type of elements in the set. It is determined by 1–1 correspondences. By its very nature, in order to be independent of cats and sheep and other things, the cardinal number "three" must be abstract. At the risk of being repetitious we say once again—the concept of number is an abstraction; numbers were conceived by the mind of man and exist only in the mind of man.

Suppose we are given a particular set b. Let A now denote the collection of all sets which can be placed into 1–1 correspondence with b. In order to belong to A a set c must satisfy the defining property of A, i.e., it must be possible to put c into 1–1 correspondence with b. All sets which belong to A share this property in common. This common property of all sets in A is called a *cardinal number*. Since any set in A determines A, we will not lose any generality by restricting attention to a particular set in A—say, a pile of stones. Hereafter, for the sake of simplicity and concreteness we will use piles of stones as representatives of cardinal numbers. Thus all "possible" piles of stones represent all cardinal numbers. (This restricts our cardinal numbers to so-called "finite" cardinals. However, it is possible to extend the definition.) Two piles of stones in 1–1 correspondence with each other represent the same cardinal number. The symbol $_o{}^o_o$ is obviously not a pile of stones, but this book is already going to be quite a weighty tome so we shall use the symbol to represent the pile of stones which is in 1–1 correspondence with the circles in the symbol. Various symbols may be used to represent cardinal numbers. We shall, for the present, use these circles, but we shall develop a better notation later. The symbol $^o_o{}^o_o$, of course, represents the pile of stones in 1–1 correspondence with the circles in it.

EXERCISES

1. Let A be the set of all sets which can be put into 1–1 correspondence with the set $\{_o{}^o_o\}$. Familiarize yourself with the defining property of A by taking several sets and determining whether or not they belong to A.

2. Show that if a set of apples is in 1–1 correspondence with a given set of stones and a set of bull elephants is in 1–1 correspondence with the same set of stones, then the set of apples is in 1–1 correspondence with the set of bull elephants.

3. Find a set which is in 1–1 correspondence with the set $\{_o{}^o_o\}$. Are there other 1–1 correspondences between these two sets besides the one you gave? How many?

4. Can you give a property, distinct from the defining property, which all sets in A possess in common?

1.4. ADDITION OF CARDINAL NUMBERS

We are now ready to consider the set of all cardinal numbers and to define on it the binary operation of addition. A *binary operation* on the set of cardinal numbers is a rule which associates with any pair of cardinal numbers a unique third cardinal number; or (by our convention in the preceding section) a rule which associates with any two given piles of stones a unique third pile of stones. Binary means the operation is defined on pairs of numbers only—no more and no less. The binary operation of addition on these cardinal numbers is defined as follows: If A and B are cardinal numbers then the sum $C = A + B$ is defined as the cardinal number which has as a representation the pile of stones obtained by placing pile a on pile b; where a is a pile of stones representing A, and b is a pile of stones representing B.

Note that if a' is another pile of stones representing A, and b' is another pile of stones representing B; then a' is in 1–1 correspondence with a, and b' is in 1–1 correspondence with b. Therefore the pile obtained by placing a' on b' is in 1–1 correspondence with the pile obtained by placing a on b. Thus this procedure leads to a unique cardinal number C.

We read $A + B$ as "A plus B" and may think of it as being obtained by adding A to B.

Hereafter we deal mainly with the piles of stones which are representations of cardinal numbers. With this in mind, we have the following: *To add two given piles of stones place the first pile of stones upon the second.* We are assuming that, when we are given two piles of stones, we are given a first pile and a second pile. The notation for addition will be the sign "$+$." In terms of the symbols we are presently using, this binary operation of addition may be illustrated by the following example

$$\overset{\circ}{\underset{\circ\ \circ}{\circ}}\ \circ\ +\ \overset{\circ\ \circ}{\underset{\circ\ \circ}{\circ}}\ =\ \overset{\circ}{\underset{\circ\ \circ}{\circ\ \circ}}\ \circ\ =\ \overset{\circ\circ\circ\circ}{\circ\circ\circ\circ}$$

(The first "$=$" is by definition of "$+$" and the second "$=$" comes from the fact that the last two piles of stones can be put into a 1–1 correspondence. Note also that the notation $\overset{\circ}{\underset{\circ\ \circ}{\circ}}\ \circ\ +\ \overset{\circ\ \circ}{\underset{\circ\ \circ}{\circ}}$ indicates that $\overset{\circ}{\underset{\circ\ \circ}{\circ}}\ \circ$ is the first pile and that $\overset{\circ\ \circ}{\underset{\circ\ \circ}{\circ}}$ is the second pile.) From the fact that

$$\overset{\circ}{\underset{\circ\ \circ}{\circ}}\ \circ\ +\ \overset{\circ\ \circ}{\underset{\circ\ \circ}{\circ}}\ =\ \overset{\circ}{\underset{\circ\ \circ}{\circ\ \circ}}\ \circ\ =\ \overset{\circ\circ\circ\circ}{\circ\circ\circ\circ}\quad \text{and} \quad \overset{\circ\ \circ}{\underset{\circ\ \circ}{\circ}}\ +\ \overset{\circ\ \circ}{\underset{\circ\ \circ}{\circ}}\ =\ \overset{\circ\ \circ}{\underset{\circ\ \circ}{\circ}}\ =\ \overset{\circ\circ\circ\circ}{\circ\circ\circ\circ}$$

we get $\begin{smallmatrix}&o\\o&\\&o\end{smallmatrix} + \begin{smallmatrix}o&o\\&o\\o&o\end{smallmatrix} = \begin{smallmatrix}o&o\\&o\\o&o\end{smallmatrix} + \begin{smallmatrix}&o\\o&\\&o\end{smallmatrix}$. This result does not come as a great surprise to us for we have long been familiar with it. It was perplexing to most of us, though, when we first noted this property.

How can you give a reasonable answer to a child who asks, " why is five plus three equal to three plus five?" The answer "because both are equal to eight" would be highly unsatisfactory. The child knows that both are equal to eight. What he is probably trying to say is that for every pair of numbers "*a*" and "*b*" that he has tried, $a + b$ and $b + a$ give the same results. He would like to know if this will always be the case and, if so, why. A satisfactory answer can be given in terms of piles of stones, which is one reason we are considering piles of stones here. More formally, we have the *commutative law of addition for cardinal numbers;* i.e., *if a and b are cardinal numbers then $a + b = b + a$.* Observe that *b* is not necessarily distinct from *a*. To see the validity of the commutative law we note that whether we put the first pile of stones upon the second or the second pile of stones upon the first, the resulting piles of stones in either case consist of precisely the same stones, and hence can be put into 1–1 correspondence, and so by our definition have the same cardinal number. The commutative law of addition states that *a* added to *b* gives the same sum as *b* added to *a*. This result is by no means as trivial as we might first think. Certainly "adding" sulphuric acid to water does not give the same result as "adding" water to sulphuric acid. "Putting on" our socks first and then our shoes does not give the same result as "putting on" our shoes first and then our socks. While these are somewhat artificial examples of noncommutative processes, there are many genuine arithmetic examples and the interested reader is referred to the exercises in Section 3.1. There is no general universal law which says that all operations are commutative, therefore, we must verify in each particular case whether or not a given kind of operation is commutative.

Since our operation of addition is a binary operation we can add only two numbers at a time. It follows then that any sum of more than two numbers is at the moment undefined and hence meaningless. For example, $\begin{smallmatrix}&o\\o&\\&o\end{smallmatrix} + \begin{smallmatrix}o&o\\&o\\o&o\end{smallmatrix}$ $+ \begin{smallmatrix}o&o\\&o\\o&o\end{smallmatrix}$ is undefined. We could introduce grouping symbols, thus, $\left(\begin{smallmatrix}&o\\o&\\&o\end{smallmatrix} + \begin{smallmatrix}o&o\\&o\\o&o\end{smallmatrix}\right)$ $+ \begin{smallmatrix}o&o\\&o\\o&o\end{smallmatrix}$, i.e., we first add $\begin{smallmatrix}&o\\o&\\&o\end{smallmatrix}$ to $\begin{smallmatrix}o&o\\&o\\o&o\end{smallmatrix}$ and then add the result to $\begin{smallmatrix}o&o\\&o\\o&o\end{smallmatrix}$. On the other hand we could introduce grouping symbols, thus, $\begin{smallmatrix}&o\\o&\\&o\end{smallmatrix} + \left(\begin{smallmatrix}o&o\\o&o\\&o\end{smallmatrix} + \begin{smallmatrix}o&o\\&o\\o&o\end{smallmatrix}\right)$; i.e., we add $\begin{smallmatrix}&o\\o&\\&o\end{smallmatrix}$ to the result of adding $\begin{smallmatrix}o&o\\o&o\end{smallmatrix}$ to $\begin{smallmatrix}o&o\\&o\\o&o\end{smallmatrix}$. It happens in this case that each gives the same final result, $\begin{smallmatrix}o&o&o&o&o&o\\o&o&o&o&o&o\end{smallmatrix}$. Again this is a special case of a more general result. *If a, b, and c are cardinal numbers, then $(a + b) + c = a + (b + c)$, (the associative law of addition for cardinal numbers).* To see that this law is true we note that $(a + b) + c$ directs us to place pile *a* on pile *b* and then to place the resulting pile on pile *c*; while $a + (b + c)$ directs us to place pile b on pile c and then to place pile a on this result. Since each of these directions result in forming a single pile of stones consisting of the same stones, there is an obvious 1–1 correspondence between the two piles so that the answer is the same cardinal number. We understand, of course, that the arrangement of the stones in a pile is unimportant, and that any two piles which are in a 1–1 correspondence represent the same cardinal number. The notation $a = b$ means "a" and "b" are symbols which represent the same object. When we write ooo $=$ 8 $=$ 8 we are asserting that the symbols "ooo," "8," and "8" all represent the same cardinal number, although the symbols are clearly distinguishable and hence are different numerals (see Section 1.1).

If a, b, and c are cardinal numbers, we define $a + b + c$ to mean either $a + (b + c)$ or $(a + b) + c$. This gives a unique meaning to $a + b + c$ by virtue of the associative law.

EXERCISES

1. In how many ways can grouping symbols be introduced in $a + b + c + d$ so that the result would be meaningful for the binary operation of addition? Two possibilities would be $(a + b) + (c + d)$ and $a + [(b + c) + d]$. Note that $(b + a) + (c + d)$ would not be acceptable because the order has been changed.

2. Do you think each possible grouping in Exercise 1 would give the same sum? Why?

3. What does $\left(\substack{\circ \\ \circ \, \circ} + \substack{\circ \, \circ \\ \circ \, \circ}\right) + \substack{\circ \, \circ \\ \circ \\ \circ \, \circ}$ "direct" us to do?

4. What does $\substack{\circ \\ \circ \, \circ} + \left(\substack{\circ \, \circ \\ \circ \, \circ} + \substack{\circ \, \circ \\ \circ \\ \circ \, \circ}\right)$ "direct" us to do?

5. What are some advantages of the numerals we are using at present?

6. What are some disadvantages of the numerals we are using at present?

1.5. MULTIPLICATION OF CARDINAL NUMBERS

We have seen that when three cardinal numbers are added, the answer is the same no matter how they are associated; hence, we may omit the grouping symbols. (Exercise 1 in the previous set of exercises indicated that a similar property is true for four numbers.) It can be shown that when we are adding any number of cardinal numbers the result will be the same regardless of the way that they are associated. Therefore, with this in mind we shall write $a + b + c + d$ instead of something like $[(a + b) + c] + d$.

We now define a second binary operation on the set of cardinal numbers, the operation called *multiplication*. If A and B are cardinal numbers, they determine a unique third cardinal number C called the product of A and B (denoted by $A \times B$, $A \cdot B$, or simply AB) as follows. The product of A and B is defined to be the sum of "A" "B's", i.e.,

$$A \cdot B = \underbrace{B + B + \cdots + B}_{\text{"}A\text{" numbers}}$$

If a is a pile of stones representing A, and b is a pile of stones representing B, then (assuming of course, that we have an adequate supply of stones) we can think of $A \cdot B$ as being represented by $a \cdot b$ where $a \cdot b$ is a rectangular array of stones consisting of A piles of B stones each. Or we can think of getting a representative for $A \cdot B$ by replacing each stone in a by a pile of B stones. Thus if $a = \circ\,\circ$ and $b = {}_\circ{}^\circ{}_\circ$, then $a \cdot b = {}_\circ{}^\circ{}_\circ\,{}_\circ{}^\circ{}_\circ$. More generally for any cardinal numbers A, B

$$a \cdot b = A \left\{ \begin{array}{cccc} \overbrace{}^{B} \\ \circ \quad \circ \quad \cdots \quad \circ \\ \circ \quad \circ \quad \cdots \quad \circ \\ \vdots \\ \vdots \\ \vdots \\ \circ \quad \circ \quad \cdots \quad \circ \end{array} \right.$$

while

$$b \cdot a = B \left\{ \begin{array}{cccc} \overbrace{}^{A} \\ \circ \quad \circ \quad \cdots \quad \circ \\ \circ \quad \circ \quad \cdots \quad \circ \\ \vdots \\ \vdots \\ \vdots \\ \circ \quad \circ \quad \cdots \quad \circ \end{array} \right.$$

We have previously observed that addition is commutative. The question naturally arises now as to whether or not multiplication is commutative. What is your answer to this question? Can you prove your answer? Note that we may associate the stones in the first column of $a \cdot b$ with those of the first row of $b \cdot a$, those of the second column of $a \cdot b$ with those of the second row of $b \cdot a$, etc., until finally the stones of the bth column of $a \cdot b$ are associated with those of the bth row of $b \cdot a$. Since each column of $a \cdot b$ and each row of $b \cdot a$ have exactly a stones, it is clear that the correspondence thus indicated can be made in a 1–1 fashion. Since this 1–1 correspondence exists it follows that $a \cdot b = b \cdot a$ and we have verified the *commutative law for multiplication of cardinal numbers: If A and B are cardinal numbers then $A \cdot B = B \cdot A$.*

Hereafter we deal mainly with the piles of stones which are representations of cardinal numbers and agree to identify a with A. *The associative law of multiplication for cardinal numbers states that if a, b, and c are cardinal numbers then $a \cdot (b \cdot c) = (a \cdot b) \cdot c$.*

To verify this law, note again that performing the operation $a \cdot b$ replaces each stone in a by a pile of b stones. Consider the array below.

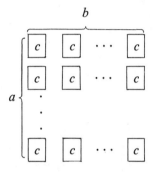

This array consists of a rows and b columns of rectangles with c stones in each rectangle. We observe that we have $a \cdot b$ rectangles where each rectangle contains c stones; i.e., we may think of starting with $a \cdot b$ stones and then replacing each stone by a pile of c stones. But this is precisely the product $(a \cdot b) \cdot c$. On the other hand each row consists of b piles of c stones each, i.e., of $b \cdot c$ stones. But this is repeated "a" times since there are a rows, which gives $a \cdot (b \cdot c)$. Hence $a \cdot (b \cdot c) = (a \cdot b) \cdot c$.

In particular we may show that $(\text{o o}) \cdot (\substack{\text{o} \\ \text{o} \text{ o}} \cdot \substack{\text{o o} \\ \text{o o}}) = (\text{o o} \cdot \substack{\text{o} \\ \text{o} \text{ o}}) \cdot \substack{\text{o o} \\ \text{o o}}$ by means of the array

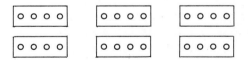

We have seen that both addition and multiplication have commutative and associative laws. There is, moreover, a law which connects the two operations. This is known as *the distributive law of multiplication with respect to addition and states that if a, b, and c are cardinal numbers, then $a \cdot (b + c) = (a \cdot b) + (a \cdot c)$.* For example, $\text{o o} \cdot (\substack{\text{o} \\ \text{o} \text{ o}} + \substack{\text{o o} \\ \text{o o}}) = (\text{o o} \cdot \substack{\text{o} \\ \text{o} \text{ o}}) + (\text{o o} \cdot \substack{\text{o o} \\ \text{o o}})$.

To verify this rule, consider the arrays below

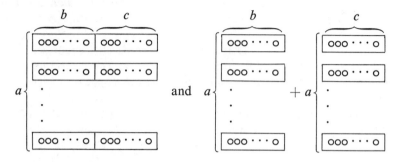

and recall that

$$\underbrace{\boxed{\text{ooo} \cdots \text{o}}}_{b} + \underbrace{\boxed{\text{ooo} \cdots \text{o}}}_{c} = \boxed{\underbrace{\text{ooo} \cdots \text{o}}_{b} \mid \underbrace{\text{ooo} \cdots \text{o}}_{c}}$$

In particular we may show that $\text{o o} \cdot \left(\begin{smallmatrix}\text{o}\\\text{o}\ \text{o}\end{smallmatrix} + \begin{smallmatrix}\text{o o}\\\text{o o}\end{smallmatrix}\right) = \left(\text{o o} \cdot \begin{smallmatrix}\text{o}\\\text{o}\ \text{o}\end{smallmatrix}\right) + \left(\text{o o} \cdot \begin{smallmatrix}\text{o o}\\\text{o o}\end{smallmatrix}\right)$ by means of the arrays

$$\boxed{\text{o o o} \mid \text{o o o o}} \quad = \quad \boxed{\text{o o o}} \quad + \quad \boxed{\text{o o o o}}$$

$$\boxed{\text{o o o} \mid \text{o o o o}} \qquad \boxed{\text{o o o}} \qquad \boxed{\text{o o o o}}$$

Let us insert a note of caution. It is very easy to feel that the commutative and associative laws are so well known (after all we've been using them since we first started arithmetic in elementary school) that they need hardly be mentioned at this stage, let alone belabored as much as we have done. We hasten, however, to point out that a careful understanding of these laws is essential to comprehending arithmetic processes as well as more advanced mathematics. We therefore urge the student not to confuse a superficial recollection that "you get the same answer no matter what order you do things in" with the precise statement of these laws and an understanding of them.

EXERCISES

1. Using rectangular arrays of stones as in the proof of the commutative law of multiplication, show that $\text{o o} \times \begin{smallmatrix}\text{o}\\\text{o}\ \text{o}\end{smallmatrix} = \begin{smallmatrix}\text{o}\\\text{o}\ \text{o}\end{smallmatrix} \times \text{o o}$.

2. Using rectangular arrays of stones as in the proof of the associative law of multiplication, show that (o o × $_o{}^o{}_o$) × $_o^{o\ o}{}_o$ = o o × ($_o{}^o{}_o$ × $_o^{o\ o}{}_o$).

3. Using rectangular arrays of stones as in the proof of the distributive law, show that o o × ($_o{}^o{}_o$ + $_o^{o\ o}{}_o$) = (o o × $_o{}^o{}_o$) + (o o × $_o^{o\ o}{}_o$).

4. Prove that if a, b, c are cardinal numbers, then $(b + c) \cdot a = (b \cdot a) + (c \cdot a)$, (i.e., the distributive law is valid on both sides).

1.6. POSITIONAL NOTATION

The notation for cardinal numbers that we have been using has the advantage of clarity. It can be understood by literate peoples of all nations. But it has the great disadvantage of becoming extremely cumbersome when the numbers become large. Hence we would like to develop a better system of notation. The reader may have wondered why we have tarried so long in developing the conventional notation. The explanation is that we need the operations of addition and multiplication in order to do so.

Let us suppose that an astute individual with the knowledge now at our disposal wishes to develop a better system of notation for the cardinal numbers. He must invent a new symbol for each cardinal number. We list our old symbols and then below them the new symbols he devises

o, o o, $_o{}^o{}_o$, $_o^{o\ o}{}_o$, . . .

$\mathbf{I}$, $\perp$, $\divideontimes$, $\daleth$, . . .   (read el, tee, star, eff, respectively)

The particular symbols used here are not intrinsically important—any other simple symbols would serve as well.

Our astute individual now realizes that he will have an infinite number of new symbols to create, a task which would be difficult even for one of his astuteness. He wisely decides to create one more new symbol and then to obtain all other symbols from these given ones plus the fact that, in the order he has arranged them, each cardinal number is obtained from the preceding by adding one stone to the pile. Thus $\mathbf{I} + \mathbf{I} = \perp$, $\perp + \mathbf{I} = \divideontimes$, and $\divideontimes + \mathbf{I} = \daleth$. For $_o^{o\ o}{}_o$ $= \daleth + \mathbf{I}$ he decides on the symbol $\Box$ (read flag).

Sometimes the symbol $\Box$ (or something like it) is assigned to the cardinal number $_{ooooo}^{ooooo}$ with the explanation that this corresponds to the number of fingers we have. If this explanation is correct, then the choice we have made would correspond to that of a one-armed race. Hence, at times, we might refer to the *one-handed system* or the *two-handed system*. However, we have a special reason for not taking the conventional choice for $\Box$. Our choice makes it much easier for a student to distinguish between a memorized knowledge of certain results and an understanding of how one arrives at these results.

Continuing our process yields succeeding symbols as follows

$$o, \; oo, \; \begin{smallmatrix}o\\o\;o\end{smallmatrix}, \; \begin{smallmatrix}oo\\oo\end{smallmatrix}, \; \begin{smallmatrix}o\;o\\o\;o\\o\;o\end{smallmatrix}, \; \begin{smallmatrix}ooo\\ooo\end{smallmatrix}, \; \begin{smallmatrix}ooo\\ooo\end{smallmatrix}, \; \begin{smallmatrix}oooo\\oooo\end{smallmatrix}, \; \begin{smallmatrix}oooo\\oooo\end{smallmatrix}, \; \begin{smallmatrix}ooooo\\ooooo\end{smallmatrix}, \dots$$

$$\mathsf{I}, \; \perp, \; \ast, \; \exists, \; \mathsf{P}, \; \mathsf{P} + \mathsf{I}, \; \mathsf{P} + \perp, \; \mathsf{P} + \ast, \; \mathsf{P} + \exists, \; \mathsf{P} + \mathsf{P}, \dots$$

Note that for any cardinal number a we have $\mathsf{I} \cdot a = a \cdot \mathsf{I} = a$. For if we take either a piles of I stones each or I piles of a stones, we obtain a pile of a stones. So that, in particular we have $\mathsf{P} = \mathsf{I} \cdot \mathsf{P}$. Hence the symbol

$$\begin{aligned} \mathsf{P} + \mathsf{P} &= (\mathsf{I} \cdot \mathsf{P}) + (\mathsf{I} \cdot \mathsf{P}) \\ &= (\mathsf{I} + \mathsf{I}) \cdot \mathsf{P} \\ &= \perp \cdot \mathsf{P} \end{aligned}$$

by the distributive law.

Let us now write a list of the first few cardinal numbers in our new notation

$$\mathsf{I}, \perp, \ast, \exists, \mathsf{P}, \mathsf{P} + \mathsf{I}, \mathsf{P} + \perp, \mathsf{P} + \ast, \mathsf{P} + \exists, \perp \cdot \mathsf{P}, (\perp \cdot \mathsf{P}) + \mathsf{I},$$
$$(\perp \cdot \mathsf{P}) + \perp, (\perp \cdot \mathsf{P}) + \ast, (\perp \cdot \mathsf{P}) + \exists, \ast \cdot \mathsf{P}, \dots$$

Because of the associative laws for addition and multiplication we may, as we have observed, omit grouping symbols in sums and in products without ambiguity. However, this does not apply to expressions involving both sums and products. Since $(\perp \cdot \mathsf{P}) + \mathsf{I}$ and $\perp \cdot (\mathsf{P} + \mathsf{I})$ are different numbers, then the meaning of $\perp \cdot \mathsf{P} + \mathsf{I}$ is not clear. We use the symbol '$(\perp \cdot \mathsf{P}) + \mathsf{I}$' more often than we use the symbol '$\perp \cdot (\mathsf{P} + \mathsf{I})$'. Hence, to make matters easier for ourselves, we adopt the convention that $\perp \cdot \mathsf{P} + \mathsf{I}$ will denote the number $(\perp \cdot \mathsf{P}) + \mathsf{I}$. Analogously $\perp \cdot (\mathsf{P} \cdot \mathsf{P}) + \exists \cdot \mathsf{P} + \ast$, e.g., will denote the number $[\perp \cdot (\mathsf{P} \cdot \mathsf{P})] + [\exists \cdot \mathsf{P}] + \ast$, etc.

This notation is an improvement over the preceding notation, but it is still possible to improve it. If one has a numeral such as $(\perp \cdot \mathsf{P} \cdot \mathsf{P}) + (\exists \cdot \mathsf{P}) + \mathsf{I}$, one can agree to preserve this same order and to leave out all the multiplication and addition symbols as well as the P's and write $\perp \exists \mathsf{I}$ instead of the more cumbersome numeral above. This is a tremendous improvement but unfortunately it presents some problems. For example, if one writes $\ast \exists$ for $(\ast \cdot \mathsf{P} \mathsf{P}) + \exists$, he must also do so for $\ast \cdot \mathsf{P} + \exists$ and $(\ast \cdot \mathsf{P} \cdot \mathsf{P}) + (\exists \cdot \mathsf{P})$, etc., thus resulting in an ambiguous meaning. This ambiguity can be resolved by a simple yet ingenious device. Do you know what it is?

In all the previous numeral systems that we have discussed we have failed to provide a numeral to indicate the cardinality of a certain basic set. This set is the empty set; i.e., a set with no elements—in terms of our piles of stones it is a pile of stones with no stones in it. We adjoin the symbol □ (read square) to represent the cardinal number of the empty set. We need to notice how to add and multiply by this new number. Clearly $\square + a = a + \square = a$ for any cardinal number a, for if we add no stones to a given pile we retain the original pile. On the other hand for any cardinal number a we have $a \cdot \square = \square \cdot a = \square$, for if we take no piles of a stones or a piles of no stones we have no stones.

We can now use our new symbol to rule out the ambiguity mentioned above. We can think of writing $(\maltese \cdot \mathsf{P} \cdot \mathsf{P}) + \dashv$ as $(\maltese \cdot \mathsf{P} \cdot \mathsf{P}) + (\square \cdot \mathsf{P})$ $+ \dashv$ because of the properties of □ listed previously, and similarly $(\maltese \cdot \mathsf{P} \cdot \mathsf{P}) + (\dashv \cdot \mathsf{P})$ can be written as $(\maltese \cdot \mathsf{P} \cdot \mathsf{P}) + (\dashv \cdot \mathsf{P}) + \square$ so that when the addition and multiplication symbols and the P's are omitted, the resulting symbols are distinguishable.

Utilizing this procedure we can now write the first, several cardinal numbers as follows

$$\mathsf{I}, \perp, \maltese, \dashv, \mathsf{I}\,\square, \mathsf{II}, \mathsf{I}\perp, \mathsf{I}\maltese, \mathsf{I}\dashv, \perp\square,$$
$$\perp\mathsf{I}, \perp\perp, \perp\maltese, \perp\dashv, \maltese\square, \maltese\mathsf{I}, \ldots$$

Notice that we now have a collection of symbols with which we can indicate the cardinality of any pile of stones. In addition we use only a few basic symbols which can be quickly learned and written in a fairly small amount of space.

The basic idea of the new notation is that the location of a digit determines its meaning (recall that we agreed to preserve the original order of our symbols). For this reason we call our new notation *positional notation*. Although it is simple, this idea is of great importance and is a comparatively recent addition to civilization. Because of positional notation a school child of today can perform computations that could be handled by only a few learned men in the middle ages. To emphasize this point try multiplying LII by LXXIV using Roman numerals. We now have enough knowledge at our disposal to find the sum and product of any two given numbers. In order to accomplish this efficiently we need a thorough understanding of the associative, commutative, and distributive laws. To be able to quote them is not enough—we must be able to apply these laws. Hence, we consider examples and exercises designed to enhance our understanding of the laws before proceeding to sums and products.

Recall that $(\perp + \maltese) + \dashv$ "directs" us to first add $\perp$ to $\maltese$ and then add the result to $\dashv$, while $\perp + (\maltese + \dashv)$ "directs" us to first add $\maltese$ to $\dashv$ and then add $\perp$ to the result.

EXAMPLE I. Using either the commutative or associative law of addition to justify each step, show that $(\bot + ✶) + ⊣ = ⊣ + (\bot + ✶)$.

We start with the left side and reduce it to the right. We could equally well start with the right side and reduce it to the left. However we could not start by assuming the two sides are equal, for that is what we wish to show.

$$
\begin{aligned}
(\bot + ✶) + ⊣ &= \bot + (✶ + ⊣) && \text{by associative law of addition} \\
&= \bot + (⊣ + ✶) && \text{by commutative law of addition} \\
&= (\bot + ⊣) + ✶ && \text{by associative law of addition} \\
&= (⊣ + \bot) + ✶ && \text{by commutative law of addition} \\
&= ⊣ + (\bot + ✶) && \text{by associative law of addition}
\end{aligned}
$$

Throughout Example I we have thought of $\bot$, $✶$, and $⊣$ as three distinct numbers. In particular we have been thinking of $\bot + ✶$ as the sum of the two distinct numbers $\bot$ and $✶$. However we do not need to do so. Since addition is a binary operation on the set of cardinal numbers, $\bot + ✶$ is the name of a unique cardinal number and we may so regard it. To show that we are thinking of $\bot + ✶$ as a single number we could replace it by I □. But this utilizes the addition table for the digits, and we would like to avoid this. Hence we will use a bar, $\overline{\bot + ✶}$, to denote that we are regarding $\bot + ✶$ as a single entity. Thus $\bot + ✶$ denotes the sum of the two numbers $\bot$ and $✶$, while $\overline{\bot + ✶}$ denotes one cardinal number.

Note that the associative law of addition is applied to three numbers as illustrated in the first equation in Example I, while the commutative law of addition is applied to two numbers as illustrated by the second equation in Example I.

Before the commutative or associative laws of addition could be stated we had to know that addition is a binary operation, so we have certainly implicitly used this fact in Example I. However, we could have used this fact explicitly. To illustrate this we work Example I by a different method.

EXAMPLE ⊥. Using either the commutative or associative law of addition (or the fact that addition is a binary operation) to justify each step, show that

$$(\bot + ✶) + ⊣ = ⊣ + (\bot + ✶)$$

$$
\begin{aligned}
(\bot + ✶) + ⊣ &= \overline{(\bot + ✶)} + ⊣ && \text{since addition is a binary operation} \\
&= ⊣ + \overline{(\bot + ✶)} && \text{by commutative law of addition} \\
&= ⊣ + (\bot + ✶) && \text{since addition is a binary operation}
\end{aligned}
$$

Note that in the distributive law whether $b + c$ is to be regarded as a single number or whether b and c are to be regarded as distinct numbers depends on which side of the equation we take. See Exercise ⊥ □.

EXAMPLE ✶. Using either the commutative or associative law of multiplication to justify each step, show that

$(\perp \times \text{✶}) \times \dashv = \perp \times (\dashv \times \text{✶})$

$(\perp \times \text{✶}) \times \dashv = \perp \times (\text{✶} \times \dashv)$ by associative law of multiplication

$\qquad\qquad\quad = \perp \times (\dashv \times \text{✶})$ by commutative law of multiplication

EXERCISES

Using either the commutative or associative laws of addition and multiplication to justify each step, show that

|. $(\perp + \text{✶}) + \dashv = \perp + (\dashv + \text{✶})$

⊥. $(\perp + \text{✶}) + \dashv = \dashv + (\perp + \text{✶})$

✶. $(\perp + \text{✶}) + \dashv = \dashv + (\text{✶} + \perp)$

⊣. $(\perp + \text{✶}) + \dashv = \text{✶} + (\dashv + \perp)$

| □. $(\perp \times \text{✶}) \times \dashv = \dashv \times (\perp \times \text{✶})$

| |. $(\perp \times \text{✶}) \times \dashv = \dashv \times (\text{✶} \times \perp)$

| ⊥. $(\perp \times \text{✶}) \times \dashv = \text{✶} \times (\dashv \times \perp)$

| ✶. $(\perp + \text{✶}) + (\dashv + \text{✶}) = (\text{✶} + \text{✶}) + (\dashv + \perp)$

| ⊣. $\perp + [\text{✶} + (\dashv + \perp)] = [(\perp + \text{✶}) + \dashv] + \perp$

⊥ □. Using the bar notation, state both distributive laws carefully.

2

2.1. ADDITION IN POSITIONAL NOTATION

Since the sum of two numbers is unique, then given two numbers, say o o and ₀°₀, the numeral 'o o + ₀°₀' is a perfectly good name for the sum of these two numbers. We should notice that many of our numbers have precisely this kind of name. For example, we say for 106, "a hundred and six." In some cases we have condensed the names so that we say fifty-six to mean fifty and six. The French, however, refer to the card game usually called "blackjack" as "vingt et un," twenty and one. The Germans use the commutative law and say "vier und zwanzig," four and twenty. Recall in this connection the nursery rhyme about "four and twenty blackbirds baked in a pie." However, *finding the sum* of the numbers o o and ₀°₀ usually refers to the process by which the numeral 'o o + ₀°₀' is replaced by the numeral '°o°'. Similarly, finding the sum of ⊥ and ✶ means replacing the numeral '⊥ + ✶' by the numeral 'I □.' By actually placing one pile of stones upon another, we can determine the following *addition table for numbers whose standard numeral has one digit*. (A *digit* in the one-handed system is one of the symbols □, I, ⊥, ✶, ꓱ.)

+	□	I	⊥	✶	ꓱ
□	□	I	⊥	✶	ꓱ
I	I	⊥	✶	ꓱ	I□
⊥	⊥	✶	ꓱ	I□	II
✶	✶	ꓱ	I□	II	I⊥
ꓱ	ꓱ	I□	II	I⊥	I✶

operations on numbers

19

The entry **II** in the third row and fifth column indicates that "⊥ + ⊣ = **II**."
The entry **II** in the fifth row and third column indicates that "⊣ + ⊥ = **II**."
The commutative law of addition ensures that the table is symmetric about the diagonal from the upper left-hand corner to the lower right-hand corner.

Let us apply our knowledge of positional notation and the various laws that pertain to the binary operations of addition and multiplication to obtain a systematic procedure for replacing the numeral denoting the sum of two numbers by a desired numeral, which we might call the *standard numeral*. It is difficult to define the standard numeral precisely and we shall not attempt to do so. However, in the simple cases we consider here, there is no question as to which numeral is desired.

We first derive the following formula

$$(a + b) + (c + d) = (a + c) + (b + d) \tag{1}$$

For

$$
\begin{aligned}
(a + b) + (c + d) &= (a + b) + \overline{(c + d)} && \text{since addition is a binary operation} \\
&= a + (b + \overline{c + d}) && \text{by associative law of addition} \\
&= a + (\overline{c + d} + b) && \text{by commutative law of addition} \\
&= (a + \overline{c + d}) + b && \text{by associative law of addition} \\
&= [a + (c + d)] + b && \text{since addition is a binary operation} \\
&= [(a + c) + d] + b && \text{by associative law of addition} \\
&= [\overline{(a + c)} + d] + b && \text{since addition is a binary operation} \\
&= \overline{(a + c)} + (d + b) && \text{by associative law of addition} \\
&= \overline{(a + c)} + (b + d) && \text{by commutative law of addition} \\
&= (a + c) + (b + d) && \text{since addition is a binary operation}
\end{aligned}
$$

We can now utilize this formula in finding the standard numeral of the sum of two numbers.

EXAMPLE 1.

$$
\begin{aligned}
(\mathbf{I}\,⊥) + ⊥ &= (\mathbf{I} \cdot \mathsf{P} + ⊥) + ⊥ \\
&\quad\text{positional notation} \\
&= (\mathbf{I} \cdot \mathsf{P} + ⊥) + (\square + ⊥) \\
&\quad\text{property of } \square \\
&= (\mathbf{I} \cdot \mathsf{P} + \square) + (⊥ + ⊥) \\
&\quad\text{Formula 1} \\
&= \mathbf{I} \cdot \mathsf{P} + (⊥ + ⊥) \\
&\quad\text{property of } \square \\
&= \mathbf{I} \cdot \mathsf{P} + ⊣ \\
&\quad\text{addition table for digits} \\
&= \mathbf{I}\,⊣. \\
&\quad\text{positional notation}
\end{aligned}
$$

EXAMPLE 2.

$$\mathbf{I} \perp + \mathbf{II} = (\mathbf{I} \cdot \mathsf{P} + \perp) + (\mathbf{I} \cdot \mathsf{P} + \mathbf{I})$$
positional notation

$$= (\mathbf{I} \cdot \mathsf{P} + \mathbf{I} \cdot \mathsf{P}) + (\perp + \mathbf{I})$$
Formula 1

$$= (\mathbf{I} + \mathbf{I}) \cdot \mathsf{P} + (\perp + \mathbf{I})$$
distributive law

$$= \quad \perp \cdot \mathsf{P} + \ast$$
addition table for digits

$$= \quad \perp \ast$$
positional notation

EXAMPLE 3.

$$\mathbf{I} \perp + \exists = (\mathbf{I} \cdot \mathsf{P} + \perp) + \exists$$
positional notation

$$= (\mathbf{I} \cdot \mathsf{P} + \perp) + (\square + \exists)$$
property of $\square$

$$= (\mathbf{I} \cdot \mathsf{P} + \square) + (\perp + \exists)$$
Formula 1

$$= (\mathbf{I} \cdot \mathsf{P} + \square) + (\mathbf{II})$$
addition table for digits

$$= (\mathbf{I} \cdot \mathsf{P} + \square) + (\mathbf{I} \cdot \mathsf{P} + \mathbf{I})$$
positional notation

$$= (\mathbf{I} \cdot \mathsf{P} + \mathbf{I} \cdot \mathsf{P}) + (\square + \mathbf{I})$$
Formula 1

$$= (\mathbf{I} + \mathbf{I}) \cdot \mathsf{P} + (\square + \mathbf{I})$$
distributive law

$$= \quad \perp \cdot \mathsf{P} + \mathbf{I}$$
addition table for digits

$$= \quad \perp \mathbf{I}.$$
positional notation

Careful consideration of our steps shows us that the associative and commutative laws of addition permit us to rearrange a sum in any desired order. We note that the standard numeral for the sum of two digits is either a one or two digit numeral (as given in the addition table for digits). Hence we can shorten the procedures to the following

$$
\begin{array}{ccc}
(1') \; \mathbf{I} \perp & (2') \; \mathbf{I} \perp & (3') \; \mathbf{I} \perp \\
\underline{\quad \perp} & \underline{\quad \mathbf{II}} & \underline{\quad \exists} \\
\mathbf{I} \, \exists & \perp \ast & \mathbf{II} \\
& & \mathbf{I} \\
& & \perp \mathbf{I}
\end{array}
$$

EXERCISES

|. Replace each numeral below by its standard numeral giving justification for each step taken (as in Examples 1, 2, and 3).

  (a) | ⊥ + |
  (b) | ⊥ + ✳
  (c) ⊥ ✳ + ⊣
  (d) ⊥ ✳ + ⊥ |

⊥. Jane says that when a one digit number is added to a one digit number the sum will be either a one digit number or a two digit number. Correct Jane's error.

✳. Replace each numeral below by its standard numeral by the simplified procedure indicated above in examples (1′), (2′), (3′).

  (a) the numerals in Exercise |
  (b) | ⊣ ✳ + ✳ ⊥ |
  (c) ⊥ | ✳ ⊣ + ⊣ ⊥ | ✳

⊣. Explain briefly the reasons for your procedures in problem ✳.

2.2. SUBTRACTION IN POSITIONAL NOTATION

As soon as we become proficient in adding numbers (and in some cases even before then) we are asked questions such as "the sum of what number and ⊥ equals ⊣ ?" This kind of question is a natural one and occurs throughout mathematics. A mathematician invents a (perhaps very complicated) transformation on a set of objects, and then he wants to know "to what can I apply this transformation to get such and such an answer?" This "inverse" problem is almost always harder than the direct problem, both psychologically as well as in the techniques needed. We are meeting it here in perhaps its simplest form—no doubt most of you were able to answer the question above quite rapidly.

How does one attack such a problem? One way is by trial and error. Take a number, add it to ⊥ and if the result is not ⊣, discard the number you took and try another. When (and if) you finally find one that works, you've solved the problem. One might compare this process to that followed by an individual with a ring containing a large number of keys—he frantically selects them at random trying to find one that will open a certain lock. One can improve the process by making the selections systematically and noting which keys don't work so that the same key doesn't get tried several times. In fact, computing machines solve some problems in this manner. They simply try numbers (extremely rapidly) until they find one that works.

When we have a large number of similar problems to solve, it helps to have a more direct method. We start by inventing words and symbols so that we may ask the problem differently. Instead of saying "what number must be added to $\perp$ to get $\daleth$?" we may ask "what is $\perp$ *subtracted* from $\daleth$?" or "what is *the difference* of $\daleth$ and $\perp$?" or "what is $\daleth$ *minus* $\perp$?" Symbolically the (unique) number which added to a gives b is written as $b - a$.

Replacing the numeral $\daleth - \perp$ with the standard numeral $\perp$ is called subtraction. It can be shown, fortunately, that for any two cardinal numbers a and b, there is at most one cardinal number c such that $a + c = b$. Is there always one?

To subtract small numbers from each other we might use the addition table in Section 2.1. For example, $\mathbf{I}\,\square - \maltese$ can be found by looking down the $\maltese$ column until $\mathbf{I}\,\square$ is found and seeing that it is in the $\perp$ row; hence $\mathbf{I}\,\square - \maltese = \perp$. To continue the direct approach we could construct a subtraction table, but whatever table we have would only contain so many entries and there are many more subtraction problems. We notice two rather straightforward facts. First, for any number a we have $a - a = \square$; since $\square$ is obviously the answer to the question "what must be added to a to get a?" Secondly, for any number a we have $a - \square = a$; since $a + \square = a$. We now verify that the distributive law in the form $a(b - c) = ab - ac$, is valid. We begin by considering the number $a(b - c) + ac$ which equals $a[(b - c) + c]$ by the distributive law for addition. Now since $b - c$ is the number which added to c gives b

$$(b - c) + c = b \quad \text{and} \quad a[(b - c) + c] = ab$$

or

$$a \cdot (b - c) + ac = ab$$

Thus we see that $a(b - c)$ is the number which added to ac gives ab or $a(b - c) = ab - ac$, which is what we are trying to show.

When each of the numbers $(a - c)$, $(b - d)$, and $(a + b) - (c + d)$ exists then we have Formula 1

$$(a + b) - (c + d) = (a - c) + (b - d)$$

To see that this is true note that

$$(a - c) + c = a \quad \text{and} \quad (b - d) + d = b$$

so that

$$(a - c) + (b - d) + (c + d) = (a - c) + c + (b - d) + d = a + b$$

Thus $(a-c)+(b-d)$ is the number which added to $(c+d)$ gives $(a+b)$ or

$$(a-c)+(b-d)=(a+b)-(c+d)$$

as was to be shown. We are particularly interested in the case when a, b, c, and d are numbers whose standard numeral is a digit in which case the formula says that given the standard numeral for two numbers we can subtract one number from the other by subtracting the corresponding digits in the standard numerals (assuming of course that all these operations are possible). For example, to subtract $I\ast$ from $\ast\dashv$, we write

$$\ast\dashv - I\ast = (\ast\cdot P + \dashv) - (I\cdot P + \ast)$$
$$= (\ast\cdot P - I\cdot P) + (\dashv - \ast)$$

But by the distributive law for subtraction

$$(\ast\cdot P - I\cdot P) = (\ast - I)\cdot P$$

(see Exercise I). Hence

$$\ast\dashv - I\ast = (\ast - I)\cdot P + (\dashv - \ast) = \bot\cdot P + I + \bot\,I$$

When we become proficient and understand the process very well we see that it can be abbreviated by merely writing the numeral of the number to be subtracted below the numeral of the other, drawing a line under the problem, "subtracting corresponding digits," and writing the result under the line so that we have

$$\begin{array}{r} \ast\ \dashv \\ I\ \ast \\ \hline \bot\ I \end{array}$$

Unfortunately many people are taught subtraction by this abbreviated process without the procedure being justified, nor the details understood, and with the usual unsatisfactory results.

There is another complication which arises to plague young arithmetic students and their erstwhile teachers which we illustrate with the following example. Find the difference $\dashv\bot - I\ast$. If we follow the procedure above, we obtain

$$\dashv\bot - I\ast = (\dashv\cdot P + \bot) - (I\cdot P + \ast)$$
$$= (\dashv\cdot P - I\cdot P) + (\bot - \ast)$$

and we note that $\perp - ✶$ is not a cardinal number. Does this mean that Formula 1 is wrong? No, if you look back, you will note that in stating Formula 1 we stipulated that each of the component parts existed. Hence we present two alternative methods.

First we may write

$$Ⅎ\perp = Ⅎ \cdot P + \perp$$
$$= (✶ + I) \cdot P + \perp$$
$$= (✶ \cdot P + I \cdot P) + \perp$$
$$= ✶ \cdot P + (I \cdot P + \perp)$$
$$= ✶ \cdot P + (I \perp)$$

so that

$$Ⅎ\perp - I✶ = (✶ \cdot P + I \perp) - I✶$$
$$= (✶ \cdot P + I \perp) - (I \cdot P + ✶)$$
$$= (✶ - I) \cdot P + (I \perp - ✶)$$
$$= \perp \cdot P + Ⅎ = \perp Ⅎ$$

This is the so-called (but somewhat misnamed) "borrowing" method. It consists of taking a P from the number denoted by the $Ⅎ$ digit to build up the $\perp$ to $I \perp$ so that we might subtract $✶$ from it.

The second method makes use of the fact that $(a - b) = (a + c) - (b + c)$ which we may derive from Formula 1. We write

$$Ⅎ \perp - I✶ = (Ⅎ \perp + P) - (I✶ + P)$$
$$= [(Ⅎ \cdot P + \perp) + P] - [(I \cdot P + ✶) + P]$$
$$= [(Ⅎ \cdot P) + (\perp + P)] - [I \cdot P + (✶ + P)]$$
$$= [(Ⅎ \cdot P + (P + \perp)] - [(I \cdot P + I \cdot P) + ✶]$$
$$= (Ⅎ \cdot P + I \perp) - (\perp \cdot P + ✶)$$
$$= (Ⅎ \cdot P - \perp \cdot P) + (I \perp - ✶) = \perp \cdot P + Ⅎ = \perp Ⅎ$$

This method might be called the "carrying" method inasmuch as we add a P to each of $Ⅎ \perp$ and $I✶$, but keep it with the $\perp$ in the first numeral and "carry" it over to increase the I to a $\perp$ in the second. Note that both methods serve the same purpose—i.e., to modify the problem so that Formula 1 may be used. Note also that one can abbreviate the notation used in doing this first example by writing

$$\frac{Ⅎ\perp}{-I✶} = \frac{\overset{I}{✶}\perp}{-I✶} = \perp Ⅎ$$

or more concisely by changing the digits on the original problem by drawing a line there and then writing the new digits nearby, viz.

$$
\begin{array}{r}
✳\ \ \mathbf{I} \\
丮\ \ \bot \\
-\mathbf{I}\ \ ✳ \\
\hline
\bot\ \ \exists
\end{array}
$$

or more sophisticatedly by only mentally changing the digits so that the entire calculation appears as

$$
\begin{array}{r}
\exists\ \ \bot \\
-\mathbf{I}\ \ ✳ \\
\hline
\bot\ \ \exists
\end{array}
$$

The foregoing utilized the borrowing method. For the carrying method the calculation is

$$
\begin{array}{r}
\exists\ \ \bot \\
-\mathbf{I}\ \ ✳ \\
\hline
\end{array}
\quad = \quad
\begin{array}{r}
\exists\ \ {}^{\mathbf{I}}\bot \\
-\bot\ \ ✳ \\
\hline
\bot\ \ \exists
\end{array}
$$

and, when the work is done mentally, one merely writes

$$
\begin{array}{r}
\exists\ \ \bot \\
-\mathbf{I}\ \ ✳ \\
\hline
\bot\ \ \exists
\end{array}
$$

again.

It is of course, possible to extend these methods to problems of increased complexity (and the student is given an opportunity to do so in the following exercises) but all the theory needed has previously been developed. As mentioned earlier it is possible to construct a subtraction table, but the authors feel that it is more important to emphasize the definition of subtraction than it is to develop speed in getting answers; therefore, consider the absence of a subtraction table helpful in this connection.

EXERCISES

1. Show that the distributive law holds for subtraction, i.e., if $a - b$ exists then $a \cdot c - b \cdot c = (a - b) \cdot c$.

⊥. Find the standard numeral by the carrying method

(a) ⅃ | − ⊥ ✶
(b) ⅃ ⊥ − ✶ ⊥
(c) ✶ ✶ − ⊥ ⅃

✶. Find the standard numeral of the numbers in Exercise ⊥ by the borrowing method. (Give sufficient explanation so that your answer here differs from that above.)

⅃. Suppose one is given numbers *a*, *b* whose standard numerals contain more than two digits. How can one find the standard numeral for *a* − *b*?

| □. Find the standard numeral by the carrying method of

(a) ✶ ⅃ ⊥ − ⊥ ✶ ✶
(b) ✶ □ | − | ⊥ ⅃
(c) ⅃ ⊥ ✶ | − ⅃ ✶

||. Find the standard numeral of the numbers in Exercise | □ by the borrowing method.

2.3. MULTIPLICATION IN POSITIONAL NOTATION

We are now faced with the problem of finding the standard numeral for the product of two given numbers. We make use of three facts that we know: first, $| \cdot n = n$ for all n; second, the distributive law; and third, we know how to add. For example

$$\bot \cdot \daleth = (| + |) \cdot \daleth = \daleth + \daleth = | \ast$$

Now knowing what $\bot \cdot \daleth$ is, we find

$$\ast \cdot \daleth = (\bot + |) \cdot \daleth = \bot \cdot \daleth + | \cdot \daleth = | \ast + \daleth = \bot \bot$$

In this manner we can work up and find the standard numeral for any given number multiplied by ⅃, and, in a similar manner, the product of any two given numbers.

This kind of process occurs in many places in mathematics and is worth examining. The idea is that we know how to do something with $|$, and if, when we know how to do it with a number n, we can find how to do it with $n + |$; by using these two skills we can find how to do it with any given number.

What we have done so far is very satisfying. We have convinced ourselves that given two numbers (enough time and incentive) we can multiply them, i.e., find the standard numeral of their product. Our method, however, is rather impractical in that to calculate the product of two numbers, we may first have to calculate other products. In other words, if we need to do many multiplication problems, we need a faster and more efficient way to do them. First, using the method above to calculate the entries, we construct a multiplication table for the numbers with one digit numerals, viz.

·	I	⊥	✳	⊣
I	I	⊥	✳	⊣
⊥	⊥	⊣	II	I✳
✳	✳	II	I⊣	⊥⊥
⊣	⊣	I✳	⊥⊥	✳I

Next, since we are often going to use the table and since we are interested in speed of calculation, we should memorize the table.

We make use of the fact that the standard numeral of **I** □ times a given number is the standard numeral of the given number with a "□" added on the end of it. Why is this so? (See Exercise 3.) For example, **I** □ · **I** □ = **I** □□. By your old friend the associative law, multiplying by **I** □□ is equivalent to multiplying by **I** □ and then multiplying by **I** □ again. Thus the standard numeral of **I** □□ times a given number is the standard numeral of the given number with two □'s adjoined on the end of it.

In a similar manner we may show that multiplying by **I** □ □ □ adds three □'s, etc. With this in mind let's try multiplying larger numbers.

EXAMPLE 1.

$$
\begin{aligned}
✳ · ⊥ ⊣ &= ✳ · (⊥ □ + ⊣) \\
&= ✳ · (⊥ □) + ✳ · ⊣ \\
&= (✳ · ⊥) · \mathbf{I} □ + ✳ · ⊣ \\
&= \mathbf{II} · \mathbf{I} □ + ⊥ ⊥ \\
&= \mathbf{II} □ + ⊥ ⊥ \\
&= \mathbf{I} ✳ ⊥
\end{aligned}
$$

We might have arranged the work vertically as

$$
\begin{array}{r}
✳ · ⊥ ⊣ = ⊥ □ + ⊣ \\
✳ \\
\hline
\mathbf{II} □ + ⊥ ⊥ = \mathbf{I} ✳ ⊥
\end{array}
$$

or, as you may recall from grammar school days, the following abbreviated fashion is possible

$$\begin{array}{r} \perp\ \daleth \\ \times \\ \hline |\times\perp \end{array}$$

This is done by saying (to yourself) something like "$\times$ times $\daleth$ is $\perp\ \perp$, put down $\perp$ and carry $\perp$, $\times$ times $\perp$ is $\|$ and the $\perp$ we carry makes $|\times$" which we write in front of the $\perp$ getting the answer $|\times\perp$. Why does this work?

Let us now examine what happens when two numbers, each with two digit numerals, are multiplied.

EXAMPLE 2.

$$\begin{aligned}
\perp\times\cdot|\daleth &= (\perp\square+\times)\cdot|\daleth \\
&= (\perp\square\cdot|\daleth)+(\times\cdot|\daleth) \\
&= \perp\square\cdot(|\square+\daleth)+\times\cdot(|\square+\daleth) \\
&= \perp\square\cdot|\square+|\square\cdot\perp\cdot\daleth+\times\cdot|\square+\times\cdot\daleth \\
&= \perp\square\square+|\times\square+\times\square+\perp\perp \\
&= \daleth\times\perp
\end{aligned}$$

or vertically

$$\begin{array}{r}
\perp\times\cdot|\daleth = |\square+\daleth \\
\perp\square+\times \\
\hline
\perp\perp\ \rangle \\
\times\square\ \rangle \\
|\times\square\ \rangle \\
\perp\square\square\ \rangle \\
\hline
\daleth\times\perp
\end{array}$$

or by omitting the $\square$'s and doing some of the work mentally, i.e., by adding the numbers in braces, we have the familiar process

$$\begin{array}{r}
|\ \daleth \\
\perp\times \\
\hline
|\square\perp \\
\times\times \\
\hline
\daleth\times\perp
\end{array}$$

Note the importance of positional notation in multiplication. Positional notation (and the fundamental laws) enables one who has learned a few products (see the preceding table) to multiply any pair of numbers given in the form of standard numerals. We might mention that the familiar multiplication process that you know is by no means universally used. There are variations used by people in other countries, and some of these will be exhibited later.

It is also worth noting that multiplying wasn't always this easy, and until comparatively recently even the mathematicians were unable to multiply large numbers quickly.

Up to this point we have been using our own special number system. We feel that this has been worthwhile for a number of reasons. It is quite difficult for most people, at the college level, to think of arithmetic as new and exciting and worth analyzing. We feel that using different symbols and a different base (i.e., a different choice for P; see also Section 3.3) partially remedies this problem. Furthermore, it gives prospective teachers a general idea of the problems faced by youngsters to whom the numbers and numerals are still new.

By now, however, we believe that the points mentioned above have been made, and inasmuch as the subsequent material is a little more involved, we are mainly going to use the usual numerals, hereafter. The differences are that we have ten rather than five symbols and that you (and we) are more familiar with them.

EXERCISES

1. Find the standard numeral of the following numbers
   (a) $\perp \dashv \cdot \divideontimes \mathsf{I}$ (c) $\divideontimes \dashv \cdot \perp \mathsf{I}$
   (b) $\perp \mathsf{I} \cdot \dashv \divideontimes$ (d) $\divideontimes \perp \cdot \mathsf{I} \dashv$

2. Go through each step in Exercise 1 in detail as is done in the Example.

3. John says that to multiply a number by $\mathsf{I} \square$ simply annex a $\square$ at the end of the number. Correct John's error.

2.4. THE ORDERING OF THE COUNTING NUMBERS

So far we have considered only cardinal numbers—the numbers of sets. Moreover, we have arranged these numbers in a line in the so-called "natural" ordering, $0, 1, 2, 3, \ldots$. In this particular arrangement these numbers possess additional properties. For example, we know that 4 follows 3 and precedes 5. This set of numbers will be called the set of counting numbers. Sometimes we wish to consider the non-zero numbers in this set, i.e., 1, 2, 3, ... These numbers will be called the *natural* numbers.

The cardinal number 4 is the number of the set $\begin{smallmatrix} \circ & \circ \\ \circ & \circ \end{smallmatrix}$. It is independent of all other numbers. Yet when most of us think of 4 we picture this number as being sandwiched in between 3 and 5—i.e., we think of 4 as a number which is not independent of all other numbers but occurs in a definite position in the natural arrangement. By the process of *counting* the *elements* of *a non-empty set* is meant the process of effecting a 1–1 correspondence between the elements of the given set and the first n natural numbers. We say that such a set has n elements. If the set is empty, we say it has 0 elements. We observe that 5 is the cardinal number of the set $\{1, 2, 3, 4, 5\}$, 6 is the cardinal number of the set $\{1, 2, 3, 4, 5, 6\}$, and n is the cardinal number of the set $\{1, 2, 3, \ldots, n\}$.

To determine the cardinal number of the set ○ ○ / ○ ○ we may count the elements by giving a 1–1 correspondence between these elements and a certain set of natural numbers. We usually give this correspondence by "naming" the elements of the given set with numbers. Thus we say one, two, three, four, five and "name" the objects simultaneously

$$①②$$
$$③$$
$$④⑤$$

Thus the set ○ ○ / ○ ○ matches the set $\{1, 2, 3, 4, 5\}$, and as has been observed the cardinal number of this set is 5. Note that there are many ways to count. For example, the set could also have been counted

$$④③$$
$$②$$
$$①⑤$$

In how many ways can this set be counted? Of course, this counting process is the reason we call these particular numbers the counting numbers.

Let us consider some additional properties of counting numbers. We write $a < b$, read "a is less than b" if a precedes b in the natural arrangement, i.e., $0, 1, \ldots, a, \ldots, b, \ldots$. If we count the numbers that follow a up to and including b, we obtain a number c such that $b = a + c$. We use this as a definition. The counting number a *is less than* the counting number b, notation $a < b$, if and only if there is a natural number c such that $b = a + c$. We observe that the binary relation $<$ has the *transitive property*, i.e., if $a < b$ and $b < c$ it follows that $a < c$. Since $a < b$ there is a natural number d such that $b = a + d$. Since $b < c$ there is a natural number e such that $c = b + e$. Hence

$$c = b + e = (a + d) + e = a + (d + e)$$

Thus there is a natural number, i.e., $d + e$, such that $c = a + (d + e)$ and hence $a < c$.

Suppose $a < b$. Then there is a natural number, say d, such that $a + d = b$. Now

$$(a + c) + d = (a + d) + c = b + c$$

Hence $a + c < b + c$. Moreover, $bc = ac + dc$. Hence $ac < bc$. We will need this binary relation of $<$ in order to give the division algorithm of the next section. The term "binary" tells us that this relation is a property between two numbers. The word "algorithm" simply denotes a process for doing something. Division algorithm denotes a process of "doing" division.

There are two additional properties of natural numbers that are frequently used in more advanced work in mathematics. We merely mention these. One of these properties is that any (nonvacuous) set of natural numbers contains a first element, i.e., a number a such that $a < x$ for all numbers x in the set different from a. Because it has this property, we say that the set of natural numbers is *well-ordered*. The other property is called the *principle of mathematical induction*. This states that any set of natural numbers with the properties

(a) the number 1 is in the set;
(b) if a number k is in the set then the number $k + 1$ is in the set

must contain all the natural numbers. Mathematical induction is a method that is often used for mathematical proof. Curiously enough, mathematical induction is not an inductive method of proof but is a deductive method of proof. We mention also that these last two properties are equivalent, i.e., we may prove either one by using the other (see Exercise 5). In advanced mathematics courses one or the other property is assumed as part of the definition of the counting numbers.

A set A is said to be a *subset* of the set B if every element of A is an element of B. Since every even counting number is a counting number, the set of even counting numbers is a subset of the set of counting numbers. Also any set is a subset of itself. If A is a subset of B and B is a subset of A then it follows that $A = B$. The set A is said to be a *proper subset* of the set B if: (a) A is a subset of B, (b) A is not the empty set, and (c) B contains at least one element that is not contained in A. An alternative to (c) would be to say that B is *not* a subset of A. The set of even counting numbers is a subset of itself, but it is not a proper subset of itself. On the other hand, the set of even counting numbers is a proper subset of the set of counting numbers. We might observe that if A is a proper subset of B, and B is a proper subset of C, then it follows that A is a proper subset of C.

Note that if $a < b$ then $a \neq b$ and the set of stones in a can be put into 1–1 correspondence with a subset of the stones in b, but the set of stones in b cannot be put into 1–1 correspondence with a subset of the set of stones in a. A more sophisticated definition of "$a < b$" could be phrased in this fashion.

EXERCISES

1. Now $a > b$ is defined to mean $b < a$. If a and b are counting numbers and $a > b$, prove that $a \cdot a > b \cdot b$.

2. Let a and b be natural numbers. Show that $a < b$ if and only if the set of stones which represents a can be put into 1–1 correspondence with a proper subset of the set of stones which represents b.

3. If a and c are natural numbers and $a + c = b$ show that $a < b$.

4. Show that if a and b are distinct natural numbers then $a > b$ if and and only if $a - b$ is a natural number.

5. The entire set of natural numbers has a first element (i.e., the number 1). Show that every nonempty set of natural numbers contains a first element, assuming the principle of mathematical induction. (This is a difficult problem. The average student should ignore it.)

2.5. DIVISORS, DIVISION, AND THE DIVISION ALGORITHM

In this section we consider counting numbers and will refer to them simply as numbers.

Suppose a, b, and c are numbers and $a = bc$. Then we say b and c are *divisors* or *factors* of a, and a is a *multiple* of both b and c. Since $30 = 15 \cdot 2$, then 15 and 2 are factors of 30, 30 is a multiple of 2, and 30 is a multiple of 15. We observe that 1 is a divisor of every number and that every number is a multiple of 1.

We have previously defined $a - b$ as the unique number which added to b gives a, provided there is such a number. Thus subtraction "undoes" addition and is, in a sense, an inverse operation of addition. Similarly we now define $a \div b$ (read a divided by b), where $b \neq 0$, to be the unique number which when multiplied by b gives a, provided there is such a number. Thus if $a = bc$ where a, b, c, are numbers and $b \neq 0$, then $a \div b = c$. Hence division "undoes" multiplication and is, in a sense, an inverse operation of multiplication. We note that if a and b are numbers, $b \neq 0$, then the symbol $a \div b$ makes sense if and only if b is a factor of a. Since $18 = 2 \cdot 9$ then $18 \div 2 = 9$.

The set of natural numbers possesses the "Archimedean property;" i.e., if a and b are natural numbers then there exists a natural number q such that $aq > b$ (see Exercise 5).

The meaning of the word "division" is usually extended to include more than an inverse operation of multiplication. In fact one gives such a broad meaning to the word division that any number can be divided by any number, excluding only division by 0. (Why do we exclude division by 0?) We state this more precisely as follows

Division Algorithm. If a and b are counting numbers, $b \neq 0$, there exist unique counting numbers q and r such that $a = bq + r$ where $r < b$. We call a the *dividend*, b the *divisor*, q the *quotient*, and r the *remainder*.

Proof:
If $a < b$ we may take $q = 0$ and $r = a$, and have $a = b \cdot 0 + a$. If $a = b$ then we may take $q = 1$ and $r = 0$, $a = b \cdot 1 + 0$. So let us suppose $a > b$. We consider the multiples of b, i.e., b, $2b$, $3b$, etc., which become arbitrarily large and hence certainly will be larger than a eventually. Suppose that kb is the last multiple of b which is less than or equal to a, i.e., $kb \leq a$ but $(k + 1)b > a$. Then if $r = a - kb$, $r < b$ and $a = kb + r$. Thus there always exist numbers q and r such that $a = bq + r$ where $r < b$.

To show uniqueness of q and r suppose $a = bq_1 + r_1$ and also $a = bq_2 + r_2$ where $r_1 < b$ and $r_2 < b$. Then we have $bq_1 + r_1 = bq_2 + r_2$ since each is equal to a. Now if $q_1 > q_2$, then $q_1 \geq q_2 + 1$. Thus $bq_1 \geq b(q_2 + 1) = bq_2 + b$ which is greater than $bq_2 + r_2$ since $b > r_2$. Hence $bq_1 + r_1$ would be greater than $bq_2 + r_2$ which contradicts the assumption that $bq_1 + r_1 = bq_2 + r_2$. Therefore, it is wrong to assume $q_1 > q_2$ and by a similar argument it is wrong to assume $q_2 > q_1$. Therefore, q_1 must equal q_2 and we have

$$bq_1 + r_1 = bq_1 + r_2$$

so that

$$bq_1 - bq_1 + r_1 = bq_1 - bq_1 + r_2$$

or

$$r_1 = r_2.$$

Since q_1 and q_2 are equal and r_1 and r_2 are equal we have shown uniqueness.

Some students might have difficulty following this mathematical proof. Let us return to piles of stones to help clarify matters. We suppose a and b are counting numbers and $a > b$. This says the set of stones which represents a contains more stones than the set of stones which represents b. Hence we may remove a set of b stones from the larger pile. If there are more than b stones left in the pile then we may remove a second set of b stones. If there are still more than b stones left in the pile, then we may remove a third set of b stones. If there are still more than b stones left in the pile, then we may remove a fourth set from the pile. Eventually there are less than b stones left in the pile—the remaining stones, if any, are the remainder. If no stones are left, the remainder is 0. The number of sets of b stones that we have removed is the quotient. For example, let $a = 19$ and $b = 3$. On removing three stones at a time from the pile of 19 stones we form a rectangular array with them as follows

$$\begin{array}{cccccc} \circ & \circ & \circ & \circ & \circ & \circ \\ \circ & \circ & \circ & \circ & \circ & \circ \\ \circ & \circ & \circ & \circ & \circ & \circ \end{array}$$

and observe there is one stone left in the original pile. Thus the quotient is 6 and the remainder is 1.

EXERCISES

1. Let $a = 18$ and $b = 3$ and form a rectangular array as above. Show that $18 \div 3 = 6$, since $18 = 3 \cdot 6$ by our definition of multiplication in terms of piles of stones. *Note:* division is the inverse of multiplication in terms of these operations on piles of stones.

2. Let $a = 18$ and $b = 3$. Form the difference $18 - 3$ by removing three stones from the pile of 18 stones. Show that $18 - 3 = 15$ since $18 = 3 + 15$. *Note:* subtraction is the inverse of addition in terms of these operations on piles of stones.

3. Explain why we exclude division by 0.

4. Show that $aq \geqq q$ for all natural numbers a and q.

5. Utilizing Exercise 4 show that the Archimedian property holds for the natural numbers.

2.6. DIVISION IN POSITIONAL NOTATION

As observed in Section 2.5 in the division algorithm, given any two counting numbers a, b, with $b \neq 0$, there exist unique counting numbers q and r such that $a = b \cdot q + r$ where r is smaller than b. If one starts with a pile of a stones and removes q piles of b stones each, there will be r stones left in the original pile. Since $r < b$, one cannot remove b stones from this pile. In other words, to divide a by b one subtracts b from a as many times as possible. The number of subtractions performed gives the quotient, and the number that is left is the remainder.

At first glance this seems like a simple way to determine the standard numeral for the quotient and remainder. We mentally follow this procedure to divide 7 by 3 and see that $7 = 3 \cdot 2 + 1$. However on second thought it is not so simple when we consider 70 divided by 3 or 700 divided by 3. In these latter cases there are simply too many subtractions to perform conveniently one at a time. The phrase "one at a time" is the key. As noted earlier $10 \cdot 3 = 30$ and $100 \cdot 3 = 300$. It is not so simple to subtract 3, ten times from 70, but it is quite easy to subtract 30 from 70 taking advantage of positional notation and the fundamental laws as we did in Section 2.2. Similar remarks apply even more forcefully to the problem of subtracting 3, 100 times from 700, versus the problem of subtracting 300 from 700. Since our system of positional notation is based on powers of 10, the most efficient way to determine how many times 3 can be subtracted from a natural number will be to utilize the products of 3 by the powers of 10. For example, let us consider the problem of determining the standard numerals for the quotient and remainder when 700 is divided by 3. Considering $3 = 3 \cdot 1$, $30 = 3 \cdot 10$, $300 = 3 \cdot 100$, $3000 = 3 \cdot 1000$, etc., we see that 300 is the largest product of 3 by a power of 10 that can be subtracted from 700. We subtract 300 from 700 as many times as possible, i.e., two.

$$
\begin{array}{r}
700 \\
300 \\
\hline
400 \\
300 \\
\hline
100
\end{array}
$$

"The second verse is the same as the first." We see that 30 is the largest product of 3 by a power of 10 that can be subtracted from 100. We subtract 30 as many times as possible from 100, i.e., three.

$$
\begin{array}{r}
100 \\
30 \\
\hline
70 \\
30 \\
\hline
40 \\
30 \\
\hline
10
\end{array}
$$

The largest product of 3 by a power of 10 that can be subtracted from 10 is 3. We subtract 3 from 10 as many times as possible, i.e., three.

$$
\begin{array}{r}
10 \\
3 \\
\hline
7 \\
3 \\
\hline
4 \\
3 \\
\hline
1
\end{array}
$$

Since $1 < 3$ it is no longer possible to subtract 3. Recapitulating, we subtracted 100 3's, 100 3's, 10 3's, 10 3's, 10 3's, 1 3's, 1 3's, 1 3's for a total of 233 3's. Thus $700 = 3 \cdot 233 + 1$.

Since '7' in '700' is in the 100's slot, each time 3 is subtracted from this 7, 300 is subtracted from the number. Hence we may omit the 0's in 300 and write the following

$$
\begin{array}{r}
700 \\
3 \\
\hline
400 \\
3 \\
\hline
100
\end{array}
$$

But it does not take much mental agility to see that we can subtract 3 from 7 two times, and that since $2 \cdot 3 = 6$ and $7 - 6 = 1$, 100 will be left. We might indicate this by

$$
\begin{array}{r}
2 \\
3\overline{)700} \\
6 \\
\hline
100
\end{array}
$$

Similarly we can subtract 3 from 10 three times since $3 \cdot 3 = 9$ and $10 - 9 = 1$. As this '1' is in the 10's slot, 10 will be left. In other words 30 has been subtracted 3 times from 100. We continue by the following

$$
\begin{array}{r}
23 \\
3\overline{)700} \\
6 \\
\hline
100 \\
9 \\
\hline
10
\end{array}
$$

Continuation of the process yields

$$
\begin{array}{r}
233 \\
3\overline{)700} \\
6 \\
\hline
100 \\
9 \\
\hline
10 \\
9 \\
\hline
1
\end{array}
$$

This process is generally taught to school children in this country under the name of long division.

Since it is simple to divide mentally by a single digit, we may simply write

$$\begin{array}{r} 233 \\ \hline 3\overline{)700} \end{array} \qquad \text{remainder 1}$$

This process is taught to some, but by no means to all, of the school children in this country under the name of short division.

A further refinement of this process is taught in France and Germany, but is not generally taught in this country. It consists of combining the multiplication and subtraction steps in this process. By utilizing the carry-add method of subtraction no great mental agility is required. The scheme would appear as follows

$$\begin{array}{r} 233 \\ \hline 3\overline{)700} \\ 10 \\ 10 \\ 1 \end{array}$$

Let us illustrate by a slightly more complicated example and divide 34 into 7000 by this process (which is called the French method of long division).

$$\begin{array}{r} 205 \\ \hline 34\overline{)7000} \\ 200 \\ 30 \end{array}$$

We think 34 into 70 goes 2 times and write 2 on the top. Then $2 \cdot 4 = 8$ and 2 makes 10, write 2 and carry 1; $2 \cdot 3 = 6$ and the 1 that was carried makes 7, $7 + 0 = 7$ so write nothing. Now we "bring down" a zero. Since 34 does not go into 20 we write 0 on the top and "bring down" another 0. Since 34 goes 5 times into 200 we write 5 on top. We think $5 \cdot 4 = 20$ and 0 makes 20, write 0 and carry 2. Then $5 \cdot 3 = 15$ and the 2 that was carried makes 17, $17 + 3 = 20$, write 3. Thus we see that $7000 = 34 \cdot 205 + 30$.

EXERCISES

1. Find the quotient q and the remainder r in each of the following cases. Explain each step that you take.

(a) $a = 35$, $b = 8$ (e) $a = 0$, $b = 7$
(b) $a = 350$, $b = 8$ (f) $a = 35$, $b = 12$
(c) $a = 3500$, $b = 8$ (g) $a = 350$, $b = 12$
(d) $a = 35$, $b = 7$ (h) $a = 3500$, $b = 12$

2. Find the quotient and remainder in each of the following cases, using the French method. Explanations need not be given.

   (a) $a = 72345$, $b = 89$ (c) $a = 123456789$, $b = 9876$
   (b) $a = 723450$, $b = 890$ (d) $a = 59621345$, $b = 6967$

3. Explain how one proceeds from division by a number whose standard numeral contains one digit to division by a number whose standard numeral contains more than one digit.

2.7. OTHER PROCEDURES FOR MULTIPLICATION AND DIVISION

We recall that the proper phrase to use when asking someone to change 5×7 to 35 ought to be something like "what is the standard numeral for 5×7?" However, deeply ingrained in common usage are such statements as: "What is the product of 5 and 7?" "Multiply 5 by 7", or "How much is 5×7?". We note that "5×7" is a perfectly good (though flippant) answer to any of these questions. We point out again that when one writes "5×7" he has already "multiplied" the two numbers, and that what is really wanted is the standard numeral for the product. In this section we, too, will use the conventional phrases where no ambiguity will result and speak of multiplication and division when we mean finding the standard numeral of products and quotients.

Recently a young housewife we know was quite upset to discover that her fourth-grade daughter was doing long division by a process completely unfamiliar to the mother. She was convinced that the process was wrong and that her daughter was not being taught well. Many people believe that there is only one way to multiply numbers and that there is something sacred about the process of long division that they learned. It is true that the multiplication and division methods commonly taught in United States schools are very efficient processes—it is also true that they are by no means unique. It is our intention here to describe several methods of multiplying and dividing (including the one that upset the fourth-grader's mother). It is hoped that all this will lead to a better understanding of these arithmetical processes.

The key to most multiplication schemes is the distributive law. Using it on the product $(a + b) \cdot (c + d)$ and regarding, for the first step, $(a + b)$ as one number, we get

$$(a + b) \cdot (c + d) = (a + b)c + (a + b)d$$

Now "unfreezing" $(a + b)$ and distributing on the other side, we get

$$(a + b)c = ac + bc \quad \text{and} \quad (a + b)d = ad + bd$$

Thus

$$(a + b)(c + d) = ac + bc + ad + bd$$

or the sum of each of the terms in the first factor multiplied by each term in the second factor. We apply this to the product 29×42 by thinking of 29×42 as

$$(20 + 9) \cdot (40 + 2) = 20 \times 40 + 9 \times 40 + 20 \times 2 + 9 \times 2$$
$$= 800 + 360 + 40 + 18 = 1218$$

This process may be systematized in a number of ways. The requirements of a good system are that it keeps the mental work to a minimum, and yet limits the amount of writing. Perhaps the simplest system is the one which simply is the distributive law with the work arranged vertically for ease in addition. The problem above would appear as

EXAMPLE 1.

$$
\begin{array}{r}
29 \\
42 \\
\hline
800 \\
360 \\
40 \\
18 \\
\hline
1218 \\
\end{array}
$$

This could be extended to larger numbers as in

EXAMPLE 2.

$$
\begin{array}{r}
387 \\
65 \\
\hline
18000 \\
4800 \\
420 \\
1500 \\
400 \\
35 \\
\hline
25155 \\
\end{array}
$$

Note that the partial products need not be put down in any special order. One can go from left to right, or any other way as long as he is careful to get all the partial products. We may eliminate writing many of the zeros by an arrangement called the *grating* method. To illustrate this method we rework the problem in Example 2. We draw a 3 by 2 rectangle (because there are 3 digits in one factor and 2 in the other) and draw in the diagonal lines as illustrated.

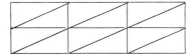

We write the digits 3, 8, and 7 across the top of the diagram (one above each little rectangle), and the digits 6 and 5 down the right side. Now each digit on the top is multiplied by each digit on the right and the product is entered in the rectangle they determine. Finally the partial products are added "diagonally" (see diagram) working from right to left, and the answer is read off along the left side and bottom of the diagram.

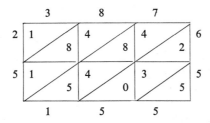

In some respects this is a better system of multiplication than the one we commonly use. It requires no carrying while multiplying and the position of the digits is kept for you with little effort.

We exhibit next another device for multiplying. This one has the advantage of requiring only proficiency in addition and the ability to multiply and divide by 2. We illustrate how this method may be used to multiply 38×23.

38	23	
19	46	46
9	92	92
4	184	
2	368	
1	736	736

The work is arranged in three columns. One factor is put in the first column the other in the second. The number in the first column is halved (with possible remainder disregarded), the one in the second column doubled and this process is repeated until the number in the first column is *1*. Then, for each *odd* number in the first column, the corresponding number in the second column is entered in the third column. The sum of the entries in the third column is the required answer.

This process has been ascribed to African natives and/or Russian peasants and often appears in books containing mathematical games and recreations. It becomes quite cumbersome when the numbers are large, but it is included here as a curiosity and because it illustrates several principles.

Let us examine what actually happened in the calculation above

$$
\begin{aligned}
(38)(23) &= (19 \cdot 2)(23) = (19)(2 \cdot 23) = (19)(46) \\
&= (18 + 1)(46) = (18)(46) + 1(46) = (9 \cdot 2)(46) + 46 \\
&= 9(92) + 46 = (8 + 1)(92) + 46 = (8)(92) + 92 + 46 \\
&= (4 \cdot 2)(92) + 92 + 46 = 4(184) + 92 + 46 \\
&= (2 \cdot 2)(184) + 92 + 46 = 2(368) + 92 + 46 \\
&= 736 + 92 + 46 = 874
\end{aligned}
$$

Notice that this process which has been called "doubling and halving" is based on the associative law for multiplication and the distributive law.

In multiplying two digit numbers it is relatively easy to do the computation mentally and write only the answer. The idea is based on the fact that $(10a + b) \times (10c + d) = 100ac + 10(ad + bc) + bd$. This means that the product is equal to the sum of: (a) the product of the units digits, (b) 10 times the sum of the "cross products" of the digits (i.e., the units digit of one times the tens digit of the other plus the tens digit of one times the unit digit of the other), and (c) 100 times the product of the tens digits. We illustrate with an example.

EXAMPLE 3. Multiply 27 and 34.

We say, "4 times 7 is 28"; put down 8 and carry 2. Next, 4 times 2 is 8, 3 times 7 is 21, and 8, 21, and the 2 we carried are 31; put down 1 and carry 3. Then 3 times 2 is 6 and the 3 we carried are 9; put down 9. The product is 918.

This method may be extended to multiplication of larger numbers, but the amount of mental computation increases rapidly as the number of digits increases and is usually impractical without considerable practice.

EXERCISES

1. By using the method of Examples 1 and 2 find the product of:
   (a) 39 and 847
   (b) 2615 and 934

2. Using the grating method find:

   (a) 67×286
   (b) 9864×482

3. Use the grating method to find the product of the numbers $\times \perp \dashv$ and $\dashv \mid \perp \perp$.

4. Using the "African natives-Russian peasants" method find:

   (a) 48×23
   (b) 53×34

5. Writing only the final answer, multiply:

   (a) 23 and 32
   (b) 67 and 59

6. A multiplying device used by people who know the multiplication table only up to 5×5 goes as follows: To multiply two numbers between 5 and 10 subtract 5 from one of the numbers and raise this many fingers on one hand; then subtract 5 from the other number and raise this many fingers on the other hand. Then multiply the number of fingers not raised on one hand by the number of fingers not raised on the other hand. Then the units digit of this number is the units digit of the answer. The tens digit of the answer is obtained by adding the tens digit, if any, of this number to the total number of raised fingers. For example, to multiply 8 by 6 subtract 5 from 8 and then raise three fingers on the left hand; subtract 5 from 6 and raise one finger on the right hand. Then there are two fingers on the left hand not raised and there are four fingers on the right hand not raised and so the units of the answer is the units digit of $4 \cdot 2 = 8$; while the tens digit of the answer will be the number of raised fingers or $3 + 1 = 4$.

   (a) Using this method multiply 8 by 7, 9 by 6, and 5 by 10.
   (b) Explain why the method gives a correct result.

7. Consider the sequence of numbers $1, 2, 4, 8, 16, 32, 64, \ldots$, where each number after the first is obtained by doubling the preceding. Now any counting number can be expressed uniquely as a sum of numbers from this list where no number in this list is used more than once. For example, $21 = 16 + 4 + 1$. To see this, suppose we are given the number n and know that k_1 is the largest number in this list which is less than or equal to n. We note that $2k_1 > n$ and so $n - k_1 < k_1$. Now let k_2 be the largest integer in the list which is less than or equal to $n - k_1$. Clearly $k_2 < k_1$. Continuing in this manner we see that $n = k_1 + k_2 + \cdots + k_r$ where $k_1, k_2, \ldots, k_r$ are uniquely determined because at each stage we have only one choice for k_i. Using this representation, and assuming we know how to add, the product of two counting numbers may be obtained. For example, $23 \cdot 37 = (16 + 4 + 2 + 1) \cdot 37 = 16 \cdot 37 + 4 \cdot 37 + 2 \cdot 37 + 1 \cdot 37$.

Using addition only, we may obtain the products of the numbers in our list by 37 as follows:

$$37 = 1 \cdot 37$$
$$37 = 1 \cdot 37$$
$$74 = 2 \cdot 37$$
$$148 = 4 \cdot 37$$
$$296 = 8 \cdot 37$$
$$592 = 16 \cdot 37$$

where each number after the first is the sum of all numbers above it. Then $23 \cdot 37 = 592 + 148 + 74 + 37 = 851$.

(a) Using this method multiply 21 by 19, 53 by 38, and 38 by 53.
(b) What effect does changing the order of the factors have upon the work involved?

We recall that the division algorithm says that for any two counting numbers a and b, $b \neq 0$, there are unique counting numbers q and r such that $a = bq + r$ and r is less than b. Finding q and r is called dividing a by b; q is called the quotient and r is called the remainder. In practice one finds q and r in several steps. He finds a, q_1 and r_1 so that $a = bq_1 + r_1$. If r_1 is smaller than b he is finished; if not he finds q_2 and r_2 so that $r_1 = bq_2 + r_2$. Similarly if r_2 is not smaller than b he finds q_3 and r_3 so that $r_2 = bq_3 + r_3$. He continues this process till he arrives at r_n which is smaller than b. Now he knows that

$$a = bq_1 + r_1$$
$$= bq_1 + (bq_2 + r_2)$$
$$= bq_1 + bq_2 + (bq_3 + r_3)$$
$$= bq_1 + bq_2 + bq_3 + \cdots + bq_n + r_n$$
$$= b(q_1 + q_2 + \cdots + q_n) + r_n$$

Now letting

$$q = q_1 + q_2 + \cdots + q_n \quad \text{and} \quad r = r_n$$

completes the problem. Hence the only question remaining is how does one determine q_1 and r_1, q_2 and r_2, etc. Theoretically it doesn't matter—one can guess at the q's (or take them to be 1, as in the piles of stones at the end of Section 2.5). Actually, of course, by selecting the q's carefully the work is tremendously shortened. Consider the following example.

EXAMPLE 4. Divide 579 by 28.

Here $a = 579$ and $b = 28$. To find q_1 one thinks of replacing 28 by 30. Now $30 \times 20 = 600$ which is larger than 579; so let $q_1 = 10$. We have $bq_1 = 28 \times 10 = 280$ and $r_1 = a - bq_1 = 579 - 280 = 299$. It is now easy to let $q_2 = 10$ so $299 = 28 \times 10 + r_2$ and $r_2 = 299 - 280 = 19$ which is smaller than $b = 28$. Thus $579 = 28(10) + 28(10) + 19$ or

$579 = 28(20) + 19$ or 579 divided by 28 is 20 with a remainder of 19. The preceding calculation can be written more compactly as

$$
\begin{array}{r}
28\overline{)579} \quad 10 \\
280 \\
\hline
299 \quad 10 \\
280 \\
\hline
\end{array}
$$

remainder $\overline{19} \ | \ \overline{20}$ quotient

Note that the only "mistake" that can be made (aside from computational ones) is to guess too large for the q's. To avoid this is the reason for using 30 as a "trial divisor."

This is the method that the young mother, mentioned at the beginning of this section, found so strange and novel. It is, without question, less efficient than the usual system of long division. It illustrates, perhaps a little more clearly, what is going on, and it has the advantage of requiring less mental work than the usual method.

Note that in the usual method q_1 is selected so that its first digit (reading from the left) is the same as that of q's, then q_2 is chosen so that its first digit is q's second, etc. Thus in this method we get a digit of the quotient for each step of the procedure. The method described in the previous paragraph permits a little more latitude, but still is fairly conservative in that there should be a relatively small number of steps. Let's look at an example where the guessing is "wilder" and less well organized.

EXAMPLE 5. Divide 82714 by 53.

$$
\begin{array}{r}
53\overline{)82714} \quad 17 \\
901 \\
\hline
81813 \quad 103 \\
5459 \\
\hline
76354 \quad 2 \\
106 \\
\hline
76248 \quad 1001 \\
53053 \\
\hline
23195 \quad 53 \\
2809 \\
\hline
20386 \quad 322 \\
17066 \\
\hline
3320 \quad 60 \\
3180 \\
\hline
140 \quad 2 \\
106 \\
\hline
34 \quad 1560 \\
\end{array}
$$

Here the first guess is 17—not very close to 1560 yet it is still possible to continue and find q and r. Note in particular that the work is more involved—it took eight steps and we had to perform more complicated multiplications (on a sheet of scratch paper for those we can't do mentally).

EXERCISES

1. By the method illustrated above divide 3545 by 26.

2. Divide 3545 by 26 by the usual method. Indicate what q_1, r_1, q_2, r_2, etc., are in this problem. Which method do you prefer?

3. Divide 3545 by 26 using the French method. How does it compare with the other methods?

4. Divide 5280 by 17 starting with $q_1 = 23$.

3

3.1. DIVISORS AND COMMON DIVISORS

The ancient Greeks are purported to have reserved number theory for the sons of the nobility—they considered it too precious to be taught to the sons of tradesmen. The sons of the tradesmen were taught a form of mechanical tallying. Although our notation used in arithmetic in elementary schools is vastly different from and superior to that of the ancient Greeks, it is unfortunate that our philosophy of teaching seems to stress mechanical manipulation. Our sons are not likely to study number theory prior to entering college, unless some curriculum innovation such as that envisaged by the School Mathematics Study Group takes place. While the contents of this section can properly be entitled "Number Theory," let it be noted that we delve but slightly into the topic.

We will review some material from Section 2.5. If a, b, and c are counting numbers and $a = bc$; then, we say b is a *divisor* (or *factor*) of a, c is a *divisor* (or, *factor*) of a, a is a *multiple* of b, and a is a *multiple* of c. It is customary to state that b is a divisor of a (notation $b \mid a$) and c is a divisor of a, also. Note that if $b \neq 0$ then we can *divide a* by b obtaining $a = bq + r$ by the division algorithm. Then a is a multiple of b if and only if $r = 0$. To be more explicit, the counting number b is a *divisor* of the counting number a if there exists a counting number c such that $a = bc$. Since $0 = 0 \cdot a$ then 0 is a divisor of 0 and 0 is a multiple of 0. However, we never divide by 0 for even in the case of

number theory

"0 divided by 0" where division is actually possible, the quotient is not unique. One must keep in mind the fine distinction between "divide" and "divisor." If a is a counting number and b is a nonzero counting number then we can "divide" a by b, but b is not in general a "divisor" of a. On the other hand 0 is a "divisor" of 0 but we never "divide" by 0.

LEMMA 1. If a, b, c, d, e are counting numbers, $b = ad$, $c = ae$, and $b > c$, then $d > e$.

Proof:

We know that $d = e$, $d > e$ or $d < e$. If $d \leq e$ then $ad \leq ae$ or $b \leq c$, a contradiction. Hence we must have $d > e$.

THEOREM 1. Let a, b, c, be counting numbers.

(i) If $a \mid b$ and $a \mid c$ then $a \mid b + c$.
(ii) If $a \mid b$ and $a \mid c$ and $b - c$ exists, then $a \mid b - c$.
(iii) If $a \mid b$ and $b \mid c$ then $a \mid c$.

Proof:

(*i*) Since $a \mid b$ there is a counting number k such that $b = ka$. Since $a \mid c$ there is a counting number r such that $c = ra$. Hence $b + c = ka + ra = (k + r)a$.

Thus there is a counting number, $k + r$, which when multiplied by a yields $b + c$. By definition then, $a \mid (b + c)$.

(ii) After an application of the Lemma 1, the proof is similar to that of (i) and is left for the reader.

(iii) Since $a \mid b$ and $b \mid c$ then there exist counting numbers b and r such that $b = ka$ and $c = rb$. Hence $c = rb = r(ka) = (rk)a$. That is, $a \mid c$.

LEMMA 2. $a - (b - c) = (a - b) + c$.

Proof:

$[(a - b) + c] + (b - c) = (a - b) + [c + (b - c)] = (a - b) + b = a$. Hence $(a - b) + c$ is the number which added to $b - c$ gives a, i.e., $a - (b - c)$.

COROLLARY. Let a, b, c be counting numbers.

(i) If $a \mid b$ and $a \mid b + c$ then $a \mid c$.
(ii) If $a \mid b$ and $a \mid b - c$ then $a \mid c$.
   The proof is left to the reader.

We can now deduce some consequences of positional notation by considering the standard numerals of counting numbers. In order to simplify the notation, we will consider special cases. Let us take the number 2345.

We know that this denotes $2 \cdot 1000 + 3 \cdot 100 + 4 \cdot 10 + 5$. Since we observe by Theorem 1 that 10 is a divisor of 10, 100, and 1000, then

$$10 \mid (2 \cdot 1000 + 3 \cdot 100 + 4 \cdot 10)$$

Now $5 \mid 10$ and also $5 \mid (2 \cdot 1000 + 3 \cdot 100 + 4 \cdot 10)$. But $5 \mid 5$ so

$$5 \mid [(2 \cdot 1000 + 3 \cdot 100 + 4 \cdot 10) + 5]$$

i.e., $5 \mid 2345$. It is not much of a generalization to show that 5 is a divisor of a given counting number if, and only if, the number represented by the last digit in its standard numeral is divisible by 5. Since the only numbers whose standard numeral consists of a single digit which are divisible by 5 are 0 and 5, the counting numbers divisible by 5 are those whose standard numerals end in 0 or 5. Note that we have been using the units slot of a standard numeral as the "end" of the numeral and have called it the "last" digit. It could equally well be called the "first" digit of the standard numeral, but we prefer to call it the "last" digit. The only property of the number 5 we have used in the argument is that it is a divisor of 10. What other numbers are divisors of 10? What can you deduce?

We can also write the number 2345 as $(2 \cdot 1000 + 3 \cdot 100) + 45$. In a fashion similar to the above we see that $100 \mid 100$ and $100 \mid 1000$ so that $100 \mid (2 \cdot 1000 + 3 \cdot 100)$. Since $25 \mid 100$, then $25 \mid (2 \cdot 1000 + 3 \cdot 100)$. Hence 25 will divide 2345 if and only if it divides 45. We see that, in general, 25 divides a given counting number if and only if 25 divides the number composed of the last two digits of the standard numeral of the given number. What other 1 and 2 digit divisors does 100 have? What can you deduce?

Note that $125 \mid 1000$. Does this give you a clue as to how to determine whether or not 125 divides a given counting number by examination of its standard numeral? What other divisors does 1000 have whose standard numerals have 1, 2, or 3 digits? What else can you deduce?

A very nice device for testing whether a number is divisible by 9 can be established by means of the following theorem.

THEOREM 2. Let a, b be counting numbers, $a = 9q + r$ where q, r are counting numbers. Then $9 \mid (a + b)$ if and only if $9 \mid (r + b)$.

Proof:

Since $a + b = (9q + r) + b = 9q + (r + b)$, this theorem follows from the preceding theorem and corollary.

Now to see if $9 \mid 2345$ we note that

$$4 \cdot 10 = 4 \cdot (10 - 1) + 4 \qquad 3 \cdot 100 = 3 \cdot (100 - 1) + 3$$

$$2 \cdot 1000 = 2 \cdot (1000 - 1) + 2$$

Moreover

$$10 - 1 = 9 \qquad 100 - 1 = 99 \qquad 1000 - 1 = 999$$

Hence we see that

$$
\begin{aligned}
2345 &= 2 \cdot 1000 + 3 \cdot 100 + 4 \cdot 10 + 5 \\
&= 2 \cdot (1000 - 1) + 2 + 3 \cdot (100 - 1) + 3 + 4 \cdot (10 - 1) + 4 + 5 \\
&= 2 \cdot (1000 - 1) + 3 \cdot (100 - 1) + 4 \cdot (10 - 1) + 2 + 3 + 4 + 5 \\
&= (2 \cdot 999 + 3 \cdot 99 + 4 \cdot 9) + (2 + 3 + 4 + 5)
\end{aligned}
$$

Since $9 \mid 9$, $9 \mid 99$, and $9 \mid 999$ we see that $9 \mid (2 \cdot 999 + 3 \cdot 99 + 4 \cdot 9)$. Hence $9 \mid 2345$ if and only if $9 \mid (2 + 3 + 4 + 5)$, (incidentally it does not).

More generally if a number n has four digits in its standard numeral it can be written in the form $1000a + 100b + 10c + d$ where a, b, c, and d are, respectively, its thousands digit, hundreds digit, tens digit, and units digit. Since

$$1000a = 999a + a \qquad 100b = 99b + b \qquad 10c = 9c + c$$

we have

$$
\begin{aligned}
n &= 999a + a + 99b + b + 9c + c + d \\
&= 999a + 99b + 9c + a + b + c + d \\
&= 9(111a + 11b + c) + (a + b + c + d)
\end{aligned}
$$

Thus applying Theorem 2, we see that n is divisible by 9 if and only if $a + b + c + d$ is divisible by 9. Since similar proofs can be made for numbers which have 1, 2, 3, 5, 6, 7, ... digits in their standard numerals, we now know that 9 divides a given counting number if and only if 9 divides the "sum of the digits" of its standard numeral. (Strictly speaking, since digits are numerals, the phrase in quotation marks is not correct.)

Note that Theorem 2 may also be used to reduce the work in determining whether 9 divides the sum of the digits of a given numeral. So that in determining, e.g., whether 9 divides $2 + 3 + 4 + 5$ we note that $2 + 3 + 4 = 9$ so that 9 divides $2 + 3 + 4 + 5$ if and only if it divides 5 (which it still doesn't). One can learn to discard, mentally, those digits whose sums are multiples of 9 and consider only the remaining ones. This is one of several processes which have been called "casting out nines" and is sometimes a useful device in mental arithmetic.

EXERCISES

1. Prove part (ii) of Theorem 1.

2. Prove the Corollary to Theorem 1.

3. What counting numbers are divisors of 0?

4. What counting numbers does 0 divide?

5. How can you deduce that the sum of two even counting numbers is an even counting number? (Recall that a counting number is even if it contains 2 as a factor.)

6. Let a be an odd counting number and b an even counting number. Is $a + b$ odd or even?

7. Let S be the sum of an even number of odd counting numbers. Is S even or odd?

8. Let S be the sum of an odd number of odd counting numbers. Is S even or odd?

Suppose a and $b \neq 0$ are counting numbers and $a \mid b$. Then, if $a \neq b$, $a < b$. As there are only a finite number of counting numbers smaller than b, there are only a finite number of divisors of b. That is, the set of divisors of a nonzero counting number b is a finite set.

Now suppose a and $b \neq 0$ are counting numbers and c is a divisor common to a and b, i.e., $c \mid a$ and $c \mid b$. Since there are only a finite number of divisors of b, then it follows there are only a finite number of counting numbers which divide both a and b. But any finite set of numbers has a largest element. This, then, is the largest counting number which divides both a and b. It is called the greatest common divisor of a and b; it is abbreviated as g.c.d. of a and b; it is denoted by (a, b). We will consider a more sophisticated definition of g.c.d. later.

This proof asserts that there is such a thing as the g.c.d. of two counting numbers a and b, which are not both 0 and that you may determine it by examining the set of all divisors of a and the set of all divisors of b and then picking out the elements common to these two sets. We then select the largest element in this new set and it is (a, b).

Some two thousand years ago Euclid gave a proof of the result above which was superior in many ways to this proof. For instance, Euclid's proof applies not only to counting numbers but also to polynomials over a field (whatever these might be) while this proof does not. But also Euclid's method is much simpler than our method for finding the g.c.d. of large counting numbers. In fact Euclid's method is the only method which might be termed "practical" for finding the g.c.d. of large counting numbers. This process of Euclid was taught to the school children in the "Gay Nineties," and is called the *Euclidian algorithm*. An algorithm is a process for doing something. So, the Euclidian algorithm denotes the process used by Euclid to find the g.c.d. of two counting numbers. Let us now look at Euclid's proof.

Suppose a and $b \neq 0$ are counting numbers. Then by the division algorithm there are unique counting numbers q and r such that $a = bq + r$ where $0 \leq r < b$. Now any divisor common to b and r divides a by Theorem 1, and hence is a divisor common to a and b. On the other hand, $r = a - bq$ and so any divisor common to a and b divides r by the same theorem. Thus the set of divisors common to a and b is the same as the set of divisors common to b and r. In particular, then $(a, b) = (b, r)$. If $r \neq 0$, then by the division algorithm there are unique counting numbers q_1 and r_1 such that $b = q_1 r + r_1$ where $0 \leq r_1 < r$. As above we have $(b, r) = (r, r_1)$. If $r_1 \neq 0$, then by the division algorithm there are unique counting numbers q_2, r_2 such that $r = q_2 r_1 + r_2$ where $0 \leq r_2 < r_1$. Then $(r, r_1) = (r_1, r_2)$ where $0 \leq r_2 < r_1 < r < b$. Since there are only a finite number of counting numbers smaller than b, the process must terminate in a finite number of steps, i.e., the remainder at some stage, say r_{k+1} must be 0. Suppose then, $r_k \neq 0$ but $r_{k+1} = 0$. Then $(a, b) = (b, r) = (r, r_1) = (r_1, r_2) = \cdots = (r_k, r_{k+1}) = (r_k, 0)$. It is not hard to convince ourselves that $(r_k, 0) = r_k$ (see Exercise 8). But then $(a, b) = r_k$. We have divided b into a, divided the remainder into b, and continued the process of dividing the remainder into the previous divisor until a remainder of 0 is obtained. Then the divisor used to obtain this 0 remainder is the g.c.d. of a and b.

EXAMPLE 1. Find the g.c.d. of 247 and 221 by the Euclidian algorithm. Our work is shown below.

$$
\begin{array}{r}
1 \\
221\,\overline{)247} \\
221 \quad 8 \\
\hline
26\,\overline{)221} \\
208 \quad 2 \\
\hline
13\,\overline{)26} \\
26 \\
\hline
0
\end{array}
$$

We see that $13 = (221, 247)$. In fact, we see that $(247, 221) = (221, 26) = (26, 13) = (13, 0) = 13$.

EXAMPLE 2. Find the g.c.d. of 247 and 221 by the factoring method.

Surprisingly, it is not so easy to determine all the divisors of a counting number. There are 247 possible divisors of 247, i.e., the counting numbers $1, 2, 3, \ldots, 247$. While we could try each of these in turn, there are better methods which we will discuss in more detail later. For the moment let us simply assert that $\{1, 13, 19, 247\}$ is the set of divisors of 247 and $\{1, 13, 17, 221\}$ is the set of divisors of 221. By inspection we see that $\{1, 13\}$ is the set of divisors common to 247 and 221 and that 13 is the $(247, 221)$.

Now let us consider in more detail some points pertinent to the method of factoring. To classify the counting numbers by the type of factors they possess we divide the set of counting numbers into four subsets, no two of which have an element in common. The first subset contains the single element 0 which we term the *additive identity*. The second subset contains the single element 1, which we term the *multiplicative identity*. The third subset contains all *primes*. The counting number a is a *prime* if for *every* pair of counting numbers b, c, such that $a = bc$ it is true that $b = 1$ or $c = 1$ but not both b and c are 1. The fourth subset contains all *composites*. The counting number a is called composite if $a \neq 0$ and there exists counting numbers b, c, such that $a = bc$ where neither b nor c is 1. We note that $a \neq 0$ is a prime if, excluding 1, no counting number smaller than a divides a.

Some two hundred and fifty years before the birth of Christ, Eratosthenes used this fact to determine all primes $\leq$ a given counting number. The process is known as the "Sieve of Eratosthenes." Let us illustrate it by finding all primes ≤ 41. We first make a list of the nonzero counting numbers from 1 through 41, 1, 2, 3, 4, 5, 6, 7, 8, 9, 10, 11, 12, 13, 14, 15, 16, ... , 41. Since 1 is not a prime we scratch it off, thus, 1, 2, 3, 4, 5, ... , 41. Then we see that, excluding 1, no number smaller than 2 divides 2 and so 2 is a prime. But the multiples of 2, other than 2 are not primes and so we scratch them off. Our list will then look like this! 1, 2, 3, 4, 5, 6, 7, 8, 9, 10, 11, 12, 13, 14, 15, 16, 17, 18, 19, 20, 21, 22, 23, 24, 25, 26, 27, 28, 29, 30, 31, 32, 33, 34, 35, 36, 37, 38, 39, 40, 41. Now we see that, excluding 1, no number smaller than 3 divides 3 and no number smaller than 5 divides 5. Thus 3 and 5 are primes. Scratching off the multiples of 3 and 5, other than 3 and 5, gives the list 1, 2, 3, 4, 5, 6, 7, 8, 9, 10, 11, 12, 13, 14, 15, 16, 17, 18, 19, 20, 21, 22, 23, 24, 25, 26, 27, 28, 29, 30, 31, 32, 33, 34, 35, 36, 37, 38, 39, 40, 41. Crossing off multiples of 7, 11, etc., result in no new deletions. Hence the primes ≤ 41 are 2, 3, 5, 7, 11, 13, 17, 19, 23, 29, 31, 37, and 41.

EXERCISES

1. Suppose a is a counting number between 90 and 120, and no prime ≤ 11 is a factor of a. Show that a is a prime.

2. Find all primes between 90 and 120.

3. Is the sum of two primes: (a) always, (b) sometimes, or (c) never a prime?

4. Is the product of two primes: (a) always, (b) sometimes, or (c) never a prime?

5. Find the number of times that 3 will divide the product of the counting numbers 1 through 50.

6. Find the g.c.d. of:

(a) 221 and 247

(b) 667 and 713

(c) 1517 and 1591

(d) 3127 and 3233

(e) 4757 and 4891

(f) 5767 and 6059

7. Find the g.c.d. of:

(a) 143, 187, and 209

(b) 7081, 6497, and 7811

8. Show $(a, 0) = a$ where $a \neq 0$.

3.2. MULTIPLES AND COMMON MULTIPLES

We first consider the set of nonzero common multiples of two given natural numbers. Since every nonempty set of natural numbers contains a least number, there is a least number in this set of multiples of the given natural numbers which we call the *least common multiple* of the two given natural numbers. Thus, as the name implies, the least common multiple of two given natural numbers a and b is the smallest natural number which is a multiple of both a and b. In particular the product ab is a common multiple of a and b, but it is not necessarily the smallest common multiple. Mathematicians use a more sophisticated definition of least common multiple which we give at the end of this section. We denote the least common multiple of a and b by l.c.m. of a and b or by $[a, b]$. The set of common divisors of the counting numbers a and b is finite while the set of common multiples of a and b is infinite. Thus it is not easy, in general, to determine the l.c.m. of a and b and it will be helpful for us to develop more theory. We can easily see by inspection that $[2, 3] = 6$ and that $[4, 6] = 12$, but it is not so easy to determine $[1517, 1591]$.

One consequence of the Euclidian algorithm is that the greatest common divisor of two counting numbers may be expressed as a difference of the counting numbers. For example, let us use the Euclidian algorithm to determine $(18, 48)$. We have

$$48 = 2 \cdot 18 + 12 \qquad 18 = 1 \cdot 12 + 6 \qquad 12 = 2 \cdot 6 + 0$$

so that $(18, 48) = 6$. But from $6 = 18 - 12$ and $12 = 48 - 2 \cdot 18$ we obtain

$$6 = 18 - 12 = 18 - (48 - 2 \cdot 18)$$
$$= 18 - 48 + 2 \cdot 18 = 3 \cdot 18 - 48$$

Since $3 \cdot 18$ is a multiple of 18 and $48 = 1 \cdot 48$ is a multiple of 48 we have 6, the g.c.d. of 18 and 48 expressed as a difference of multiples of 18 and 48. The reader may verify that $6 = 17 \cdot 48 - 45 \cdot 18$. It may be shown by one familiar with the contents of Chapter 5 that both representations of the g.c.d are always possible.* Hence, we may state the following theorem.

> THEOREM 1. If a and $b \neq 0$ are counting numbers and $d = (a, b)$ then there are counting numbers r and s such that $d = ra - sb$.

We recall that the only factors of a prime counting number are 1 and the prime itself. Hence the only common divisors of a and p, where p is a prime, are 1 and p. Thus either $p \mid a$ or $(p, a) = 1$ if p is a prime.

> THEOREM 2. If p is a prime and $p \mid ab$ then $p \mid a$ or $p \mid b$.
>
> If $p \mid a$ then the conclusion is satisfied. If $p \nmid a$ then $(p, a) = 1$. Hence by Theorem 1 there are counting numbers r and s such that $1 = rp - sa$. On multiplication by b we obtain $b = (rb)p - s(ab)$. Since $p \mid ab$ and p divides any multiple of p we see that $p \mid (rb)p - s(ab)$, i.e., $p \mid b$. Thus the conclusion $p \mid a$ or $p \mid b$ is always satisfied. Note that the hypothesis p as a prime is essential. For $4 \mid 2 \cdot 6$ but $4 \nmid 2$ nor does 4 divide 6. On the otherhand, 3 is a prime and $3 \nmid 20$ and $3 \nmid 49$ so we can conclude $3 \nmid 20 \cdot 49$.

We recall that if a is a composite counting number then there are counting numbers $b \neq 1$ and $c \neq 1$ such that $a = bc$. It follows that b and c are smaller than a. Since there are only a finite number of counting numbers smaller than $s \neq 0$ then there are only a finite number of factors of a non-zero counting number. If a is a composite number then there exist counting numbers $b \neq 1$ and $c \neq 1$ such that $a = bc$. If b and c are primes we have a expressed as a product of primes. If one of these factors is not a prime we can express it as a product of smaller counting numbers neither of which is 1. Eventually we have a expressed as a product of primes.

> THEOREM 3. Every composite number can be expressed as a product of primes and the primes are unique (except for the order in which we write them).
>
> As we have observed, any composite counting number may be expressed as a product of primes. Our only problem is to show that the factorization is unique. Thus let us suppose we have two factorizations, and to show that they must be the same suppose $a = p_1 \times p_2 \times \cdots \times p_r = q_1 \times q_2 \times \cdots \times q_s$ where $p_1, \ldots, p_r$ and $q_1, \ldots, q_s$ are primes. Since p_1 is a prime and $p_1 \mid q_1 \times q_2 \times \cdots \times q_s$, it follows from Theorem 2 that p_1 is a factor of one of $q_1, q_2, \ldots, q_s$. We lose no generality in supposing $p_1 \mid q_1$. But as p_1 and q_1 are both primes p_1 is a factor of q_1 only if $p_1 = q_1$. Thus $p_1 \times p_2 \times \cdots \times p_r = p_1 \times q_2 \times \cdots \times q_s$ and hence we obtain $p_2 \cdots p_r = q_2 \cdots q_s$ (see Exercise 1). Continuation of this same argument shows that $r = s$ and each of the p's is equal to one of the q's.

---

* By adding and subtracting $18 \cdot 48$ we obtain $6 = 3 \cdot 18 - 1 \cdot 48 = (3 - 48) \cdot 18 - (1 - 18) \cdot 48 = 17 \cdot 48 - 45 \cdot 18$.

This theorem is sometimes called the *Unique Factorization Theorem* or the *Fundamental Theorem of Arithmetic*.

Sometimes some of us think that this theorem is trivial, because everyone knows that factorization into primes is unique. But this fact is certainly not obvious. Consider the set of even counting numbers under ordinary multiplication. Remember we are considering *only* the numbers 2, 4, 6, 8, ..., etc., and no others. The teacher says to factor 36; Susie gets $6 \cdot 6$ while Frank gets $2 \cdot 18$. A unique factorization into primes does not exist in this system. But we have the comforting assurance from Theorem 3 that unique factorization into primes does exist in the set of *all* counting numbers. We can write 12 as $2 \cdot 2 \cdot 3$, or $2 \cdot 3 \cdot 2$, or $3 \cdot 2 \cdot 2$; there are no other possibilities. The order in which we write the factors 2, 2, and 3 is immaterial by virtue of the commutative and associative laws of multiplication.

Now let us return to consideration of $[a, b]$. If $(a, b) = d$, $a = a_1 d$, and $b = b_1 d$, then $a_1 b_1 d$ is a common multiple of a and b. We claim, in fact, that it is the least common multiple of a and b because it divides every common multiple. For if m is a common multiple of a and b, $m = ka = tb$, then $ka_1 d = tb_1 d$ or $ka_1 = tb_1$. If a_1 is a prime then $a_1 \nmid b_1$ for otherwise d would not be the *greatest* common divisor of a and b. Hence, by Theorem 2, $a_1 \mid t$. If a_1 is not a prime then by the same reasoning every prime factor in a_1 must divide t. We conclude that a_1 is a factor of t, say $t = sa_1$. But then $ka_1 = tb_1 = sa_1 b_1$ and so $m = s(a_1 b_1 d)$ as we wished to show. Since this gives us a convenient means (the Euclidian algorithm) of calculating the least common multiple of two counting numbers we state the result as a theorem.

THEOREM 4. If $a \neq 0$ and $b \neq 0$ are counting numbers then $[a, b] = \dfrac{a \cdot b}{(a, b)}$.

In closing we mention the more sophisticated way in which mathematicians define g.c.d. and l.c.m. If $a \neq 0$ and $b \neq 0$ are counting numbers then the greatest common divisor of a and b is a counting number d which divides both a and b and which has the property that every common divisor of a and b divides d; the least common multiple of a and b is a counting number m which is a multiple of both a and b and which divides every common multiple of a and b. In this text we will not use either of these definitions.

EXERCISES

1. If a, b, and c are natural numbers and $ab = ac$ show that $b = c$.

2. Find:

(a) [1517, 1519]	(d) [3127, 3233]
(b) [221, 247]	(e) [4757, 4891]
(c) [667, 713]	(f) [5767, 6059]

3. If the least common multiple of three natural numbers a, b, c is defined to be the smallest integer which is a common multiple of a, b, c and is denoted by $[a, b, c]$, show that $[a, b, c] = [a, [b, c]]$ so that the Euclidian algorithm may still be applied.

4. Find:

(a) [142, 181, 209]

(b) [7081, 6497, 7811]

3.3. LANGUAGE TRANSLATION OR CHANGE OF BASE

We have thus far considered two systems of numerals or two languages. The language depends on our choice for flag. One which we might call the "one-handed language" was based on five symbols while the other was the more familiar "two-handed language." It is possible (and, surprisingly enough, sometimes desirable) to use systems of numerals based on other choices for flag. We could, as we did for the one-handed language invent new symbols, but the common practice is to use the old symbols whenever possible and attach new meanings to them. In this section we examine some of these languages and investigate the inter-relationships between different systems.

The simplest system, which is called the binary system, utilizes two basic symbols (why not one?). We will use 0 and 1 for these symbols and we list the first several numerals together with the corresponding piles of stones

```
                                             o o
                               o      o o     o
             o      o o     o o    o o     o o
      0      1      10      11     100     101
```

Thus in this language the name for the number of fingers that one has on his right hand is 101. Note that the individual digits have the same meaning as before but that the combinations of them which occur in our positional notation do not. The number $\substack{o \\ oo}$, for example, has the name '3' in the two-handed system while it has the name '11' in the binary system. Systems of numerals are, in effect, languages and replacing '3' in the two-handed system by '11' in the binary system is simply a matter of language translation—they are different names for the same number. With the possibility of more than one language the question of notation arises.

The numeral '11' always denotes the same number as the numeral '1 · ⊓ + 1' by virtue of positional notation. But the number 11 in the two-handed system is one more than the number of fingers on both hands, while the number 11 in the binary system is two less than the number of fingers on the right hand. We have been tacitly assuming that everyone agrees on the meaning of "one" and "two"—consider the phrases "two-handed system" and the "two less than the number of fingers on the right hand," for instance. More particularly this is based on the familiarity we all have with the two-handed system which we have utilized since childhood. Hence we agree that the two-handed language is our standard language, and that all numerals hereafter will be in this language unless explicitly stated otherwise. One particular convention that we will use is to state the language by means of a subscript denoting the base. Thus $(11)_2 = (3)_{10}$ will state that the number whose name is '11' in the binary language has the name '3' in the two-handed language. Some books express this equivalence of names by means of the equation $(11)_{two} = (3)_{ten}$, but we prefer the previous notation. A word of caution—read the numeral '11' as "one, one" and not as "eleven." The reason for this is that "eleven" has much stronger connotations for most of us than does "one, one" and hence is more likely to engender confusion. Similarly, read '25' as "two, five," '100' as "one, zero, zero," etc.

In the base 3, or ternary, system we use the symbols 0, 1, and 2 and write the first ten numerals as 1, 2, 10, 11, 12, 20, 21, 22, 100, 101. We can also use these standard symbols (i.e., the digits 0, 1, 2, 3, 4, 5, 6, 7, 8, 9) for the other systems whose bases are less than ten. We run into difficulties when we use a base greater than ten (why?) and have to invent new symbols. For example, if we use the base 12 (called the duo-decimal system—there is actually a "Duo-decimal Society" whose purpose is the establishment of the base 12 system as the standard one) we need new symbols for ten and eleven. We shall use T and E, respectively, so that the first twenty-five numerals in the base 12 are, 1, 2, 3, 4, 5, 6, 7, 8, 9, T, E, 10, 11, 12, 13, 14, 15, 16, 17, 18, 19, $1T$, $1E$, 20, 21.

Anyone who understands positional notation should be able to mentally translate small numbers from one language to another. Thus, $(3)_{10} = (11)_2 = (10)_3$; or $(17)_{10} = (21)_8 = (32)_5 = (101)_4$. Translate 17 to the binary language; or, to phrase it as a question, $(17)_{10} = (?)_2$. Note that 2 is a "Naughty" word in the binary language, i.e., '2' is a symbol which cannot be used in this language. Thus the student who writes $(6)_{10} = (22)_2$ is making a number of errors. It is desirable to do some of these problems to remind us of the significance of positional notation. Thus let the reader pause and fill in the blanks

$$(21)_{10} = (\quad)_9 = (\quad)_6 = (\quad)_3 = (\quad)_7 = (\quad)_8$$
$$= (\quad)_2 = (\quad)_5 = (\quad)_4 = (\quad)_{17} = (\quad)_{13} = (\quad)_{12}$$

We might observe that, for example

$$(345)_6 = 3 \cdot 36 + 4 \cdot 6 + 5$$
$$= 108 + 24 + 5 = 137$$

so that $(345)_6 = (137)_{10}$. How did we know that 137 is in the base 10 language?

EXERCISES

1. $(1101)_2 = (?)_{10}$.

2. How would you write 11 in the binary system?

3. Write the binary numerals for 2, 4, 8, and 16. What do you deduce?

4. Write the ternary numerals for 3, 9, 27, and 81.

5. What base 10 numeral is $(123)_4$?

6. Add the base 2 numbers 1101 and 1011. Subtract 1011 from 1101 (base 2).

7. If someone says "just as sure as 2 and 2 are 11," what base is he using?

8. If you wanted to write the number "five" for someone and you didn't know which base he was using, how could you do it?

To translate larger numbers from one base to another requires more technique, but again the ideas are based upon positional notation. We note that writing a number m in the base b means writing it in the form

$$a_0 b^n + a_1 b^{n-1} + \cdots + a_{n-1} b + a_n *$$

where each of the a_i's is less than b. For example, $(3145)_7$ means

$$3(7)^3 + 1(7)^2 + 4(7) + 5$$

This observation offers us a rather systematic way of converting numbers from one base to another. For if

$$m = a_0 b^n + a_1 b^{n-1} + \cdots + a_{n-1} b + a_n$$

where each a_1 is less than b, then dividing m by b will leave a remainder of a_n no matter in which base m is written. Then, since $a_n < b$, its standard numeral in base b will be a digit. Note that the quotient of the division is

$$a_0 b^{n-1} + a_1 b^{n-2} + \cdots + a_{n-1}$$

so if this is divided by b the remainder is a_{n-1}, the next digit. Proceeding in this manner we get the base b numeral for m.

* The reader not familiar with exponents may look ahead to Section 8.1.

EXAMPLE 3.
$$29 = (?)_3$$
Now
$$29 = 3 \cdot 9 + 2$$
$$9 = 3 \cdot 3 + 0$$
$$3 = 3 \cdot 1 + 0$$
$$1 = 3 \cdot 0 + 1$$
$$\therefore \quad 29 = 1(3)^3 + 0(3)^2 + 0(3) + 2, \text{ or } 29 = (1002)_3$$

As an alternative procedure we could work from the other end by considering the powers of the base b.

EXAMPLE 4. $(237)_{10} = (?)_7$. The powers of 7 are 7, $7^2 = 49$, $7^3 = 346$, etc. Since $346 > 237$ the largest power of 7 contained in 237 is 49. Now $237 - 4 \cdot 49 = 237 - 196 = 41$. Similarly $41 = 7 \cdot 5 + 6$. Thus

$$237 = 4 \cdot 49 + 5 \cdot 7 + 6 = 4 \cdot 7^2 + 5 \cdot 7 + 6 = (456)_7.$$

Most people, not being familiar with sums, products, etc., in different bases will translate back and forth between the base 10 and the one in which they are working in the course of a problem.

It is very good practice to do simple arithmetic problems in other bases. Bright youngsters are particularly interested in this, and the notions of "carrying" and "borrowing" become more clearly understood when done more generally.

EXAMPLE 5. Multiply the base 5 numbers 42 and 34.
We write

$$
\begin{array}{r}
42 \\
34 \\
\hline
323 \\
231 \\
\hline
3133
\end{array}
$$

and mentally say things like "four times two is eight," but in the base 5, this becomes one three. Therefore put down three and carry one. Four times four is sixteen and one is seventeen, but in the base 5 this becomes three two, etc.

EXERCISES

1. What is a "one digit number"? A "two digit number"? Are you sure?

2. $(2345)_7 + (6556)_7 = (?)_7$

3. $(2345)_8 + (6556)_8 = (?)_8$

4. $(6556)_7 - (2345)_7 = (?)_7$

5. $(6556)_8 - (2345)_8 = (?)_8$

6. $(345)_7 \cdot (556)_7 = (?)_7$

7. $(345)_8 \cdot (556)_8 = (?)_8$

8. $(2343)_7 \div (12)_7 = (?)_7$

9. $(2344)_6 \div (12)_6 = (?)_6$

10. $(2345)_6 = (?)_{10}$

11. $(2345)_{10} = (?)_6$

12. $(2345)_6 = (?)_{12}$

13. $(89E)_{12} \cdot (72)_{12} = (?)_{12}$

4

4.1. SET NOMENCLATURE

We have had occasion before to speak of sets of stones, sets of bull elephants, sets of numerals, sets of numbers—the notion of set is a primitive and useful concept. In this section we want to discuss sets in general, examine what can be done with them, and introduce some notation.

We think of a set as being known when we have given a method for determining what belongs to the set and what does not. More precisely, we think of a set as being determined when we have some defining property that distinguishes among a given collection of elements those elements which belong to the set and those which do not belong. For example, given the collection of all living creatures we might speak of the set of United States citizens. Given any living creature one could, presumably distinguish between those which are citizens of the United States and those which are not. Thus every living creature would either belong or not belong to the set and no living creature could both belong and not belong to the set. This does *not* constitute a definition of a set—we accept the notion of set as intuitively known. In fact, no one as yet has given a satisfactory definition of a set because, as Bertrand Russell has pointed out, some logical difficulties arise.

Although the notion of set is intuitive, a particular set such as "the set of cardinal numbers" is quite explicit and should have a universal meaning. A particular set may be defined by listing its elements explicitly (e.g., we might let the set A be the numbers

sets

1, 2, 3, 4, and 5), or by giving the characteristic properties that its elements possess (e.g., the aforementioned set of United States citizens).

If s is an element of the set S (traditionally, but not always, one uses capital letters for the names of sets and lower case letters for the names of elements of sets) we sometimes say "s is a member of S" or "s belongs to S" and, symbolically, we write "$s \in S$."

If A and B are sets, we are sometimes interested in a set called $A \cup B$ (read A union B). The set $A \cup B$ is defined as the set which consists of all elements of A and all elements of B. An equivalent definition would be to say $x \in A \cup B$ if (and only if) $x \in A$ or $x \in B$. The word "or" is used ambiguously in the English language (see Exercises 1 and 2). We use it in the sense that at least one of the alternatives is true—this is expressed in legal documents by "and/or." That is when we say "$x \in A$ or $x \in B$," we mean at least one of the following is true: (a) $x \in A$, (b) $x \in B$, (c) x belongs to both A and B. Some logicians call this an "inclusive or" as opposed to an "exclusive or" which means one or the other but not both. We also define $A \cap B$ (read A intersect B) to be the set which consists of all elements common to both A and B, or, equivalently, $x \in A \cap B$ if (and only if) $x \in A$ and $x \in B$. Thus the elements of $A \cup B$ are those elements which belong to A or to B (or to both A and B), while the elements of $A \cap B$ are those elements which belong to both A and B.

EXAMPLE 1. If A is the set of all odd counting numbers and B is the set of all even counting numbers then $A \cup B$ is the set of all counting numbers. While $A \cap B$ is a set which has no elements in it. We call such a set the *empty set* or *vacuous set* and denote it by $\emptyset$. Thus $A \cap B = \emptyset$.

EXAMPLE 2. If $A = \{1, 2, 3, 4\}$ (the braces denote the set consisting of the elements enumerated within them), and $B = \{3, 4, 5\}$, then $A \cup B = \{1, 2, 3, 4, 5\}$ and $A \cap B = \{3, 4\}$.

We next define a *subset* of a set as follows: a set A is a subset of a set B (written $A \subset B$) if each element of A is an element of B. We sometimes read "$A \subset B$" as "A is contained in B" and alternatively we write $B \supset A$ (read B contains A). Notice that any set is a subset of itself. To say that the set A is not a subset of the set B would mean there is some element in A which is not in B. The word "some" is equivalent to the phrase "at least one." Thus if A is not a subset of B there must be at least one element in A which is not in B. Since the empty set has no elements we cannot show that it is not a subset of any given set. We agree that the empty set, $\emptyset$, is a subset of every set.

Note that the symbols "$A \subset B$" represent a sentence, "A is a subset of B," unlike "$A \cup B$" which is merely the name of a set. Similarly "$\in$" is a relation between an element of a set and a set. Note also that the element a and the set, $\{a\}$, consisting of the single element a are logically distinct. We can write $a \in \{a\}$ but it is not correct to write $a \subset \{a\}$, or we can say that 2 is an even number but $\{2\}$ is not even a number, much less an even number.

We mentioned that when thinking of sets one first begins with a given collection of objects. This given set is called the *universal set* and contains as subsets all sets that we will deal with in some particular context. The universal set could change from one problem to the next. Indeed the universal sets chosen by two different persons working on the same problem might well be different. If one is considering sets of odd counting numbers, even counting numbers, counting numbers divisible by three, etc., the universal set might be the set of all counting numbers. If one is talking about sets of people with red hair, blue eyes, birthmarks, etc., the universal set might be the set of all people.

With respect to the universal set, which we temporarily call U, we now define for each subset A of U a set called the *complement* of A (written $\tilde{A}$) by saying an element x of U is in $\tilde{A}$ if (and only if) x is not a member of A. In other words, the complement of A consists of precisely those elements of U which are not elements of A.

If we are given a universal set U, this determines a set whose elements are the subsets of U. For example, if $U = \{a, b, c\}$, then the subsets of U are $\{a, b, c\}$, $\{a, b\}$, $\{a, c\}$, $\{b, c\}$, $\{a\}$, $\{b\}$, $\{c\}$, and $\emptyset$. In this connection we may think of "$\sim$" as a unary operation on the set of subsets of U—to each subset of U it assigns a unique subset of U. Now "$\cup$" is a binary operation on the set of subsets of U—to each pair of subsets, A and B, of U is assigned a unique subset of U, i.e., $A \cup B$. Similarly "$\cap$" is a binary operation on the subsets of U.

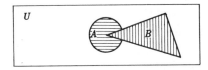
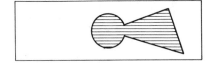

Figure 4-1   Figure 4-2

Let us illustrate some of these concepts by means of pictures called *Venn diagrams*, which are named after an English mathematician, John Venn. For example, let the set of points inside the rectangle denote U, those inside the circle A, and those inside the triangle B (Fig. 4.1). Then the set $A \cup B$ may be represented as in Fig. 4.2, the set $A \cap B$ as shown in Fig. 4.3, and the set $\tilde{A}$ as shown in Fig. 4.4, where in each case the shaded area represents the set in question.

If $C \subset D$ the Venn diagram might look like Fig. 4.5. Note that each

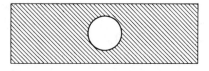

Figure 4-3   Figure 4-4

element of *C* is an element of *D* and that this is indicated by drawing *C* inside of *D*.

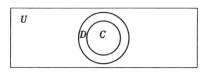

Figure 4-5

We wish to remark that while Venn diagrams, like other pictorial representations, are often extremely helpful, their indiscriminate use will sometimes lead to difficulties. The reason for this is that the moment you draw a picture you specialize the problem. Analogously it is helpful for a dictionary to have a picture of a chair, beside the definition; however, the picture may represent only one type of chair whereas the word "chair" includes all types.

EXERCISES

1. Explain the meaning of the word "or" in each of the following statements.
   (a) A child is either a boy or a girl.
   (b) Podunk College buys cars only if they cost less than $2,000 or are Fords.
   (c) The answer is "6 feet or 72 inches."
   (d) A football team may score by means of touchdowns or field goals.
   (e) This bill may be paid by cash or check.

2. Draw a Venn diagram which illustrates each of the following:
   (a) $A \cap B = \emptyset$ (c) $\tilde{A} = \emptyset$
   (b) $A \cup B = B$ (d) $A \cap B = A \cap C$ but $B \neq C$

3. If $A \subset B$, what can you say about:
   (a) $A \cup B$
   (b) $A \cap B$
   (c) $\tilde{A}$ and $\tilde{B}$

4. What sets are:
   (a) $\widetilde{(\tilde{A})}$
   (b) $\widetilde{A \cup B}$
   (c) $\widetilde{A \cap B}$

5. If $A \subset B$ and $B \subset C$ what can you say about A in relation to C?

6. If $A \cap B = \emptyset$, what can you say about $\tilde{A}$ and $\tilde{B}$?

7. If $U = \{a, b, c, d\}$, list the subsets of U.

Many English sentences can be expressed in set language. For example, "Football players are athletes" states that the set of football players is a subset of the set of athletes. We can also use sets in drawing conclusions. Given the statements "Math courses are hard courses" and "Hard courses have good teachers," what can be concluded? What we do here is to take the set of all courses as the universal set. Then we let A be the set of math courses, B the set of hard courses, and C the set of courses with good teachers. Then the first sentence says $A \subset B$, the second says $B \subset C$, and we apply the preceding Exercise 5 to get $A \subset C$, which says "Math courses have good teachers." We hasten to point out that we cannot, in general, expect the conclusion to be a true statement unless the given statements are true themselves. In general we do not decide whether the given statements are true, we merely decide what logical conclusion can be deduced from them. Similar analyses can be made for more involved problems. Some of the best known of these are due to Lewis Carroll (Charles Dodgson), an English mathematician who is perhaps better known as the author of *Alice in Wonderland*. The idea in these problems is to arrive at the "best possible" conclusion; i.e., one which utilizes all the hypotheses (the given statements).

EXAMPLE 3.

(a) Babies are illogical.
(b) Nobody is despised who can manage a crocodile.
(c) Illogical persons are despised.

We assume that everyone is either a baby or not a baby, logical or illogical, despised or not despised, and either can or cannot manage a crocodile. We take the set of all persons as the universal set, A as the set of babies, B as the set of illogical persons, C as the set of despised persons, and D as the set of persons who can manage a crocodile. Then statement (a) is equivalent to stating $A \subset B$ and statement (c) is equivalent to stating $B \subset C$. From $A \subset B$ and $B \subset C$ we could deduce that $A \subset C$, but this is not a "best possible" deduction since it has not utilized statement (b). Statement (b) is equivalent to stating "no one in the set of despised persons is in the set of persons who can manage a crocodile" or, more briefly, "$C \cap D = \emptyset$." From $A \subset C$ and $C \cap D = \emptyset$ we deduce that $A \cap D = \emptyset$. We could then state "No baby can manage a crocodile" (no element of A is an element of D) or "No one who can manage a crocodile is a baby" (no element of D is an element of A). In lieu of writing these set relations explicitly we could pictorially represent them on a Venn diagram as in Fig. 4.6. The circle A being inside of circle B shows

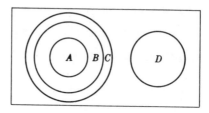

Figure 4-6

that $A \subset B$. Similarly the circle B being on the inside of circle C shows that $B \subset C$. The circle D being on the outside of circle C shows that $C \cap D = \emptyset$. We see that circle D is on the outside of circle A or that $A \cap D = \emptyset$, and hence this conclusion is the same as our preceding one.

EXERCISES (LEWIS CARROLL)

Find a conclusion:

1. All cats understand French.
   Some chickens are cats.

2. Nothing intelligible ever puzzles me.
   Logic puzzles me.

Are these conclusions correct?

3. No doctors are enthusiastic.
   You are enthusiastic.
   ∴ You are not a doctor.

4. I saw it in a newspaper.
   All newspapers tell lies.
   ∴ It was a lie.

5. All who are anxious to learn work hard.
   Some of these boys work hard.
   ∴ Some of these boys are anxious to learn.

6. No thieves are honest.
   Some dishonest people are found out.
   ∴ Some thieves are found out.

Find the "best" conclusions:

7. My gardener is well worth listening to on military subjects.
   No one can remember the battle of Waterloo unless he is very old.
   No one is really worth listening to on military subjects unless he can remember the battle of Waterloo.

8. All of my sons are slim.
   No child of mine is healthy who takes no exercise.
   All gluttons who are children of mine are fat.
   No daughter of mine takes any exercise.

9. Promise breakers are untrustworthy.
   Wine drinkers are very communicative.
   A man who keeps his promises is honest.
   No teetotalers are pawnbrokers.
   One can always trust a very communicative person.

4.2. COUNTING AND SETS

If a given set can be put into a 1–1 correspondence with the first n counting numbers then we can count the elements of the given set and we say that the set has n elements. (In fact, this is why the counting numbers are called the "counting" numbers.) Such a set is called a *finite* set. In this section we restrict attention to finite sets and consider some of the consequences of applying the process of counting to such sets. We will use the notation $c(A)$ (read "cardinal number of A") to denote the number of elements in a finite set A and so $c(A)$ will be a counting number. We usually find it convenient to consider the vacuous set as a finite set and to write $c(A) = 0$ when A is the empty set.

Many authors start with abstract set theory, and use the concepts of union and complement to define addition and subtraction. More particularly if a is $c(A)$ and b is $c(B)$, and $A \cap B = \emptyset$, we can say that $a + b = c(A \cup B)$. We point out that A and B must be *disjoint* (i.e., $A \cap B = \emptyset$) to make $c(A \cup B) = c(A) + c(B)$. Note also that this is essentially the way we defined "$+$" except that we used sets of stones. While the abstract set approach may be more elegant, we feel that pedagogically the use of concrete (no pun intended) sets at the beginning is to be preferred.

Since A and $\tilde{A}$ are disjoint, $c(A) + c(\tilde{A}) = c(A \cup \tilde{A}) = c(U)$. Thus $c(\tilde{A}) = c(U) - c(A)$, and this fact may be used to define subtraction. It is also possible to define multiplication by means of abstract set theory as we shall point out in Section 14.2.

EXAMPLE 1. A certain class has 43 students, 12 of whom are unusually smart, and 31 of whom are girls. Let $A =$ the set of boys in the class, $B =$ the set of girls in the class, and $C =$ the set of unusually smart students.

(a) Describe the sets $A \cup B, A \cup C, B \cup C, A \cap B, A \cap C, B \cap C$

(b) Find $c(A), c(A \cap B)$, and $c(A \cup C)$

(a) We note that $A \cup B$ would be the set consisting of the boys in the class together with the girls in the class, i.e., the set consisting of all students in the class. Similarly $A \cup C$ would be the set consisting of all the boys together with the unusually smart girls; $B \cup C$ would be the set consisting of all the girls together with the unusually smart boys; $A \cap B$ would be the set consisting of the boys who are also girls, i.e., it would be the vacuous set; $A \cap C$ would be the set consisting of the unusually smart boys; while $B \cap C$ would be the set consisting of the unusually smart girls.

(b) Since there are 43 students, 31 of whom are girls, the remaining 12 must be boys. Thus $c(A) = 12$.

Since $A \cap B$ is empty, $c(A \cap B) = 0$.

As $A \cup C$ contains all the boys and there are 12 boys, then $c(A \cup C) \geq$ 12. If all of these boys are unusually smart then $A \cup C = A = C$ and $c(A \cup C) = 12$. If none of the boys are unusually smart, then the 12 unusually smart students must be girls so $c(A \cup C) = 24$. If some of the unusually smart students are boys, then $c(A \cup B) < 24$. We summarize by stating $12 \leq c(A \cup C) \leq 24$. This means that any one of the counting numbers 12, 13, . . . , 24 are possible answers for $c(A \cup C)$ for particular sets A and C satisfying the stipulated conditions of the problem.

Suppose A and B are sets and $x \in A \cup B$. Then exactly one of the three following possibilities must hold

(i) $x \in A$ and $x \in B$, i.e., $x \in A \cap B$
(ii) $x \in A$ and $x \notin B$ ("$\notin$" is read "does not belong to")
(iii) $x \notin A$ and $x \in B$

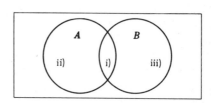

Figure 4-7

The situation is represented pictorially on a Venn diagram in Fig. 4.7. If we count the elements in A and then count the elements in B, we have counted the elements in $A \cap B$ twice. It follows that

$$c(A \cup B) = c(A) + c(B) - c(A \cap B) \tag{1}$$

EXAMPLE 2. In a group of 25 coffee drinkers 8 people prefer their coffee black (with neither cream nor sugar), 10 take cream with their coffee, and 12 take sugar with their coffee. How many people in the group take both cream and sugar?

At first glance we might think this question is unreasonable, but closer scrutiny proves that this is not the case. Let us take as a universal set this particular group of 25 coffee drinkers; let A be the set of these coffee drinkers who take cream and let B be the set of these coffee drinkers who take sugar. Then $A \cup B$ would be the set of these coffee drinkers who take either cream or sugar and since $25 - 8 = 17$, we see that $c(A \cup B) = 17$. Since $c(A) = 10$ and $c(B) = 12$ we have on substituting in (1) the result $17 = 10 + 12 - c(A \cap B) = 22 - c(A \cap B)$. But this says that 17 is the unique counting number which, when added to $c(A \cap B)$, gives 22 and hence $c(A \cap B) = 5$. As $A \cap B$ is the set of these coffee drinkers who take both cream and sugar we have the desired result.

Suppose A, B, and C are sets and $x \in A \cup B \cup C$. Then exactly one of the following possibilities must hold

$$
\begin{array}{llll}
\text{(i)} \ x \in A & x \in B & x \in C, & \text{i.e. } x \in A \cap B \cap C \\
\text{(ii)} \ x \in A & x \in B & x \notin C \ , & \text{i.e. } x \in A \cap B \cap \tilde{C} \\
\text{(iii)} \ x \in A & x \notin B & x \in C, & \text{i.e. } x \in A \cap \tilde{B} \cap C \\
\text{(iv)} \ x \notin A & x \in B & x \in C, & \text{i.e. } x \in \tilde{A} \cap B \cap C \\
\text{(v)} \ x \in A & x \notin B & x \notin C, & \text{i.e. } x \in A \cap \tilde{B} \cap \tilde{C} \\
\text{(vi)} \ x \notin A & x \in B & x \notin C, & \text{i.e. } x \in \tilde{A} \cap B \cap \tilde{C} \\
\text{(vii)} \ x \notin A & x \notin B & x \in C, & \text{i.e. } x \in \tilde{A} \cap \tilde{B} \cap C
\end{array}
$$

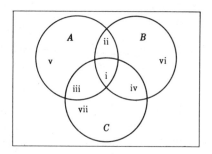

Figure 4-8

The various possibilities are represented by regions on a Venn diagram in Fig. 4.8.

EXAMPLE 3. A pollster, stating that there is one in every crowd, reports that among 100 male college students there is one who likes neither blondes, brunettes, nor redheads. But, he says, 60 like blondes, 55 like brunettes, 40 like redheads, 26 like blondes and brunettes, 25 like blondes and redheads, 20 like brunettes and redheads, while 8 like blondes, brunettes, and redheads. He concludes that gentlemen prefer blondes. Do you agree with him? Explain.

Let A = the set of these students who like blondes, B = the set of these students who like brunettes, and C = the set of these students who like redheads. Then $c(A \cup B \cup C) = 100 - 1 = 99$. We can also count the elements in $c(A \cup B \cup C)$ by adding the number of elements in each of the seven regions, since no element is in two of these regions. We fill in these as shown in Fig. 4.9.

We are given that the number of elements in region (i) is 8. Since there are 26 who like blondes and brunettes, then $c(A \cap B) = 26$ and there are $26 - 8 = 18$ in region (ii). Similarly there are $25 - 8 = 17$ in region

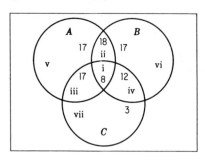

Figure 4-9

(iii) and $20 - 8 = 12$ in region (iv). Since $c(A) = 60$ there are $60 - (8 + 18 + 17) = 60 - 43 = 17$ in region (v). Similarly there are $55 - (8 + 18 + 12) = 17$ in region (vi) and $40 - (8 + 17 + 12) = 3$ in region (vii). Thus, in all seven regions, there are $8 + 18 + 17 + 12 + 17 + 17 + 3 = 92$ students. But this says that $c(A \cup B \cup C) = 92$ which contradicts the fact that $c(A \cup B \cup C) = 99$. This contradiction shows that the figures quoted are not possible and hence we should be skeptical of any conclusions made from them.

If we count the elements in A, B, and C, then we have counted the elements in region (i) three times, the elements in region (ii) twice, the elements in region (iii) twice, the elements in region (iv) twice and the elements in region (v), (vi), (vii) once each. Since $A \cap B$ is represented by region (i) plus region (ii), $A \cap C$ is represented by region (i) plus region (iii), $B \cap C$ is represented by region (i) plus region (iv), and $A \cap B \cap C$ is represented by region (i) we deduce that

$$c(A \cup B \cup C) = c(A) + c(B) + c(C) - c(A \cap B) - c(A \cap C)$$
$$- c(B \cap C) + c(A \cap B \cap C) \quad (2)$$

We could have observed that $c(A) = 60$, $c(B) = 55$, $c(C) = 40$, $c(A \cap B) = 26$, $c(A \cap C) = 25$, $c(B \cap C) = 20$, while $c(A \cap B \cap C) = 8$, and substituted these values in (2) to obtain $c(A \cup B \cup C) = 60 + 55 + 40 - 26 - 25 - 20 + 8 = 92$. Thus we would have arrived at the same contradiction we had previously noted.

Consider the Venn diagram in Fig. 4.10, where the given circular regions denote sets A and B, the region shaded with horizontal lines denotes $\tilde{A}$ and the region shaded with vertical lines denotes $\tilde{B}$. We observe that the region representing $\tilde{A} \cap \tilde{B}$ is the same as the region representing $\widetilde{A \cup B}$ and that the region representing $\tilde{A} \cup \tilde{B}$ is the same as the region representing $\widetilde{A \cap B}$. It is in fact true that $\tilde{A} \cap \tilde{B} = \widetilde{A \cup B}$ and that $\tilde{A} \cup \tilde{B} = \widetilde{A \cap B}$, these results being known as de Morgan's Laws. Moreover the results can be extended so that $\tilde{A} \cup \tilde{B} \cup \tilde{C} = \widetilde{(A \cap B \cap C)}$, $\tilde{A} \cup \tilde{B} \cup \tilde{C} \cup \tilde{D} = \widetilde{(A \cap B \cap C \cap D)}$, etc.

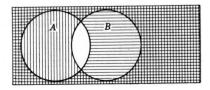

Figure 4-10

It is sometimes advantageous to make use of the complements of sets when working problems. While the following example may be worked without resort to complements, we feel it is instructive to use complements.

EXAMPLE 4. Out of 100 members of a certain P.T.A. at least 70 drink coffee and at least 40 drink tea. How many drink both coffee and tea?

We take as a universal set the set consisting of the 100 P.T.A. members, let A be the set of those members who drink coffee, and B the set of those members who drink tea. Then $\tilde{A}$ is the set of those members who do not drink coffee, $\tilde{B}$ is the set of those members who do not drink tea, $c(A) \geq 70$, $c(B) \geq 40$, $c(\tilde{A}) \leq 30$, and $c(\tilde{B}) \leq 60$. Now $c(\tilde{A} \cup \tilde{B}) = c(\tilde{A}) + c(\tilde{B}) - c(\tilde{A} \cap \tilde{B})$ and so $c(\tilde{A} \cup \tilde{B}) \leq c(\tilde{A}) + c(\tilde{B}) \leq 30 + 60 = 90$. But $\tilde{A} \cup \tilde{B} = \widetilde{A \cap B}$ and so $c(\widetilde{A \cap B}) \leq 90$ and hence $C(A \cap B) \geq 10$. Thus we can assert the rather surprising result that at least 10 members of this particular P.T.A. group drink both coffee and tea.

EXERCISES

1. (Joint associateship examination for actuaries, 1935) Certain data were obtained from a study of a group of 1000 employees in a cotton mill. Their race, sex, and marital status were unofficially reported as follows: 525 colored lives; 312 male lives; 470 married lives; 42 colored males; 147 married colored; 86 married males; 25 married colored males. Test this classification to determine whether the numbers reported in the various groups are consistent.*

2. (Lewis Carroll) In a very hotly fought battle, at least 70 per cent of the combatants lost an eye; at least 75 per cent, an ear; at least 80 per cent, an arm; at least 85 per cent, a leg. How many lost all four members.*

3. A penny, a nickel, and a quarter are tossed together 100 times. The penny turns up heads on 70 tosses, the nickel turns up heads on 50 tosses, and the quarter turns up heads on 56 tosses. The penny and nickel are heads together exactly 31 times, while the nickel and quarter are heads together 28 times. Prove that all three coins turned up heads together at least nine times, and that all three coins turned up tails together at most eleven times.*

4. If A and B are finite sets what can you say about the relative sizes of $c(A)$, $c(A \cap B)$, and $c(A \cup B)$?

5. If $A = B$, what can you say about $c(A)$ and $c(B)$?

6. If $c(A) = c(B)$ what can you say about A and B?

7. If $c(A) = c(A \cup B)$ what can you say about A and B?

8. If $c(A) = c(A \cap B)$ what can you say about A and B?

9. If $c(A \cap B) = c(A \cup B)$ what can you say about A and B?

10. A certain senior class at Recreation University has 100 members. Fifty of them have had no courses in either Math, Science, or Foreign Languages; 75 have had no Foreign Language courses; and 80 have had no Science courses. How many have had Math courses?

* Exercises 1, 2, 3 are from Birkoff and MacLane, *A Survey of Modern Algebra* (New York: The Macmillan Company, 1941).

5

We have already considered the binary operations of addition and multiplication on the set of counting numbers. We had observed that "binary" refers to the fact that these operations connect two numbers —no more and no less. But we have not defined an abstract binary operation on a set. We do so now: a *binary operation on a set A* is a correspondence which associates with each ordered pair of elements of A a unique element of A. The phrase "ordered pair" means that there is a first element and a second element. We might phrase this more precisely by stating that $\oplus$, say, is a binary operation on the set A if for each $a, b \in A$, $a \oplus b$ is a unique element of A. In this notation a is the first element and b is the second element. Note that $a \oplus b$ and $b \oplus a$ might be different elements.

The symbol $\oplus$ simply denotes a binary operation on some set—it might denote either ordinary addition or multiplication on the set of counting numbers. It could not denote ordinary subtraction on the set of counting numbers because, e.g., $2 - 3$ is not a counting number. It could denote the operation of union on the collection of subsets of a given set E. For if this collection is denoted by F and if $A, B \in F$ then $A \cup B$ is a unique member of F. Similarly it could denote the operation of intersection on the members of F, for if $A, B \in F$ then $A \cap B$ is a unique member of F. Since $A \cup B = B \cup A$ the operation of union is commutative, and since $A \cup (B \cup C) = (A \cup B) \cup C$ the operation of union is associative. We tacitly used both of these facts in

enlarging the number system

75

Chapter 4. For example, we wrote $A \cup B \cup C$. What fact did we tacitly assume in this case?

So far all of the operations that we have considered have been both commutative and associative. Let us make up some binary operations, each denoted by $\oplus$, on the set of counting numbers, some of which will not be commutative and some of which will not be associative.

EXAMPLE 1. Let us define $\oplus$ by $a \oplus b = a(b \cdot b)$. For instance $2 \oplus 3 = 2(3 \cdot 3) = 18$, while $3 \oplus 2 = 3(2 \cdot 2) = 12$. Since $2 \oplus 3 \neq 3 \oplus 2$ this particular binary operation $\oplus$ is not commutative.

EXAMPLE 2. We define $\oplus$ by $a \oplus b = (a \cdot a)(b \cdot b)$. Note that $b \oplus a = (b \cdot b)(a \cdot a)$. Since $(a \cdot a)(b \cdot b) = (b \cdot b)(a \cdot a)$, we see that this binary operation $\oplus$ is commutative.
As
$$(3 \oplus 2) \oplus 4 = (3 \cdot 3)(2 \cdot 2) \oplus 4 = 36 \oplus 4$$
$$= (36 \cdot 36)(4 \cdot 4) = 20736$$
while
$$3 \oplus (2 \oplus 4) = 3 \oplus (2 \cdot 2)(4 \cdot 4)$$
$$= 3 \oplus 64 = (3 \cdot 3)(64 \cdot 64) = 11664$$

we see that this binary operation $\oplus$ is not associative. In fact we observe that

$$(a \oplus b) \oplus c = (a \cdot a)(b \cdot b) \oplus c = (a \cdot a \cdot a \cdot a)(b \cdot b \cdot b \cdot b)(c \cdot c)$$

while

$$a \oplus (b \oplus c) = a \oplus (b \cdot b)(c \cdot c) = (a \cdot a)(b \cdot b \cdot b \cdot b)(c \cdot c \cdot c \cdot c).$$

Hence we see that it is not necessarily true that

$$a \oplus (b \oplus c) = (a \oplus b) \oplus c.$$

Sometimes a set will have a special element, called an identity element, with respect to a given binary operation. For example, 0 is an identity element with respect to addition on the set of counting numbers since $0 + a = a + 0 = a$ for all counting numbers a. Again 1 is an identity element with respect to multiplication on the set of counting numbers since $1 \cdot a = a \cdot 1 = a$ for all counting numbers a. We say that e is in *identity element with respect to the binary operation $\oplus$ on the set A if $e \oplus a = a \oplus e = a$ for all $a \in A$.*

EXAMPLE 3. Define $\oplus$ on the set of counting numbers by $a \oplus b = a + b + ab$ for all counting numbers a, b. For example, $2 \oplus 3 = 2 + 3 + 2 \cdot 3 = 11$. We observe that $a \oplus 0 = a + 0 + a \cdot 0 = a$ and $0 \oplus a = 0 + a + 0 \cdot a = a$ for all counting numbers a. Hence 0 is an identity element with respect to $\oplus$ on the set of counting numbers.

EXERCISES

1. Is ordinary multiplication a binary operation on the set of odd counting numbers? Ordinary addition?

2. Is ordinary addition a binary operation on the set of all even counting numbers? Ordinary multiplication?

3. Is the operation defined in Example 3 commutative? Associative?

4. Does the operation of union on the set of all subsets of a given set have an identity element? The operation of intersection?

Determine whether or not the following are binary operations defined on the set of counting numbers. If so, determine whether or not they (a) are commutative; (b) are associative; (c) have an identity element.

5. $a \oplus b = a + b + ab$

6. $a \oplus b = a + b - ab$

7. $a \oplus b = a \cdot a + b$

8. $a \oplus b = a$

9. $a \oplus b = b$

10. $a \oplus b = a - b$

11. $a \oplus b = a \cdot a$

12. $a \oplus b = b + 1$

13. $a \oplus b =$ the remainder obtained when $a + b$ is divided by 10

14. If A is any finite set of natural numbers, then max $\{A\}$ means the largest member of A and min $\{A\}$ means the smallest member of $\{A\}$ (where of course the largest member of a set consisting of one element is that element). It is relatively easy to establish that if A is not empty, max $\{A\}$ and min $\{A\}$ exist. Investigate the operations $a \oplus b =$ max $\{a, b\}$ and $a \oplus b =$ min $\{a, b\}$.

5.2. THE SET OF INTEGERS

We have observed that subtraction is not a binary operation on the set of counting numbers, although addition is. It would be desirable to have a set of numbers on which both addition and subtraction are operations. Moreover this set of numbers should, in some sense, include the counting numbers. We would like to retain the numbers we have at present, together with the properties they possess, while extending the system by the inclusion of other numbers in such a fashion that subtraction will be an operation on the new set. Such a procedure can be rigorously followed, but is beyond the scope of this book. We merely assume the result. The interested reader might refer to John E. Hofstrom, *Basic Concepts in Modern Mathematics* (Reading, Mass.: Addison Wesley Publishing Co., Inc., 1961), pp. 95–113.

In particular we assume the existence of a set called the set of *integers*, which has the properties enumerated below.

A1. Addition, notation $+$, is a binary operation on the set of integers.

A2. Addition is associative, i.e., if a, b, c are integers then $a + (b + c) = (a + b) + c$.

A3. There is a (unique) identity element for addition denoted by 0; i.e., if a is an integer then $a + 0 = 0 + a = a$.

A4. For each integer a there is a (unique) inverse (denoted by $\bar{a}$) with respect to the identity, i.e., $a + \bar{a} = \bar{a} + a = 0$.

A5. Addition is commutative, i.e., if a, b are integers then $a + b = b + a$.

The notation A1 reminds us that this is postulate 1 for addition, just as the postulate M1, which follows, reminds us that it is postulate 1 for multiplication.

M1. Multiplication, notation $\cdot$, is a binary operation on the set of integers.

M2. Multiplication is associative, i.e., if a, b, c are integers then $a \cdot (b \cdot c) = (a \cdot b) \cdot c$.

M3. There is a (unique) identity element for multiplication, denoted by 1; i.e., if a is an integer then $a \cdot 1 = 1 \cdot a = a$.

M5. Multiplication is commutative, i.e., if a, b are integers then $a \cdot b = b \cdot a$.

Note that M1 is the analogue of A1, M2 is the analogue of A2, M3 is the analogue of A3, and M5 is the analogue of A5. We might remember these by operation, associative, identity, inverse, and commutative, respectively, and that A stands for addition whereas M stands for multiplication. Thus M1 would state that multiplication is a binary operation while A3 would state there exists an identity element for addition. It is much shorter to write "A3," say, as the reason for a given step rather than "there exists an identity element for addition." Why did we omit M4, the analogue of A4?

D1. The distributive law, i.e., if a, b, c are integers then $a \cdot (b + c) = (a \cdot b) + (a \cdot c)$.

Two additional properties possessed by the set of integers are as follows:

I1. The additive identity is distinct from the multiplicative identity, i.e. $0 \neq 1$.

I2. If a, b are integers and $ab = 0$ then $a = 0$ or $b = 0$.

Now the set of counting numbers possessed properties A1, A2, A3, A5, M1, M2, M3, M5, D1, I1, I2. Hence the only new property, assumed to date, is A4. The additive inverse of an element is frequently called the *opposite* of the element. In other words "$\bar{a}$" is read "opposite of a." Thus the *opposite of a denotes the unique element which when added to a yields* 0. We may regard the set of integers as consisting of the counting numbers together with their opposites since the sum of a counting number and the opposite of a counting number is either a counting number or the opposite of a counting number. We have extended the set of counting numbers to the set of integers by adjoining the set of opposites of counting numbers. Thus we consider the set of integers to contain the set of counting numbers as a subset. If a and b are counting numbers then $a + b$ and $a \cdot b$ have the same meaning whether we regard a and b as counting numbers or as integers. Professional mathematicians would use a more sophisticated approach to the topic above; however, we feel that the simplified version is more suitable for our purposes.

We will not give a complete list of the properties necessary to characterize the integers. In particular there is an order relation of $<$ on the system of integers which we will discuss in more detail in the section on ordered fields. Furthermore, the principle of mathematical induction (which we mentioned earlier) is true for certain subsets of the integers. The integers also have additional properties with which we will not be concerned in this text.

The inquisitive reader might wonder what has happened to subtraction, since we have not mentioned it in our list of postulates. We will, as before, define subtraction in terms of addition, but we will first improve our understanding of postulate A4—a necessity for an appreciation of this definition. Hence let us examine the notion of opposite more closely.

If a is an integer then $\bar{a}$ denotes the opposite of a. That is, by A4, $\bar{a}$ is the unique integer such that: (1) $a + \bar{a} = \bar{a} + a = 0$. Now $\bar{\bar{a}} = \overline{(\bar{a})}$ denotes the unique integer which when added to $\bar{a}$ gives 0, i.e., (2) $\bar{\bar{a}} + \bar{a} = \bar{a} + \bar{\bar{a}} = 0$. On comparing (2) with (1) we see that a is one integer which added to $\bar{a}$ gives 0 and hence, utilizing the uniqueness, we have $\bar{\bar{a}} = a$. (In the more conventional notation our conclusion would be written as $-(-a) = a$. Many teachers have wondered how to prove the assertion. As we see, it is an immediate consequence of A4.)

Note that

$$b + (a + \bar{b}) \underset{\text{A5}}{=} b + (\bar{b} + a) \underset{\text{A2}}{=} (b + \bar{b}) + a \underset{\text{A4}}{=} 0 + a \underset{\text{A3}}{=} a$$

Thus $a + \bar{b}$ is an integer which, when added to b, yields a, for any integers a, b. We have just observed that one integer which added to b yields a, is $a + \bar{b}$. Let us show that this is the only such integer. For if x is an integer such that $b + x = a$ then

$$\underset{\text{A3}}{x = 0 + x} = \underset{\text{A4}}{(\bar{b} + b) + x} = \underset{\text{A2}}{\bar{b} + (b + x)} = \bar{b} + a = \underset{\text{A5}}{a + \bar{b}}$$

We define $a - b$ to be the unique integer which added to b yields a, i.e., $b + (a - b) = (a - b) + b = a$. We have shown that $a - b = a + \bar{b}$ and hence that subtraction is a binary operation on the set of integers.

We know that $a + 0 = 0 + a = a$ for all integers a by A3. Suppose that b and c are any two particular integers with the property that $b + c = c$. Then, we claim, $b = 0$. For we know there is an integer $\bar{c}$ such that $c + \bar{c} = 0$ by A4 and so

$$(b + c) + \bar{c} = c + \bar{c}$$

or

$$0 = (b + c) + \bar{c} = b + (c + \bar{c}) = b + 0 = b$$

i.e., $b = 0$. (Give the reasons which make each step in this argument permissible.) In particular, then, $b + c = c$ for one integer c implies that $b + a = a$ for all integers a. We could have utilized this fact to prove that the identity element 0 is unique instead of postulating this uniqueness.

In terms of piles of stones it is easy to see that $0 \cdot a = 0$ where a is a counting number, as we had observed earlier. However when a is a nonzero counting number what can be said of $0 \cdot \bar{a}$? There is no longer any connection with piles of stones and the answer now is not so obvious. However one fact we have mentioned in the previous paragraph provides an answer. Thus observe that $0 + 0 = 0$ and so $a \cdot (0 + 0) = a \cdot 0$ or $a \cdot 0 + a \cdot 0 = a \cdot 0$. But if we let $b = c = a \cdot 0$ then we have $b + c = c$ and so $b = 0$, i.e., $a \cdot 0 = 0$ for all integers a. Of course $0 \cdot a = 0$ also. We can now prove the following theorem.

THEOREM 1. If a and b are integers then $a \cdot \bar{b} = \bar{a} \cdot b = \overline{a \cdot b}$.

For $a \cdot \bar{b} + ab = a(\bar{b} + b) = a \cdot 0 = 0$ and so by the uniqueness of $\overline{ab}$ we have $a \cdot \bar{b} = \overline{ab}$. Similarly $\bar{a}b + ab = (\bar{a} + a)b = 0 \cdot b = 0$ and so $\bar{a}b = \overline{ab}$.

THEOREM 2. If a and b are integers then $\bar{a} \cdot \bar{b} = a \cdot b$.

For $\bar{a} \cdot \bar{b} + \overline{a \cdot b} = \bar{a} \cdot \bar{b} + \bar{a} \cdot b$ (by Theorem 1) $= \bar{a} \cdot (\bar{b} + b) = \bar{a} \cdot 0 = 0$ and, since we know that $a \cdot b$ is the unique opposite of $\overline{a \cdot b}$, we have that $\bar{a} \cdot \bar{b} = a \cdot b$.

The material in this chapter is very important—it appears in mathematics at all levels. One cannot deal with numbers without being familiar with the properties of the numbers; and agreement on the properties requires an explicit formulation of them. In more abstract work in mathematics (and other sciences) where more general types of numbers are used this same postulational approach is used. This postulational approach is one of the central ideas of modern mathematics.

Some people have difficulties, both actual and psychological, with mathematical concepts such as are discussed in this chapter. The abstractness of the ideas presented offers little or nothing to visualize. These people, accordingly, are convinced that they are dealing with meaningless symbols and are tempted to use this as an excuse for giving up. The authors hasten to reassure the readers that the material presented here (as well as elsewhere in the book) has a large number of practical applications and is in effect no more abstract than the basic number concepts discussed heretofore. The difference is due mainly to the familiarity which most of us have with the counting numbers. From earliest childhood we have had experiences counting various objects, and this lifelong use has deluded us into believing that the counting numbers are actual entities. If you ask someone to think of "four," they will probably visualize the numeral "4." In other words, because of long usage, we are able to attribute to a symbol such as "4" the properties of the abstract concept of "fourness" and, what is more, we are able to use the symbol in various applications of the concept. What we need to do is to become familiar with these new numbers and learn their properties. They will then seem more natural and far less formidable. In this connection it might be interesting to read the first two paragraphs of the preface of Sherman K. Stein, *Mathematics, The Man-Made Universe*. San Francisco: W. H. Freeman & Company, 1963. Stein points out that mathematics is actually concrete whereas the physical world is abstract.

We offer the following model of the integers. Imagine the natural numbers written in their usual order in a horizontal line. Then directly beneath each number is written its opposite. This takes care of all the integers with the exception of zero which is its own opposite. To indicate this we put "0" midway between the lines of numbers and on the left so that we have the following array.

$$1, 2, 3, 4, 5, \ldots$$
$$0$$
$$\bar{1}, \bar{2}, \bar{3}, \bar{4}, \bar{5}, \ldots$$

Note that each number is in the same column as its opposite.

Another model consists of thinking of all the integers as being in a horizontal line with zero in the middle, the natural numbers going out to the right, and their opposites to the left as below.

$$\ldots, \bar{5}, \bar{4}, \bar{3}, \bar{2}, \bar{1}, 0, 1, 2, 3, 4, 5, \ldots$$

With this representation one application of the integers is quite apparent. We can imagine a starting point on a long, straight road as being designated by 0; points 1, 2, 3, etc., miles down the road as being designated by the numbers 1, 2, 3, etc.; while points on the other side of the starting point are represented by $\bar{1}, \bar{2}, \bar{3}$, etc.

In this application it is easy to see that to go from the point labeled '$\bar{2}$' to the point labeled '3' one has to go 5 miles to the right, or $3 - \bar{2} = 3 + \bar{\bar{2}} = 3 + 2 = 5$. Similarly, adding 2 and 4 produces the number which is the label of the point obtained by going 2 miles to the right of the point labeled '4' (or 4 miles to the right of the point labeled '2'). Many teachers use this application (or one like it) to justify the "rules" for adding or subtracting positive and negative integers. We hasten to point out that while the application is illustrative and, perhaps, reassuring, it is the application and not conversely.

EXERCISES

1. Without looking at the text write down postulates A1, A2, A3, A4, A5, M1, M2, M3, M5, D1, I1, I2.

2. State postulate M4 as the analogue of A4.

3. Show that $\bar{5} + 2 = \overline{5 + \bar{2}}$. (*Hint:* add $5 + \bar{2}$ to $\bar{5} + 2$.)

4. Show that $\bar{5} + \bar{2} = \overline{5 + 2}$.

5. If a and b are counting numbers will $a - b$ necessarily be a counting number? When will $a - b$ be a counting number?

6. Show that $\bar{a} + b = \overline{a + \bar{b}}$.

7. Show that $\bar{a} + \bar{b} = \overline{a + b}$.

8. Utilizing the method by which Theorem 1 is proved show that $2 \cdot \bar{3} = \bar{2} \cdot 3 = \overline{2 \cdot 3}$.

9. Is it true that $\bar{2} \cdot \bar{3} = \overline{2 \cdot 3}$?

10. Is it true that $\bar{\bar{2}} \cdot \bar{3} = \overline{2 \cdot 3}$?

5.3. THE FIELD OF RATIONAL NUMBERS (FRACTIONS)

We had mentioned that we could think of passing from the counting numbers to the integers by "adjoining" the set of opposites of counting numbers. We did not lose any essential properties in the process; indeed, we gained an important new property—subtraction is a binary operation on the new set whereas it was not a binary operation on the old set. Our second verse is very much the same as the first. Starting with the set of integers we "adjoin" the set of "reciprocals" of the nonzero integers and then we adjoin the set of products of integers by reciprocals of nonzero integers in such a way that we do not lose any essential properties in the process. The reciprocal of a nonzero number b is to be the unique number designated by the symbol b^{-1} such that $b \cdot b^{-1} = b^{-1} \cdot b = 1$. That is, the reciprocal of b is the multiplicative inverse of b. As before we gain an important new property. Whereas division is not a binary operation on the set of integers it is almost a binary operation on the new set. As we shall see, division by 0 is not generally possible. However, if 0 is excluded then division is a binary operation on the remaining members of the new set. This new set is called the *set of rational numbers.* Addition, subtraction, and multiplication are binary operations on this set and, excluding 0, division is also a binary operation. Every element has an opposite, every nonzero element has a reciprocal, the associative and commutative laws hold for both addition and multiplication, and the distributive law holds. A set of numbers with these properties is called a field—we will give a more precise definition later. If a is an integer and b is a nonzero integer then the reciprocal of b is sometimes denoted by $1/b$ and the product of a and the reciprocal of b is denoted by ab^{-1} or a/b.

We postulate the existence of a set, R (which we may think of as the set of integers together with the reciprocals of the nonzero integers and products of integers and reciprocals of integers), together with a binary operation of addition and a binary operation of multiplication, which satisfy the following postulates.

A1. If $a \in R$, $b \in R$ then $a + b \in R$, i.e., addition is a binary operation on R.

A2. If $a \in R$, $b \in R$, $c \in R$ then $a + (b + c) = (a + b) + c$; i.e., addition is associative.

A3. There is a unique element $0 \in R$ such that $0 + a = a + 0 = a$ for all $a \in R$, i.e., 0 is a unique additive identity.

A4. If $a \in R$ then there exists a unique element $\bar{a} \in R$, called the opposite of a, such that $a + \bar{a} = \bar{a} + a = 0$, i.e., each element a of R has a unique additive inverse element with respect to 0.

A5. If $a \in R$, $b \in R$ then $a + b = b + a$, i.e., addition is commutative.

M1. If $a \in R$, $b \in R$ then $a \cdot b \in R$, i.e., multiplication is a binary operation on R.

M2. If $a \in R$, $b \in R$, $c \in R$ then $a \cdot (b \cdot c) = (a \cdot b) \cdot c$, i.e., multiplication is associative.

M3. There is a unique element $1 \in R$ such that $1 \cdot a = a \cdot 1 = a$ for all $a \in R$, i.e., 1 is a unique multiplicative identity.

M4. If $a \in R$, $a \neq 0$, then there exists a unique element a^{-1}, called the reciprocal of a, such that $a \cdot a^{-1} = a^{-1} \cdot a = 1$, i.e., each nonzero element of R has a unique multiplicative inverse element with respect to 1.

M5. If $a \in R$, $b \in R$, then $a \cdot b = b \cdot a$, i.e., multiplication is commutative.

D1. If $a \in R$, $b \in R$, $c \in R$ then $a \cdot (b + c) = a \cdot b + a \cdot c$, i.e., the distributive law holds in R.

I1. $0 \neq 1$.

A set R which satisfies the above postulates for addition and multiplication is called a *field*. Thus we will frequently speak of the set of rational numbers as the field of rational numbers.

Any set with a binary operation which is associative, with an identity element, and with inverses with respect to the identity is called a *group*. If the operation is also commutative it is called a *commutative* or *abelian* group. Thus a field is, in particular, an abelian group with respect to addition, and the nonzero elements of a field form an abelian group with respect to multiplication. Groups are important in many phases of modern mathematics and are the subject of considerable research activity. The concept of a group is, moreover, beginning to be introduced in experimental mathematics courses on the elementary and high school level. We give a definition here of group to partially satisfy the curiosity of these persons who have seen the word in their outside reading and wish to learn its meaning.

It is not necessary to list I2 as a postulate for a field, because this follows from the other postulates.

I2. If $a \in R$, $b \in R$, and $ab = 0$ then $a = 0$ or $b = 0$.

Proof: Suppose $ab = 0$. If $b = 0$ then our conclusion is satisfied. If $b \neq 0$ then the reciprocal $1/b$ exists and so $(ab) \cdot \dfrac{1}{b} = 0 \cdot \dfrac{1}{b}$. Now $(ab) \cdot \dfrac{1}{b} = a\left(b \cdot \dfrac{1}{b}\right) = a \cdot 1 = a$. Also $0 \cdot \dfrac{1}{b} = 0$ (by the same argument which showed that $0 \cdot a = 0$ for all integers a). Hence, we see that $a = 0$ so either $a = 0$ or $b = 0$.

notation usually employed this would be written as $(-a) \cdot (-b) = a \cdot b$. Too many students quote the content of this theorem as stating that the product of two negative numbers is a positive number, whereas the theorem has little to do with positive or negative numbers. It merely states that the product of the opposite of a with the opposite of b is the same as the product of a with b. It is a property that is valid in all fields and it is by no means true that all fields have positive numbers. Those fields which have positive numbers will be considered in this section. Perhaps one reason for some of the misconceptions is that positive (and negative) numbers are generally left undefined. We will hereby rectify this situation.

Suppose that the field R contains a set of elements P with the following properties.

1. Trichotomy Principle. If $a \in R$ then exactly one of the following three possibilities holds: (i) $a = 0$, (ii) $a \in P$, (iii) $\bar{a} \in P$.

2. Addition and multiplication are binary operations on P, i.e., if $a, b \in P$ then $a + b \in P$ and $a \cdot b \in P$.

Then R is said to be an *ordered field*. Moreover the elements in P are called *positive numbers* and the opposites of the elements in P are called *negative numbers*, i.e., a is negative if $a = \bar{b}$ where $b \in P$. We observe that 1, the multiplicative identity, is an element of P. Since $1 \neq 0$, then either $1 \in P$ or $\bar{1} \in P$. If $\bar{1} \in P$ then since $\bar{1} \cdot \bar{1} = 1 \cdot 1 = 1$, we would have by property 2 that $1 \in P$, which would contradict property 1. Hence $\bar{1}$ is not in P and so $\bar{\bar{1}} = 1 \in P$. The reader familiar with complex numbers might realize that this indicates how he may show that the complex numbers do not form an ordered field. If he is not acquainted with the complex field then he may pass over this parenthetical insertion. [The complex number i with the property that $i^2 = -1$ (we are using -1 in lieu of $\bar{1}$ here to make matters look more familiar) is not equal to 0. Thus if there is a set P of complex numbers with the two properties enumerated above then either $i \in P$ or $-i \in P$. We know that $1 \in P$ and so -1 does not belong to P. But if $i \in P$ then $i \cdot i = -1 \in P$ which is a contradiction since both 1 and -1 cannot belong to P. Hence it must be true that $-i \in P$. But this also implies that $(-i) \cdot (-i) = -1 \in P$ which leads to the same contradiction. Thus the supposition that there is a set P of complex numbers with these two properties leads to a contradiction, and therefore the complex field is not ordered and one cannot speak of a positive complex number.]

When we say that a field contains positive numbers then we mean that there is a set P of elements of the field satisfying the two properties enumerated above. The statement "a is positive" is equivalent to the statement "$a \in P$." The statement "a is negative" is equivalent to the statement

"$\bar{a} \in P$." The statement "$a = 0$" is equivalent to the statement "neither $a \in P$ nor $\bar{a} \in P$." Of course we are assuming that a is an element of the field in each case.

Once we know what positive numbers are (but not before) than we can define the relationship of one number being "greater than" another. Thus we define a to be *greater than* b, notation $a > b$, to mean that $a - b$ is positive. Since $a - 0 = a$ then the statement "a is positive" is equivalent to the statement "$a > 0$." It is customary to define a to be *less than* b, notation $a < b$, if $b > a$. We can then think of reading $a < b$ from either left to right or right to left—it is comprehensible either way.

Let us now show that the set of rational numbers forms an ordered field. We already know that this set is a field—we merely need to show that the order properties 1 and 2 are satisfied by some set P. We first decide what elements have to be in P and then show that the resulting set will suffice. As was already observed it must be true that $1 \in P$ and so $1 + 1 = 2 \in P$, $1 + 2 = 3 \in P$, and, in fact, every natural number must be in P. Let us consider, e.g., 3^{-1} the reciprocal of 3. Since $3^{-1} \neq 0$ then either $\overline{(3^{-1})} \in P$ or $3^{-1} \in P$. If $\overline{(3^{-1})} \in P$ then $3 \cdot \overline{(3^{-1})} \in P$ or $\overline{3 \cdot (3^{-1})} = \bar{1} \in P$, but, as we had observed earlier, this is a contradiction. Hence we conclude $3^{-1} \in P$. A similar argument shows that the reciprocal of every natural number must be in P. Hence if a and b are natural numbers then $a \cdot b^{-1} = a/b$ must be in P. But this is sufficient to determine P. We define P to consist of all rational numbers which can be written in the form a/b where a and b are natural numbers. Then this set P satisfies the two order properties; in fact, it is the only set of rational numbers which satisfies these two properties.

By property 2 the product of two positive numbers is positive. Suppose that c and d are negative numbers; then $c = \bar{a}$ and $d = \bar{b}$ where a and b are positive. Hence $c \cdot d = \bar{a} \cdot \bar{b} = a \cdot b$ which is positive. That is, we have finally proved that the product of two negative numbers is positive. Can you show that the product of a positive number and a negative number is negative?

The following theorem, sometimes referred to as the cancellation law for multiplication, holds in any field.

THEOREM 1. If a, b, c are in a field, $a \neq 0$, and $ab = ac$ then $b = c$.

Proof:
Since $a \neq 0$ then the reciprocal of a, a^{-1}, exists. Hence $a^{-1}(ab) = a^{-1}(ac)$ or $(a^{-1}a)b = (a^{-1}a)c$ or $1 \cdot b = 1 \cdot c$ or $b = c$.

EXAMPLE 1. Show that $(3)^{-1} = \overline{(3^{-1})}$.
We observe that $3 \cdot (3)^{-1} = 1$ by definition of reciprocal and that $3 \cdot \overline{(3^{-1})} = 3 \cdot (3^{-1}) = 1$ and so $3 \cdot (3)^{-1} = 3 \cdot \overline{(3^{-1})}$. Hence, by applying Theorem 1; since $3 \neq 0$, $(3)^{-1} = \overline{(3^{-1})}$.

EXAMPLE 2. Show that $\dfrac{2}{3} = \dfrac{\bar{2}}{3} = \overline{\left(\dfrac{2}{3}\right)}$.

Note that

$$\frac{2}{3} + \frac{2}{3} = 2 \cdot (3)^{-1} + 2 \cdot 3^{-1}$$
$$= 2 \cdot [(\bar{3})^{-1} + 3^{-1}]$$
$$= 2 \cdot [(\overline{3^{-1}}) + 3^{-1}]$$
$$= 2[0] = 0$$

Hence by the uniqueness of $\overline{\left(\dfrac{2}{3}\right)}$ we have $\dfrac{2}{3} = \overline{\left(\dfrac{2}{3}\right)}$.

Similarly

$$\frac{\bar{2}}{3} + \frac{2}{3} = \bar{2} \cdot 3^{-1} + 2 \cdot 3^{-1} = (\bar{2} + 2) \cdot 3^{-1} = 0 \cdot 3^{-1} = 0$$

and so by the uniqueness of $\overline{\left(\dfrac{2}{3}\right)}$ we have $\dfrac{\bar{2}}{3} = \overline{\left(\dfrac{2}{3}\right)}$.

EXAMPLE 3. Show that if $b \neq 0$, $c \neq 0$, then $(bc)^{-1} = b^{-1}c^{-1}$. We have $(bc)(b^{-1}c^{-1}) = (bb^{-1})(cc^{-1}) = 1 \cdot 1 = 1$ and so by the uniqueness of $(bc)^{-1}$ we have $(bc)^{-1} = b^{-1}c^{-1}$.

EXAMPLE 4. Show that if $c \neq 0$ then $(a/b) = (ac/bc)$. (We are assuming, of course, that $b \neq 0$ when we write a/b.)
For

$$\frac{ac}{bc} = (ac)(bc)^{-1} = ac \cdot b^{-1} \cdot c^{-1} = (ab^{-1})(cc^{-1})$$
$$= (ab^{-1}) \cdot 1 = ab^{-1} = \frac{a}{b}$$

EXAMPLE 5. Show that $(a/b)(c/d) = \dfrac{ac}{bd}$. We have

$$\frac{a}{b} \cdot \frac{c}{d} = (a \cdot b^{-1})(c \cdot d^{-1}) = (ac)(b^{-1}d^{-1}) = (ac)(bd)^{-1} = \frac{ac}{bd}.$$

EXAMPLE 6. Show that

$$\frac{a}{b} + \frac{c}{d} = \frac{ad + bc}{bd}.$$

Note that

$$\frac{ad + bc}{bd} = (ad + bc)(bd)^{-1} = (ad + bc)(b^{-1}d^{-1})$$
$$= (ad)(b^{-1}d^{-1}) + (bc)(b^{-1}d^{-1}) = ab^{-1} + cd^{-1} = \frac{a}{b} + \frac{c}{d}.$$

EXERCISES

1. Let us think of the integers as stations along the single track of a monorail,

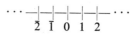

Then "$a < b$" will be equivalent to saying "a is to the left of b." Verify this by showing that if a is to the left of b then there is a "positive" number which when "added" to a gives b.

2. We have observed that $\bar{\bar{2}} = 2$. In the more conventional (and less clear) notation this would state $- -2 = 2$. Think of the first sign as directing us to head the monorail car to the left and the second sign as directing us to put it in reverse. "Show" that this results in going two units to the right.

3. Show that $\frac{2}{4} = \frac{1}{2}$.

4. Show that $\frac{2}{6} = \frac{3}{9}$.

5. Express $\frac{2}{5} + \frac{1}{2}$ as a fraction. What results are you using?

6. Express $\frac{3}{8} + \frac{1}{12}$ as a fraction. What results are you using?

7. Show that $a/b = c/d$ if and only if $a \cdot d = b \cdot c$ and $b \neq 0, d \neq 0$.

8. $(a^{-1} + b^{-1})^{-1} = ?$

9. What can you say about x and y if $x^{-1} = y^{-1}$?

10. Express $(a/b) - (c/d)$ as a fraction where a, b, c, and d are integers, $b \neq 0, d \neq 0$.

Many applications in mathematics make use of the order properties in terms of "inequalities" (i.e., statements that one number is larger than another). We look now at some of the basic arithmetic of inequalities.

THEOREM 1. If $a > b$, then $a + c > b + c$.

Proof:

$$(a + c) - (b + c) = (a + c) + \overline{(b + c)} = a + c + \bar{b} + \bar{c}$$
$$= a + \bar{b} + c + \bar{c} = a + \bar{b} = a - b,$$

which is positive because $a > b$. Therefore $a + c > b + c$.

If a and b are counting numbers then this theorem says that if one pile has more stones in it than a second, and if the same number of stones is added to each pile, then the first pile still has more stones than the second.

THEOREM 2. If $a > b$, and $c > 0$, then $ac > bc$.

Proof:
$ac - bc = ac + \overline{bc} = ac + \bar{b}c = (a + \bar{b})c = (a - b)c$ is positive because both $(a - b)$ and c are. Therefore $ac > bc$.

Note carefully that this theorem, unlike the previous one, requires that c be positive. In fact if $c < 0$, we can show that $ac < bc$.

THEOREM 3. If $a < b$ and $b < c$, then $a < c$.

Proof:

$$c - a = (c - a) + (b - b) = (c + \bar{a}) + (b + \bar{b})$$
$$= c + \bar{b} + b + \bar{a} = (c - b) + (b - a)$$

which is positive because both $c - b$ and $b - a$ are positive. Hence $c > a$ as was to be shown.

EXERCISES

1. Show: If $a > b$ and $c < 0$, then $ac < bc$.

2. Show: If $a > b$ and $b > 0$, then $a^{-1} < b^{-1}$.

3. Show: If $a > b$, $\bar{a} < \bar{b}$.

4. Show: If $0 > a > b$, then $(b)^{-1} > (a)^{-1}$.

5. Show: If $a < b < 0$, then $a \cdot a > b \cdot b$.

6

The statement "The number which added to b gives a" occurs so often that we devised a notation for it, i.e., $a - b$. Phrases such as "seven more than a number," "two less than a number," and "twice a number" also occur frequently. For example, one might state, "Seven more than a number is eleven," and then ask, "What is the number?" A school child would probably answer "four." Again, one might state, "Two less than a number is eleven," and then ask, "What is the number?" A school child would probably answer "thirteen." Finally, one might state, "Twice a number is eleven," and then ask, "What is the number?" A school child might answer, "There is no such number," or, he might answer, "Eleven over two," depending on whether or not he was familiar with rational numbers.

Once again consider the phrase "seven more than a number." We might ask "To what does the word 'number' refer?" The school child of sufficient maturity might answer, "a rational number." If pressed to be more specific he might add, "any rational number." Now consider the sentence, "A number, which added to its opposite gives one." To what does the word "number" in this sentence refer? The school child who is thoughtful as well as mature might delay his answer and then state "It doesn't stand for anything." When is a number not a number? It is quite convenient to use some letter, say, x, as being synonymous with "number." Then "seven more than a number" could

applications involving rational numbers

be replaced by $7 + x$ (or $x + 7$); "two less than a number" could be replaced by $x - 2$ (but not by $2 - x$); "twice a number" could be replaced by $2x$ (or $x \cdot 2$).

Similarly the sentence "Seven more than a number is eleven" could be replaced by $7 + x = 11$. As before we would agree that x, in this case, stands for the number 4. On the other hand the sentence "A number which added to its opposite gives one" could be replaced by $x + \bar{x} = 1$. We would agree that x cannot represent a number in this case. However if x doesn't represent a number, what does it represent? Since addition is a binary operation on numbers, $x + \bar{x}$ does not make sense unless both x and $\bar{x}$ are numbers.

One way out of this dilemma is to introduce the concept of variable over the field of rational numbers. We say x is a *variable* over the set of rational numbers if we understand that x, in whatever expression it occurs, is to be replaced by each rational number in some order. Thus given that $x + 7 = 11$ and x is a variable over the rational field we think of replacing x by each rational number. We think $1 + 7 = 11$, $2 + 7 = 11$, $3 + 7 = 11$, $4 + 7 = 11$, $\overline{10} + 7 = 11$, $\frac{3}{2} + 7 = 11$, etc. The numbers $4 + 7$ and 11 are the same whereas the numbers $1 + 7$ and 11 are not the same. Thus if we replace the variable x in $x + 7 = 11$ by 4 we get a valid or true statement, whereas if we replace x by 1 we get an invalid or false statement. The set of rational numbers which yield a valid statement when put in place of x is called the *truth set* or *solution set* of the equation. Thus the truth set of the equation $x + 7 = 11$ is $\{4\}$. In a similar fashion we see that the truth set of the equation $x + \bar{x} = 1$ is the empty set. However the variable x in the equation $x + \bar{x} = 1$ stands for precisely the same thing as it does in the equation $x + 7 = 11$. Indeed the variable x over the rational field stands for precisely the same thing regardless of the context in which it appears.

Some textbooks have phrases such as "seven more than two times a number." This is ambiguous; it could mean "(seven more than two) times a number" or it could equally well mean "seven more than (two times a number)." Note that the use of grouping symbols eliminates the ambiguity. The phrase "$7 + 2x$" has precisely the same ambiguity; it could mean "$(7 + 2) \cdot x$" or it could mean "$7 + (2x)$." We make the agreement now that henceforth "$7 + 2x$" is to mean "$7 + (2x)$." When we intend "$(7 + 2) \cdot x$" we will *not* omit the grouping symbols. In general, then, if a and b are rational numbers "$ax + b$" denotes "$(ax) + b$" and we understand what is meant by assertions such as "$375 = 3 \cdot 100 + 7 \cdot 10 + 5$." In instances such as these, and perhaps a few others, we find it convenient to omit grouping symbols. Some books state a "Rule of Precedence" implying that all mathematicians agree that multiplication and division take priority over addition and subtraction. It might be hard to find any mathematicians—much less all—agreeing on such a rule. Thus does $12 \cdot 2 \div 3 \cdot 4$ designate 2 or 32?

Again, how does one perform the division before the addition in $10 \div (2 + 3)$? At any rate the proper use of grouping symbols eliminates all ambiguity and it is undoubtedly true that persons skilled in mathematics are more prone to use grouping symbols copiously than less well-trained persons.

If a and b are rational numbers and x is a variable over the rational field then equations of the form $ax = b$, or which can be reduced to this form are called *linear equations*. Thus if $7x - 3 = 2x + 2$, then upon adding 3 to both sides we obtain $7x = 2x + 5$, then upon subtracting $2x$ from both sides we obtain $5x = 5$ and then upon dividing both sides by 5 we obtain $x = 1$. This does not permit us to conclude that if $x = 1$ then $7x - 3 = 2x + 2$. In other words our work to date does not tell us that 1 is an element of the solution set of $7x - 3 = 2x + 2$. On the contrary it states that no number other than 1 can be in the solution set. We can observe that $7 \cdot 1 - 3 = 2 \cdot 1 + 2$ which tells us 1 is in the solution set. Or we could work backward, if $x = 1$ then $5x = 5$, $7x = 2x + 5$, and $7x - 3 = 2x + 2$, which would also permit us to conclude that 1 is in the solution set. Between the two we can conclude that the solution set of $7x - 3 = 2x + 2$ is $\{1\}$. Observe that if $5x = 5$ we might multiply both sides by $\frac{1}{5}$ to obtain $x = 1$ (instead of dividing both sides by 5 as we did previously). From $7x = 2x + 5$ we could obtain $5x = 5$ by adding $\overline{2x}$ to both sides (instead of subtracting $2x$ from both sides as we did previously). Dividing by a is equivalent to multiplying by a^{-1}, adding a is equivalent to subtracting $\bar{a}$, subtracting a is equivalent to adding, $\bar{a}$, and multiplying by a (provided $a \neq 0$) is equivalent to dividing by a^{-1}.

Let us look at this example once more. If $7x - 3 = 2x + 2$ then $7x = 2x + 5$. Hence the solution set of $7x - 3 = 2x + 2$ is a subset of the solution set of $7x = 2x + 5$. If $7x = 2x + 5$ then $5x = 5$. Hence the solution set of $7x = 2x + 5$ is a subset of the solution set of $5x = 5$. If $5x = 5$ then $x = 1$. Hence the solution set of $5x = 5$ is a subset of the solution set of $x = 1$. But it is clear that the solution set of $x = 1$ is $\{1\}$. Hence the solution set of $7x - 3 = 2x + 2$ is the vacuous set or it is the set $\{1\}$. We can verify by direct substitution that $\{1\}$ is a subset of the solution set of $7x - 3 = 2x + 2$, and hence $\{1\} =$ the solution set of $7x - 3 = 2x + 2$. Or, as before, by working backward we can see that the solution set of $x = 1$ is a subset of the solution set of $7x - 3 = 2x + 2$ and hence these two sets are equal.

EXAMPLE 1. Solve (i.e., find the solution set over the rational field of) the equation $\frac{2}{3}x + \frac{7}{5} = \frac{4}{11}x - \frac{5}{2}$.

Since the l.c.m. of 2, 3, 5, 11 is 330 we can eliminate fractions by multiplying both sides of the equation by 330. Thus if $\frac{2}{3}x + \frac{7}{5} = \frac{4}{11}x - \frac{5}{2}$ then $220x + 462 = 120x - 575$, or $100x = -1037$ or $x = -\frac{1037}{100}$. Thus our desired solution set is a subset of $\{-\frac{1037}{100}\}$. On working backward we see that the two solution sets are equal.

EXERCISES

1. Solve: $ax = b$ [*Hint:* Consider cases (i) $a \neq 0$; (ii) $a = 0$, $b = 0$; (iii) $a = 0$, $b \neq 0$].

2. Explain why it is permissible to add the same number to both sides of an equation.

3. Explain why it is permissible to subtract the same number from both sides of an equation.

4. Explain the following calculation. Given the equation $2x = 7$, we multiply both sides by x getting $2 \cdot x \cdot x = 7x$ and note that 0 is a solution to the new equation but does not belong to the original solution set.

5. Solve: $3/x = 2/x$

6. Solve: $5x + 2 = 2x + 3x + 2$

7. Solve: $x = \bar{x}$

8. Solve: $x = x^{-1}$

9. Simplify: $3 - (2 - x)$

10. Simplify: $(2 + x^{-1})^{-1}$

6.2. SYSTEMS OF LINEAR EQUATIONS

If you ask someone to find two numbers whose sum is 7, you will probably get answers like 5 and 2, 3 and 4, or 6 and 1. If you press them for more answers, they may finally come up with pairs like 7 and 0, -3 and 10, or $2\frac{1}{2}$ and $4\frac{1}{2}$. Finally you may be able to convince them that there is no limit to the different answers you can get to this question by using numbers from the field of rationals. A little more involved question is "Find two numbers so that (2 times the first) minus (3 times the second) is 1." This may be written more compactly as "Find solutions to the equation $2x - 3y = 1$." Notice that 2 and 1 is a solution (although 1 and 2 is not) as are $\frac{1}{2}$ and 0 and -1 and -1. Again the number of answers is unlimited. We point out that these answers are ordered pairs; i.e., each answer is a pair of numbers and it may make a difference which number comes first in the pair. We will have more to say about ordered pairs in a later chapter of this book.

It is possible to ask if there is a solution common to two equations; e.g.

$$\begin{cases} x + y = 7 \\ 2x - 3y = 1 \end{cases}$$

This means to find a pair of numbers which will satisfy both equations. In other words the solution set of the system

$$\begin{cases} x + y = 7 \\ 2x - 3y = 1 \end{cases}$$

is the intersection of the solution set of the first equation with that of the second. It is possible that this intersection may be empty in which case there is no common solution; however, in this case there is a solution and we will proceed to find it. Note that if certain values of x and y, say, x_1 and y_1 satisfy both equations of our system, then in particular $x_1 + y_1 = 7$ and $2x_1 + 2y_1 = 14$. Moreover $2x_1 - 3y_1 = 1$. Now if we subtract from both sides of this last equation the number 14, we get $2x_1 - 3y_1 - 14 = 1 - 14$. But $14 = 2x_1 + 2y_1$ so we may rewrite the previous equation as $2x_1 - 3y_1 - (2x_1 + 2y_1) = 1 - 14$ which simplifies to $5y_1 = \overline{13}$. Now we have shown that if x_1 and y_1 satisfy the system

$$\begin{cases} x + y = 7 \\ 2x - 3y = 1 \end{cases}$$

then in particular $x_1 + y_1 = 7$ and $5y_1 = \overline{13}$. Thus any solution of the system

$$\begin{cases} x + y = 7 \\ 2x - 3y = 1 \end{cases}$$

is also a solution of the system

$$\begin{cases} x + y = 7 \\ 5y = \overline{13} \end{cases}$$

i.e., the solution set of the first system is a subset of the solution set of the second system. Again if x_1 and y_1 satisfy the second system, then $x_1 + y_1 = 7$ and $5y_1 = \overline{13}$. If $x_1 + y_1 = 7$ then $2x_1 + 2y_1 = 14$, and if $5y_1 = \overline{13}$, then $5y_1 + 14 = \overline{13} + 14$. Replacing the 14 on the left-hand side of the equation by $2x_1 + 2y_1$ (which is 14) gives $2x_1 + 2y_1 + 5y_1 = \overline{13} + 14$ which simplifies to $2x_1 - 3y_1 = 1$. So any solution of the second system is a solution of the first. That is both systems have the same solution set; thus, if we know the solutions of the second system we would know the solutions of the first. The second system, moreover, is easy to solve. If x and y must be such that $5y = \overline{13}$, then y must be $\frac{13}{5}$. If y is $\frac{13}{5}$ and $x + y = 7$, then $x + \frac{13}{5} = 7$ and $x = \frac{22}{5}$. Finally substituting these values for x and y in the second system shows that they do satisfy the equations.

An alternative approach which would not require substitution of values in the system is to observe that the solution set of the system

$$\begin{cases} x = \frac{22}{5} \\ y = \frac{13}{5} \end{cases}$$

is obvious. Since this system is equivalent to the original system we have found our desired solution set.

We have gone into considerable detail in the example above to justify the general procedure we will use to solve systems of equations. Two systems are called equivalent if the solution sets of both systems are the same. Our procedure consists of replacing one system by an equivalent system which is easier to solve. It is possible to modify the argument given in the example to show the following assertion. If we start with a given system of equations and obtain a new system by any of the following means:

1. Interchanging two equations.

2. Multiplying one equation by a nonzero number k (i.e., replacing $a = b$ by $ka = kb$).

3. Replacing one equation by the sum of it and another from the system (i.e., if $a = b$ is an equation and $c = d$ is another equation, then we replace $a = b$ by $a + c = b + d$),

then an equivalent system results. Note that one may combine steps 2 and 3 and thus replace one equation by the sum of it and a multiple of one of the others in the system.

A system is called triangular if each equation has at least one less variable than the preceding one. A triangular system can be readily solved. Our method is to replace the given system by an equivalent triangular system and find the solutions from the latter. Notice that in the example above the second system is a triangular one.

It is possible to use our methods on systems consisting of n equations with n variables (or even m equations with n variables). It may be instructive to examine a system of three equations in three unknowns.

EXAMPLE 1. Solve over the rational field the system

$$\begin{cases} 2x + y + 3z = \bar{1} \\ 3x + \bar{1}y + 2z = 1 \\ 5x + 2y + 4z = \bar{3} \end{cases}$$

It is convenient to obtain a system in which there is a 1 (or $\bar{1}$) as the coefficient of x in the first equation. One way to accomplish this would be to multiply the first equation by $\frac{1}{2}$. As this would introduce a number of fractional terms for coefficients we usually take a method that is somewhat less direct. We might add $\bar{2}$ times the first equation to the third (i.e., we multiply each side of the first equation by $\bar{2}$ and then add the resulting equation to the third equation) and then interchange the first and third equations. We might add $\bar{1}$ times the first equation to the second and then interchange the first and second equations. However, we prefer to add $\bar{1}$ times the second equation to the first yielding the equivalent system

$$\begin{cases} \bar{1}x + 2y + z = \bar{2} \\ 3x + \bar{1}y + 2z = 1 \\ 5x + 2y + 4z = \bar{5} \end{cases}$$

We now add 3 times the first equation to the second and then 5 times the first equation to the third yielding the equivalent system

$$\begin{cases} \bar{1}x + 2y + z = \bar{2} \\ \phantom{\bar{1}x +} 5y + 5z = \bar{5} \\ \phantom{\bar{1}x +} 12y + 9z = \overline{15} \end{cases}$$

We would now like to get a 1 (or a $\bar{1}$) as the coefficient of y in the second equation. We could add $\bar{2}$ times the second equation to the third and then $\bar{2}$ times the third equation to the second. However we prefer to multiply the second equation by $\frac{1}{5}$. This gives the equivalent system

$$\begin{cases} \bar{1}x + 2y + z = \bar{2} \\ \phantom{\bar{1}x + 1} y + z = \bar{1} \\ \phantom{\bar{1}x +} 12y + 9z = \overline{15} \end{cases}$$

If we now add $\overline{12}$ times the second equation to the third equation we obtain the equivalent system

$$\begin{cases} \bar{1}x + 2y + z = \bar{2} \\ \phantom{\bar{1}x +} y + z = \bar{1} \\ \phantom{\bar{1}x + 2y +} 3z = 3 \end{cases}$$

But this system is triangular and hence can readily be solved. From the last equation we find that $z = 1$. Putting $z = 1$ in the second equation yields $y + 1 = \bar{1}$ or $y = \bar{2}$. Putting $z = 1$ and $y = \bar{2}$ in the first equation yields $\bar{1}x + \bar{4} + 1 = \bar{2}$ or $\bar{1}x = 1$ or $x = \bar{1}$. We conclude that $x = \bar{1}$, $y = \bar{2}$, $z = 1$ gives the solution of our original system of equations.

It is convenient to use detached coefficients in the solution and omit the symbols for the variables x, y, z as well as the addition, multiplication, and equal signs. Then the original system would look like this

$$\begin{bmatrix} 2 & 1 & 3 & \vdots & \bar{1} \\ 3 & \bar{1} & 2 & \vdots & 1 \\ 5 & 2 & 4 & \vdots & \bar{5} \end{bmatrix}$$

By utilizing an eraser we can perform our operations one by one on this system and finally wind up with the array

$$\begin{bmatrix} \bar{1} & 2 & 1 & \vdots & \bar{2} \\ 0 & 1 & 1 & \vdots & \bar{1} \\ 0 & 0 & 3 & \vdots & 3 \end{bmatrix}$$

Although it is convenient to use an eraser on arrays such as these, once an error is made one must generally start from the beginning again. It is sometimes advantageous to add a check column consisting of the sum of the other elements in the respective rows. Then our array for the original would look like this

$$\begin{bmatrix} 2 & 1 & 3 & \vdots & \bar{1} & 5 \\ 3 & \bar{1} & 2 & \vdots & 1 & 5 \\ 5 & 2 & 4 & \vdots & \bar{5} & 6 \end{bmatrix}$$

When we add $\bar{1}$ times the second row to the first we obtain the array

$$\begin{bmatrix} \bar{1} & 2 & 1 & \vdots & \bar{2} & 0 \\ 3 & \bar{1} & 2 & \vdots & 1 & 5 \\ 5 & 2 & 4 & \vdots & \bar{5} & 6 \end{bmatrix}$$

Since $\bar{1} + 2 + 1 + \bar{2} = 0$ and there is a 0 in the last column of the first row, our work checks. This does not mean it is impossible for us to have an error, but it does mean that an error is rather unlikely and that we can obtain a check for each step of our procedure, if desired.

In the first paragraph of this section we considered the question of finding some solutions to the equation $2x - 3y = 1$ over the rational field. Suppose we had been asked to *solve* the equation rather than to find some solution for it. In other words we must find *all* solutions of the equation. We can let y be any rational number, say, $y = a$. Then $x = (1 + 3a)/2$. Hence $x = (1 + 3a)/2$, $y = a$ is a solution for every rational number a. Conversely if $y = a$ is part of a solution, then the original equation tells us that $x = (1 + 3a)/2$. That is, every solution has the form $x = (1 + 3a)/2$, $y = a$ where a is a rational number. A variable used in this fashion is usually called a *parameter;* we say a is a parameter over the rational field. We could equally well have let $x = b$ and then obtained $y = (\bar{1} + 2b)/3$, where b is a parameter over the rational field. Or we could have let $x = \bar{1} + t$ and then found

$y = (3 + 2t)/3$. Sometimes parameters are helpful in solving systems of linear equations as in the following example.

EXAMPLE 2. Solve over the rational field the system

$$\begin{cases} 2x - 3y = 1 \\ 4x - 6y = 2 \end{cases}$$

Adding $\bar{2}$ times the first equation to the second gives the equivalent system whose array is

$$\begin{bmatrix} 2 & 3 & \vdots & 1 \\ 0 & 0 & \vdots & 0 \end{bmatrix}$$

Since the second equation puts no restriction on y, we can let $y = a$ where a is a parameter over the rational field. Then $x = (1 + 3a)/2$.

EXERCISES

Solve over the rational field the systems:

1. $\begin{cases} x + y = 5 \\ x - y = 3 \end{cases}$

2. $\begin{cases} 2x + 3y = 5 \\ 4x + 5y = 9 \end{cases}$

3. $\begin{cases} 2x - y = 4 \\ 2y - 4x + 8 = 0 \end{cases}$

4. $\begin{cases} 2x + 3y = 5 \\ 6x + 9y = 10 \end{cases}$

5. $\begin{cases} x + 2y + z = 2 \\ 2x + y + z = 1 \\ 3x - 2y - 2z = 5 \end{cases}$

6. Find two rational numbers whose sum is twelve, and such that three times the first is two more than twice the second.

7. Solve over the rational field the system

$$\begin{cases} 2x - y = 1 \\ y + 2z = 5 \\ 3x + z = 7 \end{cases}$$

8. Prove that replacing an equation in a system by the difference of it and one of the others results in an equivalent system.

9. Solve over the rational field the system

$$\begin{cases} x + 2y + 3z + 4w = 7 \\ 3x - y - z - 2w = 4 \\ 3x - 5y + 4z = 10 \\ y + 5z - 6w = 2 \end{cases}$$

10. Solve over the rational field the system

$$\begin{cases} x + 3y + 2z = 4 \\ y - 2x - z = 1 \\ z + 3x + 2y = 0 \end{cases}$$

6.3. SOME APPLICATIONS OF LINEAR EQUATIONS

Many problems can be solved through use of linear equations or systems of linear equations. We illustrate by an example.

EXAMPLE 1. A man is now three times as old as his son. In seven years his age will be four years more than twice that of his son. How old are they now?

SOLUTION A. Let x denote the age of the son now in years. Then $3x$ denotes the age of the man now in years. Moreover $3x + 7 =$ the age of the man seven years from now and $x + 7 =$ the age of the son seven years from now. Hence we obtain from the second sentence in the problem the equation $3x + 7 = 2(x + 7) + 4$. The solution set of this equation is 11. Hence the son is 11 years old and the man is 33 years old. Note that x, as used here, does *not* denote a variable.

SOLUTION B. Let x denote the age of the son now in years and let y denote the age of the man now in years. The first sentence in the problem yields the equation $y = 3x$ while the second sentence in the problem yields the equation $y + 7 = 2(x + 7) + 4$. Solving the system

$$\begin{cases} y = 3x \\ y + 7 = 2x + 18 \end{cases}$$

yields the solution $x = 11$, $y = 33$, in agreement with our previous result. Note that neither x nor y denote variables in this case.

Sometimes, as in the next example, it seems better not to set up a formal equation.

‡EXAMPLE 2. A hare makes 3 leaps to the dog's 2, but 3 of the dog's leaps are equal to 7 of the hare's. If the hare has a start of 60 of her leaps, how many leaps must the hound make to overtake the hare? [*Note:* Selected exercises and examples are by J. W. Nicholson, *An Advanced Arithmetic* (New Orleans: F. F. Hansel & Brothers, 1889); these are marked with a dagger.]

We observe that while the dog makes 6 leaps the hare makes 9 leaps. But 6 dog leaps are equal to 14 hare leaps, and so each time the dog makes 6 leaps he gains 5 hare leaps on the hare. Hence to gain 60 hare leaps he must make 12 sets of 6 leaps or 72 dog leaps.

Some problems in the exercises below, such as numbers 1 and 2, might not have much to do with linear equations, but nonetheless we feel their inclusion here is desirable.

EXERCISES

1. Write the integer twelve thousand twelve hundred and twelve.

2. Which is greater, six dozen dozen or a half dozen dozen?

3. A piece of wire 7 ft long is to be cut into two pieces so that one piece will be two-thirds as long as the other. Find the length of each piece.

4. Find two counting numbers whose sum is 45, and such that when the larger is divided by the smaller the quotient is 3 and the remainder is 1.

5. A man has a pocketful of nickels and dimes and has twice as many dimes as nickels. How many dimes and how many nickels does he have if the change in his pocket totals $5.

6. If a brick and a half weighs a pound and a half more than half a brick, how much does a brick weigh?

7. The sum of the digits of a "two digit number" is 11. If the digits are reversed, the number is increased by 9. What is the number?

8. Fifteen more than twice a number is 37 less than half of the number. What is the number?

9. The inscription on a tombstone reads: "For half of my life I was a bachelor, for five years of married life I had no children, for one third of my life I was married, and I was three times my oldest child's age when my wife died." How old was the man when he died?

10. My daughter and I were born in September. When her birthday is on a Tuesday mine comes later on a Thursday. The sum of the dates is fifteen. When is my birthday?

11. The hands of a clock are pointing in exactly the same direction at 12 o'clock. When exactly do they next point in the same direction?

‡12. A, B, and C own 108 horses, of which B owns 2 times as many as A, and C, 3 times as many as B, how many does each own?

‡13. A man went from A to B, then from B to A, and then from A to B, at the rates of 36, 15, and 48 miles per day, respectively, and traveled the distance each time in an exact number of days; find the least possible distance from A to B.

‡14. *B* is $\frac{1}{4}$ older than *A*, and $\frac{1}{6}$ younger than *C*, and *C* is 12 years older than *A*, what are their ages?

‡15. After paying out $\frac{1}{4}$ and $\frac{1}{5}$ of my money, I had $16 more than I had spent; what had I at first?

‡16. Forty-eight stones are placed in a straight line and extend a distance of 175 ft; some of them are 3 ft, some 5 ft, and others 6 ft in length; how many of each kind are there?

‡17. A fox is 60 ft ahead of a hound, but the hound runs 12 ft while the fox runs 10 ft; how far will the fox run before the hound catches him?

18. A snail crawling up a pole 10 ft high climbs 3 ft every day and slips back 2 ft every night. How long will it take him to reach the top?

19. A watermelon weighs $\frac{4}{5}$ of its weight, plus $\frac{4}{5}$ of a pound. How many pounds does it weigh?

20. If a herring and a half cost a cent and a half, how much will a dozen and a half herrings cost?

21. A bottle and a cork cost $1.10, and the bottle costs $1.00 more than the cork. How much does each cost?

22. How many minutes would it take to cut a strip of cloth 50 yd long into strips 1 yd long if each cut takes 1 min?

23. After cutting off $\frac{1}{10}$ of a piece of cloth, a merchant had 100 yd left. How many yards did he have at first?

24. If an apple just balances in weight with $\frac{3}{4}$ of an apple of the same weight, and $\frac{3}{4}$ of an ounce, how much does the apple weigh?

25. There were two Arabs who sat down to eat, one with 5 loaves and the other with 3, all the loaves having the same value. Just as they were about to begin, a third Arab came along and proposed to eat with them, promising to pay 8 cents for his part of the meal. If they ate equally and consumed all the bread, how should the 8 cents be divided?

26. A man had 5 pieces of chain, each having 3 links. He asked a blacksmith how much he would charge to make them into 1 piece of chain. The blacksmith replied that he charged 2 cents to cut a link and 2 cents to weld or fasten a link together. How much was the blacksmith's charge?

27. A mule and a horse were carrying some bales of cloth. The mule said to the horse, "If you give me one of your bales, I shall carry as many as you." "If you give me one of yours," replied the horse, "I shall carry twice as many as you." How many bales was each carrying?

28. A man sold his farm for $5000, which is what it cost him, then bought it back for $4500, and then sold it again for $5500. How much did he gain?

29. A man with $1.00 wanted $1.25. He pawned the $1.00 for 75 cents and then sold the pawn ticket for 50 cents. He then had his $1.25. Who lost in the transaction?

30. In a certain town 3 % of the inhabitants are one-legged and half of the others go barefoot. How many shoes are necessary?

6.4. AVERAGE AND PERCENTAGE

The average of two numbers is defined to be half of their sum (see Chapter 13). This definition can be extended so that the average of n numbers means their sum divided by n. If x and y are two numbers with x smaller than y, their average z is a number midway between x and y in the sense that $y - z = z - x$. To see this, note that $z = (x + y)/2$; so

$$z - x = \frac{x + y}{2} - x = \frac{x + y - 2x}{2} = \frac{y - x}{2}$$

and

$$y - z = y - \frac{x + y}{2} = \frac{2y - (x + y)}{2}$$
$$= \frac{2y - x - y}{2}$$
$$= \frac{y - x}{2}$$

Similarly most of us have a vague intuitive feeling that the average of several numbers is a number sort of in the middle of them. The definition above makes this vagueness precise. Accordingly if a teacher wants to find the class average on a test she gives, she adds all the test scores and divides by the number of people taking the test. Every teacher also usually gets questions like "What do I have to make on the next test to pass the course?"

EXAMPLE 1. A passing grade is 70. Joe Smith has made test grades of 65, 80, and 56. If there is one more test, and all the tests are weighted equally, what score does he need to make to have a passing average?

Let x be a variable indicating the possible scores on the last test. We wish to determine x so that

$$\frac{65 + 80 + 56 + x}{4} \geq 70$$

If this is so, $65 + 80 + 56 + x$ must be greater than or equal to 280. If this is so, x must be $\geq 280 - 201 = 79$. Further if $x \geq 79$, $65 + 80 + 56 + x$ will be ≥ 280 and

$$\frac{65 + 80 + 56 + x}{4} \geq 70$$

as was desired.

There is a set of problems, called mixture problems, which can be considered as problems involving averages. We illustrate with an example.

EXAMPLE 2. A grocer mixes 5 pounds of nuts which sell for 30¢ per pound and 10 pounds of nuts which sell for 50¢ per pound. At what rate should he sell the mixture?

We are looking for the average of 15 numbers, 5 of which are 30, and 10 of which are 50. The result is clearly

$$\frac{5 \times 30 + 10 \times 50}{15} = \frac{650}{15} = \frac{130}{3} = 43\tfrac{1}{3}$$

Each pound of the mixture should thus be sold for $43\tfrac{1}{3}$¢.

The use of percentages arose because it is often convenient to express a number as a fraction with a denominator of 100. Having done this, it is then easy to suppress the denominator and add the words "per cent" or the symbol %. Thus $\tfrac{1}{5} = \tfrac{20}{100} = 20$ per cent and $2\tfrac{1}{2} = \tfrac{5}{2} = \tfrac{250}{100} = 250\%$. There are some numbers that cannot be written as fractions with a denominator of 100. For example, $\tfrac{1}{3}$. If we try to determine x so that $x/100 = \tfrac{1}{3}$, we find $x = 33\tfrac{1}{3}$. It is common practice to avoid this difficulty by saying $\tfrac{1}{3} = 33\tfrac{1}{3}\%$. In this manner every rational number may be written as a percentage. The usual problems involving per cent are illustrated in the following example.

EXAMPLE 3. (a) Find $22\tfrac{2}{9}\%$ of 79. We have

$$22\tfrac{2}{9}\% \text{ of } 79 = \frac{22\tfrac{2}{9}}{100} \cdot 79 = \frac{2}{9} \cdot 79 = \frac{158}{9} = 17\tfrac{5}{9}.$$

(b) $22\tfrac{2}{9}\%$ of what number $= 79$. As above $22\tfrac{2}{9}\%$ of a number $= \tfrac{2}{9}$ of the number. But if $\tfrac{2}{9}$ of the number $= 79$ then $\tfrac{1}{9}$ of the number $= \tfrac{79}{2}$ and so the number $= 9(\tfrac{79}{2}) = \tfrac{711}{2} = 355\tfrac{1}{2}$. (c) $22\tfrac{2}{9}$ is what per cent of 79? If a certain per cent of 79 $= 22\tfrac{2}{9}$ then this certain per cent

$$= \frac{22\tfrac{2}{9}}{79} = \frac{200}{9 \cdot 79} = \frac{200}{711} = \frac{200}{711}(100)\% = 28\tfrac{92}{711}\%$$

Many problems involve completing a particular task in a certain period of time. We have called these "job" problems. The following two examples illustrate this type of problem. If 10 men mow 20 acres in 3 hr, then one man would mow two acres in 3 hr, or one man would mow 20 acres in 30 hr. Similarly 100 men would mow 200 acres in 3 hr or 100 men would mow 20 acres in $\frac{3}{10}$ hr. If one man can complete a certain task in four days, then in one day he would complete $\frac{1}{4}$ of the task. These statements are reasonable only with the proper assumptions—we agree that everyone works at a constant rate, that all men do the same amount of work in the same time, that no one gets in any one else's way so that doubling the number of men halves the time required for a job, etc.

‡EXAMPLE 4. If 12 men mow 25 acres of grass in two days of $10\frac{1}{2}$ hr, how many men will it require to mow 80 acres in six days of $9\frac{3}{5}$ hr? If 12 men mow 25 acres in 21 hr, then

$$1 \text{ man mows } \frac{25}{12} \text{ acres in 21 hr,}$$

$$1 \text{ man mows } \frac{25}{12 \cdot 21} \text{ acres in 1 hr}$$

$$1 \text{ man mows } \frac{6 \cdot 48}{5} \cdot \frac{25}{12 \cdot 21} \text{ acres in } \frac{6 \cdot 48}{5} \text{ hr}$$

or

$$1 \text{ man mows } \frac{40}{7} \text{ acres in } \frac{6 \cdot 48}{5} \text{ hr}$$

hence

$$14 \text{ men mow 80 acres in } \frac{6 \cdot 48}{5} \text{ hr}$$

EXAMPLE 5. If pipe A can fill a pool in 3 hr, pipe B in 4 hr, and pipe C in 5 hr, how long will it take to fill the pool if all three pipes are used?

In 1 hr pipe A fills $\frac{1}{3}$ of the pool, pipe B fills $\frac{1}{4}$ of the pool and pipe C fills $\frac{1}{5}$ of the pool. Hence in 1 hr all three pipes fill $\frac{1}{3} + \frac{1}{4} + \frac{1}{5} = \frac{47}{60}$ of the pool. Thus it would take

$$\frac{1}{47/60} = \frac{60}{47} \text{ hr}$$

to fill the pool.

Moreover, problems involving mixtures can be handled by consideration of the average value of the mixture. We illustrate by an example.

EXAMPLE 6. Candies worth 20¢, 28¢ and 32¢ a pound, respectively, are to be mixed so as to form 30 pounds of a mixture worth 25¢ per pound. How much of each might be taken? (Use all three kinds of candy.)

The average price of the mixture is 25¢ per pound. Each time we take 1 pound of the 20¢ candy we miss the average price by -5¢; each time we take 1 pound of the 28¢ candy we miss the average price by $+3$¢; each time we take one pound of the 32¢ candy we miss the average price by $+7$¢. We put this information down in chart form as follows: average price = 25¢ per pound,

20¢	28¢	32¢
-5¢	$+3$¢	$+7$¢

Our idea is to mix the candies so that the mixture differs from the average price by 0¢. Then we shall have a mixture worth 25¢ per pound. We see that 3 pounds of 20¢ candy will miss the average by -15¢ and that 5 pounds of 28¢ candy will miss the average by $+15$¢. Hence by taking 3 pounds of 20¢ candy and 5 pounds of 28¢ candy we will have 8 pounds of a mixture which differs by 0¢ from the average, i.e., the mixture is worth 25¢ per pound. Similarly we may take 7 pounds of 20¢ and 5 pounds of 32¢ to obtain a mixture worth 25¢ per pound. Thus by taking $3 + 7 = 10$ pounds of 20¢ candy, 5 pounds of 28¢ candy, and 5 pounds of 32¢ candy we obtain 20 pounds of a mixture worth 25¢ per pound. Thus $\frac{10}{20} = \frac{1}{2}$ of the total is 20¢ candy, $\frac{5}{20} = \frac{1}{4}$ of the total is 28¢ candy, and $\frac{5}{20} = \frac{1}{4}$ of the total is 32¢ candy. Hence we could obtain 30 pounds total by taking $\frac{1}{2}(30) = 15$ pounds at 20¢, $\frac{1}{4}(30) = 7\frac{1}{2}$ pounds at 28¢, and $\frac{1}{4}(30) = 7\frac{1}{2}$ pounds at 32¢.

Alternatively we might observe that $7 + 3 = 10$ and $2 \cdot 5 = 10$. Hence we might take 1 pound of 28¢ candy, 1 pound of 32¢ candy, and 2 pounds of 20¢ candy to obtain a "balanced" mixture. This happens to give the same answer as we just obtained. However whenever there are as many as 3 items to mix there is an unlimited number of ways to mix them. All that we ask here is to find *one* way to combine them. This explains the phrasing "How many pounds of each kind *might* be taken?" instead of something like "How many kinds of each kind *must* be taken?" All possible solutions may be found by setting up and solving a system of linear equations. Can you find all possible solutions to Example 6?

EXERCISES

1. How many pounds of 20¢ candy and 40¢ candy should be mixed to form 24 pounds of a mixture worth 25¢ per pound?

‡2. What is the average monthly wage of a clerk who receives $36 a month for the first three months, $48 a month for the next four months, and $60 a month for the next five months?

‡3. A father gave 15 % of his money to his son, 25 % of the remainder to his daughter, and had $15,300 left; how much had he at first?

‡4. For what must I sell a horse, which cost me $125, to gain $6\frac{2}{3}$ %?

‡5. If four boys can build a fence in 15 hr, how long will it take six boys to build it?

‡6. A and B can do a certain work in $4\frac{4}{5}$ days, A and C in 6 days, and B and C in 8 days; in how many days can each do the work?

7. How much pure alcohol could be added to 12 gal of a mixture containing 15 % alcohol to obtain a mixture containing 25 % alcohol?

‡8. By working 8 hr a day 25 men can do a certain work in 24 days; how many hours a day must 30 men work for 16 days to do the same work?

9. During a three day sale of slightly used left-handed shoe horns a store sold 500 units at 15 % profit (of the cost price) the first day, 1000 units at 10 % profit the second day, and 2000 units at 5 % profit the third day. What was the per cent profit for the sale?

10. A car radiator holds 15 quarts. At the beginning of the winter it has two quarts of antifreeze in it. Sometime later one quart of the mixture is drained and replaced by a quart of antifreeze. What now is the percentage of antifreeze in the radiator?

11. If A can do a certain job in 3 hr, B in 5 hr, and C in 7 hr, how long will it take to do the job if all three work together?

12. State the assumptions you made before working Exercise 11. Consider the case where A and B are males and C is a female dressed in a Bikini. Consider the case where the job consists of memorizing a piece of poetry.

‡13. A, B, and C engage to hoe an acre of corn for $5.00. A alone can hoe it in 48 hr; B, in 36 hr; and C, in 24 hr. A works alone 10 hr, then A and B work together 6 hr, when C begins and all work together till the job is finished. How much of the $5.00 should each receive?

14. Ship A can cross the ocean in five days, ship B in seven days, and ship C in nine days. How long will it take them to cross the ocean if they all cross together?

15. A can climb a certain mountain in 12 hr; B, in 15 hr; and C, in 19 hr. How long will it take them to climb the mountain if they all climb together?

‡16. How long will provisions sufficient for 475 men for 56 days last 133 men?

‡17. If 10 men earn $90 in four days, how much will 16 men earn in five days?

‡18. If 35 men earn $462.00 in six days, in how many days can 55 men earn $484.00?

‡19. If 15 men perform a piece of work in 24 hr, how many men can perform another piece of work nine times as great in $\frac{1}{5}$ of the time?

‡20. If five men earn $155.00 in a week, how much will nine men earn in the same time?

‡21. How long will it take 15 men to perform a work which 21 men can do in 35 days?

‡22. A grocer desires to mix four kinds of sugar worth 5, 7, 10, and 12 cents a pound so that the mixture should be worth 9 cents a pound; how much of each could be taken?

‡23. Dried fruits worth 9, 12, 15, and 18 cents a pound are combined in a mixture worth 14 cents a pound; find the proportional weights of the different kinds.

‡24. In what proportion could syrups worth 40, 45, 50, and 64 cents per gallon be mixed so that the mixture may have an average value of 48 cents per gallon?

‡25. A farmer has hogs worth $10, $6, and $4 a head; what number of each could he sell to obtain an average price of $8 a head?

‡26. A grocer has sugars worth 5, 6, 9, and 12 cents a pound; how much of each could be take to form a mixture of 60 pounds, worth 8 cents a pound?

‡27. A paid $100 for 100 head of hogs, pigs, and chickens. The hogs cost $9 each; the pigs $4 each; the chickens $½ each; how many of each did he buy?

‡28. How much candy at 9, 11, and 14 cents a pound will form a mixture of 56 pounds, worth 12 cents a pound?

‡29. A, B, and C together receive $94 for doing a work which A alone could do in 6 days, B in 8 days, and C in 10 days; how much is each entitled to?

‡30. A barrel of vinegar lost 20 % by leakage, and was sold by volume for 40 % above cost price. What was the gain per cent?

‡31. How much more money has A than B if $2\frac{7}{9}$ % of A's or $3\frac{1}{3}$ % of B's is $5.00?

‡32. A certain article of consumption is subject to a duty of 6 cents a pound but in consequence of a reduction of the duty the consumption increased $\frac{1}{2}$, but the revenue fell $\frac{1}{3}$; what was the duty per pound after the reduction?

‡33. If $\frac{7}{8}$ of a yard of silk costs \$2.10, what will $\frac{3}{5}$ of a yard cost?

‡34. If 12 men can build a wall in 35 days, how long will it take 21 men to build the wall?

‡35. In an examination A made $54\frac{1}{6}\%$ and B made $62\frac{1}{2}\%$. If B answered 75 questions, how many questions did A answer?

36. Two identical glasses are $\frac{2}{3}$ full of wine and water, respectively. One takes a teaspoonful of wine from the wine glass, pours it into the water and stirs thoroughly; then, he takes a teaspoonful of the mixture and pours it into the wine glass. Is there more wine in the water glass or more water in the wine glass?

6.5. "SEND MORE MONEY"

It may come as a surprise to some people that there is recreational mathematics—mathematical games, puzzles, etc., fit into this category. In fact, some mathematicians treat their work as a game and think of mathematics as a collection of puzzle like problems. The authors are not completely unsympathetic with this view; they feel that many people are attracted to mathematics by its challenge to puzzle solvers. Too often this intriguing facet of mathematics is not presented to children who are learning arithmetic, and as a result much of grade school mathematics is uninteresting, dull, and repetitive.

Some problems which are extremely effective in increasing understanding and facility with arithmetic processes as well as being recreational are presented here. The general idea is that letters are used for digits in an arithmetic example and the problem is to determine which letters stand for which digits. The word "digit" is used rather loosely in this section, but we feel that the reader will have little trouble in deciding on the intended meaning. Often the letters spell out words which are related but this is not necessary and merely gives the problem flavor. There are some usual assumptions made—if a letter is repeated it stands for the same digit each time; two different letters represent two different digits (but the appearance of a digit such as '2' in a problem does not rule out the possibility of a letter representing the same number); and, unless stated otherwise, the numerals are to the base ten.

EXAMPLE 1. Determine the digits in the addition problem

$$
\begin{array}{r}
\text{ME} \\
\text{MY} \\
\hline
\text{EYE}
\end{array}
$$

This problem is readily solved by noting that since the sum of two two-digit numbers is less then 200, E must be the digit '1'; since the sum of

Y and E has E as its units digit, Y must be 0; and M + M = EY = 10 implies that M is 5.

The problems can, of course, become much more involved. Sometimes they have more than one solution (in which case you are supposed to find them all), and sometimes they don't have any solution (in which case you are supposed to prove that this is the case). However, from an æsthetic viewpoint (and mathematicians are quite æsthetic), the best problems are those with exactly one solution. Let's try a more involved problem.

EXAMPLE 2. Find the digits in the long division problem

```
          HIS
       _____
    IF)TOOT
       IF
       ____
       HHO
       HHH
       ____
        FT
        FT
        __
```

One quickly sees that H must be 1. Why? Now note that I times IF = HHH = 111. Since the only nontrivial factors of 111 are 3 and 37, one sees that I is 3 and F is 7. The rest of the problem is easy and is left for the reader.

EXERCISES

1. Complete Example 2.

Determine the digits in each of the following:

2. $\dfrac{\text{BUM}}{\text{CAB}} = \text{C}$ if A = 3

3. The addition problem:

```
          SEND
          MORE
         _____
         MONEY
```

4.
```
                 IRK
             _____
      DAY)RADARS
          RIDE
          ____
           OKR
           DAY
           ____
           ARMS
           ARMS
           ____
```

5. The multiplication problem: (1ABCDE) × 3 = ABCDE1 where 1 is one.

6. The multiplication problem: 2(HEADS) = BETTER.

7. If (FOUR) + (ONE) = FIVE and 2(FOUR + $\frac{1}{2}$) = NINE.

8. Given that FOUR + 12 is a perfect square, solve the addition

> FIFTY
> FOUR
> FOUR
> TWO
> ―――
> SIXTY

Exercise 8 is from the *American Mathematical Monthly*, No. 4, Vol. 68, p. 378.

9. Given that s = 9, solve the addition

> THREE
> THREE
> ONE
> ―――
> SEVEN

6.6. OTHER BASES

Most of the problems considered in this section can be most easily solved by utilizing bases other than 10. Let us consider first a rather simple game. Eleven stones are placed in a pile; each of two players alternating turns picks up either one or two stones until they are all picked up. The winner is the one who picks up the last stone. (The mechanics of the game are sometimes revised to putting down stones instead of picking them up; making marks on paper or a blackboard; or simply adding one or two orally and trying to reach 11.) It is easily seen that, if on your next to last turn you leave three stones, you are assured of winning. For if your opponent takes one, you can take two stones; if he takes two, you can take the last one. This maneuver suggests that the number three is important in this game, and indeed it is. Write the number of remaining stones in the ternary (or base 3) system. If you leave a number of stones whose ternary representation has a zero in the units place, when your opponent removes one or two stones, the units digit will become 2 or 1 respectively. Then when you remove two or one, respectively, the units digit is once again 0. Therefore, if you continue in this manner, the units digit is 0 only after your turn—thus you will pick up the last stone as desired. In particular if the game starts with 11 stones (102 in base 3) as suggested above, and it is your play you should take two stones leaving $(100)_3$ and then continue as indicated. If it is not your first play, then your only chance is to wait for a wrong play on your opponent's part.

A slightly more involved version of this game, which is always popular with youngsters as soon as they can add with facility, is the "100 game." Here the idea is to reach 100. A move is made by adding 1, 2, 3, 4, 5, 6, 7, 8, 9, 10, or 11 to the previous total. The game starts at zero. The player who can say "100" in his turn wins. The player who moves first is guaranteed a win provided he plays correctly. It is customary to let a youngster begin first until he learns the principles of the game. Then change the rule from adding numbers up to 11 to adding numbers up to 8 or to 13. This gives good practice in mental arithmetic when one is trying to win.

A perennially popular game which has recently been reintroduced in elementary school is age cards. For example, the set of three cards given here would suffice for an ordinary first grade class.

$$
\begin{array}{ccc}
A & B & C \\
\boxed{\begin{array}{cc} 1 & 5 \\ 3 & 7 \end{array}} &
\boxed{\begin{array}{cc} 2 & 6 \\ 3 & 7 \end{array}} &
\boxed{\begin{array}{cc} 4 & 6 \\ 5 & 7 \end{array}}
\end{array}
$$

The person holding the cards asks a pupil in the class to tell him on which cards his own age appears. For example, the pupil might say his age appears on cards B and C. Then the person with the cards tells him that his age is 6. How does he know that the pupil's age is 6?

Let us now consider the artificially created problem of determining the smallest number of weights to weigh 1, 2, 3, . . . , n ounces on a pan balance. We agree that we will always put the weights on one side of the pan and the object to be weighed on the other. We only weigh integral numbers of ounces —no half-ounces or other fractional quantities. Thus to weigh 1, 2, 3, or 4 ounces we could have weights of: (a) 1, 1, 2 or (b) 1, 1, 3 or (c) 1, 2, 3 or (d) 1, 2, 4. However (b) is more efficient than (a) for it weighs 1, 2, 3, 4, or 5 ounces whereas (a) weighs only up to 4 ounces. Similarly (c) weighs up to 6 ounces whereas (d) weighs up to 7 ounces. It is clear that for an arbitrary n we will need a system of maximum efficiency. We must have a weight of 1 ounce. To weigh 2 ounces we have our choice of an additional 1 ounce or a 2 ounce weight. For maximum efficiency we choose the 2 ounce weight. Then we can weigh 1, 2, or 3 ounces. To weigh 4 ounces we choose a 4 ounce weight for maximum efficiency. Then we can weigh 1, 2, 3, 4, 5, 6, or 7 ounces. By continuing in this fashion we see that the number of weights needed is the number of digits in the binary numeral for n.

Perhaps the most involved game of this sort is the ancient game of Nim. Again there is a system which will win against any player (provided the right person has the first move)—in fact, some machines have been built to play and win at Nim. At the start of this game there are several piles of stones (or other markers). The first player takes up any number of stones from any one (and only one) of the piles of stones. He must take at least one stone. The second player takes up any number of remaining stones from any one of the piles. This is repeated until all the stones are picked up and the player who picks up the last stone is the winner. The game may be varied by changing the number of stones in any pile and/or changing the number of piles.

Let us illustrate the procedure by using 24 markers divided into three piles containing 5, 7, and 12 markers. Let us express the number of markers in our piles in the binary system. Thus we get the array

$$1100$$
$$111$$
$$101$$

Since we are restricted on any one move to removing markers from a single pile, in a certain sense all that we can do is to remove 1's, add 1's, or shift 1's in *one* of the three rows. Thus, if there are an even number of 1's in every column when a player starts his move, he cannot possibly remove the last marker. The player making the first move here could achieve this desirable state by replacing 1100 by 10

$$10$$
$$\overline{1100}$$
$$111$$
$$101$$

i.e., remove all but 2 markers from the pile containing 12. Then there are two 1's in the first column, two in the second, and two in the third. Since each of these is an even number, our opponent cannot win in his next move. Moreover our opponent has to remove at least one marker and all markers he removes must be from the same pile. This results in replacing one or more 1's in the row designating this pile with 0's, and possibly one or more 0's with a 1. Now each column has an even number of 1's in it, so removing a 1 from any column leaves an odd number of 1's in that column. Hence, after our opponent's move there is at least one column with an odd number of 1's in it. By removing a 1 from or adding a 1 to each column in which there is an odd number of 1's, we have again reached the situation where each column has an even number of 1's in it. We can always accomplish this by working on a single row, and so we are set to continue the game toward our ultimate victory. Of course, if our opponent has the first move, then he has the advantage in this case. To follow these instructions one must be proficient in changing from base 10 to the binary system and vice versa.

If we had split the 24 markers into three piles containing eight each, then the resulting binary array would look like

$$1000$$
$$1000$$
$$1000$$

Hence, in this case, the desired state of an even number of 1's in each column could be obtained by removing all markers in one of the piles

~~1000~~
1000
1000

If we had started with four piles of six markers each, we would have

110
110
110
110

Since the columns already contain an even number of 1's, whoever goes first will lose if the second player plays correctly!

EXERCISES

1. Play several games of Nim with an opponent.

2. Suppose the rules of Nim are changed so that the one who takes the last marker loses. Discuss your strategy.

3. Suppose we wish to weigh $1, 2, \ldots, n$ ounces on a pan balance where we can put the weights on either pan. What would be the smallest number of weights possible, and what is the connection with the ternary system? (Observe that by putting a one ounce weight with the object to be weighed and a 3 ounce weight in the other pan, then we can weigh an object of 2 ounces. Thus 1 and 3 ounce weights will weigh 1, 2, 3, or 4 ounce objects.)

4. In a decimal system of coins one would have coins of values 1¢, 10¢, 100¢, etc. In a ternary system one would have coins of values 1¢, 3¢, 9¢, etc. A salesman needs to make change of $1, 2, \ldots, 100$ cents. In what system of coins would he carry the smallest number of coins?

5. How many coins are required to make 84¢ in a base 3 coin system? A base 5 coin system? A base 9 coin system?

6. Explain how to win in the 100 game if numbers up to 11 are added; if numbers up to 8 are added; if numbers up to 13 are added.

7. Assume that a particular freshman class has no student in it who is older than 23 years of age. Make a set of age cards for this class. Explain the connection of these age cards with the binary system.

8. Thirteen coins are given, one of which is counterfeit and lighter than the rest. Determine the smallest number of weighings on a pan balance which will certainly suffice to find the counterfeit coin.

9. Substitute 80 coins (instead of thirteen) in Exercise 8.

10. Substitute n coins (instead of thirteen) in Exercise 8. What is the connection between the ternary system and the answer to this exercise?

6.7. MAGIC SQUARES AND MISCELLANY

A magic square is a square array of counting numbers where each row, column, and diagonal has the same total. Let us see if we can construct a magic square of order 3 with the digits 1, 2, 3, 4, 5, 6, 7, 8, 9. The average of these digits is 5 and $3 \cdot 5 = 15$. Hence let us try to construct a 3 by 3 magic square in which each row, column, and diagonal totals 15. Let us first write the triples of digits whose sum is 15; 1, 5, 9; 1, 6, 8; 2, 4, 9; 2, 5, 8; 2, 6, 7; 3, 4, 8; 3, 5, 7; and 4, 5, 6. There are three rows, three columns, and two diagonals so that we will require eight triples of digits, and we have this many in our list above.

We observe that the center digit in the square is in the second row, the second column, and both diagonals. The only digit which occurs in four triples is 5—hence we must have 5 in the middle

$$
\begin{array}{ccc}
\underline{} & \underline{} & \underline{} \\
\underline{} & 5 & \underline{} \\
\underline{} & \underline{} & \underline{}
\end{array}
$$

The element in the first row and first column is also in one diagonal, and hence could not be 1 because 1 only appears in two triples. However 2 (and 8) and 4 (and 6) appear in three triples, but no other digits appear in three triples. Thus there are only the eight possibilities

```
2 — 6     2 — 4     8 — 6     6 — 2
— 5 —     — 5 —     — 5 —     — 5 —
4 — 8     6 — 8     4 — 2     8 — 4

6 — 8     4 — 2     4 — 8     8 — 4
— 5 —     — 5 —     — 5 —     — 5 —
2 — 4     8 — 6     2 — 6     6 — 2
```

anyone of which will work. As a matter of fact the remaining four digits are completely determined by the five digits we have placed and are

```
2 7 6     2 9 4     8 1 6     6 7 2
9 5 1     7 5 3     3 5 7     1 5 9
4 3 8     6 1 8     4 9 2     8 3 4

6 1 8     4 9 2     4 3 8     8 3 4
7 5 3     3 5 7     9 5 1     1 5 9
2 9 4     8 1 6     2 7 6     6 7 2
```

respectively. These are not essentially different—in fact, since there are only eight triples which total 15 and since we use eight triples, there is essentially only one magic square of order 3 which totals 15.

The other exercises below, like magic squares, have been with us through the years and many of them have been favorites of children. They are offered here for a number of reasons: they are interesting and fun to do; they indicate the kind of thinking that is useful in mathematics (and in other disciplines requiring logic); and (for the most part) they are applications of the rational number field.

EXERCISES

1. What would happen if we added two to each element in our 3 by 3 magic square?

2. Can one construct a 3 by 3 magic square from the first nine odd numbers?

3. Construct a 3 by 3 magic square from the counting numbers 1, 4, 7 10, 13, 16, 19, 22, and 25.

4. Construct a 4 by 4 magic square from the numbers 1 through 16.

5. A cook, standing by the river, has a five quart can and a three quart can and needs four quarts of water for a recipe. Give at least two ways in which he can obtain the four quarts.

6. How can one obtain two quarts of water by utilizing a five quart and a three quart can?

7. Three missionaries and three cannibals wish to cross a river by utilizing a boat which only holds two men. It is not safe if, at any time, the number of cannibals is larger than the number of missionaries. Can this group safely cross the river?

8. Three women, two of whom are blindfolded and the third of whom is blind, are seated at a table. From a box containing two red and three green hats, three hats are selected and one is placed on each of the women. Then the blindfold is removed from one of the women and, after glancing at the hats of the other two women, she states that she does not know the color of her hat. Then the blindfold is removed from the second woman and, after glancing at the hats of the other two women, she states that she does not know the color of her hat either. Whereupon the blind woman immediately gives the color of the hat she is wearing. What color is it?

9. A certain valley is inhabited by two tribes called A and B. Tribe A always lies, whereas Tribe B never lies. An explorer, on meeting a group of three natives, asked the first native what tribe he was from.

The native replied, "Un glub gooble goo" in his native tongue since he could understand but not speak English. Then the explorer asked the second native, "What did he say?". The reply was, "He says he is from Tribe *A*." Then the explorer asked the third native "What did he (the first native) say?". The reply was, "He says he is from Tribe *B*." What tribes are the two English speaking natives from?

10. Discuss the logic.

    (a) Heat expands things and cold contracts things. It is hotter in the summer than it is in the winter. Therefore the days are longer in the summer than in the winter.

    (b) All roads going west go to California. This road does not go west and therefore does not go to California.

    (c) A man measured a steel rod with a steel ruler on the hottest and coldest days of the year. He found the two results to be the same and so concluded that temperature has no effect on the length of a steel rod.

    (d) The average graduate of Princeton has $3\frac{1}{5}$ children. The average graduate of Vassar has $2\frac{1}{3}$ children. Hence men have more children than women. Does it necessarily follow that a Princeton graduate married a non-Vassar graduate?

11. A man points at a picture hanging on the wall and says: "Brothers and sisters have I none, but this man's father is my fathers son." Whose picture is it?

12. A traveler in the valley of Exercise 9 comes to a fork in the road and wants to know which way he should go to reach the city. One of the inhabitants is nearby. Can you think of one question the man can ask the native to determine the correct road no matter which tribe the native is from?

13. Take a stack of 10 cards. Put the top card on the bottom of the stack and throw the next one away. Put the next card on the bottom and throw away the one after that. Repeat this procedure until only one card remains. What was the position of this card in the original stack?

14. Every morning at 8 a.m. (local time) a train leaves New York bound for San Francisco. Every evening at 6 p.m. a train leaves San Francisco for New York. If each trip takes exactly five days, how many trains going the other way are met by a train going from New York to San Francisco?

15. Three men and their wives are marooned on a desert island with a boat that carries only two people. Each of the women is so devastatingly beautiful that she cannot be in the presence of any man unless her husband is also present. (This means on the island, on the land, or in the boat.) Only one of the women knows how to operate the

boat, but all of the men do. How do they all reach the mainland safely?

16. One coin out of 12 coins is counterfeit. Using a pan balance determine in not more than three weighings which coin is bad and whether it is heavier or lighter than the others.

17. Out of 10 coin manufacturers one produces a product which is always 10 % off in weight while the products of the others are always exactly of the right weight—one ounce. With one weighing on a calibrated scale determine who manufactures the defective coins.

18. A man sells half of his supply of oranges plus half an orange; then sells half of the remaining supply plus half an orange; and repeats this procedure with three more customers—at which time all of his oranges are gone. How many did he have to start with? (We might mention that no oranges were cut before, during, or after the transaction.)

7

7.1. INFINITE SETS AND PROCESSES

A set is called *finite* if it is empty or if there is a natural number n such that the elements of the set can be put into a 1–1 correspondence with the natural numbers from 1 through n. In other words a set is finite if there is a counting number which tells how many elements are in the set.

A set is called *infinite* if it is not finite. Most of the sets we are used to are finite sets, and accordingly, we are sometimes surprised at properties that infinite sets have. Perhaps the first infinite set that most of us become aware of is the set of counting numbers. A common question of little children is "What is the largest number there is?" When they find out there is no largest number, it is nearly always with some regret. However, it is just this property of no largest number that is responsible for some of the interesting things that can be done with the counting numbers, as we shall see.

Notice that a set may have a largest element and still be infinite. In fact the rational numbers between zero and one, including zero and one, is an example of a set that has both a smallest and largest element and is infinite.

A rather surprising property of infinite sets is that they may be put into a 1–1 correspondence with a proper subset of themselves. To illustrate this, let A be the set of all natural numbers and B be the set of all even natural numbers. Clearly B is a proper subset of A and yet, if we associate with each number n in A, the number $2n$ in B, we see that this puts A and B into 1–1

decimals and the field of real numbers

correspondence. To put it more strikingly—there are just as many even natural numbers as there are natural numbers altogether.

Another seemingly paradoxical situation is illustrated in the following example. A child who likes ice cream very much is given a dish of it. Because he wishes to preserve it as long as possible, he eats half of it, waits a minute, and then eats half of what remains. He continues this procedure—each time eating half of the remaining ice cream. Will he ever finish it?

Assuming a number of things (which are necessary for the sake of the problem)—the ice cream doesn't melt, the boy has nothing else to do and doesn't get tired or quit, he is able to separate the ice cream into two parts even when the portion becomes very small, etc.—then the answer is no, he will never finish it. Thus he has a nonending supply of ice cream. Notice that the total amount of ice cream remains the same (no matter how it is divided)—what happens is that it is broken up into an infinite number of portions.

We wish to point out that the example above also illustrates what we call here an *infinite process*. That is, we find something, and, having found it, use it to get something else. We continue this indefinitely, in the sense that, whenever we get to a certain stage in the procedure, we have a definite method of going on to the next stage, and there is always a next stage. In the example above, of course, the step taken at each point is to eat half of the remaining ice cream.

Another example of an infinite process is the following. Form a sequence (or list) of numbers by starting with the number 3 and finding the next number at each stage by multiplying the last number by 2 and adding 5. Thus the list starts off as 3, 11, 27, 59, ... Notice that from each number we can rather easily obtain the next number, but it is impossible to write down the whole list (among other reasons, we don't have enough time or paper). Nevertheless, and this is the importance of what we've been doing, we may consider the list as being completely determined as soon as we have the directions for constructing it.

EXERCISES

1. State whether each of the following sets is finite, infinite, or that this cannot be determined.

   (a) all cars in the United States

   (b) the integers greater than a million

   (c) the integers less than a million

   (d) the bricks in all the houses, buildings, roads, etc., on earth

(e) the grains of sand on all the beaches, sand bars, sand boxes, and spinach in the world

(f) the stars in the universe

(g) all the people who have lived, are living, or will live in the world.

2. A sequence of numbers is determined by saying that the nth number is obtained by squaring the $(n - 1)$th number, adding 1, and then taking the units digit of this sum as the new number. Write the first 10 numbers in the sequence if the first number is 8.

3. (Paradox of Zeno) The famous warrior Achilles can run ten times as fast as a tortoise. If the tortoise is given 100 yd head start, then Achilles (it is said) can never catch the tortoise for whenever Achilles gets to where the tortoise was, the tortoise has moved further on. Explain.

4. A package of cereal has a picture of the package on it. How many pictures of the package are there? Can you think of similar situations?

7.2. DECIMALS

One of the nice things about fractions whose denominators are powers of 10 is that they are easy to decompose into the sum of fractions whose numerators are digits. For example

$$\frac{537}{1000} = \frac{500}{1000} + \frac{30}{1000} + \frac{7}{1000} = \frac{5}{10} + \frac{3}{100} + \frac{7}{1000}$$

Since we can read off this decomposition without difficulty, it is customary not to bother writing the denominators, but to make use of the so-called decimal notation. This consists of writing $\frac{5}{10}$ as .5, $\frac{3}{100}$ as .03, $\frac{7}{1000}$ as .007, or $\frac{537}{1000}$ as .537. This is an extension of our positional notation, so that the numeral 23.45, e.g., means two tens plus three units plus four tenths plus five hundredths. The period is called a decimal point and serves as a position indicator (some of the Europeans, incidentally, use a comma for the decimal point). Such numerals may be called decimals, and, since they represent rational numbers, we can derive processes for finding decimal numerals for the sum or product of two decimals (The phrase "sum or product of two decimals" means the sum or product of the two numbers which have these given decimals as their standard numerals. This terminology is convenient to use and should not cause confusion at this stage.)

EXAMPLE 1. Add 3.578 and 24.69.

$$(3.578) + (24.69) = \left(3 + \frac{5}{10} + \frac{7}{100} + \frac{8}{1000}\right) + \left(24 + \frac{6}{10} + \frac{9}{100}\right)$$

$$= (3 + 24) + \left(\frac{5}{10} + \frac{6}{10}\right) + \left(\frac{7}{100} + \frac{9}{100}\right) + \frac{8}{1000} = 27 + \frac{11}{10} + \frac{16}{100} + \frac{8}{1000}$$

$$= 27 + \left(1 + \frac{1}{10}\right) + \left(\frac{1}{10} + \frac{6}{100}\right) + \frac{8}{1000} = 28 + \frac{2}{10} + \frac{6}{100} + \frac{8}{1000}$$

$$= 28.268$$

This calculation may be considerably shortened by writing one numeral below the other so that the decimal points, as well as the corresponding units, tens, tenths, etc., digits are in a vertical line and adding, viz.

$$\begin{array}{r} 3.578 \\ 24.69 \\ \hline 28.268 \end{array}$$

Note, however, that the shortened version actually duplicates the longer calculation although the details are obscured.

EXAMPLE 2. Multiply (5.7) by (.36).

$$(5.7)(.36) = \left(5 + \frac{7}{10}\right)\left(\frac{3}{10} + \frac{6}{100}\right)$$

$$= 5\left(\frac{3}{10}\right) + 5\left(\frac{6}{100}\right) + \left(\frac{7}{10}\right)\left(\frac{3}{10}\right) + \left(\frac{7}{10}\right)\left(\frac{6}{100}\right)$$

$$= \frac{15}{10} + \frac{30}{100} + \frac{21}{100} + \frac{42}{1000}$$

$$= \left(1 + \frac{5}{10}\right) + \left(\frac{3}{10} + \frac{0}{100}\right) + \left(\frac{2}{10} + \frac{1}{100}\right) + \left(\frac{4}{100} + \frac{2}{1000}\right)$$

$$= 1 + \frac{10}{10} + \frac{5}{100} + \frac{2}{1000} = 1 + 1 + \frac{5}{100} + \frac{2}{1000} = 2.052$$

or in compressed form

$$\begin{array}{r} 5.7 \\ .36 \\ \hline 342 \\ 171 \\ \hline 2.052 \end{array}$$

Note that the remark at the end of Example 1 applies here as well. The usual rule given in elementary schools for determining the number of decimal places in the answer is to use the sum of the number of decimal places in each factor. Why does this work?

We have seen that decimals represent rational numbers, but a difficulty arises if we attempt to express all rational numbers as decimals. The number $\frac{1}{3}$ is seen to lie between $\frac{3}{10}$ and $\frac{4}{10}$, between $\frac{33}{100}$ and $\frac{34}{100}$, and between $\frac{333}{1000}$ and $\frac{334}{1000}$. In fact for any natural number n we find that

$$\underbrace{.333\ldots33}_{n\ \text{digits}} < \tfrac{1}{3} < \underbrace{.333\ldots34}_{n\ \text{digits}}$$

so that there is no decimal equal to $\frac{1}{3}$. To overcome this difficulty we introduce *infinite decimal expansions*, i.e., unending decimals. Now with each positive rational number x we associate the infinite decimal expansion obtained as follows. First find the largest integer a so that $a \leq x$. Next find the largest integer a_1 so that $a + a_1/10 = a + .a_1 \leq x$. We let a_2 be the largest integer so that $a + a_1/10 + a_2/100 = a + .a_1a_2 \leq x$. Suppose we have already determined $a + .a_1a_2\cdots a_i$. We let a_{i+1} be the largest integer so that $a + .a_1a_2\cdots a_ia_{i+1} \leq x$. This is an infinite process of the kind discussed in Section 7.1—thus we may consider the infinite decimal expansion completely determined although we never write more than a few digits in it.

The infinite decimal expansion for a negative number n is defined to be the opposite of the infinite decimal expansion for $\bar{n}$, i.e., it is the infinite decimal expansion for $\bar{n}$ with a bar over it (or a minus sign in front of it—if you think the bar is too long).

It is clear that any finite decimal (or integer) may be considered as an infinite decimal expansion by putting "0's" for the rest of the digits. In view of what was said earlier it is clear that the decimal expansion (from now on we drop the word infinite but consider all expansions infinite) for $\frac{1}{3}$ is .333 $\cdots$ where each digit is a "3."

We wish to make a field of the set of all decimal expansions and will discuss this in Section 7.3. However, we need a few arithmetic properties of decimal expansions now. So we make at this time those definitions which enable us to proceed.

We point out that the product of 10 and any finite decimal can be obtained by "moving the decimal point one digit to the right." (State this more carefully.) We, accordingly, define the product of 10 and any decimal expansion to be the resulting decimal expansion obtained by moving the decimal point one digit to the right. Similarly the effect of multiplying by 100, 1000, or 10 $\cdots$ 0 (n 0's) is to move the decimal point of any decimal expansion 2, 3, or n places to the right

The sum of two decimal expansions is to be that decimal expansion whose nth decimal place consists of the units digit of the sum of the digits in the nth place in the two given expansions—or that digit increased by 1 if there is a carry from the digits to the right. Notice again that whenever you know how to find the nth digit of a decimal expansion, you know how to find all of them, and hence the decimal expansion is determined. A similar definition is made for subtraction.

The reader might work up to subtracting one infinite decimal expansion from another by first subtracting one finite decimal expansion from another by going from left to right instead of proceeding from right to left as is usually done. In the last century many expert calculators habitually used this method of subtraction because it is reputed to be faster than the conventional methods.

Suppose 2.173 is a number which agrees with the first four digits of some decimal expansion and 10.468 agrees with the first five digits of another decimal expansion. We notice that $(2.173)(10.468) = 22.746964$. If we calculate $(2.174)(10.469)$ we get 22.759606. We see, therefore, that if a is any rational number between 2.173 and 2.174, and b is any rational number between 10.468 and 10.469, then ab is between 22.746964 and 22.759606. But any rational number whose first four digits are 2.173 is between 2.173 and 2.174, and any rational number whose first five digits are 10.468 is between 10.468 and 10.469; therefore, the product of such rational numbers will be between 22.746964 and 22.759606, and we may say that the first three digits of such a product will be 22.7 (the next digit is either a '4' or '5'). We accordingly define the first three digits of the product of the two decimal expansions mentioned in the first sentence of this paragraph to be 22.7. Notice that no matter how many additional digits of the decimal expansions we include, the resulting numbers will be between 2.173 and 2.174 and between 10.468 and 10.469 so that their product will have as its first three digits 22.7.

More generally two decimal expansions may be "multiplied" by letting the nth decimal place of the product be that digit which results in the nth place of the product of "suitable" finite decimal approximations to the given decimal expansions. The finite decimal approximations consist of the first several digits of the decimal expansions and are deemed suitable when adding more digits does not affect the nth decimal place of the product.

Let us look a little more closely at the problem of adding two decimal expansions. Suppose the nth digit of one decimal is 6 and the nth digit of the other is 7. Then the nth digit of the sum is either 4 or 3 depending on whether there is or is not a carry from the digits to the right. To determine this we examine the $n + 1$st digits. If their sum is 10 or more, then the nth digit of the sum is 4. If their sum is 8 or less, the nth digit is 3. If their sum is 9, we must look at the $n + 2$nd digits. If their sum is 9, we must look at the $n + 3$rd digits, etc. Two possibilities exist. Either all the sums of the digits from the $n + 1$st on are 9 (in which case the nth digit of the sum is 3); or eventually we reach a first place where the sum of the $n + p$th isn't 9 (in which case the nth digit of the sum is 3 if the sum of the $n + p$th digits is 8 or less, or the nth digit of the sum is 4 if the sum of the $n + p$th digits is 10 or more).

In any event we notice that the nth digit of the sum can be determined by using finite decimal approximations to the given infinite decimals, and using more decimal places in the approximation does not affect any of the first n digits in the sum.

The problem of dividing a decimal expansion by another is handled in a similar fashion. To find the nth digit of the quotient we use sufficiently close finite decimal approximations to the divisor and dividend and find the nth digit of their quotient. Since we can do this for any n, we may consider the quotient determined.

If a decimal expansion is to be divided by an integer, we proceed by an extension of the usual division process. We illustrate this and also indicate (at the same time) how to find the decimal expansion associated with a given rational number.

EXAMPLE 3. Divide 3 by 14 or find the decimal expansion of $\frac{3}{14}$. The largest integer a, such that $a(14) < 3$, is 0. The largest digit a_1, such that $a_1/10\,(14) < 3$, is 2. So the decimal expansion for $\frac{3}{14}$ begins with 0.2. We can continue in this manner but the calculation can be more quickly effected by long division. We begin by considering 3 as the decimal expansion $3.000\ldots$.

```
          .214285714
     14)3.000000000 · · ·
        2 8
        ̄ ̄ ̄
         20
         14
         ̄ ̄
          60
          56
          ̄ ̄
          40
          28
          ̄ ̄
          120
          112
          ̄ ̄ ̄
           80
           70
           ̄ ̄
           100
            98
            ̄ ̄
            20
            14
            ̄ ̄
             60
             56
             ̄ ̄
              4 · · ·
```

It is clear that the decimal expansion of $\frac{3}{14}$ will continue to repeat and so is $.2142857142857142857\ldots$. We adopt the notation of putting dots over the digits to be repeated to save writing. So that we write the decimal expansion of $\frac{3}{14}$ as $.2\dot{1}4285\dot{7}$; in this notation the decimal expansion of $\frac{1}{3}$ is $.\dot{3}$.

Implicit in Example 3 is the proof that the decimal expansion of any rational number is a repeating decimal. For if the rational number is p/q (p and q positive integers) and we find its expansion by division, we write p as $p.\dot{0}$. Since there are only $q - 1$ positive integers less than q, there are only $q - 1$ possible remainders different from zero. Hence, once we get to that step in the division process at which only 0's will be "brought down," then, within q additional steps, the remainder will become zero or repeat. If the remainder is zero, the rest of the digits in the quotient are all zeros and thus repeating. If two remainders are the same, the remainders following each are the same and hence so are the corresponding digits in the quotient.

It is also true that every periodic decimal expansion represents a rational number. Let us illustrate a method of finding the rational number when given the decimal expansion.

‡EXAMPLE 4. What fraction is associated with $17.2\dot{3}\dot{4}$?

If $$d = 17.2\dot{3}\dot{4}$$

then $$10d = 172.\dot{3}\dot{4}$$

and $$1000d = 17234.\dot{3}\dot{4}$$

Therefore $$990d = 17062.\dot{0}$$

or $$990d = 17062$$

and $$d = \frac{17062}{990}$$

There is a minor difficulty which arises and which we need to resolve. We have noticed that the expansion for $\frac{1}{3}$ is $.\dot{3}$. Therefore the expansion for $\frac{1}{3} + \frac{1}{3} + \frac{1}{3}$ should be $.\dot{3} + .\dot{3} + .\dot{3}$, and hence the expansion for 1 should be $.\dot{9}$. But the expansion for 1 is $1.\dot{0}$. This apparent inconsistency can be resolved by noting the difference between $1.\dot{0} - .\dot{9}$. To determine the nth decimal place of $1.\dot{0} - .\dot{9}$ we note that the nth and $(n + 1)$th places in the calculation look like

$$\begin{array}{c} \cdots 00 \cdots \\ \cdots 99 \cdots \\ \hline 0 \end{array}$$

and that, since we need to "borrow one" to effect the subtraction in the $(n + 1)$th place, in the nth place we subtract 9 from 9 and get 0. Since we have just shown that every digit of the decimal expansion $1.\dot{0} - .\dot{9}$ is "0," it follows that $1.\dot{0} - .\dot{9} = .\dot{0}$. We can thus resolve this difficulty by identifying $1.\dot{0}$ and $\dot{9}$; i.e., we consider them as different numerals representing the same number.

Many people are surprised by the fact that these different looking decimal expansions must be equivalent. Therefore, we feel that, perhaps, another example might be in order.

EXAMPLE 5. Add $.4\dot{9}$ and $.4\dot{9}$ and then subtract $.4\dot{9}$ from the answer,

$$
\begin{array}{r}
.499\dot{9} \\
.499\dot{9} \\
\hline
.999\dot{9}
\end{array}
$$

The tenth's digit is obtained by noting that 4 and 4 = 8 and 1 carried makes 9. Each of the other digits is obtained by noting that 9 and 9 = 18 and 1 carried makes 19. Therefore the sum is $.9\dot{9}$. Clearly $.9\dot{9} - .4\dot{9} = .5\dot{0}$. So again $.4\dot{9}$ and $.5\dot{0}$ must be equivalent decimal expansions.

In fact all difficulties of this nature are resolved if we agree to identify any decimal expansion which consists of "9's" from the nth decimal place on with the decimal expansion which consists of "0's" from the nth decimal place on and whose $(n - 1)$th place has a digit one greater than the digit in the $(n - 1)$th place of the first decimal expansion.

EXERCISES

1. Consider the set of all finite decimals. Is this a field?

2. Express as a periodic decimal:

    (a) $\frac{2}{11}$ (c) $\frac{4}{7}$

    (b) $\frac{17}{8}$ (d) $\frac{18}{17}$

3. Find the fractions for each of the following numbers:

    (a) $.\dot{6}$ (c) $12.\dot{5}\dot{2}$

    (b) $.\dot{7}$ (d) $6.54\dot{3}\dot{2}\dot{1}$

4. Give an example of a non-periodic decimal expansion.

5. When working with money most people "round off" all calculation to the nearest penny. If we consider the set of all two place decimals together with the usual addition and multiplication operations (rounding off where necessary), is this a field?

6. Find:

(a) $.24\dot{5} + .4\dot{9}$ (c) $(.24\dot{5}) \div (.4\dot{9})$

(b) $(.24\dot{5})(.4\dot{9})$ (d) the average of $(1.3\dot{9})$ and $(1.4\dot{0})$

7. Consider the decimal expansion $.12345678910111213\ldots$ (where it is understood that this expansion is formed by continuing writing the standard numerals of the natural numbers in their usual order). Is this the decimal expansion for some rational number?

8. Subtract $.4\dot{9}$ from $1.\dot{0}$ and then check by adding $.4\dot{9}$ to the result to see if $1.\dot{0}$ is obtained. Explain.

9. Find the digit in the 15th decimal place of:
   (a) the sum of $.24\dot{5}$ and the number in Exercise 7.
   (b) the difference of $.24\dot{5}$ and the number in Exercise 7.

10. Find the digit in the 5th decimal place of the product of $.24\dot{5}$ and the number in Exercise 7.

11. Find the digit in the 1st decimal place of the quotient $.24\dot{5}$ divided by the number in Exercise 7.

7.3. THE FIELD OF REAL NUMBERS

The set of real numbers can be defined in terms of rational numbers and then a mathematical proof can be given that properties A1, A2, A3, A4, A5, M1, M2, M3, M4, M5, D1, I1, I2, and the order axioms are satisfied. Thus, in a sense, the real numbers are derived from the rational numbers by some mathematical process. There is, then, some mathematical process (not now known to us) that when applied to the rational numbers produces the real numbers. However, if this same process is applied again to the real numbers it will not produce a new field but will produce the real field once more. For this reason the mathematicians call the real field *complete*. As noted above the set of real numbers forms an ordered field. Thus the set of real numbers can be described as a *complete ordered field*. In fact it is essentially the *only* complete ordered field with the definition of complete given later in this section.

Since the concepts and proofs of the preceding paragraph are too advanced for this course, we take an alternative path. We simply define the set of *real numbers* as the set of (all) numbers which have a numeral that is an infinite decimal. It can be shown that, using the definitions for addition and multiplication given above, properties A1, A2, A3, A4, A5, M1, M2, M3, M4, M5, D1, I1, and I2 hold for the real numbers. To verify these properties is a burdensome task, the details are rather messy and are difficult to write down. Let us examine A5, the commutative law for addition, and see how it can be verified. If x and y are two decimal expansions, then we will show that for each natural number n, the nth digit of $x + y$ is equal to the nth digit of $y + x$. Now, as seen earlier, the nth digit of $x + y$ can be found by using finite decimal approximations to x and y. Similarly the nth digits of $y + x$ can be found using decimal approximations to y and x. Let $\tilde{x}$ and $\tilde{y}$ be finite decimal approximations to x and y such that the nth digit of $x + y$ equals the nth digit of $\tilde{x} + \tilde{y}$ and such that the nth digit of $y + x$ equals the nth digit of $\tilde{y} + \tilde{x}$. [If x' and y' are approximations to x and y, respectively, suitable to approximate $x + y$; and x'' and y'' are approximations to x and y, respectively, suitable to approximately $y + x$; then we may take $\tilde{x} = $ max (x', x'') and $\tilde{y} = $ max (y', y'').] Now since $\tilde{x}$ and $\tilde{y}$ are finite decimals, they are rational numbers and therefore commute; therefore, the nth digit of $x + y = n$th digit of $\tilde{x} + \tilde{y} = n$th digit of $\tilde{y} + \tilde{x} = n$th digit of $y + x$. Thus $x + y = y + x$ and the commutative law is established.

The foregoing suggests approaches to verifying the other field postulates (some of which are much more difficult than the above). We will not explicitly verify any of the others but assume them and say the set of all infinite decimals forms the set of real numbers.

Let us now look more closely at the field of real numbers. If one restricts the arithmetic of the real numbers to the repeating decimals, it is possible to show that one merely gets back the arithmetic of the rational numbers. This means, e.g., that if p and q are rational numbers, the decimal expansion of their sum (product, difference, or quotient) is the same as the sum (product, difference, or quotient) of their decimal expansions. In other words, we may regard the repeating decimals as numerals for the rational numbers so that the real numbers constitute another enlargement of the number system. Thus the new items in our set are the numbers which have infinite decimal expansions that are not periodic—we call these *irrational* real numbers. An irrational real number, then, is a real number which is not rational. The decimal expansion of an irrational number might have a pattern of repetition which is not cyclic, or it might not have any pattern at all.

THEOREM 1. If r is a rational number and s is an irrational number then $r + s$ and $r - s$ are irrational.

Proof:
Let $r + s = p$ so that $s = p - r$. Then if p is rational, $s = p - r$ would also be rational since subtraction is a binary operation on the rationals. But then this contradicts the assumption that s is irrational and so it must be true that p is irrational.

The proof that $r - s$ is irrational is similar.

THEOREM 2. If $r \neq 0$ is a rational number and s is an irrational number then rs, r/s, and s/r are irrational.

Proof:

Let $rs = p$ so that $s = p/r$. Then if p is rational $s = p/r$ is rational since division is a binary operation on the non-zero rationals. But this contradicts the hypothesis that s is irrational and so it must be true that p is irrational.

The proof that r/s and s/r are irrational is similar.

We have already observed in Section 6.4 that the average of two numbers lies between the two numbers. It follows that between any two rational numbers lies a rational number and, hence, no rational number is adjacent to another rational number as each integer is adjacent to the two integers which immediately precede and follow it. Neither is any real number adjacent to any other real number because between any two real numbers lies a real number. In fact we can state that between any two real numbers lies a rational number. To see this we utilize, without proof, the order properties of the infinite decimal expansion in a fashion which seems plausible. Thus, e.g., consider the real numbers $12.37894523107 \cdots$ and $12.37894617192 \ldots$. The first place in which the two numbers differ is in the 6th decimal place. We then "see" that the finite decimal 12.378946 is less than the second number and yet is larger than the first. Hence it lies between the two numbers and it is rational since it is a finite decimal.

We now examine another aspect of the differences between the real numbers and the rationals. We point out that the concepts discussed here are somewhat advanced and rather technical, and although we do not expect the general reader to follow the detailed arguments presented, we feel perhaps, that, some indication of what is involved should be presented. If S is a set of numbers, then a number x with the property $x \geq s$ for each $s \in S$ is called an *upper bound* for S. A *least upper bound* is an upper bound with the property that no smaller number is an upper bound. The property of *completeness*, mentioned earlier, is defined for the real numbers by saying it guarantees that every nonempty set of real numbers which has an upper bound has a least upper bound. One can intuitively see that the real numbers have this property by noting first that if x is an upper bound for the set S then there is an integer n which is also an upper bound. Hence there is a smallest integer which is an upper bound for S. If this smallest integer is in a particular case, 28, we note that $27.9\dot{9}\dot{9} = 28$ is an upper bound. We next examine $27.9\dot{9}$, $27.8\dot{9}$, $27.7\dot{9}$, $27.6\dot{9}$, $27.5\dot{9}$, $27.4\dot{9}$, $27.3\dot{9}$, $27.2\dot{9}$, $27.1\dot{9}$, $27.0\dot{9}$ and select the smallest of these which is an upper bound; say, $27.3\dot{9}$. We then go on to the next decimal place, look at $27.39\dot{9}$, $27.38\dot{9}, \ldots, 27.30\dot{9}$, and select the smallest of these which is an upper bound. By continuing this process we arrive at a decimal which cannot be made smaller in any decimal place and still be an upper bound, and, hence, is the least upper bound.

Now let Q be the set of all positive rational numbers r such that r^2 (where $r^2 = r \cdot r$) < 2. We note that since $a^2 > b^2$ if and only if $a > b$, and 2^2

$= 4 > 2$, then 2 is greater than any number whose square is less than 2 and hence is an upper bound for Q. However, since $(1.5)^2 = 2.25 > 2$ and $1.5 < 2$, 2 is not the least upper bound. Let q be the least upper bound for Q. We would like to show that $q^2 = 2$. If $q^2 < 2$, then $e = 2 - q^2 > 0$. Let d be a number > 0 but less than the smaller of $e/5$ and 1. Then $(q + d) > q$, but

$$(q + d)^2 = (q + d)(q + d) = q^2 + 2qd + d^2 = q^2 + d(2q + d)$$

But we noted earlier that although 2 was an upper bound, it was not the least upper bound; thus $q < 2$, $2q < 4$, and $2q + 1 < 5$. Therefore

$$q^2 + d(2q + d) < q^2 + d(2q + 1) \qquad \text{(since } d < 1\text{)}$$

which is less than

$$q^2 + d(5) < q^2 + \left(\frac{e}{5}\right)5 = q^2 + e = 2$$

We have just shown that $(q + d)^2 < 2$ and, hence, q is not an upper bound. Therefore q^2 is not less than 2. In a somewhat similar manner it can be shown that q^2 is not greater than 2 and, hence $q^2 = 2$. The usual notation for q is $\sqrt{2}$. We wish next to show that $\sqrt{2}$ is irrational.

To do this we first note that the prime factors of a counting number b^2 are the prime factors of b taken twice, and hence that every prime factor of b^2 occurs an even number of times. Now suppose that $\sqrt{2}$ is rational; then there exist integers $b \neq 0$ and a such that $\sqrt{2} = a/b$. Hence $2 = a^2/b^2$ or $2b^2 = a^2$. But then the prime number 2 appears as a factor of the counting number $2b^2$ an odd number of times while it appears as a factor of the counting number a^2 an even number of times, which is a contradiction. Hence our supposition that $\sqrt{2}$ is rational is wrong, i.e., $\sqrt{2}$ is irrational. It follows that the decimal expansion of $\sqrt{2}$ is not periodic.

EXERCISES

1. Does the numeral $.101001000100001000001\cdots$ (where each time one more 0 is inserted before the next 1 occurs) designate a rational or an irrational number?

2. If r is a rational number and s is an irrational number prove that $r - s$ is irrational.

3. If $r \neq 0$ is a rational number and s is an irrational number prove that r/s is irrational.

4. Is it true that if r is a rational number and s is an irrational number then r/s is irrational?

5. If $r \neq 0$ is rational and s is irrational, prove that s/r is irrational.

6. Is it true that the sum of two irrational numbers is necessarily irrational?

7. Is it true that the difference of two irrational numbers is necessarily irrational?

8. Is it true that the product of two irrational numbers is necessarily irrational?

9. Is it true that the quotient of two irrational numbers is necessarily irrational?

10. Find a rational number between the irrational number given in Exercise 1 and the rational number $.10100100\dot{0}\dot{1}$.

11. Is the product of two repeating decimals necessarily a repeating decimal?

7.4. INEQUALITIES AND THE REAL NUMBER LINE

It was mentioned in the last section that the real numbers are an ordered field. This means, of course, that there is a subset of the reals called P satisfying

1. If $x \in P$ and $y \in P$, then $x + y \in P$

2. If $x \in P$ and $y \in P$, then $xy \in P$

3. For each real number r exactly one of the following is true

(a) $r \in P$
(b) $\bar{r} \in P$
(c) $r = 0$

Using this set P we say $x < y$ if $y - x \in P$.

Since this order is defined the same way that the order in the rational field was defined, we have exactly the same theorems proved in exactly the same manner. Furthermore, using decimal expansions, it is comparatively easy to determine the larger of two numbers.

The numbers in P are called positive numbers. The numbers whose opposites are in P are called negative numbers. The positive and negative numbers together with 0 constitute the real numbers. There is a nice model of the real numbers which is helpful in many ways. This consists of a horizontal line extending indefinitely both to the right and left. A point is fixed on the line and labeled "0." Then P consists of the labels of the points to the right of 0 and the negative numbers are the labels of the points to the left. The integers are put in at equal intervals in their natural order (see diagram). Each point on the line is to represent a real number, and of

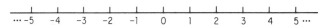

course, each real number corresponds to a point on the line. If the number x is greater than y, then the point corresponding to x is to the right of the point corresponding to y. This line is called the *real number line*. If x and y are real numbers, one sometimes mentions, rather loosely, the "point $x + y$" instead of the "point whose label is $x + y$."

Now suppose $a < b$. Then the set of all real numbers x such that $a < x < b$ is called the *open interval* from a to b and is indicated by (a, b). The set of all real numbers x such that $a \le x \le b$ is called the *closed interval* from a to b and denoted by the symbol $[a, b]$. The set of all real numbers x such that $a \le x < b$ and the set of all real numbers x such that $a < x \le b$ are called *half open intervals* and are denoted by $[a, b)$ and $(a, b]$, respectively. For each real number x, the set of all points whose labels are real numbers y such that $y > x$ is called an *open ray*. Similarly, the set of all points whose labels are real numbers y such that $y < x$, is also called an open ray. The set of all points whose labels are real numbers y such that $y \ge x$ is called a *ray* as is the set of all points whose labels are real numbers y such that $y \le x$.

On the real number line an open ray consists of all the points to the right (or left) of a given point—a ray consists of all the points to the right (or left) of a given point together with the point. Similarly an open interval consists of all labels of the points between two given points whereas a closed interval also includes the labels of the two given points.

Recall that solving an equation like $2x + 7 = 4$ means finding the set of all numbers x such that $2x + 7 = 4$. Similarly solving an inequality like $2x + 7 > 4$ means finding the set of all (real) numbers x such that $2x + 7 > 4$. This is done in the following manner.

$$\text{If } 2x + 7 > 4, \quad \text{then } 2x > 4 - 7$$

$$\text{If } 2x > 4 - 7, \quad \text{then } x > (4 - 7)\frac{1}{2} = \frac{\bar{3}}{2}$$

Thus the set of solutions of the inequality is contained in the set of all x such that $x > \frac{\bar{3}}{2}$. However, since each step above is reversible, the set of all x such that $x > \frac{\bar{3}}{2}$ is contained in the solution set, and, hence the two sets are equal. We may describe the solution set as the labels of all points on the open ray to the right of the point whose label is $\frac{3}{2}$.

EXERCISES

1. What possible sets are the intersection of two open rays?

2. What possible sets are the union of two rays?

3. What possible sets are the union of two closed intervals?

4. In words describe the set $(1, 2) \cup (2, 3)$.

5. Find and describe the solution sets of the following inequalities:
   (a) $3x - 5 < 4$ (c) $3x + 5 \leq 5x + 3$
   (b) $1 - 2x > 8$ (d) $1/x < 6$

6. Find the set of x's that satisfy both $4x - 5 < 7$ and $2x + 6 > 1$.

7. Find the set of x's that satisfy at least one of $7x + 18 < 4x - 6$ and $6 - 3x > 2$.

7.5. 1–1 CORRESPONDENCES

Those of us whose intuition has been accustomed to finite sets find that it is not reliable when dealing with infinite sets. Thus Euclid stated, "The whole is greater than the part" and numerous generations of school children have repeated this statement as a reason for certain steps. Yet, as we observed in Section 7.1, this statement is certainly false. The set of even natural numbers is only a part of the set of natural numbers because it does not contain any of the odd natural numbers. As a matter of fact we might be prone to say that there are about half as many even natural numbers as there are natural numbers. But we had observed in Section 7.1 that there is a 1–1 correspondence between the set of even natural numbers and the set of natural numbers, and hence there are exactly as many even natural numbers as natural numbers. That there can be a 1–1 correspondence between a set and a proper subset seems impossible (and it is for finite sets). In fact, this is perhaps the major difference between finite sets and infinite sets.

Since the set of rational numbers contains the integers and also many numbers which are not integers, we might have been prone to say there are obviously more fractions than integers. However we might recall the case of the even natural numbers and look more closely at this assertion. Let us restrict attention to the set of positive rational numbers and write them in the following array

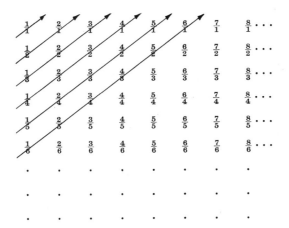

in which the nth row contains all fractions with n in the denominator and the nth column contains all fractions with n in the numerator. Some numbers are written more than once, but we are sure that every positive rational number is included in the array. In particular the fraction p/q appears in the pth column and qth row. To eliminate duplicates we may imagine putting a circle around each fraction of the form p/q where p and q are not relatively prime, i.e., where the fraction is not in lowest terms. Now we enumerate the rationals by following the path indicated by the arrows in the array skipping the encircled entries. More particularly we match the integer 1 with the first rational number, $\frac{1}{1}$; we match 2 with the 2nd, $\frac{1}{2}$; 3 with the third, $\frac{2}{1}$; 4 with the fourth, $\frac{1}{3}$; and 5 with the fifth, which is $\frac{3}{1}$ since $\frac{2}{2}$ has been circled because it is not in lowest terms. Continuing in this manner we match 6 with $\frac{1}{4}$, 7 with $\frac{2}{3}$, 8 with $\frac{3}{2}$, 9 with $\frac{4}{1}$, 10 with $\frac{1}{5}$, 11 with $\frac{5}{1}$, 12 with $\frac{1}{6}$, etc. It can be shown that if we were not to skip the encircled fractions, we would match the integer

$$i + \frac{(i+j-1)(i+j-2)}{2}$$

with the fraction i/j; hence (since we do skip) given the fraction p/q with p and q relatively prime we know that when we get to the integer

$$p + \frac{(p+q-1)(p+q-2)}{2}$$

we have already matched p/q. Thus every positive rational number is matched with some positive integer and we have indicated a 1–1 correspondence between these two sets.

Some people, at this stage of the game, jump to the conclusion that there is a 1–1 correspondence between any two infinite sets. They reason somewhat as follows. Take an element from one set and match it with an element of the other. Then repeat this step over and over again. Since there are an infinite number of elements we do not run out of elements and hence there is a 1–1 correspondence. We wish to show that this conclusion (and this line of reasoning) is wrong. There are, as a matter of fact, infinitely many infinite sets, no two of which can be put into 1–1 correspondence, but we will be content to show that there is no 1–1 correspondence between the positive integers and the positive real numbers between 0 and 1. From this it can be shown that there are "more" real numbers than there are rational numbers.

Consider the set of positive real numbers between 0 and 1, i.e., the set of proper decimal fractions. Let us agree to use $.5\dot{0}$ instead of $.49$, etc. In other words, none of the decimals has only 9's from a certain point on. If there is a 1–1 correspondence between the natural numbers and the positive reals between 0 and 1, then we can form a rectangular array in which the first row contains the decimal corresponding to 1, the second row contains the decimal corresponding to 2, etc. Then the array would look something like this

$$
\begin{array}{llllll}
.a_1 & a_2 & a_3 & a_4 & a_5 \cdots \\
.b_1 & b_2 & b_3 & b_4 & b_5 \cdots \\
.c_1 & c_2 & c_3 & c_4 & c_5 \cdots \\
.d_1 & d_2 & d_3 & d_4 & d_5 \cdots \\
\quad \cdot & \cdot & \cdot & \cdot & \cdot \\
\quad \cdot & \cdot & \cdot & \cdot & \cdot \\
\quad \cdot & \cdot & \cdot & \cdot & \cdot
\end{array}
$$

We will show that there is a proper decimal not in this list and hence that not all proper decimals are written here, as we had assumed. Thus there cannot be a 1–1 correspondence between the natural numbers and the positive proper decimals. To obtain a proper decimal not on our list we write down the proper decimal $.a_1'b_2'c_3'd_4' \cdots$ where a_1' is any digit different from a_1, 0, 9; b_2' is any digit different from b_2, 0, 9; etc. Then this proper decimal we have just written down is not on the first row of our array because $a_1' \neq a_1$; it is not on the second row because $b_2' \neq b_2$; it is not on the third row because $c_3' \neq c_3$; it is not on the fourth row because $d_4' \neq d_4$; etc. Note that at each stage we choose one digit from a collection of at least seven digits. Hence there are a great many infinite decimals not on our original list.

EXERCISES

1. Let A be the set of all real numbers x such that $0 \leq x \leq 1$ and let B be the set of all real numbers x such that $0 \leq x \leq 2$. Is there a 1–1 correspondence between A and B?

2. (a) Given triangle ABC, show geometrically that there is a 1–1 correspondence between the points in (Segment AB) $\cup$ (Segment BC) and the points in Segment AC.

   (b) Given the triangle here, show geometrically that there is a 1–1 correspondence between the points in Segment AB and the points in Segment CD.

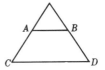

   (c) Show how each of these may be utilized in answering Exercise 1.

3. Suppose we have one cubic foot of an "ideal" paint. Theoretically how many square feet of surface could be covered?

4. A certain hotel, which has a room for each counting number, puts only one person in a room. Assume that the hotel has a person in each room and that a traveller appears at the desk. Can he be put up for the night? Explain.

7.6. APPLICATIONS

In this section we are particularly interested in working with decimal expansions in other bases. Let us look at some examples.

EXAMPLE 1. Find the decimal expansion in base 2 of the fraction $\frac{2}{3}$. We see that $\frac{2}{3} = (\frac{10}{11})_2$. By long division in base 2

$$
\begin{array}{r}
.10 \\
11{\overline{\smash{\big)}\,10.000}} \\
\underline{1\,1} \\
100 \\
\end{array}
$$

we see that $(\frac{10}{11})_2 = (.\dot{1}\dot{0})_2$.

An alternative procedure would frequently be simpler since it would avoid division in other bases. In the decimal expansion $7.23\dot{5}$, for instance, we speak of 7 as the *integral part* of the number and $.23\dot{5}$ as the *proper decimal* part of the number. As $7.23\dot{5} = 7 + .23\dot{5}$ and we already know how to convert an integer from one base to another, the integral part of a decimal expansion does not constitute a problem. The proper decimal part can be handled by the following remark. A proper decimal expansion in base b would be of the form $a_1/b + a_2/b^2 + a_3/b^3 + \cdots$. Multiplication by b yields $a_1 + a_2/b + a_3/b^2 + \cdots$, i.e., the integral part here is the first digit in the decimal expansion in base b. If we multiply the new proper decimal part $a_2/b + a_3/b^2 + \cdots$ by b we obtain $a_2 + a_3/b + \cdots$. The integral part here is the second digit of the desired decimal expansion in base b. The process may be continued indefinitely to give as many decimal places as desired.

EXAMPLE 2. Express $\frac{3}{7}$ as a decimal expansion in base 5.

$$
\begin{aligned}
5(\tfrac{3}{7}) &= \tfrac{15}{7} = 2 + \tfrac{1}{7}\\
5(\tfrac{1}{7}) &= \tfrac{5}{7} = 0 + \tfrac{5}{7}\\
5(\tfrac{5}{7}) &= \tfrac{25}{7} = 3 + \tfrac{4}{7}\\
5(\tfrac{4}{7}) &= \tfrac{20}{7} = 2 + \tfrac{6}{7}\\
5(\tfrac{6}{7}) &= \tfrac{30}{7} = 4 + \tfrac{2}{7}\\
5(\tfrac{2}{7}) &= \tfrac{10}{7} = 1 + \tfrac{3}{7}
\end{aligned}
$$

Hence we see that $\frac{3}{7} = (.\dot{2}0\dot{3}\dot{2}4\dot{1})_5$.

As mentioned earlier, a rigorous definition of an infinite decimal expansion depends on some sort of concept of the mathematical term "limit," but we do not wish to pursue this topic here. Assuming such a definition and some of its consequences, we give the following example.

EXAMPLE 3. Show that $\frac{1}{2} + \frac{1}{4} + \frac{1}{8} + \cdots = 1$. We observe that in base 2 the number we are looking for has the decimal expansion $.\dot{1}$. Working in base 2 let $d = .\dot{1}$, then $10d = 1.\dot{1}$, and upon subtracting we obtain $d = 1$. That is, the base 2 name of the number we are looking for is 1. But that is also its name in base 10. Hence we have completed the problem.

The story has been told about Karl Friedrich Gauss, the German mathematical genius whose tutor, desiring a few moments respite, told his pupils to find the sum of all the integers from 1 through 100. Gauss computed the sum mentally and immediately gave the answer. Can you? Young Gauss observed that the first integer, 1, and the last integer, 100, have a sum of 101; the second integer 2, and the next to last integer, 99, have a sum of 101; etc. Since he has 50 pairs, each with a sum of 101, the total is 50(101) or 5050. A sequence of the form $a, a + d, a + 2d, \ldots, a + nd, \ldots$ is called an *arithmetic progression*. The method of Gauss should enable you to find the sum of a finite sequence of numbers in arithmetic progression. Do you see how to find such a sum?

EXERCISES

1. State which is larger and by how much:

   (a) $\frac{2}{35}$ or $\frac{1}{17}$ (b) $\frac{3}{35}$ or $\frac{1}{12}$

2. Arrange the following numbers so that each is less than its successor.
   $\frac{16}{7}, \frac{17}{8}, \frac{7}{16}, \frac{8}{17}, -\frac{7}{16}, -\frac{8}{17}, 0, 2.1, 2.2, -1/2.1$

3. Find the standard numeral for:

   (a) $\frac{2}{35} + \frac{1}{17} + \frac{1}{12}$ (b) $\frac{4}{9} \cdot \frac{7}{25} \cdot \frac{27}{8} \cdot \frac{5}{14} \cdot \frac{17}{51}$

4. Prove irrational.

   (a) $\sqrt{3}$ (b) $\sqrt{6}$ (c) $\sqrt[3]{2}$

5. Find the decimal expansion of $17\frac{3}{7}$ in:

   (a) base 2   (b) base 3   (c) base 7

6. $(.10\dot{1}\dot{1})_2 + (3.4\dot{2}1\dot{3})_5 = (?)$

7. Find the decimal expansion in base 3 of $(.\dot{3})_5$

8. Find the standard numeral for:

   (a) $2 + 4 + 6 + \cdots + 98$ (b) $\bar{7} + \bar{3} + 1 + 5 + 9 + \cdots + 29$
   (c) $3 + 8 + 13 + \cdots + 43$

9. Find the standard numeral for:

   (a) $\frac{1}{3} + \frac{1}{9} + \frac{1}{27} + \cdots$ (b) $\frac{2}{3} + \frac{2}{9} + \frac{2}{27} + \cdots$
   (c) $\frac{5}{9} + \frac{5}{81} + \frac{5}{729} + \cdots$

10. Suppose $p_1, p_2, \ldots, p_k$ are prime counting numbers and consider the counting number $p_1 \cdot p_2 \cdots p_k + 1$. What can be said concerning the factors of this number? With these considerations, in mind, can you decide how many prime counting numbers there are?

‡11. The product of 1807 by one (natural) number a is equal to the product of 1105 by another (natural) number, b. Find the least possible values of a and b.

‡12. The prime factors of a (counting) number are 2, 3, 7, 11, and 23. Name the only three (counting) numbers between 65 and 80 that are factors of this number.

‡13. Find the only four (counting) numbers less than 1000, which when divided into 13078, will leave a remainder of 65.

‡14. A row of trees planted at equal distances from each other is 1891 ft long; what is the least possible number of trees in all if one of them is 427 ft from one end of the row and another 671 ft from the other end?

8

8.1. EXPONENTS

Much of the power of mathematics comes from its symbolism. A good symbol can be used to communicate quickly a great deal of information in a small amount of space. There is, however, a danger of becoming so enrapt in the symbols and their manipulation that we forget what they stand for and therefore use them incorrectly. This often occurs in work with exponents and radicals which are mishandled, in one way or another, by students and occasionally by their teachers and textbooks. We will attempt to avoid the usual errors in the presentation below.

Very often it is necessary to multiply a number by itself. The symbol a^2 (read a-square) means a times a, while a^3 (read a-cube, or a to the third power) means $a \cdot a \cdot a$ (where because of the associative law for multiplication we need not insert grouping symbols). Similarly a^4 (read a to the fourth power) means $a \cdot a \cdot a \cdot a$, $a^5 = a \cdot a \cdot a \cdot a \cdot a$, etc. More explicitly we define $a^1 = a$ and for any positive integer $n > 1$, we define $a^n = a \cdot a^{n-1}$. Thus knowing a^1, we can find a^2; then knowing a^2, we can find a^3, and so on through the positive integers. The symbol a^n is read a to the nth power—the number a is called the *base* while n is called the *exponent*.

THEOREM 1. For any two positive integers m and n and any real number a we have

(a) $a^n \cdot a^m = a^{n+m}$
(b) $(a^n)^m = a^{nm}$

exponents and radicals

143

(c) If $n > m$ and $a \neq 0$

$$\frac{a^n}{a^m} = a^{n-m}$$

(d) If $n < m$ and $a \neq 0$

$$\frac{a^n}{a^m} = \frac{1}{a^{m-n}}$$

Proof:

(a) $a^n \cdot a^m = a^n \cdot (a \cdot a^{m-1}) = (a^n \cdot a)a^{m-1}$

$\qquad = a^{n+1} \cdot a^{m-1} = a^{n+1} \cdot (a \cdot a^{m-2})$

$\qquad = a^{n+2}a^{m-2} = \cdots$

$\qquad = a^{n+(m-1)}a^1 = a^{n+m}$

(b) $(a^n)^m = \underbrace{a^n \cdot a^n \ldots a^n}_{m \text{ factors}} = \overbrace{a^{n+n+\cdots+n}}^{m \text{ terms}} = a^{nm}$

(c) If $n > m$, $n = (n - m) + m$ and

$$\frac{a^n}{a^m} = \frac{a^{(n-m)+m}}{a^m} = \frac{a^{(n-m)} \cdot a^m}{a^m} = a^{n-m} \cdot \frac{a^m}{a^m} = a^{n-m} \cdot 1 = a^{n-m}$$

(d) If $m > n$, $m = (m - n) + n$ and

$$\frac{a^n}{a^m} = \frac{a^n}{a^{(m-n)+n}} = \frac{a^n}{a^{m-n}a^n} = \frac{1}{a^{m-n}} \cdot \frac{a^n}{a^n} = \frac{1}{a^{m-n}}$$

We would like now to define a^0 and a^{-n} in such a manner that Theorem 1 will hold for these exponents as well. In particular by part (a) we want $a^n \cdot a^0$ to be equal to $a^{n+0} = a^n$. Hence, if $a \neq 0$, a^0 must be 1. Again by part (a) $a^n \cdot a^{-n} = a^{n+(-n)} = a^0 = 1$. Hence a^{-n} must equal $\dfrac{1}{a^n}$. Accordingly we make the following.

DEFINITION. If $a \neq 0$ and n is a positive integer, $a^0 = 1$ and $a^{-n} = 1/a^n$. If $a = 0$, a^0 and a^{-n} are not defined.

Note that the reason we cannot define zero to nonpositive powers is that we cannot divide by zero. Accordingly we make the agreement that from now on whenever we write $(a)^0$ or a^{-n} (where n is a positive integer) we will assume that a is not zero. Just as when we write x/y we are assuming that y is not zero.

Although we have chosen our definitions to fit part (a) of Theorem 1, it fortunately happens that they satisfy all of the theorem so that we have the following.

THEOREM 2. If m and n are integers and $a \neq 0$

(a) $a^m a^n = a^{m+n}$

(b) $(a^m)^n = a^{mn}$

(c) $\dfrac{a^m}{a^n} = a^{m-n} = \dfrac{1}{a^{n-m}}$

This theorem may be proved by considering the nine cases which occur when m and n are positive, negative, or zero.

Proof: Case 1. $m > 0, n > 0$

(a) and (b) follow from Theorem 1 (a) and (b) respectively

(c) If $m = n$, then

$$\frac{a^m}{a^n} = 1 \qquad a^{m-n} = a^0 = 1 \quad \text{and} \quad \frac{1}{a^{n-m}} = \frac{1}{a^0} = \frac{1}{1} = 1$$

If $m > n$ then

$$\frac{a^m}{a^n} = a^{m-n} \quad \text{and} \quad \frac{1}{a^{n-m}} = \frac{1}{a^{-(m-n)}} = \frac{1}{1/a^{m-n}} = a^{m-n}$$

If $m < n$ then

$$\frac{a^m}{a^n} = \frac{1}{a^{n-m}} \quad \text{and} \quad a^{m-n} = a^{-(n-m)} = \frac{1}{a^{n-m}}$$

Case 2. $m < 0, n < 0$, let $m = -h$ and $n = -k$ where $h > 0$ and $k > 0$

(a) $a^m \cdot a^n = a^{-h} \cdot a^{-k} = \dfrac{1}{a^h} \cdot \dfrac{1}{a^k} = \dfrac{1}{a^{h+k}} = a^{-(h+k)} = a^{-h-k} = a^{m+n}$

(b)

$$(a^m)^n = (a^{-h})^n = \left(\frac{1}{a^h}\right)^n = \left(\frac{1}{a^h}\right)^{-k} = \frac{1}{(1/a^h)^k} = \frac{1}{1/a^{hk}}$$
$$= a^{hk} = a^{(-h)(-k)} = a^{mn}$$

(c) $\dfrac{a^m}{a^n} = \dfrac{a^{-h}}{a^{-k}} = \dfrac{1/a^h}{1/a^k} = \dfrac{a^k}{a^h}$

If $k = h$ then

$$\frac{a^k}{a^h} = 1 \qquad a^{m-n} = a^{(-h)-(-k)} = a^0 = 1$$

and

$$\frac{1}{a^{n-m}} = \frac{1}{a^{(-k)-(-h)}} = \frac{1}{a^0} = 1$$

If $k < h$ then

$$\frac{a^k}{a^h} = \frac{1}{a^{h-k}} = \frac{1}{a^{-k+h}} = \frac{1}{a^{-k-(-h)}} = \frac{1}{a^{n-m}}$$

and

$$\frac{1}{a^{h-k}} = a^{-(h-k)} = a^{k-h} = a^{-h+k} = a^{-h-(-k)} = a^{m-n}$$

If $k > h$ then $\dfrac{a^k}{a^h} = a^{k-h}$ and the rest of the proof is similar to that above.

CASE 3. $m > 0$, $n < 0$. Let $n = -k$ where $k > 0$

(a)

$$a^m \cdot a^n = a^m \cdot a^{-k} = a^m \cdot \frac{1}{a^k} = \frac{a^m}{a^k}$$

Then by Case 1,

$$\frac{a^m}{a^k} = a^{m-k} = a^{m+(-k)} = a^{m+n}$$

(b) $(a^m)^n = (a^m)^{-k} = \dfrac{1}{(a^m)^k} = \dfrac{1}{a^{mk}} = a^{-(mk)} = a^{m(-k)} = a^{mn}$

(c) $\dfrac{a^m}{a^n} = \dfrac{a^m}{a^{-k}} = \dfrac{a^m}{1/a^k} = a^m \cdot a^k = a^{m+k} = a^{m-(-k)} = a^{m-n}$

and

$$a^m \cdot a^k = \frac{1}{1/a^m} \cdot \frac{1}{1/a^k} = \frac{1}{1/(a^m \cdot a^k)} = \frac{1}{1/a^{m+k}} = \frac{1}{1/a^{m-n}} = \frac{1}{a^{-(m-n)}} = \frac{1}{a^{n-m}}$$

CASE 4. $m < 0$, $n > 0$. Let $m = -h$ where $h > 0$. Then the proof is similar to that in Case 3.

There remain the five cases in which either $m = 0$ or $n = 0$. Since for any number b, $1 \cdot b = b$ and for $b \neq 0$ $b^0 = 1$, the proof of these cases is fairly simple. The details are left for the reader to fill in.

EXAMPLE 1. $(10)^3 = 10 \cdot 10 \cdot 10 = 1000$
$(-2)^5 = (-2)(-2)(-2)(-2)(-2) = -32$
$(\frac{2}{3})^4 = \frac{2}{3} \cdot \frac{2}{3} \cdot \frac{2}{3} \cdot \frac{2}{3} = \frac{16}{81}$
$10^5 \cdot 10^3 = 10^{5+3} = 10^8$

EXAMPLE 2. $(5)^{-2} = \frac{1}{5^2} = \frac{1}{25}$
$(\frac{3}{4})^{-1} = \dfrac{1}{\frac{3}{4}} = \frac{4}{3}$

EXAMPLE 3. $10^3 \cdot 10^{-5} = 10^{3-5} = 10^{-2}$
$(3^{-2})^{-4} = 3^{(-2)(-4)} = 3^8$

THEOREM 3. If each is defined, $a^n \cdot b^n = (ab)^n$

Proof:

If n is positive, $a^n \cdot b^n = (a \cdot a \dots a) \cdot (b \cdot b \dots b) = ab \cdot ab \dots ab = (ab)^n$. Note that we use the commutative and associative laws repeatedly here.

If n is zero, $a^0 \cdot b^0 = 1 \cdot 1 = 1 = (ab)^0$, and finally if n is negative let $m = -n$. Then m is positive, $n = -m$ and $a^n \cdot b^n = a^{-m} \cdot b^{-m} = 1/a^m \cdot 1/b^m = 1/a^m b^m = 1/(ab)^m = (ab)^{-m} = (ab)^n$.

EXAMPLE 4. Consider the expression

$$\frac{ab^{-1} + 2 + a^{-1}b}{a^{-1}b^{-1}}$$

with $a \neq 0$ and $b \neq 0$. We may write

$$\begin{aligned}
\frac{ab^{-1} + 2 + a^{-1}b}{a^{-1}b^{-1}} &= \frac{ab^{-1} + 2 + a^{-1}b}{(ab)^{-1}} \\
&= ab(ab^{-1} + 2 + a^{-1}b) \\
&= (ab)(ab^{-1}) + ab \cdot 2 + ab(a^{-1}b) \\
&= aabb^{-1} + 2ab + aa^{-1}bb \\
&= a^2 \cdot 1 + 2ab + 1 \cdot b^2 \\
&= a^2 + 2ab + b^2 \\
&= (a + b)^2
\end{aligned}$$

What we are trying to do here is replace the given numeral by another numeral. The notion of standard numeral is not easy to agree upon in this connection, but we make some general observations. Usually negative and zero exponents are to be replaced, compound fractions eliminated, and the expression made as short as possible. Sometimes these directions conflict with each other and then a choice must be made. The usual direction given is "simplify" or "perform the indicated operations."

EXERCISES

1. Find the standard numeral for:
   (a) $(4)^{-2}$
   (b) $(-3)^3$
   (c) $[(2,357)^7]^0$
   (d) $2^0 + 3^0$
   (e) $(2^{-1} + 3^{-1})^{-1}$

2. Perform the indicated operations (given $a \neq 0$, $b \neq 0$, $c \neq 0$). State when you use the distributive law and quote the laws of exponents you use.
   (a) $(2^{100})(\frac{1}{2})^{100}$
   (b) $3^{-4} \cdot 3^6 \cdot 3^0$

(c) $(a - b^{-1})(a + b^{-1})$

(d) $(a + b^{-1})(a^{-1} - b^{-2})$

(e) $(a + 1)(a^{-2} + a^{-1} + 1)$

(f) $\dfrac{a^{-1}b^{-1}c - abc^{-1}}{a^{-1}b^{-2}c^{-1}}$

(g) $\dfrac{ab^{-1} + 4 + a^{-1}b}{a^{-1}b^{-1}}$

3. Fill in the blanks

(a) $(a - b^{-1}) = b($ $)$

(b) $(a - b^{-1}) = a($ $)$

(c) $(a - b^{-1}) = ab($ $)$

(d) $(a - b^{-1}) = a^2b^3($ $)$

(e) $a^{-1}b^{-1}c - abc^{-1} = abc($ $)$

4. Does Theorem 3 imply that $\dfrac{a^n}{b^n} = (a/b)^n$? Explain.

5. Simplify:

(a) $(\tfrac{1}{2})^{-2}$

(b) $(-3)^{-3}$

(c) $\dfrac{a^2 + b^2}{a + b}$

(d) $(x^{-1}y^{-1})^{-2}$

(e) $(x^{-1} - y^{-1})^{-1}$

6. Is $(x + 2)^2$ ever equal to $x^2 + 4$?

7. Is $(a + b)^m$ ever equal to $a^m + b^m$?

8. Simplify:

(a) $\dfrac{\tfrac{1}{2} - \tfrac{1}{3}}{\tfrac{1}{6} + \tfrac{1}{12}}$

(b) $\dfrac{a^{-2} + b^{-3}}{a^{-3} + b^{-2}}$

9. Express as a fraction in lowest terms:

(a) $\dfrac{\tfrac{23}{5} - \tfrac{6}{37}}{\tfrac{8}{5} - \tfrac{7}{11}}$

(b) $\dfrac{\tfrac{45}{32} - \tfrac{19}{39}}{\tfrac{17}{32} + \tfrac{19}{39}}$

10. Work Exercise 9 by a method different from the one you used previously.

8.2. RADICALS

We wish in this section to examine the operation inverse to that of raising to powers. For example, we want to answer questions like "What is the number whose product with itself equals the number a?" There are two difficulties which arise in connection with this question. One is that there are numbers a such that no number has its square equal to a. Another difficulty is that if $x^2 = a$, then $(-x)^2$ is also equal to a. We get around the first difficulty if we restrict the question to nonnegative numbers a. The second difficulty can be overcome by asking for the nonnegative number whose square is a.

We presented an argument in the last chapter concerning the existence of a nonnegative number whose square is 2. We indicate below an alternative argument, somewhat more intuitive, but which has several advantages. It is easier to generalize and it actually gives the infinite decimal expansion of the desired number.

Recall again that if a and b are positive then $a > b$ if and only if $a^2 > b^2$ (see Exercise 1, Section 2.4 for part of this assertion). Then we note successively that: $1^2 = 1 < 2$ and $2^2 = 4 > 2$; $(1.4)^2 = 1.96 < 2$ and $(1.5)^2 = 2.25 > 2$; $(1.41)^2 = 1.9881 < 2$ and $(1.42)^2 = 2.0164 > 2$; $(1.414)^2 = 1.999396 < 2$ and $(1.415)^2 = 2.002225 > 2$; $(1.4142)^2 = 1.99996164 < 2$ and $(1.4143)^2 = 2.00024449 > 2$. We construct, by continuing the process above, a number $a = 1.4142\ldots$, with the property that the number a_n consisting of the first n decimal places of a is the largest n-decimal place number whose square is ≤ 2. We notice that, although the work may become quite lengthy and tedious, we can find any decimal place of a that we wish. Thus we have an infinite process which defines the number a. We notice that $(a_n)^2$ gets arbitrarily close to 2 as n increases. If we let b_n be the number obtained by increasing the nth digit of a_n by 1, $(b_n)^2$ also gets arbitrarily close to 2. In addition, for each n, we have $a_n \leq a < b_n$ so that $a_n^2 \leq a^2 < b_n^2$. Since we can, by taking large enough n's, make a_n^2 and b_n^2 as close to 2 as we like, a^2 must $= 2$. In a similar manner given any real number $x \geq 0$, we can indicate the existence of a number $y \geq 0$ such that $y^2 = x$. We note, that if $z \geq 0$ and $z^2 = x$, then $z = y$. For if $z < y$ then $z^2 < y^2$ and if $z > y$, $z^2 > y^2$. With this in mind we make the following.

DEFINITION 1. For any nonnegative real number a we define $\sqrt{a}$ (read the *square root* of a, or sometimes *radical a*) to be that unique nonnegative real number whose square is a.

THEOREM 1. $\sqrt{a}\,\sqrt{b} = \sqrt{ab}$, if $a \geq 0$, $b \geq 0$

Proof: Since $\sqrt{a} \geq 0$ and $\sqrt{b} \geq 0$, we know $\sqrt{a}\sqrt{b} \geq 0$. Now
$$(\sqrt{a}\sqrt{b})^2 = (\sqrt{a}\sqrt{b})(\sqrt{a}\sqrt{b}) = (\sqrt{a}\sqrt{a})(\sqrt{b}\sqrt{b}) = ab.$$
Hence $\sqrt{a}\sqrt{b} = \sqrt{ab}$.

Notice that while $(\sqrt{a})^2 = a$ by definition; it is not always true that $\sqrt{a^2} = a$. To see this let $a = -3$ (or any other negative number), then $\sqrt{(-3)^2} = \sqrt{9} = 3 \neq -3$.

If we are faced with the problem of finding a number whose cube is a given number, we may proceed analogously to the method above in order to show that such a number exists. In fact the situation is much nicer in this case because we do not need to restrict ourselves to the nonnegative numbers and the answer is always unique. Thus we can make the following.

DEFINITION 2. For any real number a we define $\sqrt[3]{a}$ (read the *cube root* of a) to be that unique real number whose cube is a.

In general the following definition can be shown to be meaningful.

DEFINITION 3. (a) If n is any even positive integer and a is any nonnegative real number, then $\sqrt[n]{a}$ (read the nth root of a) is defined to be that unique nonnegative number whose nth power is a. (If a is negative and n is an even integer then $\sqrt[n]{a}$ does not represent a real number.)
(b) If n is any odd positive integer and a is any number, then $\sqrt[n]{a}$ is that unique real number whose nth power is a.

Theorem 1 can be generalized to say that $\sqrt[n]{a}\sqrt[n]{b} = \sqrt[n]{ab}$, and the generalization can be proved in a similar manner.

THEOREM 2. $\sqrt[n]{\sqrt[m]{a}} = \sqrt[nm]{a}$ if $a \geq 0$ and m and n are positive integers. The proof of this theorem is straightforward and is left for the reader.

EXERCISES

1. Show that if $a < b$, $a^3 < b^3$. Use this to show that $\sqrt[3]{x}$ is unique.

2. Find the standard numeral for:

(i) $\sqrt{9 + 16}$

(ii) $\sqrt{\frac{2}{8}}$

(iii) $\sqrt[3]{-8}$

(iv) $\sqrt{\sqrt{81}}$

(v) $\sqrt{2}\sqrt{8}$

3. Show that $\sqrt{8} = 2\sqrt{2}$ and $\sqrt{32} = 4\sqrt{2}$. Use this to find another numeral for $\sqrt{2} + \sqrt{8} + \sqrt{32}$.

4. Find another numeral (as in Exercise 3) for:

    (a) $\sqrt{2} - \sqrt{8} + 3\sqrt{32}$
    (b) $\sqrt{18} + \sqrt{50}$
    (c) $\sqrt{12} - \sqrt{27} + \sqrt{75}$

5. $\dfrac{x}{\sqrt{x}} = \underline{\hspace{2cm}}$?

6. Use the method in the text to find two decimal places of $\sqrt{7}$.

7. Show that $\dfrac{\sqrt{6} + \sqrt{2}}{4} = \sqrt{\dfrac{2 + \sqrt{3}}{4}}$

8. With Exercise 7 in mind, consider the difficulty of defining standard numerals for irrational numbers which can be expressed in terms of radicals involving rational numbers, radicals involving rational numbers and other radicals, etc.*

9. Show that $\dfrac{\sqrt{6} - \sqrt{2}}{4} = \sqrt{\dfrac{2 - \sqrt{3}}{4}}$

8.3. FRACTIONAL EXPONENTS

A rather common practice is to introduce fractional exponents to be used as alternatives for radicals. For example, $\sqrt{a}$ is denoted by $a^{1/2}$, $\sqrt[3]{a}$ by $a^{1/3}$, $\sqrt[4]{a^3}$ by $a^{3/4}$, etc. While fractional exponents are useful for many purposes, extreme care must be used in defining and working with them to avoid some subtle errors. In fact if r and s are positive integers, many textbooks "define" $a^{r/s}$ to be $(a^r)^{1/s}$, i.e., $\sqrt[s]{a^r}$. This has some rather startling consequences. For instance, $-8 = (-2)^3 = (-2)^{6/2} = \sqrt{(-2)^6} = \sqrt{64} = 8$.

Let us examine this "definition" more carefully to see how this strange situation occurs. If r and s are positive integers then $a^{r/s} = \sqrt[s]{a^r}$ does not actually define the r/s power of a. For r/s is a number and this so-called definition is not independent of the numeral 'r/s' used to denote the number r/s. As noted above $\frac{3}{1} = \frac{6}{2}$ but $(-2)^{3/1} \neq (-2)^{6/2}$. However this difficulty can easily be rectified. For positive integers r, s let us define $a^{r/s}$ to be $\sqrt[q]{a^p}$ where $r/s = p/q$, p and q are positive integers, and p/q is in lowest terms.

---

* In more advanced work it is shown that there exist real numbers which cannot be expressed in terms of expressions involving radicals and rational numbers.

If q is an even integer than p must be an odd integer. Thus if $a < 0$ then $a^p < 0$. In this case $\sqrt[q]{a^p}$ does not represent a real number and hence '$a^{r/s}$' does not represent a real number, but it does in all other cases. For example, since $\sqrt{-4}$ does not represent a real number (see Definition 2(a) in preceding section and Exercise 1 at the end of this section), then $(-4)^{8/16}$ does not represent a real number. We note that by our definition $a^{1/s} = \sqrt[s]{a}$. Moreover whenever $a^{r/s}$ is a real number then $(a^r)^{1/s}$ and $(a^{1/s})^r$ are also real numbers and all three are equal (thus behaving as we would expect exponents to behave).

However, not all of our troubles have vanished. We have now defined $\sqrt[s]{a^r}$ (in Section 8.2), and $a^{r/s}$ (in this section) where r and s are positive integers and a is a real number (except in the previously mentioned case where $a < 0$ and q is a positive even integer). Unfortunately, though, the two might not be equal. For instance $\sqrt{(-1)^2} = \sqrt{1} = 1$, whereas $(-1)^{2/2} = -1$. (Note that, although $\sqrt{(-1)^2} = 1$, $(\sqrt{-1})^2$ does not represent a real number so that we cannot commute the order in which we perform these operations.) Since we have not stated that $a^{r/s} = \sqrt[s]{a^r}$ there is no reason to suppose that the two should be equal. However, many people (and some authors of texts) seem to feel this is true; it is also a convenience to be able to use exponents and radicals interchangeably at times as in the following exercises.

One alternative is to restrict a to be a positive real number. Then for all positive integers r and s we have $a^{r/s} = \sqrt[s]{a^r}$. One can define $a^{-(r/s)}$ to be $\dfrac{1}{a^{r/s}}$, a^0 to be 1, and proceed to develop the same rules of exponents we have in Section 8.1. This eliminates discussion of quantities such as $(-2)^3$ and $\sqrt[3]{-8}$ which do appear occasionally.

Another approach is sometimes used by mathematicians. (Readers who are unfamiliar with the field of complex numbers might omit this paragraph.) For any complex number a, $\sqrt{a}$ denotes the set of all complex numbers whose square is a, and $\sqrt{a} \cdot \sqrt{b}$ denotes the set of all products obtained by multiplying an element in $\sqrt{a}$ by an element in $\sqrt{b}$. Then $\sqrt{a}\sqrt{b} = \sqrt{ab}$ (see Exercise 3).

A third alternative (and the one we recommend) is to follow the approach offered in this book. We have defined $\sqrt[s]{a^r}$ in Section 8.2 and $a^{r/s}$ in this section for positive integers r and s (excluding the case previously noted). Sometimes, but not always, $\sqrt[s]{a^r} = a^{r/s}$. For any given values of a, r, and s we should have no difficulty in deciding whether or not the two are equal. We could extend our definition by defining $a^{-(r/s)}$ to be $1/a^{r/s}$ and a^0 to be 1, but positive exponents will suffice for the cases we are interested in.

EXERCISES

1. Show that $\sqrt{-4}$ does not represent a real number.

2. Show that $\sqrt[q]{a^p}$ does not represent a real number where $a < 0$, p is an odd positive integer, and q is an even positive integer.

3. Produce real numbers a, b for which it is not true that $\sqrt{a}\sqrt{b} = \sqrt{ab}$.

4. Given $a > 0$, $b > 0$, express the radicals in $3a\sqrt[3]{a}\sqrt[5]{b} + 2\sqrt[3]{a^4}\sqrt[5]{b^2} - \sqrt[3]{a^2}\sqrt[5]{b^3}$ in terms of exponents and then factor out $a^x b^y$ where x is the smallest power of a and y is the smallest power of b.

9

9.1. POINTS AND LINES

We are surrounded in our everyday lives with geometric objects, geometric terms enrich our language, and geometry plays an artistic as well as a functional part of our civilization. Thus some geometry is clearly a part of what every educated person should know, and it behooves us to have an acquaintance with the rudiments of this subject. In this chapter we will examine some of the basic concepts of geometry.

We first point out that the terms used in geometry, as well as in other branches of mathematics, have very specialized meanings, and, accordingly, need careful definitions. We have the usual difficulty of basing any definition on previously defined terms, so that we must assume as known several basic, but undefined terms. Furthermore we must assume a number of interrelationships (called axioms or postulates) among these objects. It is then possible to define new terms and prove theorems about them.

We do not wish to delve deeply into the subject, nor do we feel that a rigorous treatment of the foundations of the subject is in order. We will merely try to give a clearer understanding and appreciation of some of the geometric entities and to call attention to some aspects of the subject.

Perhaps the most basic concept is that of a point. This will, of course, be one term which we will leave undefined, but we will try to present an intuitive picture of it. When one wants to indicate a point, he sometimes makes a dot with a pencil—

geometry

155

perhaps something like the period at the end of this sentence. This fails to be a point for two reasons. First it is too big—the tip of a needle is better but it is also too big. We need the ultimate in smallness. The second reason that the dot is not a point is that we want the point to be not the dot but the position which the dot occupies.

We wish to take as our universal set of points all space (sometimes called three-space because many mathematicians work with four or higher dimensional spaces) also undefined, but you may imagine a box increasing in size until it includes the earth, planets, all the stars, in fact the whole universe—the set of all points included is called *space*. We now have space as a universal set of points, and the objects with which geometry deals are subsets of space.

At this point some authors assume the existence of certain other undefined subsets of space called *lines*. We will, however, assume as undefined something called the distance between points and use this to define lines. Either way something undefined has to be assumed, and we feel that the way we have chosen makes for a nicer presentation. We assume therefore that for any two points P and Q in space the distance from P to Q, indicated by $d(P, Q)$, is a nonnegative real number. Some of the properties that we wish our distance function to possess, and which are intuitively clear about distance as we normally think of it, are:

1. $d(P, Q) = 0$ if and only if $P = Q$—i.e., the distance from one point to a distinct second point is always a positive number.

2. $d(P, Q) = d(Q, P)$—i.e., the distance between two points is independent of which point is first.

3. If P, Q, and R are any three points in space, then $d(P, Q) + d(Q, R) \geq d(P, R)$.

In Fig. 9.1 it is clear that $d(P, Q) + d(Q, R)$ is greater than $d(P, R)$. When would $d(P, Q) + d(Q, R)$ be equal to $d(P, R)$? We use this to make a definition. The *line segment* from a point P to a distinct point Q is the set of all points X which satisfy the relationship $d(P, X) + d(X, Q) = d(P, Q)$. The points which belong to a line segment are said to be on it. The symbol $\overline{PQ}$ indicates the line segment from P to Q (assuming, of course, $P \neq Q$). The points P and Q are called *end points* of the segment, the other points of the segment are said to be *between* P and Q.

The *line* determined by P and Q with $P \neq Q$ is the set of all points X such that X is on the line segment from P to Q, or P is on the line segment from X to Q, or Q is on the line segment from X to P.

Figure 9.2 shows three types of "X's" on the line determined by P and Q. Notice that a line extends without limit in two "directions," whereas a line segment consists of two points and all of the points between them.

Someone has said that mathematics should be read with a pencil in hand

and a scratch pad close by. This is especially true of geometry; we recommend to the reader that he draw pictures freely to help in his understanding of the material. It should be pointed out, however, that a picture does not in any way constitute a proof and may even be misleading. A mathematician may make several sketches to get ideas of what possible situations can arise, then he may try to guess what the general case is and, finally, try to prove it. In fact this is the usual procedure followed by many mathematicians. Another important contribution that pictures make is in communicating ideas, and

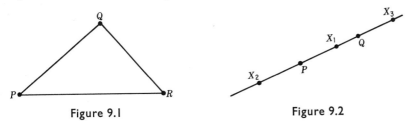

Figure 9.1   Figure 9.2

we will use them to illustrate many concepts in this chapter. Once again, the pictures are used in clarifying and illustrating, but do not replace the necessary logical and/or analytical arguments.

EXERCISES

1. If P and Q are two points, what does it mean to say $P = Q$? $P \neq Q$? $P > Q$?

2. If $P \neq Q$, compare the line segment from P to Q with the line segment from Q to P?

3. If $P \neq P'$, what can you say about the line segments from P to Q and from P' to Q? What can you say about the lines through P and Q and through P' and Q? (It is understood that $P \neq Q$ and $P' \neq Q$.)

4. Consider the line segments from P to Q and from R to S. What can their intersection be?

5. What are the possible intersections of a line and a line segment?

6. What are the possible intersections of two lines?

7. Nearly everyone has heard the statement, "A straight line is the shortest distance between two points." Criticize the statement.

9.2. LENGTH AND ITS MEASUREMENT

We have remarked earlier (in Chapter 7) that there is a 1–1 correspondence between the points on a line and the real numbers. Actually there are a great many 1–1 correspondences between these sets. We would like to exhibit one of these based on the distance concept discussed in the last section. Suppose we are given a line. We take any point A on the line and associate it with the number zero. The point A is then called the *origin* of the coordinate system. We take any other point B and associate it with the number equal to $d(A, B)$. With all other points X on the line, we associate the number $d(A, X)$ if A is not between X and B, or $-d(A, X)$ if A is between X and B (as in the case for the point C in Fig. 9.3). This has the effect of associating all points on one side of A with positive numbers and all points on the other side with negative numbers. The number associated with a point is called the *coordinate* of the point. The association of each point with its coordinate turns out to be a 1–1 correspondence between the points on the line and the real numbers.

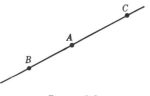

Figure 9.3

We point out that the definition made in the paragraph above depends on having a distance function between points on a line. It is also clear that any point on the line may be taken as having coordinate 0 and that either "direction" may be taken as positive. We also call attention to the fact that if one is given a coordinate system on a line (i.e., a suitable 1–1 correspondence between the points and the real numbers), this can be used to define the distance between two points. Explicitly if a is the coordinate of point A and b is the coordinate of point B, then $d(A, B)$ is defined to be $|a - b|$.

The effect of introducing a coordinate system is to make geometrical concepts numerical; i.e., it enables us to use numbers (which were created originally to count the elements of a set) to talk about spatial relationships. We will extend coordinate systems to planes and space later, but for now we will restrict ourselves to subsets of a line.

If A and B are two points on a line and the coordinate of A is a and the coordinate of B is b and $a < b$, we see that the *line segment* from A to B is the set of all points with coordinate x where $a \leq x \leq b$. This segment is designated $\overline{AB}$. The *length* of the segment $\overline{AB}$ is the distance from A to B which equals $b - a$. Notice that we distinguish between a segment $\overline{AB}$ which is a set of points, a closed interval $[a, b]$ which is a set of numbers, and the length of $\overline{AB}$ which is a number.

Now that we have the concept of length of a line segment, we can introduce the notion of measurement of a line segment. Suppose we are given a unit ruler—i.e., a portable object with two marks on it that can be placed so that one mark is at the point whose coordinate is 0 while the other is at the point whose coordinate is 1. Using this ruler, can we determine the length of a line segment the coordinates of whose end points are not given?

It should be mentioned that the kind of measurements we are describing are "theoretical" measurements. The marks on the rulers we ordinarily use have some "thickness" and so can't really represent points. Nor can our eyes detect the difference between points which are sufficiently close; so that even if we had a perfect ruler (i.e., one with a mark for each rational number) we couldn't use it. Nevertheless, it is possible to imagine that a mark made by a pencil represents a point, that close points can be distinguished, and whatever other idealizations are necessary. Thus, we can determine the length of a line segment the coordinates of whose end points are not given if the segment has an integral length (i.e., the length is an integer). For example, if we are measuring the segment $\overline{AB}$, and we place one mark on the ruler at A and note that the other mark falls at an intermediate point C on the segment, then place the first mark at C and note that the other is at B, then we know that $\overline{AB}$ is two units long.

However if A has coordinate 1 and B has coordinate 1.5, and we try to measure with our ruler, we find only that the distance between A and B is more than one and less than two units. We may try to remedy this situation by putting more marks on our ruler. By some method (see, e.g., Exercise 4, Section 5.3) we may divide a segment into any integral number of equal parts. We might divide the segment from the point with coordinate 0 to the one with coordinate 1 into, say, eight equal parts. Then placing the ruler so that the marks coincide with the points with coordinates 0 and 1, we might make new marks on the ruler coinciding with the points which subdivide the interval. This ruler could now be used to measure any length of the form $k/8$ where k is any nonnegative integer. Similarly we could construct a ruler to measure other lengths. It is easy to see that we can thus measure any rational length, but no irrational length.

Since there are many distance functions is behooves us in certain "practical" cases to have a standard distance. There are a number of these. Most of us are familiar with the terms inch, foot, mile, etc., and the relationships among them. In addition there is the metric system which is in common use in many parts of the world and which is used in scientific measurements. Although great pains are taken to make these standards as precise as possible, it is doubtful that anyone has ever seen an object exactly one inch long or that he would know it if he did see it. Nevertheless, these standards are important and serve their purpose. It is advantageous to have these different sized units of length when dealing with the measurements of various sized objects in order to avoid very large or very small numbers.

EXERCISES

1. Give a definition for the "midpoint" of a line segment.

2. Using only coordinates, can you give a criterion for the point A to be closer to B than it is to C, if all three points are on a line?

3. In fixing our ruler to measure "eights" (see Section 9.2.) how many new marks did we add?

4. Given a perfect ruler, unlimited time, and incentive could we theoretically "measure" an irrational length?

5. Using the procedure in the first paragraph of Section 9.2 show that no two distinct points on a line will be assigned the same coordinate. (*Hint*: show first that no two distinct points can have zero as a coordinate. Then examine "betweenness" relationships between two points with the same coordinate and the origin and use properties of distance.)

6. If A and B are two points on a line, show that the length of the line segment $\overline{AB}$ can be determined.

7. Give your height in miles (approximately).

8. Light travels at approximately 186,000 miles per second. A light year is the distance that light travels in one year. If the distance between two stars is 10 light years, what is the approximate distance between them in inches?

9.3. PLANES AND POLYGONS

We have noted that any two distinct points determine a line. Suppose we are given three points, A, B, and C not all on the same line. Then each pair of these points determines a line. Furthermore each pair of distinct points on the lines AB, AC, and BC determines a line, and each pair of distinct points on these lines determines a line, etc. The totality of all points on all of these lines constitutes a set called the *plane* determined by A, B, and C. For example, the point Z in Fig. 9.4 is in the plane determined by A, B, and C because it is on the line XY whereas X is on FG, Y is on DE, F is on AC, D is on AB, and G and E are on BC.

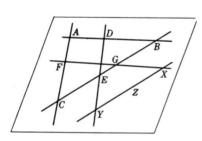

Figure 9.4

We usually visualize a plane as a "flat surface"—something like the top of a table but extending indefinitely in all directions—other approximations to portions of planes include: a pane of glass; a sheet of paper; the walls, ceiling, and floor of a room; etc.

It is easily seen that if two points belong to a plane, then the line they determine is a subset of the plane. A set of points is called a *plane set* if there is a plane which contains the set. Thus we see that any line or line segment is a plane set; moreover, any pair of intersecting lines is a plane set. Is the set of points on three intersecting lines a plane set.?

Consider now the set of points obtained by taking the union of several line segments as in Fig. 9.5.

The first segment is $\overline{A_1A_2}$, the next $\overline{A_2A_3}$, etc., and the last one is $\overline{A_{13}A_1}$. Notice that none of the line segments intersect (except at end points), and that each "A" is on exactly two segments. Such a collection of points is called a *polygon*. The A_i are called *vertices* (each one is a vertex) and the individual

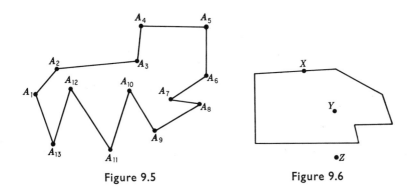

Figure 9.5   Figure 9.6

segments are called *edges* or *sides* of the polygon. Note that a polygon always has the same number of edges and vertices. In particular if there are three vertices, the polygon is a *triangle*. A four-sided polygon is a *quadrilateral;* a five-sided polygon, a *pentagon;* and a six-sided polygon, a *hexagon*.

If the polygon is a subset of a plane, the plane can be very naturally thought of as consisting of three subsets—namely the points on the polygon, the points "inside" of it, and the points "outside" of it. In Fig. 9.6, X, Y, and Z are representative points in each of these subsets, respectively. The terms "inside" and "outside" can be rigorously defined (in fact it can be proved that they exist) but we will accept the intuitive concepts of these terms. The set of points on the inside is called the *interior* of the polygon. Some people use the word "polygon" to denote the set consisting of the polygon together with its interior, but we will retain our original definition.

EXERCISES

1. The intersection of two planes can be what kinds of sets? Make a sketch of two distinct planes which have a nonnull intersection.

2. The intersection of a plane and a line can be what kinds of sets?

3. Explain why the crease that results when a piece of paper is folded is an approximation to a line segment.

4. What is the smallest number of sides that a polygon can have?

5. Make a list of common objects in which polygons appear.

6. How can you see that any triangle is a plane set?

7. Sketch a polygon which is not a plane set.

8. Sketch a polygon which has a "knot" in it.

9. What is the smallest number of sides a polygon with a knot in it can have?

9.4. PARALLEL AND PERPENDICULAR LINES

Two lines are called *parallel* if: (1) there is a plane which contains both of them and (2) their intersection is the empty set. Two line segments are called *parallel* if the lines which contain them are parallel. A *parallelogram* is a quadrilateral consisting of two pairs of parallel line segments (Fig. 9.7).

One of the properties possessed by a parallelogram is that the sides which are parallel have the same length. We reserve the phrase "two segments are

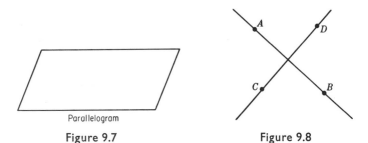

Figure 9.7   Figure 9.8

equal" to mean that the segments consist of the same points. This means that the statement (sometimes made) that the opposite sides of a parallelogram are equal is incorrect—their lengths are equal, however.

Suppose there exist distinct points A and B on one line and distinct points C and D on another line which intersects the first line, such that the distance from A to C equals the distance from A to D, and the distance from B to C equals the distance from B to D; then the lines are said to be *perpendicular* or equivalently are said to *intersect at right angles* (Fig. 9.8).

Two line segments are perpendicular if the lines which contain them are perpendicular. A triangle which has two of its sides perpendicular is called a *right triangle*. A parallelogram, two of whose sides are perpendicular, is called a *rectangle*. It can be verified that if a line intersects two parallel lines and is perpendicular to one of them, it is also perpendicular to the second so that a rectangle has several pairs of perpendicular line segments. How many? (See Fig. 9.9.)

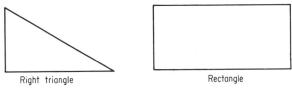

Right triangle   Rectangle

Figure 9.9

EXERCISES

1. What sort of physical examples could we use to illustrate parallel lines or line segments?

2. What sort of physical examples could we use to illustrate perpendicular lines or line segments?

3. Sketch two lines which do not intersect but are not parallel.

4. Sketch three lines each of which is parallel to the other two.

5. Is a parallelogram always a plane figure?

6. Is a quadrilateral whose opposite sides have the same length always a parallelogram?

7. A triangle is called *isosceles* if two of its sides have the same length. Can an isosceles triangle be a right triangle?

8. A triangle is called *equilateral* if all of its sides have the same length. Do you believe an equilateral triangle can be a right triangle?

9. A *rectangle* is called a square if all of its sides have the same length. Must a quadrilateral with all of its sides of the same length be a square?

10. Must a quadrilateral which is a plane set with all of its sides of the same length be a square?

9.5. AREAS ENCLOSED BY PLANE POLYGONS

A concept which is important in geometry is that of congruence. The idea is that two sets in space are congruent if, speaking loosely, they are the same "size" and "shape." We make this precise by saying two sets in space are *congruent* if there is a 1–1 correspondence between them which preserves distance. We have had occasion several times earlier to speak of 1–1 correspondences, and the reader should now have some familiarity with this concept. A correspondence between sets A and A' is called *distance preserving* if for every two points a and b in A which correspond to a' and b' in A' the distance from a to b equals the distance from a' to b'. It is sometimes intuitively helpful to imagine the correspondence between two congruent sets as being effected by moving one set so that it "coincides" with the other—keeping the distances between each pair of points fixed throughout the

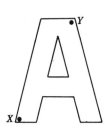 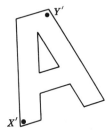

Figure 9.10

movement. For this reason these correspondences are sometimes called *rigid motions*.

In Fig. 9.10, the two sets are congruent and we can think of sliding the set at left toward the right and then turning it until it coincides with the other—in particular the points X and Y "go into" the points X' and Y', respectively. See Exercise 6 for congruent sets which can't be physically moved into each other.

We mentioned earlier that congruent sets have the same "size" and shape. In case the sets are plane sets, we express the preservation of "size" by saying the areas of congruent sets are equal.

By *area* we mean a nonnegative number associated with certain plane sets and satisfying the following properties:

1. If the set B is congruent to the set A, then the area of B equals the area of A.

2. If $A \cap B = \emptyset$, then area of $A \cup B$ equals the area of A plus the area of B.

3. The area of the interior of a rectangle is the product of the lengths of two perpendicular sides of the rectangle.

4. The area of any subset of a line is zero.

By using the properties it is possible to determine the areas of the interiors of all plane polygons, as well as for more general sets.

Note first that since a polygon is made up of line segments, we can see that its area, using properties 2 and 4, must be zero. Thus the area of a polygon together with its interior is equal to the area of the interior. We will call this the *area enclosed by the polygon,*

Let's determine the area enclosed by a right triangle. Suppose we are given the triangle (Fig. 9.11) with vertices A, B, and C so that $\overline{AB}$ is perpendicular to $\overline{BC}$. If we consider the polygon whose vertices are A, B, C, and D where $\overline{AD}$ is taken parallel to $\overline{BC}$ and $\overline{DC}$ is taken parallel to $\overline{AB}$, we have a rectangle which (by property 3) encloses an area equal to the product of the lengths $\overline{AB}$ and $\overline{BC}$. Now it is intuitively clear (and may be proved by theorems of high school geometry) that the triangle with vertices A, D, and C is congruent to the original triangle. Moreover, it is clear that the interior of the rectangle is the union of the interiors of the two triangles and the points on the segment $\overline{AC}$ between A and C. Thus, utilizing the properties of

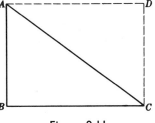

Figure 9.11

area, we have: The area enclosed by the rectangle equals the sum of the areas enclosed by the triangles (since each triangle encloses the same area, and the area of part of a line is zero). Therefore the area enclosed by the triangle with vertices A, B, and C equals $\frac{1}{2}$ the length of $\overline{AB}$ times the length of $\overline{BC}$.

Once we know how to find the area enclosed by a right triangle, we can use this to find the area enclosed by any triangle. For example, for the triangle with vertices A, B, and C below, we add the segment $\overline{AD}$ perpendicular to $\overline{BC}$. This creates two right triangles (Fig. 9.12), and the area enclosed by the original triangle is the sum of those enclosed by these two right triangles. The details of this argument are to be supplied by the reader.

Similarly we can now find the area enclosed by any plane polygon by

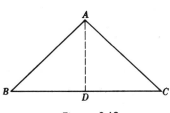

Figure 9.12

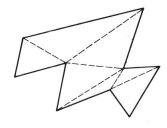

Figure 9.13

"breaking it up into triangles" as illustrated by the dotted lines for the polygon in Fig. 9.13.

EXERCISES

1. Supply the details for the process of finding the area enclosed by any triangle.

2. Is there any plane set which can't have an area? (Not just a set whose area is zero.)

3. Find the areas of the shaded sets in Fig. 9.14 (the numerals indicate the length of the various segments).

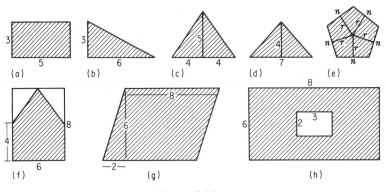

Figure 9.14

4. The midpoints of the sides of a square are the vertices of a smaller square. How does the area enclosed by the new square compare with that enclosed by the original? If the length of a side of the original square is 2, what is the length of a side of the new square?

5. What is the area of the set of points on the outside "surface" of a box whose dimensions are 2 by 3 by 4?

6. Consider the two sets in Fig. 9.15. Each has the shape of a domino

Figure 9.15

with a line segment attached. Are they congruent? Can one be moved to coincide with the other?

7. Consider the two sets in Fig. 9.16. Each is supposed to be a cube with

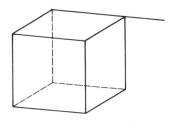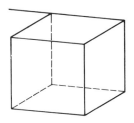

Figure 9.16

an attached line segment. Are they congruent? Can one be moved to coincide with the other?

9.6. UNITS OF AREA

In the interest of economy of language, let us adopt the phrase "rectangular region" to mean a rectangle together with its interior. Analogous to our work on length where we had several different units, we wish to explore the *possibility* of different units for the measure of area. Suppose that the rectangular region R_1 with sides of length a and b, respectively, is our unit of area and we wish to measure the area of the rectangular region R_2 with sides of length c and d, respectively. If

$$R_1 = a \quad \boxed{}$$
$$b$$

then we can subdivide it into smaller rectangular regions, e.g.

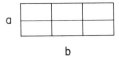
$$b$$

where each of the six smaller rectangular regions has sides of length $a/2$ and $b/3$, respectively. Thus if R_1 is too large to "fit into" R_2 then we can subdivide R_1 into smaller rectangular regions and so obtain a rectangular region which will fit into R_2. Hence let us suppose that R_1 will fit into R_2. We will illustrate what we have in mind by two numerical examples. Suppose R_1 has sides whose lengths are 1 and 2, respectively, whereas R_2 has sides of lengths 2 and 6, respectively. Then since $6 \div 2 = 3$, we can fit three rectangular regions like R_1 into R_2.

$R_1 = 1$ ▭ $R_2 = 2$ ▭▭▭

      2   6

Since $2 \div 1 = 2$ we can fit two rectangular regions in the other direction.

$R_1 = 1$ ▭ $R_2 = 2$ ▦▦▦

      2   6

Thus we see that area $R_2 = (3 \cdot 2)$ area $R_1 = 6 \cdot$ area R_1.

Suppose now R_1 is the same as before but R_2 has sides whose lengths are 2 and 7, respectively. Then $7 \div 2 = 3\frac{1}{2}$. We could divide R_1 into two smaller rectangular regions

$R_1 = 1$ ▭▭

        2

and then fit three rectangular regions like R_1 and one of the smaller rectangular regions in R_2.

$R_2 = 2$ ▭▭▭▯

             7

Then since $2 \div 1 = 2$ we can as before fit two rectangular regions in the other direction.

$R_2 =$ ▦▦▦▨

            7

We see that area $R_2 = (3\frac{1}{2} \cdot 2)$ area $R_1 = 7 \cdot$ area R_1.

Hence it seems plausible and we agree to accept as valid that if R_2 is a rectangular region with sides of lengths c and d, respectively, and R_1 is our rectangular region of unit area with sides of lengths a and b, respectively, then

1.   Area $R_2 = (c/a \cdot d/b) \cdot$ Area R_1

(where of course the sides of lengths a and c are expressed in the same units of length as are the sides of lengths b and d).

EXAMPLE 1. Suppose we take R_1 to be a rectangular region with each side of length 1; in other words, R_1 is a square region with sides of length 1. This is generally called the *unit square region* and we usually take its area as the *unit area*. Thus if the units are feet we say that the area of R_1 is 1 *square foot*; if the units are inches, we say that the area of R_1 is 1 *square inch*, etc.

Suppose we take feet as the length so that our unit area, R_1, has an area of 1 sq ft. Then if R_2 has sides of length c and d ft, respectively, we have by 1 the area of R_2 is $c \cdot d$ sq ft.

EXAMPLE 2. If we take R_1 to be a rectangular region with sides of length 1ft and 1 yd, respectively, then we might call our unit of area a *foot-yard*. Hence if R_2 has sides of length c ft and d yd, respectively, then we have by 1 the area of R_2 is $c \cdot d$ ft-yd.

EXAMPLE 3. If we take R_1 to be a rectangular region with sides whose lengths are 2 ft and 4 ft, respectively, then we do not ordinarily give our unit of area an additional name. Thus the rectangular region R_2 with sides whose lengths are 5 ft and 7 ft, respectively, would by 1 have an area of $\frac{35}{8}$ units of area.

Most of the time our unit of area is taken to be a square foot, a square inch, or something similar. Occasionally, as when we buy material by the "running foot" or rugs by the "running yard," we are in effect taking as a unit of area a rectangular region which is not a square region. At any rate, one should avoid such errors of logic as the statement that we can multiply 5 ft by 7 ft to obtain 35 sq ft because we can multiply "like units" but we cannot multiply 5 ft by 7 yd because we cannot multiply "unlike units." It is true that we cannot multiply 5 ft by 7 yd—not because we cannot multiply unlike units but because we can multiply only numbers. After all, multiplication is a binary operation on numbers. By the same token we cannot multiply 5 ft by 7 ft even though these are considered as like units by some people. However, just as we may state that a 5 ft by 7 ft rectangular region has an area of 35 sq ft, we may say that a 5 ft by 7 yd rectangular region (or one of 5 yd by 7 ft) has an area of 35 ft-yd (or 35 yd-ft).

In order to comply with the usual conventions, let us agree to take the rectangular region of unit area as a square, unless the contrary is explicitly stated. The precise units are usually left to the reader; thus, the area of a

5 ft by 7 ft rectangular region could be given in terms of square feet, square inches, square yards, square miles, or other units. It is easier in this case to use square feet; however, there is nothing inherent in the problem that would require this use.

EXERCISES

1. Recall that 1 foot = 12 inches, 1 yard = 3 feet, and 1 mile = 1760 yards. Give the area of a 5 ft by 6 ft rectangular region:
   (a) in square feet
   (b) in square inches
   (c) in square yards
   (d) in square miles

2. Give the area in Exercise 1 in foot-yards.

3. A bolt of goods 36 in. wide is sold at a price of 50¢ a "running foot" (i.e., a strip 1 ft in length cut from the bolt).
   (a) What is the cost per square foot of the material?
   (b) What is the cost per foot-yard of the material?

4. A roll of linoleum 9 ft wide is sold at a cost of $2 per "running foot."
   (a) What is the cost per square foot?
   (b) What is the cost of a 9 ft by 12 ft rug?
   (c) What is the cost of a (3 yd)-ft?
   (d) Utilizing part (c), find the cost of a 9 ft by 12 ft rug.
   (e) Which is easier, (b) or (d)? Why?

5. In a square region whose side is 1 in., how many square regions (or how much of a square region) are (is) contained whose side is:
   (a) $\frac{1}{4}$ in.
   (b) $\frac{1}{64}$ in.
   (c) 2 in.
   (d) 3 in.

6. How many square regions of side 1 in. are contained in one of side 2 in.? Are you sure?

7. If the rectangular region S has sides of lengths a and b, respectively, and the rectangular region T has sides of lengths $3a$ and $3b$, respectively, then compare the area of T with the area of S. Can you generalize this result?

8. What happens to the area of a rectangular region if its dimensions are doubled?

9. Do you know of any other common units of area? How do they compare with the units above?

9.7. CIRCLES

Suppose we consider a plane, a point P in the plane, and a positive number r. The set of all points in the plane whose distance from P is r is called a *circle* (Fig. 9.17). If Q is any point on the circle, then the line segment $\overline{PQ}$ is called a radius of the circle. Clearly the length of any radius is r. If S and T are two points on the circle, and the point $P \in \overline{ST}$, then the segment $\overline{ST}$ is called a *diameter* of the circle. It is easy to see that the length of a diameter is twice the length of a radius. The point P is called the *center* of the circle. Notice that the center of a circle is not on the circle. Quite often we wish to speak of a circle together with its interior (i.e., the points inside the circle).

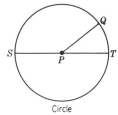

Circle

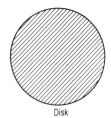

Disk

Figure 9.17   Figure 9.18

Such a set we will call a *disk* (Fig. 9.18). When we speak of the center, radius, or diameter of a disk we mean the center, radius, or diameter of the circle which together with its interior form the disk. This circle is called the *circumference* of the disk.

One historical problem is to find the length of the circumference of a disk. Hidden within this problem is the question "What is length?" That is, we have defined what we mean by the length of a line segment but not what we mean by the length of a circle (or any other "curve"). Surprising, perhaps, is the fact that such a definition is quite complicated, if it is to be made precisely, and beyond the scope of this text. We offer, however, the following intuitive idea. Imagine that we have a very fine piece of thread which we bend around to approximate as closely as possible the circle (or any other curve) whose length we are trying to find. The thread is then straightened to approximate a line segment. The length of this line segment is called the length of the circle.

By experimentation it appears that the length of the circumference of a disk is a certain multiple of the length of a diameter of the disk. This multiple is called π (the Greek letter "pi"); and most of us as school children were taught the formula $C = \pi d$ (where C and d are respectively the lengths of the circumference and a diameter of a disk). It can be established that π correct to five decimal places is 3.14159 (not withstanding the efforts of a certain state legislature to change it to 3) and that its infinite decimal expansion is non-repeating.

Another problem which arises is to find the area of a disk; one difficulty is to extend the meaning of area to include disks and other sets which are not enclosed by polygons. Again a precise solution of the problem is beyond the scope of this text, but we give an intuitive idea of the concept.

Let us attempt to define and find the area of a disk whose diameter is 2 units long. We first superimpose a square of side 2 units on the disk and subdivide the interior of the square into 4 unit squares with interiors. Next each of these square regions is subdivided into 4 square regions and the process is continued. The first three steps of this infinite process are illustrated in Fig. 9.19. Now we approximate the area of the disk by finding the areas of

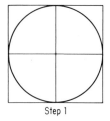
Step 1
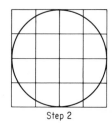
Step 2
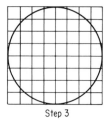
Step 3

Figure 9.19

those square regions completely in the disk. In the first step none of the square regions is contained in the disk; the first approximation is 0. (Not a very good approximation but an approximation nonetheless.) In step 2, four square regions each with area $\frac{1}{4}$ (each has length of side $\frac{1}{2}$ unit) are in the disk; the second approximation is 1. In step 3, 32 square regions each with area $\frac{1}{16}$ are in the disk; the third approximation is 2. If this process is continued the approximation can be shown to approach the number π. An alternative method is to use the areas of those square regions which intersect the disk. In steps 1 and 2 all of the regions intersect the disk so the first two approximations are 4. In step 3, 60 (all but the 4 corner regions) regions intersect the disk so that the third approximation is 60 $(\frac{1}{16}) = \frac{15}{4} = 3.75$. These approximations also approach π, but do so from above, i.e., each is greater than π but less than its predecessor. As most of you will recall, the formula for the area of a disk is πr^2 (where r is the length of the radius). In our example since the diameter is two units long, the length of the radius is 1 and the area is $\pi(1)^2 = \pi$.

It should perhaps be mentioned that, even among mathematical textbook writers, the terms previously defined are often used more loosely than we have done. For example, many people use the word "circle" to mean circle or disk, and use "radius," "diameter," and "circumference" to mean either radius, diameter, and circumference or their lengths.

EXERCISES

1. Make a list of common objects which you usually consider as circles or disks.

2. Explain why a compass "works" in sketching circles.

3. Actually try to approximate the length of the circumference of a 50¢ piece with a piece of thread and a ruler. Assuming that the diameter is 1.200 inches, approximate the length of the circumference using $\pi \cong 3.1416$. Calculate the per cent error in your measurement.

4. Using a large piece of paper, and correspondingly large units, approximate the area of a disk that you sketch with diameter 2 units long, as accurately as possible by using as many steps as you can in the process outlined in the text. To simplify the work you may restrict the work to one of the square regions in step (1) of Fig. 9.19 and multiply by 4.

5. Using the definitions prove that the length of a diameter is twice that of a radius.

9.8. ANGLES

One of the most widely used geometric terms is also the one which is perhaps least clearly defined. We refer to the word *angle*. One reason for the difficulty in making a satisfactory definition is that, as in other instances, the word is commonly used to refer to several related but distinct concepts. High school geometry books often have definitions such as, "an angle is the opening between two intersecting lines." A dictionary we recently consulted says, "an angle is the shape formed when two lines intersect in a point or the space between such lines." One difficulty in these definitions is that the words "opening," "shape," and "space" are not defined—nor, as the reader will discover, if he tries to do so, are they readily definable. In addition the word "line" is misused. If they mean "line," then, as most people will agree, there are four separate and distinct angles (whatever they may be) which are formed when two lines intersect. If they mean "line segments intersecting at an end point of each," what is the "opening" or "space" between them? Furthermore (see Fig. 9.20) is the angle "formed" by the line segments $\overline{AB}$ and $\overline{CB}$ the same as the angle formed by the line segments $\overline{A'B}$ and $\overline{C'B}$?

Before we define angles, we make some preliminary definitions. If A and B are distinct points, we define the *ray from A through B* (written $\overrightarrow{AB}$) to be the union of the set of points on the line segment $\overline{AB}$ and the set of all points X on the line AB for which B is between A and X. (This definition of ray is consistent with the definition in Section 7.4.) Pictorially (Fig. 9.21) you may imagine $\overrightarrow{AB}$ to be A and all points on the line AB that are on "the same side" of A as B is. It is easy to see why a ray is sometimes called a *half line*. Notice that $\overrightarrow{BA}$ is not equal to $\overrightarrow{AB}$, but that if $C \in \overrightarrow{AB}$ and $C \neq A$, then $\overrightarrow{AC} = \overrightarrow{AB}$.

The point A is called the *end point* of the ray $\overrightarrow{AB}$. If $\overrightarrow{AB}$ and $\overrightarrow{AC}$ are two distinct rays with a common end point, then the set $\overrightarrow{AB} \cup \overrightarrow{AC}$ is a plane set

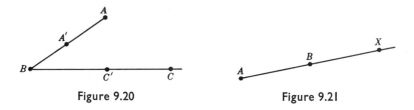

Figure 9.20   Figure 9.21

(since the lines AB and AC which contain the rays lie in a plane). Let P be the plane which contains $\overrightarrow{AB}$ and $\overrightarrow{AC}$ and let K be the complement of $\overrightarrow{AB} \cup \overrightarrow{AC}$ with P considered as the universal set. Note that in our sketches we are able to include only part of the plane and we use dotted lines to indicate the boundary of our figures although the plane is not bounded.

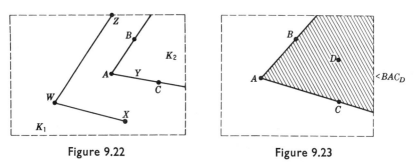

Figure 9.22   Figure 9.23

Although it seems intuitively obvious, we need to postulate that $\overrightarrow{AB} \cup \overrightarrow{AC}$ will always separate P, i.e., K will be made up of two sets K_1 and K_2 with $K_1 \cap K_2 = \emptyset$ (see Fig. 9.22), and such that if $x \in K_1$ and $y \in K_2$ then no line segment or curve exists in P from x to y which does not intersect $\overrightarrow{AB} \cup \overrightarrow{AC}$. Note, however, if we take any two points X and Z in K_1 (or any two points in K_2), we can find a point W such that $\overline{XW} \cup \overline{WZ} \subset K$. (The set $\overline{XW} \cup \overline{WZ}$ is called a *polygonal path* joining X and Z.) The sets K_1 and K_2 are called the *components* of the complement of $\overrightarrow{AB} \cup \overrightarrow{AC}$.

We are now ready to define an angle. Let A, B, C, D be four points in a plane P such that $\overrightarrow{AB} \neq \overrightarrow{AC}$ and $D \notin \overrightarrow{AB} \cup \overrightarrow{AC}$. Then by $\angle BAC_D$ (read angle BAC containing D) we shall mean the set $\overrightarrow{AB} \cup \overrightarrow{AC} \cup$ (the component of the complement of $\overrightarrow{AB} \cup \overrightarrow{AC}$ in P which contains D), i.e., the shaded set in Fig. 9.23. The rays $\overrightarrow{AB}$ and $\overrightarrow{AC}$ are called the *sides* of the angle. The point A is called the *vertex* of the angle, the component which contains D is called the *interior* of the angle, and the other component (the unshaded set) is called the *exterior* of the angle.

Notice that the designation of an angle is not unique for we may substitute any point (but A) on $\overrightarrow{AB}$ for B, or substitute any point (but A) on $\overrightarrow{AC}$ for C or we may substitute any point in the same component as D for D and still have the same angle.

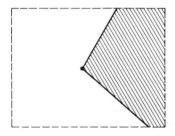 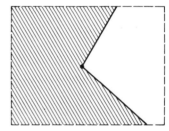

Figure 9.24

It perhaps should be mentioned that some authors define an angle as the points on two rays which have a common end point. However, since there is no distinction between the angles in Fig. 9.24, we prefer our usage.

EXERCISES

1. What kinds of sets can the intersection of two rays be?

2. Is it possible for one ray to be a proper subset of another?

3. Can one ray separate a plane? Must two distinct rays separate a plane?

4. Can a line segment separate a plane? Can two?

5. Is it possible for an angle to be the whole plane?

6. If $\overrightarrow{AB} = \overrightarrow{CD}$, what do you know about A and C? About B and D?

Associated with each angle is a number which we will call the *measure* of the angle. In defining a measure let S be a circle with center at A, the vertex of $\angle BAC_D$. Let E and F be the points of intersection of the sides of the angle and the circle. The measure of the angle will depend on the length of the arc from E to F (see Fig. 9.25) which is contained in the angle. More precisely we define the *measure* of angle $\angle BAC_D$ [written $m(\angle BAC_D)$] as the length of the arc from E to F (which is contained in the angle) divided by the length of the circumference of the circle and multiplied by 360. Thus an angle whose sides contain a diameter of a circle would have a measure of 180 since one-half of the circumference would be contained in the angle. Traditionally, the

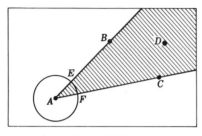

measure of an angle is followed by the word "degrees" (to distinguish this measure from others that are occasionally used) so we would say the angle in Fig. 9.26 has measure of 180 degrees (abbreviated 180°). Notice that the circle is used only in helping to find the measure of the angle so that the angle in Fig. 9.27 is an angle whose measure is 180°.

Figure 9.25

If two angles are congruent it may be established that their measures are the same. We emphasize that the angles are sets of points and are thus equal if and only if the point sets are the same, whereas their measures are implications of size of the angles and, therefore, may be equal even if the angles are not equal.

If two angles have a common edge and no other points in common they are said to be *adjacent*. The union of two adjacent angles is clearly an angle

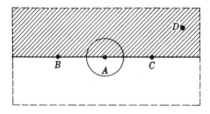

Figure 9.26

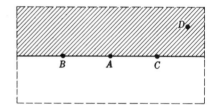

Figure 9.27

whose measure is the sum of the measures of the given angles. Thus if two lines BD and CE intersect at A, they divide the plane into four components containing the points F, G, H, and I, respectively (see Fig. 9.28). We consider $\angle BAC_F$, $\angle EAB_G$, $\angle DAE_H$, and $\angle CAD_I$. Clearly $\angle BAC_F$ and $\angle EAB_G$ are adjacent and their union $\angle EAC_G$ has measure of 180°. Also $\angle DAE_H \cup \angle EAB_G = \angle DAB_G$ which has measure of 180°. Thus

$$m(\angle BAC_F) + m(\angle EAB_G) = m(\angle DAE_H) + m(\angle EAB_G)$$

Therefore, $m(\angle BAC_F) = m(\angle DAE_H)$. Similarly we can show $m(\angle EAB_G) = m(CAD_I)$.

Now suppose that the lines BD and CE (Fig. 9.29) are perpendicular. We have already noted that $m(\angle BAE_G) + m(\angle CAB_F) = 180°$. Since $\angle BAE_G$ and $\angle CAB_F$ are "mirror images" of each other we may think of mapping each point of one into its mirror image about the common ray $\overrightarrow{AB}$. This is evidently a distance preserving mapping and therefore the two angles are congruent. Moreover they have the same measure since they are congruent

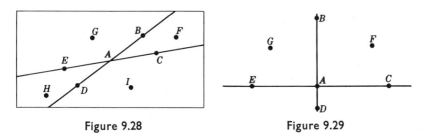

Figure 9.28   Figure 9.29

angles. Thus, $m(\angle BAE_G) = m(\angle CAB_F) = 90°$. An angle whose measure is 90° is called a *right angle* which justifies our earlier usage of the phrase "perpendicular lines intersect at right angles."

We extend our usage of the word "angle." Suppose A, B, and C are the vertices of a triangle and P is any point in the interior of the triangle (Fig. 9.30). We will then say that the triangle has angles A, B, and C where angle

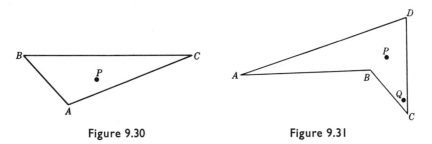

Figure 9.30   Figure 9.31

A means $\angle BAC_P$, angle B is $\angle ABC_P$ and angle C is $\angle ACB_P$. Notice that the angles of a triangle are not contained in the triangle. We can extend this definition to include angles of other plane polygons, but complications arise. For example, in the polygon pictured in Fig. 9.31 when defining angle A, $\angle DAB_Q \neq \angle DAB_P$ although P and Q are both in the interior of the polygon.

EXERCISES

1. Is there a largest measure an angle can have? A smallest? Explain.

2. Explain what is meant by the statement "The hillside has a 30° slope."

3. How could you define angle *A* in the polygon in Fig. 9.31?

4. What can you say about the measures of the angles in a rectangle?

5. Do you see why triangles and rectangles might have been given the names they have?

6. It can be shown that the sum of the measures of the angles in a triangle is 180°. If the angles in an equilateral triangle all have the same measure, what is the measure of each?

7. What is the sum of the measures of the angles of a rectangle? Of a parallelogram? Of any plane polygon with four sides?

8. A regular polygon is a plane polygon all of whose sides have the same length and all of whose angles have the same measure. What is the measure of an angle of a regular pentagon?

9.9. THREE-DIMENSIONAL GEOMETRY

Although three-dimensional objects are somewhat more difficult to visualize, sketch, and work with than two-dimensional objects, we have to

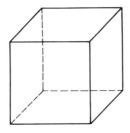

Figure 9.32

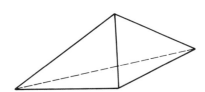

Figure 9.33

admit that we live in a three-dimensional world and cannot ignore the three-dimensional problems that arise. In this section we merely examine a few of the common sets encountered and attempt to give fairly precise definitions thereof.

One important class is called *polyhedra*. They are the three-dimensional analogues of polygons. A polygon, you will recall, is formed by putting line segments together. A polyhedron is formed by combining plane polygons, together with their interiors. More specifically, a *polyhedron* is the union of a finite number of plane polygons (with interiors) such that: (1) the intersection of any two of the polygons (with interiors) is either empty, a common vertex, or a common edge of the polygons and (2) each edge is on exactly two polygons. Perhaps the most common polyhedron is a *cube* (Fig. 9.32). It is made up of six polygons with interiors and each polygon is a square. The polygons with their interiors are called *faces* of the polyhedron. The edges and vertices of the polygons are called the edges and vertices of the polyhedron which they constitute.

A polyhedron with a minimum number of faces can be made using four triangular faces as in Fig. 9.33. This is called a *tetrahedron*.

A special kind of polyhedron can be constructed as follows. Let $A_1 A_2 A_3 \ldots A_n$ be any plane polygon. Let $A_1' A_2' A_3' \ldots A_n'$ be a polygon congruent to the original with corresponding sides parallel but in a different plane from the original polygon (Fig. 9.34).

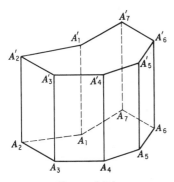
Figure 9.34

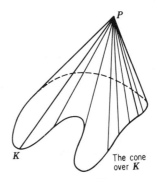
Figure 9.35

Now form polygons $A_1 A_1' A_2' A_2$, $A_2 A_2' A_3' A_3$, etc., by putting in the segments $\overline{A_1 A_1'}$, $\overline{A_2 A_2'} \ldots$, etc. The resulting polyhedron (obtained by considering all these polygons and their interiors) is called a *prism*. The two original polygons and their interiors are called the *bases* of the prism. The other polygons are all parallelograms. If they are rectangles the prism is said to be a *right prism*.

Another way of extending plane sets is as follows. Let K be any plane set and P any point not in the plane that K is in. Consider the union of all line segments $\overline{PX}$ where $X \in K$. The resulting sets (Fig. 9.35) is called a *cone* (or the *cone over K*). If K is a circle and the point P is chosen so that the line from P to the center of the circle is perpendicular to the plane of the circle, the cone is called a *right circular cone*, and its most familiar examples are an ice cream holder, and an Indian teepee (Fig. 9.36).

If we consider the set of all points in space whose distance from a point C is r, we get a set called a *sphere* (Fig. 9.37). The point C is called its *center* and r is the length of its radius.

The surface of a ball is a good approximation to a sphere. Spheres and polyhedra as we have defined them separate space into two components—what we intuitively think of as the inside and outside. The inside component is called the *interior* and when some people refer to "sphere" or "tetrahedron," they mean the sphere or tetrahedraon together with its interior.

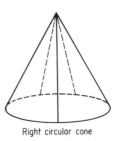

Right circular cone

Figure 9.36

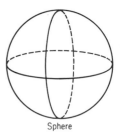

Sphere

Figure 9.37

EXERCISES

1. What familiar objects can you name as illustrations of some of the sets described in this section?

2. What kind of sets do you think can result as the intersection of a plane and a sphere?

3. In the definition of the cone what kind of object is obtained if the set K is a line segment? A triangle? A square?

4. The surface of the earth is often considered to be a sphere. If this were the case, what would the equator be?

5. The tetrahedron has four faces and the cube has six. Can you sketch a polyhedron that has five? Eight?

9.10. VOLUME

The three-dimensional analogue of area is called *volume*. The properties of volume are reminiscent of those for area. Volume is a nonnegative number associated with certain subsets of space and satisfying the following:

1. If A is congruent to B, then the volume of A = volume of B.

2. If $A \cap B = \emptyset$, then the volume of $A \cup B$ = volume of A + volume of B.

3. The volume of a cube together with its interior = the cube of the length of one of its edges. (Note the two usages of the word "cube" here.)

4. The volume of any plane set is zero.

A right prism with rectangular bases is called a *rectangular parallelepiped* but, in the interest of simplicity, we'll call it a *box*. We are interested in determining the volume enclosed by boxes. If the box has integral dimensions (such as the 3 by 4 by 5 box in Fig. 9.38) the problem of finding the volume is to find the number of 1 by 1 by 1 boxes into which the given box may be subdivided.

It is easily seen that there are $3 \cdot 4 \cdot 5$ boxes so that the volume is 60. More generally if a box has dimensions, a, b, and c, the volume it encloses is abc. It is, of course, possible (and often desirable) to introduce different

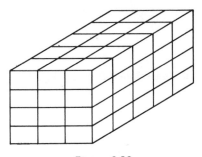

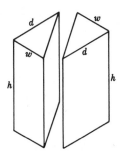

Figure 9.38   Figure 9.39

units of volume. The most common of these are cubic inches (the volume enclosed by a cube 1 in. by 1 in. by 1 in.), cubic feet (the volume enclosed by a cube 1 ft by 1 ft by 1 ft) etc.

If we are asked to find the volume of a right prism, we may use the knowledge we have about areas to assist us. First, if the base of our prism is a right triangle and its interior, then, as we did in the area case, we may consider the prism to be half of a box and hence, the volume that is enclosed is $\frac{1}{2}$ the volume enclosed by the box. Thus if the dimensions of the triangular prism are d, w, and h (as indicated in Fig. 9.39), the volume it encloses is $\frac{1}{2}$ dwh.

Since the area of the base of the triangular prism is $\frac{1}{2}$ dw, we note that the volume can be expressed as (area of base) $\times$ height.

If the base of the prism is a triangle (which is not a right triangle) with its interior, we may (as in the area problem) subdivide it into two right triangles with interiors, and then induce a subdivision of the volume enclosed by the prism into two volumes enclosed by prisms with right triangular bases (Fig. 9.40). Since the volume enclosed by each of these = area of its base $\times$ its height and the height is the same in each case, the total volume enclosed = the sum of the areas of each base $\times$ its height = the area of the total base $\times$ its height.

More generally since we can subdivide any right prism into prisms with triangular bases (Fig. 9.41), we can repeat the argument of the preceding paragraph and obtain: the volume enclosed by a right prism = the area of its base $\times$ its height.

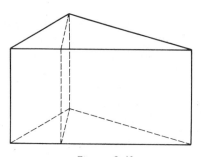

Figure 9.40

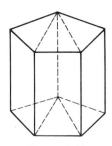

Figure 9.41

EXERCISES

1. Find the volume of a box with dimensions 1 ft by 2 ft by 3 ft in:
   (a) Cubic feet
   (b) Cubic inches
   (c) Cubic yards

2. How many cubic inches are in:
   (a) 1 cu ft?
   (b) 1 cu yd?

3. If box S has sides of length a, b, and c, respectively, and box T has sides of length $3a$, $3b$, and $3c$, respectively, compare the volume of T to that of S. Can you generalize this result?

4. How many cubic feet are in 1 cu in.?

5. If the dimensions of a box are doubled, what happens to the volume?

6. Do you know of any other common units of volumes? How do they compare with the above?

7. A tent has dimensions as shown in Fig. 9.42. What volume does it enclose?

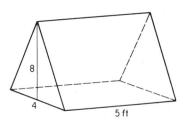

Figure 9.42

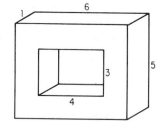

Figure 9.43

8. What volume is enclosed by a right prism whose base is the pentagon of Exercise 3(e) in Section 9.5 and whose altitude is h?

9. What is the volume enclosed by the solid in Fig. 9.43?

9.11. THE EULER CHARACTERISTIC AND REGULAR POLYHEDRA

If one counts the faces, edges, and vertices of a box, he finds six faces, 12 edges, and eight vertices; for a tetrahedron, he finds four faces, six edges, and four vertices. Is there any connection between these sets of numbers? Figure 9.44 is a prism with pentagonal faces; it has seven faces, fifteen edges,

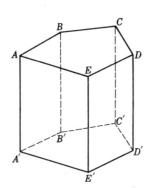

Figure 9.44

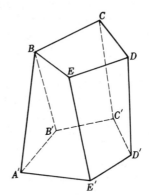

Figure 9.45

and ten vertices. Now do you see any connection? If you play around with these numbers, you might discover that in each case, the sum of the number of faces and vertices minus the number of edges is two. Will this always happen? The answer is "yes" except for polyhedra of the types illustrated in Exercise 1. If we let F, E, and V, respectively, stand for the number of faces, edges, and vertices, the number $F - E + V$ is called the *Euler Characteristic* for a given polyhedron. It is beyond the scope of this text to prove rigorously that the Euler characteristic of any polyhedron not of a type in Exercise 1 is always equal to two, but we give an indication of part of the argument.

Consider, e.g., the prism in Fig. 9.44. We replace it with the polyhedron in Fig. 9.45. You may think of replacing the edges $\overline{AB}$ and $\overline{AE}$ by $\overline{BE}$ and $\overline{A'A}$ by $A'B$. Since our new polyhedron has one less edge and one less vertex (A is gone), the Euler characteristic is unchanged. In a similar way it is possible to keep reducing the number of edges, vertices, or faces until a tetrahedron is reached. Since at each stage, the Euler characteristic remains unchanged, it is the same in the end as it was in the beginning. Since this kind of argument can be made for any polyhedron not of a type in Exercise 1, all of them have the same Euler characteristic as the tetrahedron, i.e., two.

The Euler characteristic is a very useful criterion in working with polyhedra. We will illustrate its use here to prove a theorem about regular polyhedra. A regular polyhedron is one of Euler characteristic two; each of whose faces is congruent to the others and is a regular polygon with interior; and each of whose vertices lies on exactly the same number of faces. Perhaps the most familiar example of a regular polyhedron is the cube; each of whose faces is a square with interior and each of whose vertices lies on three faces. Our problem is to identify all regular polyhedra.

We begin by noting that each vertex must lie on at least three faces. Since each vertex of a polyhedron is a vertex of at least one of the polygons, it lies on two edges, say, e_1 and e_2. But each edge lies on two faces—say, e_1 on F_1 and F_2 while e_2 is on F_3 and F_4. If $F_1 = F_3$ and $F_2 = F_4$ (or $F_1 = F_4$ and $F_2 = F_3$), then $F_1 \cap F_2$ contains e_1 and e_2 contrary to the definition of a polyhedron. Therefore at least one face, say F_3, is not equal to F_1 or F_2 and thus the given vertex lies on F_1, F_2, and F_3.

Let us suppose that we have a regular polyhedron with V vertices, F faces, and E edges; each vertex is on exactly k faces; and each face has exactly n edges. Since each face has n edges and there are F faces, we seem to have nF edges but this counts each edge twice because each edge is on two faces. Therefore $E = nF/2$. Also if each face has n edges, then each face has n vertices, and F faces would have nF vertices, but since each vertex is on k faces, $V = nF/k$. Substituting these numbers in the formula for the Euler characteristic gives

$$F - E + V = F - \frac{nF}{2} + \frac{nF}{k} = 2$$

We may write this as $F(1 - n/2 + n/k) = 2$. Now since each polygonal face has at least three edges, $n \geq 3$. If we substitute $n = 3$ in our formula we get $F(1 - \frac{3}{2} + 3/k) = 2$ or $F[(6 - k)/2k] = 2$. We had already agreed that $k \geq 3$. Since the left side of the equation must be positive, $k < 6$. Therefore $k = 3, 4,$ or 5. Substituting these values yield the following.

CASE 1. $k = 3$, $F = 4$, and $(n = 3)$. This means four triangular faces with each vertex on three faces, i.e., a regular *tetrahedron* (Fig. 9.46).

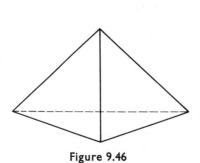
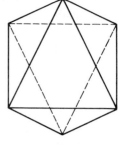

Figure 9.46   Figure 9.47

CASE 2. $k = 4$, $F = 8$, and ($n = 3$). This means eight triangular faces with each vertex on four faces. This is an *octohedron* (Fig. 9.47).

CASE 3. $k = 5$, $F = 20$, and ($n = 3$). This means 20 triangular faces with each vertex on five faces. This is called an *icosohedron* (see Exercise 4 below).

If we let $n = 4$ in the formula above, it becomes $F(1 - 2 + 4/k) = 2$ or $F[(4 - k)/k] = 2$. Since the left side of the equation must be positive $k < 4$. This means $k = 3$ and we have the following.

CASE 4. $k = 3$, $F = 6$, and ($n = 4$). This means six square faces with each vertex on three faces, i.e., a cube (Fig. 9.48).

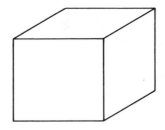

Figure 9.48

If $n = 5$, $F(1 - \frac{5}{2} + 5/k) = 2$ or $F[(10 - 3k)/2k] = 2$. It is easily seen that the only possible value for k is 3, which makes $F = 12$.

CASE 5. $k = 3$, $F = 12$, and ($n = 5$). This means 12 pentagonal faces with each vertex on three faces. This is called a *dodecahedron* (see Exercise 3 below).

If $n \geq 6$

$$F\left(1 - \frac{n}{2} + \frac{n}{k}\right) = F\left[1 + n\left(-\frac{1}{2} + \frac{1}{k}\right)\right] \leq F\left[1 + 6\left(-\frac{1}{2} + \frac{1}{k}\right)\right]$$

(because the quantity in parenthesis is negative since $k \geq 3$). Now

$$F[1 + 6(-\tfrac{1}{2} + 1/k)] = F[(6 - 2k)/k] \leq 0 \quad \text{since} \quad k \geq 3.$$

Therefore there are no solutions if $n \geq 6$ and hence no regular polyhedra with faces of six or more sides. This means we have proved the following theorem.

THEOREM 1. A regular polyhedron is either a tetrahedron, cube, octohedron, dodecahedron, or icosohedron.

EXERCISES

1. Calculate the Euler characteristic for the polyhedra in Fig. 9.49.

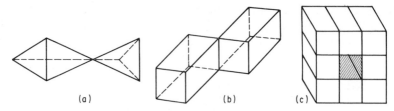

(a)   (b)   (c)

Figure 9.49

2. Construct a tetrahedron by carefully copying Fig. 9.50 on a sheet of paper, cutting it out, folding along the lines, and pasting. (The shaded areas are tabs to use for pasting.)

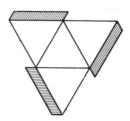

Figure 9.50

3. Construct a dodecahedron by using Fig. 9.51. (Add appropriate tabs.)

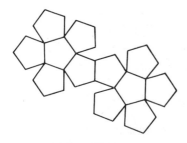

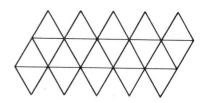

Figure 9.51   Figure 9.52

4. Construct an icosohedron using Fig. 9.52. (Add appropriate tabs.)
5. Using your own pattern construct a cube.
6. Using your own pattern construct an octohedron.

10

10.1. APPROXIMATIONS

In everyday life, approximations are used very extensively. Since a penny is the smallest monetary unit in this country, the final step in financial transactions must involve an integral number of pennies. If a local store has soup at two cans for 25¢, then we might say that soup sells for 12½¢ per can. Thus we would expect to pay 13¢ for a single can, but only $12.50 for 100 cans. If the monthly payment on our mortgage is calculated to be $120.543 then we would pay either $120.54 or $120.55, depending on the policy of the mortgage holder (or perhaps depending on the whims of the girl who makes out the bill). The man whose monthly salary is $987.53 and the man whose monthly salary is $1004.71 are both likely to say that they make $1000 per month. We use expressions such as "glass of milk" and "half an orange" which are not intended to be precise. It is highly unlikely that there are exactly 473,000 residents in a city whose population is listed as 473,000. Very large or very small numbers are likely to be approximations. We say that the distance to the sun is 93,000,000 miles or that the annual interest on our national debt is $7,000,000,000.

Although approximations are casually used in everyday life, in mathematics we wish to always distinguish between the concepts of a given number and of an approximation to this given number. For example, .33 is an approximation to the number $\frac{1}{3}$, but it is not the same as the number $\frac{1}{3}$ and hence it would be incorrect

errors and

approximations

to write .33 = $\frac{1}{3}$. Note that $3 \cdot (.33) = .99$ whereas $3 \cdot (\frac{1}{3}) = 1$ so, $\frac{1}{3}$ is certainly different from .33.

To indicate approximations we use the symbol $\approx$ (read "is approximately equal to"). Thus .33 $\approx \frac{1}{3}$. The mathematician (and others who use language with some precision of meaning) might state that the distance to the sun is about 93,000,000 miles or he might write, distance to the sun $\approx$ 93,000,000 miles.

At any rate, when a and b are numbers we will use the notation $a = b$ only when 'a' and 'b' are numerals denoting the same number. We will use the notation $a \approx b$ to mean that a is "close" to b in some sense, or that the difference $a - b$ is "small." Whether a number is large or small depends on the context. If city A and city B each have a population listed as 500,000 then we would say that population of city $A \approx$ population of city B, although in fact it might happen that city A has 10,000 more residents than city B. In this case we are regarding 10,000 as a "small" number. On the other hand if citizen A has a weekly income of $10,100 and citizen B has a weekly income of $100 then the difference between their weekly incomes is $10,000. However we would not regard $10,000 as "small" in this case and therefore we would *not* state that the weekly income of citizen $A \approx$ the weekly income of citizen B.

We have had occasion in the preceding paragraphs to talk about how close a number a is to a number b. We can determine this closeness by looking at $a - b$, but we observe that if b is larger than a, then $a - b$ is a negative number. Since we are not interested in which number is larger, but only in how close the numbers are, we introduce a device which ignores the sign of the difference.

DEFINITION. If x is any number, $|x|$ (read "the absolute value of x") is defined to be x if $x \geq 0$, and is defined to be $-x$ if $x < 0$.

Notice that this ensures that $|x|$ is always ≥ 0. In particular $|-3| = -(-3) = 3$ (since $-3 < 0$). Notice also that $|x| = |-x|$ for any number x so that $|a - b| = |b - a|$ [since $a - b = -(b - a)$]. With this device at our disposal we can now rephrase some of the previous statements to read, "a is close to b" if $|a - b|$ is small.

EXERCISES

1. Find:
  (a) $|5|$
  (b) $|-7|$
  (c) $|0|$
  (d) $|3 - 7|$
  (e) $|3| - |7|$
  (f) $-|-5|$

2. What is $\dfrac{|x|}{x}$ if:

   (a) $x > 0$
   (b) $x < 0$
   (c) $x = 0$

3. If $|x - 3| < 1$, what can you say about x?

4. If $|x + 5| > \frac{1}{2}$, what can you say about x?

5. For what real numbers x is $|3 - x| = x - 3$?

6. Solve the equation $|a| = |b|$ for a in terms of b.

7. Complete the statement: If x is a real number then $|-x| = \dots$"

8. Determine which of the three choices makes the statement correct.

   (a) $|a| + |b|$ is $\left\{\begin{array}{l}\text{always}\\\text{sometimes}\\\text{never}\end{array}\right\} = |a + b|$

   (b) $|a| + |b|$ is $\left\{\begin{array}{l}\text{always}\\\text{sometimes}\\\text{never}\end{array}\right\} > |a + b|$

   (c) $|a| + |b|$ is $\left\{\begin{array}{l}\text{always}\\\text{sometimes}\\\text{never}\end{array}\right\} < |a + b|$

   (d) $|a| + |b|$ is $\left\{\begin{array}{l}\text{always}\\\text{sometimes}\\\text{never}\end{array}\right\} \geq |a + b|$

9. Determine which of the three choices makes the statement correct.

   (a) $|a| \cdot |b|$ is $\left\{\begin{array}{l}\text{always}\\\text{sometimes}\\\text{never}\end{array}\right\} = |ab|$

   (b) $|a| \cdot |b|$ is $\left\{\begin{array}{l}\text{always}\\\text{sometimes}\\\text{never}\end{array}\right\} < |ab|$

   (c) $|a| \cdot |b|$ is $\left\{\begin{array}{l}\text{always}\\\text{sometimes}\\\text{never}\end{array}\right\} \geq |ab|$

10.2. ERROR

As observed in the preceding section the notation $a \approx b$ is inherently vague since this indicates that the difference $a - b$ is "small" and we have no clear idea of the meaning of "small." Also in the statement that a is "close" to b, we don't know what "close" means. One way to overcome this difficulty is simply to denote $a - b$ by e, and call e the *error in using b to approximate a*. Then $a = b + e$. If we now agree that the positive number f is "small," and if we somehow know that $|e| < f$, then we can then say that the error is small, or, more definitely, that b *approximates a with error e* where $|e| < f$. The terminology b approximates a with error $<f$ means that the absolute value of the error is less than f. The error e might be positive or negative so that b might be smaller than a or larger than a, but in any case $|a - b| < f$ and $b - f < a < b + f$ (also $a - f < b < a + f$).

For example, a machinist might be asked to cut a metal rod 6 in. long with an error of less than .02 of an inch. In this case $a = 6$ and $f = .02$; therefore, $6 - .02 < b < 6 + .02$. Hence the rod he makes is between 5.98 in. and 6.02 in. in length. If we change the problem slightly and present someone with a rod and ask him to measure its length, then the length he measures will be b, the approximation, whereas a the actual length is unknown. The most we can do is to determine a positive number f so that our error in measurement is less than f. Then, as before, we have that $b - f < a < b + f$. Hence true length is a concept which exists only in our mind. In actual practice one can never determine a length, but can merely determine an interval in which the length lies. If this interval is short enough, then we are satisfied with the measurement.

If b is a number which has exactly n digits to the right of the decimal point, and if every digit of b is identical with the corresponding digit of the decimal expansion of a (we agree for this purpose to use the expansion involving "zeros" instead of "nines" whenever we have a choice), we will say that *b is the number a correct to n decimal places*. For example, if $a = \frac{2}{3} = .\dot{6}$ and $b = .66$, then b is $\frac{2}{3}$ correct to two decimal places. On the other hand, if the number b has exactly n digits after the decimal and is as close to a as any other number with exactly n digits, then we say that *b is the number a rounded to n decimal places*. For example, .67 is the number $\frac{2}{3}$ rounded to two decimal places. To say that b is as close to a as any other number with n digits after the decimal means that $|a - b| \leq |a - c|$ for any number c with n decimal places. Thus $|a - b|$ is as small as possible and is certainly less than or equal to $\frac{1}{2}$ unit in the nth decimal place. We note that if b is a correct to n decimal places then $|a - b| < (.1)^n = \overbrace{.00\ldots01}^{n-1 \text{ zeros}}$.

If b is a rounded to n decimal places, then $|a - b| \leq 5(.1)^{n+1} = \overbrace{.00\ldots05}^{n \text{ zeros}}$.
Thus if we want a number a correct to n decimal places, we merely copy the decimal expansion of a as far as its nth decimal place. However if we wish a rounded to n decimal places then we must examine more than n decimal places in the decimal expansion of a. Sometimes there are two numbers with n decimal places equally close to a—this occurs when, in the decimal expansion of a, the $(n + 1)$st digit after the decimal point is 5, and all succeeding digits are 0. Thus one must make a choice. We agree to make the choice which results in the nth digit of the number rounded to n digits

being an even digit. For example, .35 and .45 rounded to one decimal place will both give .4. By making this choice we will have a uniform method of procedure and will avoid changing the nth digit in about one-half of the cases where a choice must be made.

As noted above we can't measure lengths exactly, but merely determine an interval in which the length lies. However, when this interval is small enough, then all lengths in this interval will round to the same decimal place. Hence, with a sufficiently accurate ruler, we can measure every length rounded to n decimal places for some n (the n depends on the units used, the measuring device, etc.). Thus a carpenter may measure a board as being 2 ft long and be within $\frac{1}{32}$ of an inch of the actual length. Then the board is between $24 - \frac{1}{32}$ and $24 + \frac{1}{32}$ in. long, or between 23.96875 and 24.03125 in. Hence the length, rounded to one decimal place is 24.0 in. Again, he might measure a board as being 6.0 in. long to the nearest tenth of an inch. Then, by taking $b = 6.0$, we have that $|a - b| \leq .05$, where a is the true length. Although a is unknown we have an upper bound for $|a - b|$.

Again suppose we wish to find the area of a rectangular region R with sides a and b. We measure a as 2.34 and b as 3.26 each rounded to two decimal places. For convenience we ignore the units involved in the measurements. In either case the absolute value of the error is less than .005 so that $2.335 \leq a \leq 2.345$ and $3.255 \leq b \leq 3.265$. Thus we are not entitled to state that the area of R is $(2.34)(3.26) = 7.6284$ (as is sometimes done). But we can state that $(2.235)(3.255) \leq ab \leq (2.345)(3.265)$ or that the area is between 7.274925 and 7.656425. When dealing with measurements and computations involving measurements we usually end up with inequalities rather than with equalities.

Recall that we have defined the set of all real numbers x such that $a \leq x \leq b$ where $a < b$ as the closed interval $[a, b]$. As noted above, in many measurements we obtain not a true value but an interval in which the true value lies. The length of the interval is indicative of the size of the possible error.

If we measure the length of a real estate lot and have an error of $\frac{1}{2}$ in., it is a fairly good measurement. On the other hand, if we measure the length of this page, and have an error of $\frac{1}{2}$ in., it is a rather poor measurement. This indicates that the actual size of the error does not alone show the quality of the approximation. We have said earlier that $e = |a - b|$ is the error in using b to approximate a. To give a numerical indication of the quality of the approximation, we use the ratio e/b and call it the *relative error*. When e/b is expressed as a per cent, it is called the *percentage error*.

EXAMPLE 1. If a length is measured as 50 units with a possible error of 2 units, what are the possible relative and percentage errors? The relative error is $\frac{2}{50} = .04$ and the percentage error is 4%.

EXERCISES

1. For each of the following numbers find a number which is the given number correct to three decimal places:

   (a) 3.56842   (d) $\frac{1}{7}$
   (b) 213.0098   (e) 1.2345
   (c) $\frac{2}{3}$ (f) 18.036501

2. Round off each of the numbers in Exercise 1 to three decimal places.

3. What is the error in using .33 for $\frac{1}{3}$? The relative error? The percentage error?

4. Is it true that $1 \approx 2$?

5. If the height of a building is measured as 400 ft with a possible percentage error of $1\frac{1}{2}\%$, what can you say about the actual height of the building?

6. If b is a correct to n decimals, is it true that $a - b \geq 0$?

7. If b is a correct to n decimals and c is d correct to n decimals, is it true that $b + c$ is $a + d$ correct to n decimals?

8. If b is a rounded to n decimal places and c is d rounded to n decimal places, is $b + c$ equal to $a + d$ rounded to n decimals?

10.3. DIGITAL COMPUTATION

Digital computation refers simply to computation with numbers expressed in terms of digits. Modern digital computers vary from an ordinary desk calculator up to a giant electronic brain. However they have one feature in common—namely they cannot handle numbers involving more than a certain number of digits. The limit on an ordinary desk calculator is 10 digits, the limit on a giant electronic brain is much higher, but the important point is that there is a limit. In this section we will consider some of the problems involved in digital computation.

We imagine that we have a calculator which can add, subtract, multiply, and divide digital numbers. For the sake of simplicity we suppose that the machine will take two-digit entries and will give a four-digit answer. Every entry is treated like an integer—decimal places must be kept track of by some other means. Now the associative law of multiplication assures us that $(25 \cdot 25)32 = 25 \cdot (25 \cdot 32)$. To calculate $(25 \cdot 25) \cdot 32$, we enter 25, push the multiply button, enter 25, push the multiply button and read 625 on the answer dial. For the next step we can only enter two digits so we must either calculate $620 \cdot 32$ by multiplying $62 \cdot 32$ and placing the decimal properly, or we must calculate $630 \cdot 32$. Thus we will obtain as an answer, either 19,840 or 20,160. On the other hand, $25 \cdot (25 \cdot 32)$ gives $25 \cdot 800$ or 20,000. The fact that '20,000' contains five digits whereas the answer dial on our machine has space for only four digits is the real difficulty. Otherwise we could, e.g., add 625 32's.

Next observe that on our machine $50 \cdot (25 + 25) = 50 \cdot 50 = 2500$, while $50 \cdot 25 + 50 \cdot 25 = 1250 + 1250 = 2400, 2500$, or 2600, depending on how we round off. Thus, in a sense, neither the associative law of multiplication nor the distributive law holds true on our machine. Again to find $\frac{2}{3}(35)$ we might first multiply by 2 and then divide by 3 to obtain $(2 \cdot 35) \div 3 = 70 \div 3 = 23.33$, or we might first divide by 3 and then multiply by 2 to obtain $(35 \div 3) \cdot 2 = (11.66) \cdot 2$, which has to be calculated on our machine as $12 \cdot 2 = 24$. Once more, we note that the two procedures do not give the same result.

Thus we see that the rules for computation with real numbers do not always hold for digital computation. You should be concerned with this, for although it may be problematical whether or not you will work with a computer, it is almost a certainty that you will do digital computation. Anyone who ignores the digits from a certain point on in a decimal expansion or anyone who deals with measurements is doing digital computation. This includes almost all of us; however, many of us are not aware that we have been dealing with computations of this type.

Since the results we obtain in digital computation may be close to or far from the correct result and since the result we obtain may be dependent on the order in which we have performed the operations, it is necessary for us to study the procedures in more detail. We will do so in Section 10.4.

EXERCISES

1. The instrument on a car that records the total miles travelled is an odometer (the speedometer measures the rate in miles per hour at which the car is travelling). On most cars the odometer has provision for six digits, the first of which reads tenths of miles. What is the reading on the odometer when the car has gone:

   (a) 17.36 miles?
   (b) 105,364 miles?

2. On the two-digit machine described in the text, calculate $(\frac{3}{5})(\frac{4}{7})$ in two ways. Do you get the same result both times?

3. Does the associative law for addition hold true for this two-digit machine?

4. Do the commutative laws of addition and multiplication hold on it?

5. What per cent error is possible in finding the sum of two "two-digit numbers" on this machine?

10.4. THE MAXIMUM ERROR IN SUMS, DIFFERENCES, PRODUCTS, AND QUOTIENTS

One of the major problems in approximation theory is how much of an error in the answer will be caused by errors in the numbers with which we are calculating. We examine here some of the basic aspects of this problem.

Let us suppose that b_1 is an approximation to a_1 with error less than e_1 and b_2 is an approximation to a_2 with error less than e_2, then $b_1 + b_2$ is an approximation to $a_1 + a_2$ with error less than $e_1 + e_2$ and $b_1 - b_2$ is an approximation to $a_1 - a_2$ with error less than $e_1 + e_2$.

We see that these statements are correct by noting that b_1, an approximation to a_1 with error less than e_1, means

$$b_1 - e_1 < a_1 < b_1 + e_1$$

and that similarly we have

$$b_2 - e_2 < a_2 < b_2 + e_2.$$

Now putting these together gives us

$$(b_1 - e_1) + (b_2 - e_2) < a_1 + a_2 < (b_1 + e_1) + (b_2 + e_2)$$

and rearranging

$$(b_1 + b_2) - (e_1 + e_2) < a_1 + a_2 < (b_1 + b_2) + (e_1 + e_2)$$

which says that $b_1 + b_2$ is an approximation to $a_1 + a_2$ with error less than $e_1 + e_2$. Moreover $b_2 - e_2 < a_2 < b_2 + e_2$ is equivalent to

$$-b_2 - e_2 < -a_2 < -b_2 + e_2,$$

which combined with the first inequality above gives

$$(b_1 - b_2) - (e_1 + e_2) < a_1 - a_2 < (b_1 - b_2) + (e_1 + e_2)$$

which says that $b_1 - b_2$ approximates $a_1 - a_2$ with error less than $e_1 + e_2$.

EXAMPLE 1. A survey crew measures the distance from A to B (see Fig. 10.1) as 145.23 ft, with error $<.001$ ft and the distance from B to C as 57.2 ft with error $<.05$ ft. Find the approximate distance from A to C (along the path ABC) and give an upper limit for the error of your answer.

We see that the path would be about $145.23 + 57.2 = 202.43$ ft with error $<.001 + .05 = .051$ ft. Thus the true length of the path is between 202.379 and 202.481 ft.

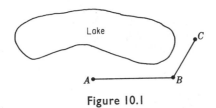

Figure 10.1

EXAMPLE 2. If A_1 rounded to the nearest hundredth is 145.23, and A_2 rounded to the nearest tenth is 57.2, find an approximation to $A_1 + A_2$ and give a maximum error for your answer.

The error in $A_1 \leq .005$ and the error in $A_2 \leq .05$. Hence we can state that $A_1 + A_2 = 202.43$ with error $\leq .055$. In other words, $202.375 \leq A_1 + A_2 \leq 202.485$.

Some texts gives "rules" involving the number of decimal places and significant figures for sums and products of approximations. Many such "rules" are about as accurate as the statement that all fat people have pleasant dispositions while all thin people are crotchety.

The easiest way to obtain a maximum error for products and quotients is to obtain upper and lower bounds for these quantities. Thus, if

$$0 < a_1 - e_1 < A_1 < a_1 + e_1$$

and

$$0 < a_2 - e_2 < A_2 < a_2 + e_2$$

then

$$(a_1 - e_1)(a_2 - e_2) < A_1A_2 < (a_1 + e_1)(a_2 + e_2)$$

and

$$\frac{a_1 - e_1}{a_2 + e_2} < \frac{A_1}{A_2} < \frac{a_1 + e_1}{a_2 - e_2}$$

In particular, if a_1 is an approximation to A_1 with error less than e_1, and a_2 is an approximation to A_2 with error $<e_2$, then these results permit us to determine upper and lower bounds for A_1A_2 and A_1/A_2 provided $A_1 > 0$ and $A_2 > 0$, even though we do not know A_1 and A_2.

EXAMPLE 3. Given that A_1 rounded to the nearest tenth is 12.6 and A_2 rounded to the nearest hundredth is 25.37, find upper and lower bounds for A_1A_2 and A_1/A_2. We observe that $12.55 \leq A_1 \leq 12.65$ and that $25.365 \leq A_2 \leq 25.375$. Hence

$$(12.55)(25.365) \leq A_1A_2 \leq (12.65)(25.375)$$

or

$$318.33075 \leq A_1A_2 \leq 320.99375$$

Thus we have a lower bound for A_1A_2, i.e., 318.33075 and an upper bound for A_1A_2, i.e., 320.99375. Since $318 < 318.33075$, then 318 is also a lower bound for A_1A_2. Since $320.99375 < 321$, then 321 is also an upper bound for A_1A_2. Thus $318 < A_1A_2 < 321$ and these bounds will be satisfactory for most of our purposes. Now $(12.6)(25.37) = 319.662$. As $321 - 319.662 = 1.338$ and $319.662 - 318 = 1.662$, then 319.662 differs from A_1A_2 by less than 1.7 (as $1.662 < 1.7$). Hence we can say that 319.662 is an approximation to A_1A_2 with error <1.7.

In a similar fashion from $12.55 \leq A_1 \leq 12.65$ and $25.365 \leq A_2 \leq 25.375$ we obtain

$$\frac{12.55}{25.375} \leq \frac{A_1}{A_2} \leq \frac{12.65}{25.365}$$

Now

$$\frac{12.55}{25.375} = .494 \ldots \quad \text{and} \quad \frac{12.65}{25.365} = .498 \ldots$$

Hence we can state that $.494 \leq A_1/A_2 \leq .499$. Since 12.6/25.37 rounded to the nearest hundredth is .497, and $.499 - .497 = .002$, whereas $.497 - .494 = .003$, we can state that .497 is an approximation to A_1/A_2 with error $<.003$.

EXERCISES

1. The sides of a rectangle are measured to the nearest tenth of a foot as 27.3 ft and 35.4 ft. Find upper and lower bounds for the area of the rectangle. Find an approximation to the area bounded by the rectangle and a maximum error for your approximation.

2. If b_1 approximates a_1 with error less than e_1, and b_2 approximates a_2 with error less than e_2, why doesn't $b_1 - b_2$ approximate $a_1 - a_2$ with error less than $e_1 - e_2$? Show by an example that this is not so.

3. If b approximates a with error less than e, show that $3b$ approximates $3a$ with error less than $3e$.

4. If b approximates a with a percentage error of less than 3 per cent, then b^2 will approximate a^2 with what percentage error?

5. If b_i approximates a_i with error $<e_i$ ($i = 1, 2, \ldots, n$), then $b_1 + b_2 + \cdots + b_n$ approximates $a_1 + a_2 + \cdots + a_n$ with error less than what number?

10.5. ESTIMATES

When estimates are made, they are made in round numbers; i.e., one doesn't usually look at a building and say, "that building is about $147\frac{1}{2}$ ft high." We say, instead, "that building is about 150 ft high." Similarly we make statements such as "New York City has about 8 million inhabitants," "his salary is about $10,000 a year," "we had to wait about an hour," "the fish I nearly caught must have weighed about five pounds," etc. The reason for this is that we are presenting these numbers as estimates and want them to be taken as such. If we say a building is about 150 ft tall, we might mean that we think the height of the building is between 130 and 170 ft. If we say it is about $147\frac{1}{2}$ ft tall, we are giving the idea that it is between 147 and 148 ft in height. Similarly few would object if the figure 8 million for New York City's population is off by a few hundred thousand. Thus we see that the estimate carries with it, more or less implicitly, a rough idea of how good an estimate it is.

On many occasions one needs to estimate the answer to a problem. There are no precise rules to follow and usually each particular problem is different; however, we shall illustrate some of the general principles.

Many times estimates are preferable because one doesn't want to go to the trouble of figuring the exact answer. A case in point might be how big a tip to leave if you are accustomed to tipping 15% at restaurants and your meal comes to $5.37. You might mentally calculate somewhat as follows: "On $5.00, 10% is 50¢ so 15% is 75¢. My bill is a little over $5.00 so that I will leave about 80¢."

Sometimes since it is impossible, for one reason or another, to calculate the exact answer to a problem, an estimate is the best you can do. For example, suppose you are going on a motor trip to visit relatives and you would like to tell them what time to expect you. You approximate as follows: "I usually average about 50 mph and the distance is 385 miles. For 400 miles, I would take about 8 hr plus about 1 hr for lunch and stops for gasoline and refreshments. If I leave shortly after 7 a.m., I should arrive at around 4 p.m."

One can use approximations to check on the accuracy of numerical computations. For example, to approximate (9.87)(16.03) you can say "9.87 is close to 10 whereas 16.03 is a little over 16; therefore, the answer should be about 160." (Actually the answer is 158.2161.) This simple procedure, in particular, will help you to detect errors such as getting the decimal point in the wrong place. Note that in this example the overestimating of the first factor and the underestimating of the second tend to cancel the respective errors; this accounts for the closeness of the approximation. One should make an effort to utilize this principle wherever practical, or if one is aware that the approximation is definitely too large (or too small), to try to compensate for this. In this connection note the preceding tipping problem.

If one is dividing, notice that increasing the dividend increases the quotient, whereas increasing the divisor decreases the quotient. Thus in this case increasing (or decreasing) both tends to give a better approximation than increasing one and decreasing the other.

EXAMPLE 1. $3118 \div 256 \approx 3000 \div 250 = 12,000 \div 1000$ (multiplying each by 4) $= 12$.

EXERCISES

1. About how many weeks have gone by since the birth of Christ?

2. About how thick is the paper on this page?

3. If your car averages about 17.5 miles per gal, gasoline costs 29.9¢ per gal, and you are going to drive from New Orleans to Chicago (about 915 miles), about what will your gasoline expenses be?

4. Approximate: $\dfrac{39.8\sqrt{857}}{588}$

5. There are about 5000 students at Subnormal Tech. If they were laid end to end, about how far would they reach?

6. A slide rule approximates the digits in the answer to a computation; the decimal point must be supplied by the user. Place the decimal point in the "answer" so that it will be approximately correct.

(a) $\dfrac{(3.547)(99.12)}{\sqrt{344.58}} \approx 189399$

(b) $\dfrac{(1975.23)(8475.4)}{.005} \approx 334817$

(c) $\dfrac{(29\frac{2}{13})(35\frac{4}{11})(485)}{.00123} \approx 40652$

(d) $\dfrac{\sqrt{1975.23}\,\sqrt{847.54}}{1758} \approx 73598$

11

11.1. INTEREST

Most persons at one time or another rent an apartment, a house, a car, a tool, or some piece of equipment, and so are familiar with the fact that the term *rent* refers to a monetary fee paid for the use of some item. Rent paid for the use of money is called *interest*. In everyday language the term "borrow" as in "borrows a car" indicates that one obtained the use of the car without payment of a fee, whereas the term "rent" as in "rents a car" indicates that one paid a fee for the use of the car. However this distinction is not usually made with respect to money so that the term "borrow" in "borrows money" does not ordinarily imply that one has obtained use of the money without payment of a fee. The quantity of money borrowed is called the *present value* of the loan (or, sometimes, the *principal*). When making a loan the borrower receives the present value and agrees to repay this amount, together with interest, in a certain length of time which is called the *period* (or *time*) of the loan.

There are two general types of interest—*simple* and *compound*. In simple interest the *rate* of interest is the amount of interest earned by \$1 in one year, expressed as a per cent. In compound interest the *rate* of interest has a slightly different meaning which we will give later. In simple interest the interest is computed only once and this (together with the principal) is paid at the termination of the period of the loan. *If more than one payment is made on a given loan then the loan is not at simple*

simple and compound interest

199

interest. In loans at compound interest (which is not simple interest), then the interest is calculated more than once and the principal on which the interest is calculated changes each time. In repaying such loans, more than one payment may be made.

Certain banks advertise 5% (per year) auto loans. For example, on a $2000 loan for 2 years they would take $[5\% \cdot (2000)]$ times 2 or $200 and call this the "interest." Then they would add this to $2000 obtaining $2200 now $2200 \div 24 \approx 91.67$ rounded to the nearest hundredth. Hence they would expect payments of $91.67 at the end of each month for 2 years. We observe that this is not simple interest because we make more than one payment on the loan. In the section on Easy Payments we will find that the compound interest rate involved in this procedure is considerably higher than 5%.

The *amount* of a loan (at either simple or compound interest) is the present value plus the interest.

11.2. SIMPLE INTEREST

Let us denote the present value by P, the amount by S, the time (in years) by t, the rate (in per cent) by r, and the interest by I. Then by definition of r and S we have

1. $I = Prt$

2. $S = P + I = P(1 + rt)$

3. $P = \dfrac{S}{1 + rt}$ (*Note:* $1 + rt \neq 0$. Why?)

Anyone familiar with percentage should have little trouble with problems on simple interest. Let us consider some examples.

EXAMPLE 1. Find the interest on $2000 at 5% for 2 years. Utilizing 1. above we have $I = Prt = (2000)(.05)(2) = 200$. Hence $I = \$200$.

Although in the past we have usually tried to avoid formulas, we will utilize them freely in this chapter.

EXAMPLE 2. If one borrows $2000 at 5% simple interest for 2 years, how much would be repaid at the termination of the loan? Utilizing 2. and Example 1, we have $S = P + I = 2000 + 200 = 2200$. Hence $S = \$2200$.

EXAMPLE 3. If one borrows money at 5% simple interest for 2 years and agrees to repay $2000 at the termination of the loan, how much cash will be received? Utilizing 3., we have

$$P = \frac{S}{1 + rt} = \frac{2000}{1 + (.05)2} = \frac{2000}{1.1} \approx 1818.18$$

Hence $P \approx \$1818.18$.

EXAMPLE 4. If one borrows $1818.18 and repays the loan by a payment of $2000 at the end of 2 years, at what simple interest rate is the loan made? From 2. we have $I = S - P$ and so $I = 2000 - 1818.18 = 181.82$. From 1. we have $r = I/Pt$ and so

$$r = \frac{181.82}{(1818.18)2} = \frac{90.91}{1818.18} \approx .050 \text{ or } 5\%$$

Hence $r \approx 5\%$.

In Example 3 the cash actually received would be $1818.18 since a penny is the smallest coin that we have. On the other hand 5 % is not exactly the same as $\dfrac{90.91}{1818.18}$ and so is not the exact answer to Example 4. Throughout this chapter we will deal mainly with approximations. Be sure to use "$\approx$" when "$=$" is not necessarily correct.

Unfortunately our time is not always given in terms of years and so some difficulties arise. Suppose that one makes a loan for a period of two months. In 1963 this could mean 59 days, 61 days, or 62 days. If one doesn't reason carefully he might think that since there are 12 months in a year, then two months is $\frac{2}{12}$ or $\frac{1}{6}$ of a year. But, as we have just observed, this reasoning is certainly fallacious. Most business transactions ignore months and express the period in terms of years or days. However the use of days also presents difficulties. For instance, 30 days is how much of a year? The answer would certainly depend on the year and would clearly be $\frac{30}{365}$ in a nonleap year and $\frac{30}{366}$ in a leap year. However, it is frequently stated, albeit somewhat roughly, that there are 30 days in a month and 12 months in a year. This would give 360 days in a year. Since many business transactions are made for periods of 30 days, 60 days, 90 days, etc., many businessmen find it convenient to assume that there are 360 days in a year. If one converts days to years by utilizing the actual number of days in the year, then the term *exact simple interest* is used. If one converts days to years under the assumption that there are 360 days in a year, then the term *ordinary simple interest* is used.

As long as the period is given in terms of years then there is no need to differentiate between ordinary and exact simple interest. If the period is given by means of dates then a further complicating factor arises. One can either calculate the actual number of days between the two given dates or one can approximate the number of days by use of the assumption that there are 30 days in a month. We are not particularly interested in this point and hence will avoid such questions in this book.

In ordinary simple interest 60 days $= \frac{60}{360} = \frac{1}{6}$ years and $\frac{1}{6}(6\%) = 1\%$.

It follows then that the ordinary simple interest on P dollars at 6% for 60 days is 1% of P. Since 1% of P can be obtained simply by moving the decimal point two places to the left, we have a simple procedure to obtain the interest in this case. But the interest for 6 days would be $\frac{1}{10}$ of this sum while the interest for 120 days would be twice this sum. By such devices we can readily approximate the ordinary simple interest at 6% for any number of days. This procedure is called the *six per cent method for calculation of simple interest*.

We are not particularly interested in the six per cent method per se, we give it to obtain some practice in routine computations and because of the simple reasoning that it requires.

EXAMPLE 5. Find the ordinary simple interest on $637.50 for 128 days at 6%. We have:

$$\text{interest for 60 days} = \$6.375.$$

Hence

$$\text{interest for 120 days} = 2(6.375) = \$12.750$$

and

$$\text{interest for 6 days} = \tfrac{1}{10}(6.375) = .6375$$

and

$$\text{interest for 2 days} = \tfrac{1}{3}(.6375) = .2125.$$

Hence

$$\text{the interest for 128 days} = 12.750 + .6375 + .2125 = 13.60$$

or the interest is $13.60.

EXAMPLE 6. Find the ordinary simple interest on $637.50 for 128 days at 5%.

As in Example 5 we see that the interest at 6% = $13.60. Hence the interest at 1% = $\tfrac{1}{6}(13.60) \approx 2.2667$ and the interest at 5% $\approx 5(2.2667) = 11.3335$. Thus the ordinary simple interest on $637.50 for 128 days at 5% is approximately $11.33.

Since a days $= \dfrac{a}{365}$ years (in a nonleap year) at exact simple interest, but a days $= \dfrac{a}{360}$ years at ordinary simple interest then exact interest will be

$$\frac{a/365}{a/360} = \frac{360}{365} = \frac{72}{73}$$

times as much as ordinary interest or ordinary interest will be $\frac{73}{72}$ times as much as exact interest in a nonleap year. Thus ordinary interest is always more than exact interest, which is another reason why merchants prefer ordinary interest. This relationship enables one to calculate exact interest by means of the six per cent rule, if desired.

EXAMPLE 7. Find the exact simple interest on $637.50 for 128 days at 5%.
As in Example 6 we see that the ordinary interest at 5% ≈ 11.3335.
Now $\frac{72}{73}I = I - (I/73)$.
As

$$\frac{11.3335}{73} \approx .1553 \quad \text{and} \quad 11.3335 - .1553 = 11.1782$$

we see that the exact interest $\approx \$11.18$.

Of course, if one thinks this procedure is too indirect, he can always use $I = Prt = (637.50)(.05)(\frac{128}{365}) \approx 11.18$ (assuming that the year in question is not a leap year).

EXERCISES

1. Find the interest on $1500 at 5% for 3 years.

2. How much money should be invested now at 4% simple interest to produce $10,000 in 5 years?

3. At what rate would a loan of $500 cost $600 to repay in 2 years?

4. How much does it cost at ordinary simple interest to borrow $100 at 6% for 45 days?

5. A man invests a total of $6000 partly at 3% and the rest at 5%. If the total interest for a year is $250, how much did he invest at each rate?

6. How long does it take an amount of money to double at 10% simple interest?

7. A man invests $100 at 1%, $100 at 2%, $100 at 3%, $100 at 4%, and $100 at 5%. At what rate could he have invested the whole $500 to earn the same interest?

11.3. DISCOUNT

A deduction from the maturity value of an obligation is termed a *discount*. If S is the maturity value and D is the discount then $P = S - D$ is called the *present value* or *proceeds* of the obligation. (The term "present value" is used not only for simple interest and discount but also for compound interest and annuities which are discussed later in this chapter. In each case it has essentially the same meaning, although, the formulas used to obtain it are quite different.) Suppose that t is the length of time in years from now until the maturity date of the obligation and d is a rate (expressed in per cent). If the discount is calculated by means of the formula $D - Sdt$ then it is called *bank discount*. (Some writers also call this *simple discount;* other writers reserve the term simple discount to describe the process of finding the present value of a given amount at simple interest as described in the preceding section.) The phrase *interest in advance* is also used to describe bank discount. We have

1. $D = Sdt$

2. $P = S - D$

3. $P = S(1 - dt)$

EXAMPLE 1. If one borrows $2000 from the bank for 2 years at a discount rate of 5 %, what is the present value?
　　Since $D = Sdt = 2000(.05)2 = 200$, we see that $P = S - D = 2000 - 200 = 1800$. Thus the present value is $1800.

The simple interest rate at which one will repay $2000 on an $1800 loan for 2 years is higher than 5 % (see Exercise 1). Hence not only is it simpler to find the present value by bank discount than it is by simple interest, but also, for a given rate the bank will make more profit.

Trade discounts are frequently given. For instance, an electronics supply house might give a discount of 40 % on television tubes to certain customers such as radio amateurs; an additional discount of 10 % if as many as 25 tubes are purchased; and an additional discount of 2 % for cash payment. This is referred to as a discount series of 40 %, 10 %, and 2 %.

EXAMPLE 2. Find a single discount equivalent to a discount series of 40 %, 10 %, and 2 %.
　　A discount of 40 % leaves 60 %, a discount of 10 % leaves 90 %, and a discount of 2 % leaves 98 %. Hence there remains $(.60)(.90)(.98) = .5292$ of the original price. Thus $1 - .5292 = .4708$ or 47.08 % is the desired single discount rate.
　　We observe that a discount series of 10 %, 2 %, and 40 % would leave $(.90)(.98)(.60)$ of the original price. We see that a discount series is independent of the order in which the discounts are given.

Our major interest in discount is as a source of computational exercises, for we need a certain amount of practice in addition, subtraction, multiplication, and division.

EXERCISES

1. Find the simple interest rate at which one borrows $1800 and pays back $2000 2 years later.

2. A certain company offers a 40% discount on certain items provided one pays a 10% tax on the original selling price. What is the resulting discount rate?

3. Find the present value of a $12,000 loan on a house for 5 years discounted at 6%.

4. If you agree to pay back $5000 3 years hence for $4000 now, what is the discount rate?

5. Find a single discount equal to the discount series 30%, 30%, and 10%.

6. A discount series of x%, 10%, and 5% is equal to a single discount of 35%. What is x?

7. Why is borrowing at a discount rate more expensive than borrowing at simple interest at the same rate?

11.4. COMPOUND INTEREST

To introduce this topic and to illustrate the general lack of knowledge about it, we describe an actual experience of an acquaintance. He desired to borrow $1000 for one year from the bank. The bank manager stated they would be glad to lend the money at 4% simple interest but that it was against the bank's policy to make such loans for periods longer than one quarter of a year. However, they could simply write this up as a new loan each quarter and the $1000 with interest could be repaid at the end of the year as desired.

At the end of the first quarter the interest owed was

$$I = Prt = 1000(.04)(\tfrac{1}{4}) = 10$$

Hence the second quarter loan was carried on the books as a $1010 loan. At the end of the second quarter the interest owed was

$$I = Prt = 1010(.04)(\tfrac{1}{4}) = 10.10$$

Hence the third quarter loan was carried on the books as a $1020.10 loan. At the end of the third quarter the interest owed was

$$I = Prt = 1020.10(.04)(\tfrac{1}{4}) \approx 10.20$$

Hence the fourth quarter loan was carried on the books as a $1030.30 loan.

At the end of the fourth quarter the interest owed was

$$I = Prt = 1030.30(.04)(\tfrac{1}{4}) \approx 10.30$$

Hence the bank stated $1040.60 was owed as full repayment of the loan.

Although it was true that each quarter's loan was calculated at simple interest, it is surprising that the bank manager referred to this loan as being made at 4% simple interest. Instead of looking at four individual loans, each made for a quarter of a year, one usually groups them together and regards this as a year loan. Such a succession of simple interest loans where in each case both the interest rate and the period are the same and where the amount of one is the present value of the next, is referred to as a *compound interest* loan. Thus this loan (is by definition) a $1000 loan at 4%, *compounded quarterly*. (Sometimes the phrase 4%, converted quarterly is used.)

For a variety of reasons almost all financial transactions such as loans, bonds, annuities, etc., are made at compound interest rather than at simple interest. Perhaps the most important reason is that equivalent payments at compound interest satisfy the transitive property, whereas equivalent payments at simple interest do not. This statement will be proved in the next section.

Let P denote the *present value*, S the *amount*, j the *compound interest rate* (in per cent), and m the *number of times per year that interest is compounded*. It is assumed that interest is compounded at least once per year. Then $i = j/m$ is *the interest rate per conversion period*. For example, in the loan previously described $P = \$1000$, $S = \$1040.60$, $j = 4\%$, $m = 4$, and $i = \dfrac{4\%}{4} = 1\%$.

At the end of the first period the amount would be $P + Pi = P(1 + i)$. At the end of the second period the amount would be

$$[P(1 + i)] \cdot (1 + i) = P(1 + i)^2$$

At the end of the third period the amount would be

$$[P(1 + i)^2] \cdot (1 + i) = P(1 + i)^3$$

At the end of n periods the amount would be $P(1 + i)^n$. Hence, we have

$$S = P(1 + i)^n \quad \text{and} \quad P = \frac{S}{(1 + i)^n} = S(1 + i)^{-n}$$

In this particular loan we would have $S = P(1 + i)^4 = 1000(1 + 1\%)^4$. Tables of approximations for $(1 + i)^n$ and $(1 + i)^{-n}$ have been computed for many values of i and n; some are included at the end of this book. By means of such tables we may obtain approximations for $(1 + i)^n$ and $(1 + i)^{-n}$ and so the previous formulas enable us to approximate S and P with relative ease.

The difference $S - P$ is usually called the *compound interest*.

EXAMPLE 1. If $1000 is borrowed for 15 years at 4%, converted semi-annually, how much will it take to repay the loan?
We see that $P = \$1000$, $j = 4\%$, $m = 2$, and so $i = \frac{4}{2}\% = 2\%$. More-over computing interest 2 times a year for 15 years shows that $n = 30$. Hence

$$S = P(1 + i)^n = 1000(1 + 2\%)^{30} \approx 1000(1.81136158) \approx \$1811.36$$

We utilized Table I to obtain an approximation to $(1 + 2\%)^{30}$.

EXAMPLE 2. If one invests $1000 at 4%, compounded semi-annually, for 15 years, how much will he then have?
Our computation will be identical with the computation in Example 1 so that the answer $\approx \$1811.36$.

EXAMPLE 3. How much should one invest now at 6%, converted monthly, to have $1000 at the end of 5 years?
We have $S = \$1000$, $j = 6\%$, $m = 12$, $i = \frac{6}{12}\% = \frac{1}{2}\%$, and $n = 5 \times 12 = 60$. Hence

$$P = S(1 + i)^{-n} = 1000(1 + \tfrac{1}{2}\%)^{-60} \approx 1000(.74137220) \approx 741.37$$

Hence, the answer $\approx \$741.37$. We obtained the approximation to $(1 + \frac{1}{2}\%)^{-60}$ from Table II.

EXERCISES

1. How much is $1000 invested at 6% for 2 years:
    (a) At simple interest?
    (b) Compounded annually?
    (c) Compounded semi-annually?
    (d) Compounded quarterly?

2. How long will it take a sum of money invested at 5% compounded semi-annually to double?

3. How much money should a parent invest at 6% compounded quarterly at the birth of a child in order to have $10,000 when the child is ready for college at age 18?

4. At what rate compounded annually will $1000 increase to $1210 in 2 years?

11.5. EQUIVALENT PAYMENTS

In a given problem we usually agree on a fixed interest rate such as 5%, compounded monthly. Sometimes the expression *money is worth* 5%, *compounded monthly*, is used. As long as the value of money remains at this rate, then there is no difference in the value of, say, $1000 now and the value of $1000(1 + \frac{5}{12}\%)^n$ dollars n periods from now, where n is a nonnegative integer. For that matter, $1000(1 + \frac{5}{12}\%)^{-n}$ dollars n periods before now also has this same value. When we say there is no difference in $1000 now and $1000(1 + \frac{5}{12}\%)^n$ dollars n periods from now, we mean that the two "dated sums" are mathematically equivalent in that one is the present value and the other is the amount of the same compound interest obligation. Hence anyone who has $1000 now could invest it at 5%, converted monthly, and have $1000(1 + \frac{5}{12}\%)^n$ dollars n periods from now. Of course if the n periods extend for 200 years, then most of us would actually prefer the $1000 now rather than the larger sum 200 years from now, but certainly not all of us would make this choice.

If money is worth $j\%$, compounded m times a year and $i = j/m$, then we say that A dollars due on one date and B dollars due n periods after (or before) this date are *equivalent* if

$$B = A(1 + i)^n \qquad (\text{or } B = A(1 + i)^{-n})$$

Thus, if A is equivalent to B then B is equivalent to A. Moreover A is equivalent to itself. Finally, as mentioned in the last section, if A is equivalent to B and B is equivalent to C, then A is equivalent to C. For $B = A(1 + i)^n$ and $C = B(1 + i)^m$ imply that

$$C = A(1 + i)^n(1 + i)^m = A(1 + i)^{m+n}$$

Mathematicians apply the term "equivalent" to a relation only when these three properties are satisfied.

The last property listed above (which is called the *transitive property*) does not hold for simple interest. Suppose we consider a fixed rate of 5%. Then $100 now is the same as $105 one year from now; $105 one year from now is the same as $110.25 two years from now; but $100 now is not the same as $110.25 two years from now. Thus it would not be proper to speak of equivalent payments at simple interest.

We deal only with *dated values*—i.e., every sum of money must have a date on which it is due. Assuming a fixed value for money, obligations on the same date may be added to get a single dated value equivalent to the original set. Obligations with different dates may be replaced by equivalent obligations with the same date and then added.

It is convenient to represent interest periods along a line with "0" denoting the present. Then m periods would mark one year. We can think of sliding dated values to the right by means of the formula $B = A(1 + i)^n$, or to the left by means of the formula, $B = A(1 + i)^{-n}$, to obtain equivalent payments.

The concept of equivalent payments is important. Many financial transactions consist of replacing one payment (or a set of payments) by an equivalent set. If someone buys a car or a house, then, he is likely to pay a certain amount down and then pay off the balance by a set of equal monthly payments. The set of monthly payments is equivalent to the balance due on the purchase date. How to obtain this type of equivalent set of payments (and the converse problem also) will be considered in the next section. We defer this because it requires some summation results that we do not yet have available.

In this section we consider some simpler problems. Let us illustrate by an example.

EXAMPLE 1. A debt of $1000 is due at the end of 10 years. Find an equivalent debt at the end of: (a) 2 years, and (b) 17 years, if money is worth 6%, $m = 4$.

Since an interest period is a quarter of a year, we use quarters on our line (Fig. 11.1).

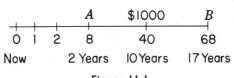

Figure 11.1

(a) Since A is $40 - 8 = 32$ periods before the $1000 payment, we see that $A = 1000(1 + 1\frac{1}{2}\%)^{-32} \approx 1000(.62099292) \approx \$620.99$.

(b) Since B is $68 - 40 = 28$ periods after the $1000 payment we see that $B = 1000(1 + 1\frac{1}{2}\%)^{28} \approx 1000(1.51722218) \approx \$1517.22$.

EXERCISES

1. If money is worth 5%, converted quarterly, then payments of $1000 at the end of $2\frac{1}{2}$ years, 3 years, $3\frac{3}{4}$ years, and $4\frac{1}{2}$ years may be equitably

replaced by:

(a) What single payment at the end of 4 years?
(b) What single payment at the end of $3\frac{1}{2}$ years?
(c) What single payment at the present time?
(d) What single payment at the end of $4\frac{1}{2}$ years?

2. What equal payments made at the end of 3 years and 4 years would equitably replace the system in Exercise 1.

11.6. ANNUITIES

House rent, payments on installment loans, so called "easy" payments on merchandise purchased, retirement pay, payments to the beneficiary of certain types of life insurance policies, and the interest payment on particular types of bonds usually result in a fixed sum paid regularly at a fixed time interval. Such a sequence of payments of fixed sums made at fixed periods of time is called an *annuity*. The word "annuity"

Figure 11.2

may have originally referred to annual payments but is now used for any time interval such as monthly, quarterly, semi-annual payments, etc. There are many types of annuities but we will consider only one type and therefore do not need to introduce terminology distinguishing among the various types. In particular we assume that the sequence of payments in an annuity is finite and the payment period (i.e., the interval between successive payments) coincides with the interest period (i.e., a year divided by the number of times per year that interest is converted). As before, we assume that interest is converted at least once per year.

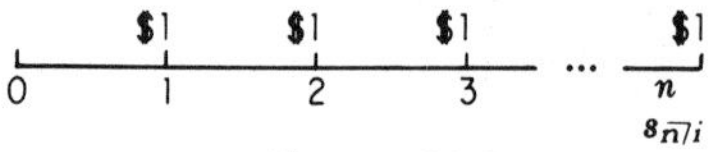

Since there are only a finite number of payments in an annuity we may denote this number by n. The amount of an annuity of n payments is the single payment at the end of n periods which is equivalent to the n payments of the annuity. Suppose that the value of money is $j\%$, converted m times per year, and that we wish to find the amount of an annuity of n payments of $1 each paid m times per year. Then $i = j/m$ will be the interest rate per payment period. We assume that the dates on which the $1 payments are made coincide with the dates on which interest is converted. The situation is illustrated in Fig 11.2, where 0 denotes the present time. Let $s_{\overline{n}|i}$ denote the amount of this annuity of $1 per period for n periods at an interest rate of i per period. By expressing each of the $1 payments as a dated value n periods from now we see that

$$s_{\overline{n}|i} = 1 + 1(1 + i) + 1(1 + i)^2 + \cdots + 1(1 + i)^{n-1}$$

On multiplying both sides by $1 + i$ we obtain

$$(1 + i)s_{\overline{n}|i} = (1 + i) + (1 + i)^2 + \cdots + (1 + i)^{n-1} + (1 + i)^n$$

On subtracting the first equation from the second we obtain

$$i \cdot s_{\overline{n}|i} = (1 + i)^n - 1$$

or

$$s_{\overline{n}|i} = \frac{(1 + i)^n - 1}{i}$$

If S denotes the amount of an annuity of R dollars per period for n periods at an interest rate of i per period then $S = Rs_{\overline{n}|i}$. Tables of approximations to $s_{\overline{n}|i}$ have been calculated for various values of n and i (see Table III). Recall that the amount in compound interest was obtained by finding a sequence of amounts at simple interest. Observe now that the amount of an annuity is obtained by finding a sequence of amounts at compound interest and then adding them together.

EXAMPLE 1. If \$100 is deposited at the end of each 6 months for 5 years in a bank which pays interest at the rate of 4%, compounded semi-annually, how much will then be in the account?

We see that $i = \frac{4}{2}\% = 2\%$ and that there are $5 \cdot 2 = 10$ payments.

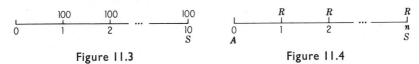

Figure 11.3   Figure 11.4

Figure 11.3 illustrates the situation. In this case $R = \$100$, $i = 2\%$, $n = 10$ so that $S = Rs_{\overline{n}|i} = 100s_{\overline{10}|2\%} \approx 100(10.94972100) \approx 1094.9721$ (using Table III). Hence $S \approx \$1094.97$. As a matter of fact $S = \$1094.97$, since this is correct to the nearest cent, but we will not always be able to ascertain whether or not we are correct to the nearest cent and so will be content with the approximation symbol.

The *present value* of an annuity of n payments is the single payment made one period before the first payment of the annuity which is equivalent to the n payments of the annuity. The situation is illustrated in Fig. 11.4, where A denotes the present value and S the amount of the annuity:

Thus

$$A = S(1 + i)^{-n} = Rs_{\overline{n}|i}(1 + i)^{-n}$$

$$= R\left[\frac{(1 + i)^n - 1}{i}\right](1 + i)^{-n}$$

$$= R\left[\frac{1 - (1 + i)^{-n}}{i}\right] = Ra_{\overline{n}|i}$$

The quantity

$$a_{\overline{n}|i} = \frac{1 - (1 + i)^{-n}}{i}$$

is approximated in Table IV.

EXAMPLE 2. What single cash deposit, made six months before the first $100 deposit in Example 1 would be equivalent to the ten $100 deposits in Example 1?

In other words, we are asked to find the present value of the annuity in Example 1. Thus

$$A = Ra_{\overline{n}|i} = 100a_{\overline{10}|2\%} \approx 100(8.98258501)$$
$$\approx 898.26 \quad \text{(using Table IV)}$$

or about $898.26.

Note that we could also have utilized the result of Example 1 and written

$$A = S(1 + i)^{-n} \approx S(1 + 2\%)^{-10} \approx (1094.9721)(.82034830)$$
$$\approx 898.25850078243$$

or about $898.26, but this is more work than the preceding method in this case.

EXAMPLE 3. Mr. Moe opens a savings account with $100 and then deposits $100 at the end of each 6 months for 5 years in a bank which pays interest at the rate of 4% converted semi-annually. How much does he then have in his account?

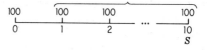

Figure 11.5

Let S denote the amount in his account at the end of 5 years. Then the last 10 payments (which are enclosed in a brace in Fig. 11.5) will amount to $Rs_{\overline{n}|i} = 100s_{\overline{10}|2\%} \approx \$1094.97$ as observed in Example 1. The first $100 payment will amount to

$$P(1 + i)^n = 100(1 + 2\%)^{10} \approx 100(1.21899442)$$

or about $121.90 on that date. Hence, the total in his account will be approximately $1094.97 + 121.90 \approx 1216.87$ or $1216.87.

A simpler way to work the problem would be to observe that we are asked to find the amount of an annuity of 11 payments. Thus $S = Ra_{\overline{n}|i} = 100s_{\overline{11}|2\%} \approx 100(12.16871542) \approx 1216.871542$ or about \$1216.87.

EXAMPLE 4. Mrs. Moe opens a savings account in the same bank and at the same time as her husband, who is mentioned in Example 3. Although she makes no further deposits, she has the same amount in the bank at the end of 5 years as her husband does. How much did she deposit?

Let us refer to Fig. 11.5 in Example 3. The value of the initial \$100 deposit at the time of the initial deposit is clearly \$100. The value of the remaining 10 \$100 deposits at the time of the initial deposit is approximately \$898.26 as computed in Example 2. Hence the desired deposit is approximately 100 + 898.26 or \$998.26.

EXERCISES

1. Mr. Moe will deposit \$100 at the end of each quarter in a fund that earns interest at the rate of 4%, converted quarterly. How much will be in the fund at the end of 10 years if at present: (a) he has nothing in the account; (b) he has \$1000 in the account?

2. At the present what single deposit by Mrs. Moe in the same fund as her husband in Exercise 1 will give her the same amount in her fund at the end of 10 years that her husband has in his in: Case 1 (a); Case 1 (b)?

3. A color television set can be purchased by paying \$100 down and then \$50 at the end of each month for one year. What is the equivalent cash price of the set if money is worth 6%, converted monthly?

4. Find the amount and present value of an annuity of 30 quarterly payments of \$500 each if interest is at 5%, converted quarterly.

5. The amount of an annuity payable quarterly for 16 years is \$1000. Find the present value if money is worth 6%, compounded quarterly.

6. The present value of an annuity payable monthly for 6 years is \$1000. Find the amount if money is worth 6%, compounded monthly.

7. A chair is purchased by paying \$10 down and then \$10 at the end of each month for 8 months. What is the equivalent cash price of the chair if money is worth 6%, converted monthly?

8. Mr. Moe deposits \$100 at the beginning of each quarter for one year in a fund that earns interest at the rate of 4%, converted quarterly. How much is in the fund at the end of the year? (Be careful on this one).

9. Mr. Moe, on his son's fifteenth birthday, wishes to deposit with a trust company a sum sufficient to provide him with regular monthly

payments of $100 for 4 years, the first payment coming one month after his seventeenth birthday (while he is attending college). How much should he deposit if interest is at 6 %, converted monthly?

11.7. "EASY PAYMENTS"

Almost everyone at some time or the other in his life either buys or sells something or repays or makes a loan on the installment plan. The conditions on the payments often conceal the true interest rate that is being paid. Many people shop for bargains in merchandise, yet surprisingly few people shop for bargains in money. Several years ago, two students each purchased a used car for approximately the same price at about the same time. One borrowed the money from a loan company and one borrowed the money from the bank; each repaid the loan in eighteen months. While discussing the matter just after the loans had been repaid, they discovered that one of them had paid several times as much interest as the other. This was quite obvious from the beginning since each had repaid his loan with 18 equal monthly installments, and the monthly payments of one were considerably higher than the monthly payments of the other. Yet, one of these purchasers had neglected to "shop" for money and had not observed that he was paying more.

To determine the actual interest rate charged on installment plans requires finding the interest rate on an annuity when the present value, term, and periodic payments are known. This can be approximated rather closely through use of logarithms, or a somewhat rougher approximation can be obtained with less effort through a process known as "linear interpolation." We will not discuss either method but will be content with upper and lower bounds for the rate which we can obtain directly from our tables.

> EXAMPLE 1. A loan of $1000 is repaid by 12 monthly installments of $100 each. What interest rate, converted monthly, is charged?
> We have $A = Ra_{\overline{n}|i}$, where $A = 1000$, $R = 100$, and $n = 12$. Thus $1000 = 100a_{\overline{12}|i}$ or $a_{\overline{12}|i} = \frac{1000}{100} = 10.0000$. Using the line in Table III where $n = 12$ we see that $a_{\overline{12}|2\frac{3}{4}\%} \approx 10.1042\ 0366$; whereas $a_{\overline{12}|3\%} \approx 9.9540\ 0399$. Since $a_{\overline{n}|i}$, for a fixed n, decreases steadily as i increases, we see that i is between $2\frac{3}{4}\%$ and 3%. Thus $j = 12i$ is between 33% and 36%, converted monthly.

Sometimes the installment price is placed on the merchandise and a discount is given for cash. If the cash discount listed matches the true cash price, then the interest rate charged for installment buying can be calculated.

> EXAMPLE 2. An article with a price tag of $100 can be paid for by payments of $9 at the end of each month for one year. If a 10 % discount is allowed

for cash (and this gives the actual cash price) what interest rate is charged
for time payments?

Since 10% of 100 = 10, we see that $A = 100 - 10 = 90$. As $n = 12$
and $R = 9$, we have that $90 = 9a_{\overline{12}|i}$ or $a_{\overline{12}|i} = 10.0000$. Then, as in
Example 1, we find that j is between 33% and 36% converted monthly.

Sometimes the price on a tag indicates the cash price and a "carrying"
charge is added for term payments.

EXAMPLE 3. An article has a tag indicating its cash price is $90. For term
payments a carrying charge of 20% is added, then the total is divided by
12 to give the monthly payments for one year. What interest charge is
made for term payments in this case?

As 20% of 90 = 18 and 90 + 18 = 108 and 108 ÷ 12 = 9, we see
that payments of $9 at the end of each month for one year will pay for
the article. As the cash price is $90, we have $A = 90$, $n = 12$, $R = 9$,
and $90 = 9a_{\overline{12}|i}$, or, as in Example 1, j is between 33% and 36%, converted
monthly.

In general if a dealer neither gives a cash discount nor adds on a carrying
charge, then it is advantageous to a customer to delay his payments as long
as possible. (This does *not* mean to delay payments beyond the deadline
stated by the contract.)

More often than not stores require some type of down payment with any
form of term payment. This is reflected in the exercises below, but was
omitted from the examples so as to make them easier to follow.

EXERCISES

1. An article whose cash price is $100 is sold for a down payment of $10
   followed by payments of $9 at the end of each month for one year.
   What interest rate, converted monthly, is charged?

2. An article with a price tag of $110 can be purchased by a down payment
   of $10 followed by payments of $9 at the end of each month for one
   year. If a 10% discount is allowed for cash (and this gives the actual
   cash price) what interest rate converted monthly is charged for term
   payments?

3. An article has a tag indicating that its cash price is $100. For term
   payments a carrying charge of 10% is added, a down payment of 10%
   of this total is required, and then the remaining balance is divided by
   12 to give the monthly payments for one year. What interest rate,
   converted monthly, is charged?

4. It is fairly common to see advertisements for cars, appliances, etc., to be paid for by so much down and so much a month without any mention of the number of months. Does this seem reasonable to you?

5. One student who found the situation in Exercise 4 reasonable was asked why. He replied that he would continue to make monthly payments until "the article was paid for." Is this a reasonable answer to you?

12

12.1. ENUMERATING POSSIBILITIES

Those persons who take time to reflect upon the fact realize that we dwell in a world of uncertainty rather than in one of certainty. This does not mean that we are trying to be purveyors of gloom but simply that there are few if any future events whose occurrence we can guarantee with incontrovertible logic. We deal in the realm of the probable and the improbable rather than in that of the certain.

Many of our everyday decisions are based on a rather vague feeling about probability. We say, "It probably won't rain," "For a dollar I have a good chance of winning a $3000 automobile," "I'd better accept this date with Tom; Dick probably won't ask me," "Surely we won't have another quiz in Math today," etc.

Moreover, probability, more precisely applied, plays a more serious and important part in our lives. We are tested, graded, passed or failed, given jobs or fired, all by applications (hopefully correct) of probability. A doctor when recommending medication or surgery bases his decision, perhaps, on a test which consists of using probability to determine the patient's condition from a small sample of blood. Many of the recent scientific achievements are dependent on careful applications of probability.

Thus there is a reason for us to give a precise meaning to the "probability" of an event occurring. We will do this, for the simplest case at least, in the following sections. In particular we will only consider the case where there is but a finite number

probability

of possibilities. It will be necessary for us to count the possibilities to utilize our definition of probability so that we will first consider methods of enumerating the various possibilities.

We may choose various lists of possibilities, but whatever category we choose must be exhaustive—i.e., the various types of possibilities that we list must be all-inclusive. The phrase *set of logical possibilities* is sometimes used to describe such a list. If $A_1, A_2, \ldots, A_n$ are sets no two of which have an element in common, and if $A = A_1 \cup A_2 \cup \cdots \cup A_n$, then we say that $A_1, \ldots, A_n$ forms a partition of A. The statement that a list of possibilities is exhaustive means that the subsets determined by our list of possibilities form a partition of the set of all possibilities of the particular type we are considering.

The list of exercises at the end of this section is designed to give practice in constructing exhaustive lists of possibilities and in counting the number of elements of various subsets of the set of all possibilities of some particular type.[1]

EXAMPLE 1. Given two urns: the first of which contains three black balls and one white ball; whereas the second urn contains two white balls and three black balls. Someone selects an urn at random and draws two balls in succession from it (without replacing a ball). What are the logical possibilities?

SOLUTION 1. We give a pictorial representation of one set of logical possibilities by means of a diagram called a *tree* (see Fig. 12.1). At the

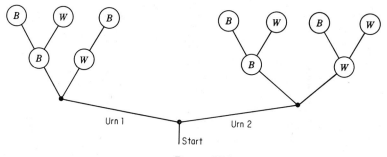

Figure 12.1

first stage he chooses either urn 1 or urn 2 so that there are two branches. At the second stage he chooses either a black ball (denoted by (B)) or a white ball (denoted by (W)) so there are two branches from each branch point. At the third stage there are one or two branches from each branch

---
[1] More extensive material of this type can be found in Kemeny, Snell, and Thompson, *Introduction to Finite Mathematics* (Englewood Cliffs, N.J.: Prentice-Hall, Inc., 1957).

point, depending on the possibilities. Note that all points at each stage lie on the same horizontal line.

SOLUTION 2. We choose another set of logical possibilities, one which would yield a finer analysis than is given by the set in Solution 1. However this analysis would be unnecessarily complicated for certain problems.

Once more we utilize a tree to illustrate the analysis (Fig. 12.2). We suppose the balls in each urn are distinguishable and denote them by numbers. There are seven logical possibilities in the list of Solution 1 and 32 logical possibilities in the list of Solution 2.

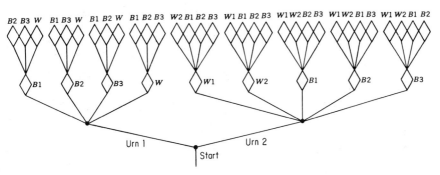

Figure 12.2

SOLUTION 3. In lieu of using a tree, we might use a table to form our list. Thus, for the logical possibilities in Solution 1 we could use the form below.

Case	Urn	First Ball	Second Ball
1	1	black	black
2	1	black	white
3	1	white	black
4	2	black	black
5	2	black	white
6	2	white	black
7	2	white	white

SOLUTION 4. We could also have formed a table corresponding to the set of logical possibilities in Solution 2.

Case	Urn	First Ball	Second Ball
1	1	black no. 1	black no. 2
2	1	black no. 1	black no. 3
3	1	black no. 1	white
4	1	black no. 2	black no. 1

(continued on next page)

Case	Urn	First Ball	Second Ball
5	1	black no. 2	black no. 3
6	1	black no. 2	white
7	1	black no. 3	black no. 1
8	1	black no. 3	black no. 2
9	1	black no. 3	white
10	1	white	black no. 1
11	1	white	black no. 2
12	1	white	black no. 3
13	2	white no. 1	white no. 2
14	2	white no. 1	black no. 1
15	2	white no. 1	black no. 2
16	2	white no. 1	black no. 3
17	2	white no. 2	white no. 1
18	2	white no. 2	black no. 1
19	2	white no. 2	black no. 2
20	2	white no. 2	black no. 3
21	2	black no. 1	white no. 1
22	2	black no. 1	white no. 2
23	2	black no. 1	black no. 2
24	2	black no. 1	black no. 3
25	2	black no. 2	white no. 1
26	2	black no. 2	white no. 2
27	2	black no. 2	black no. 1
28	2	black no. 2	black no. 3
29	2	black no. 3	white no. 1
30	2	black no. 3	white no. 2
31	2	black no. 3	black no. 1
32	2	black no. 3	black no. 2

EXERCISES

1. Extend Solution 1 to the case where three balls are drawn.

2. If an urn is chosen at random from two urns and then 2 balls are successively drawn (without replacement) from it, where one urn contains one black ball and two white balls, while the other contains one white ball and three black balls, list the logical possibilities. Utilize both a tree and a table.

3. Using your solution to Exercise 1, answer the following questions:

   (a) In how many cases do we draw one white ball?
   (b) In how many cases do we draw two white balls?

(c) In how many cases do we draw three white balls?

(d) In how many cases do we draw one black ball?

(e) In how many cases do we draw two black balls?

(f) In how many cases do we draw three black balls?

4. A man is contemplating the purchase of one of three pieces of property. Each piece of property will either increase, decrease, or remain the same in value. List the logical possibilities.

5. A man decides to select a novel from a group of five novels on the shelf. After selecting a novel he either reads it or does not read it. List the logical possibilities.

12.2. INTRODUCTION TO PERMUTATIONS AND COMBINATIONS

When you dash madly for the phone only to discover that it is a wrong number and someone who meant to dial 4713, dialed 4173, you might note philosophically that they permuted the digits 7 and 1. A *permutation* is an arrangement of objects where the order of the objects is important. For example, rearrangements of the letter in the word "DARE" might make it "READ" or "DEAR" or a combination not recognizable as an English word.

We are interested in calculating the number of permutations possible in certain situations.

EXAMPLE 1. Suppose a girl has three sweaters and four skirts. How many different outfits can she wear?

To do this problem we note that with sweater number 1 she can wear any of four skirts and that the same is true with sweaters numbers 2 and 3. Thus with any one of the three sweaters she can wear any one of the four skirts and so there are $3 \times 4 = 12$ outfits. We assume that the choice of the skirt is independent of the choice of the sweater.

Now suppose we have a row of four chairs and we consider the number of distinct ways in which four given people can sit in the chairs. Any one of the four can sit in the first chair. Thus the first chair can be filled in four ways. After someone is seated in the first chair, any one of the remaining three can sit in the second; then either of the remaining two in the third; and finally the remaining person in the last chair. Thus the chairs can be filled in

$$4 \times 3 \times 2 \times 1 = 24 \text{ ways.}$$

Note that this problem is not materially (except for the wear and tear on the furniture) changed if we are merely required to find the number of ways to put the four people in a line; or give them numbers 1 through 4; or select a president, vice president, secretary, and treasurer among them; or even find the number of ways we can count them (remember 1–1 correspondences introduced at the beginning of the book). This problem (in any of its forms) is called finding the number of *permutations of a set of four objects*.

If we are asked to determine in how many ways we can fill the four chairs from a group of eight people, we proceed in similar manner. We have a choice of eight people for the first chair, seven for the second, six for the third, and five for the fourth. Thus we can fill the seats in $8 \times 7 \times 6 \times 5 = 1680$ ways. This is called the number of *permutations of eight objects taken four at a time*.

Sometimes the order is not important as in the following problem.

> EXAMPLE 2. How many different sums of money can be made from a collection consisting of a silver dollar, a quarter, a dime, a nickel, and a penny, if two coins are used at a time?
>
> One way of doing this problem is to list all the possible sums and count them. Note that e.g., the sum of a quarter and a dime is the same as that of a dime and a quarter. This suggests the following way of doing the problem. We can pick the first coin in any of five ways and then the second in four ways, but this counts a dime and a quarter as different from a quarter and a dime so that the answer we get in this manner is exactly twice as large as it should be (we count each sum twice; once with one coin first and then with the other coin first). Hence we get the correct answer by dividing by two—i.e., $(5 \times 4) \div 2 = 10$. This problem illustrates finding the number of *combinations of five objects taken two at a time*.

Combinations are used when the order doesn't matter—permutations when the order is important.

EXERCISES

1. The Smith family consists of six people. It is decided that they shall take a bath in a different order each Saturday night (whether they need it or not). How long can this go on?

2. How many four digit telephone numbers are there? Can you do this problem an easy way? (It is permissible for the first digit to be 0.)

3. Mr. Jones has children named "Eenie," "Meenie," Minie," and "Henry" (his wife didn't want any Moe). In how many ways can he take two of his children to the show?

4. How many different sums of money can be made from the collection in Example 2 if we use three coins at a time?

5. How many four letter code words can be made from the letters in the word "CAREFUL."

It is possible to find more involved problems in permutations and combinations. We examine some of the possibilities.

EXAMPLE 3. In how many distinguishable ways can we permute the letters in the word "COWBOY"?

We can arrange the six letters in $6 \cdot 5 \cdot 4 \cdot 3 \cdot 2 \cdot 1 = 720$ ways, but we won't be able to distinguish between arrangements which have the "O's" interchanged, therefore, this number is twice as large as it should be and the correct answer is $\frac{720}{2} = 360$.

EXAMPLE 4. From a set of 10 distinguishable cards, four are taken. In how many different ways can this be done.

This problem asks for the number of combinations of 10 objects taken four at a time. The number of permutations of 10 objects taken four at a time is $10 \cdot 9 \cdot 8 \cdot 7$, but this number is too large. How much too large? Each collection of four objects gets counted, as a permutation, $4 \cdot 3 \cdot 2 \cdot 1$ times and we only want to count it once. Hence, the correct answer is $(10 \cdot 9 \cdot 8 \cdot 7)/(4 \cdot 3 \cdot 2 \cdot 1) = 210$.

We have considered procedures for counting the elements of certain sets. These procedures, or modifications of them, will suffice for the following exercises.

EXERCISES

1. In how many ways can a committee of four be selected from 5 freshmen, eight sophomores, four juniors, and six seniors, if it must contain one of each?

2. In how many ways can a party of 12 people be divided into three groups of seven, three, and two?

3. In how many ways can the letters in "Mississippi" be arranged?

4. How many different sums of money can be formed from a penny, nickel, dime, quarter, and half-dollar?

5. In how many ways can eight boys and 3 girls be seated in a row if the girls are not to be separated?

6. A committee of six is to be selected from eight men and seven women. In how many ways can it be done so as to contain three or fewer women?

7. Ima Scholar lives seven blocks east and five blocks south of school. In how many ways can she walk home without going out of her way?

8. How many radio stations can there be if each must have call letters consisting of three or four letters the first of which must be a "W" or "K".

9. In how many ways can the committee in Exercise 6 be selected so as to contain at least three women?

10. In how many ways can four books on the same subject be selected from six algebra and nine trigonometry books?

11. In how many ways can the letters in "Illinois" be arranged? Be careful with this exercise.

12.3. PERMUTATIONS

We were introduced to the notion of permutations in Section 12.2 and worked simple problems there without benefit of formulas. However, here we will consider a greater variety of problems and it will be desirable to formalize our procedures somewhat through application of certain basic results.

We introduce first a mathematical abbreviation. Many times in mathematics, and particularly in this chapter, it is necessary to talk about the number which results when the integers from 1 to n are multiplied. We indicate this number by writing n with an exclamation mark after it, viz., $n!$. This symbol is read "n factorial." Thus 5! indicates not surprise, but $1 \cdot 2 \cdot 3 \cdot 4 \cdot 5 = 120$. It is convenient to extend the definition and agree that $0! = 1$. It is also worthwhile to note that for any positive integer n we have $n! = n(n - 1)!$

Suppose that we have n distinct objects which we desire to arrange in a straight line. We may put any one of the n objects in the first spot, any one of the remaining $n - 1$ objects in the second spot, any one of the remaining $n - 2$ objects in the third spot, etc. Since our choice at each stage is independent of the previous choices there are $n(n - 1)(n - 2) \cdots 2 \cdot 1 = n!$ possible arrangements or *permutations* of n distinct objects. If we start with n objects, a of which are indistinguishable, while the remaining $n - a$ objects are distinct, then as just observed there are $n!$ possible arrangements. However these arrangements are not all distinguishable. In particular any rearrangement of the a indistinguishable objects will leave no visible change. As there are $a!$ such rearrangements then $n!/a!$ would be the total number of distinguishable permutations of n objects, a of which are indistinguishable and the remaining (if any) are distinguishable.

A similar argument shows that if we start with n objects, a_1 of which are alike, a_2 of which are alike but different from the a_1's, . . . , a_r of which are alike but different from the a_1's, a_2's, . . . , a_{r-1}'s, and the remaining (if any) are distinguishable and different from any of the a_i's for $i = 1, 2, . . . , r$, then the number of distinguishable permutations is $n!/(a_1! \, a_2! \ldots a_r!)$

Sometimes, we don't use all of the objects each time. Suppose we have n distinguishable objects and for some $r < n$ wish to arrange r of these n objects in a line. We could put any one of the n objects in the first spot, any one of the remaining $n - 1$ objects in the second spot, and so on down to any one of the remaining $n - (r - 1)$ objects in the rth spot. Since our choice at any stage is independent of the previous choices, there are

$$n(n - 1) \cdots [n - (r - 1)] = \frac{n!}{(n - r)!}$$

such arrangements. They are called the *permutations of n objects taken r at a time*. Note that although the right-hand side of the preceding equation might be simpler to remember, the left-hand side is simpler to calculate. The symbol P_r^n will be used to denote the number of permutations of n distinguishable objects taken r at a time.

> EXAMPLE 1. (a) How many permutations are there of the letters in the word *beaux*?
> (b) How many of these permutations begin and end with a vowel?
> (c) How many have consonants in the even places?
> (d) How many do not have *a* as their middle letter?

(a) $P_5^5 = 5! = 120$.

(b) There are three choices for the first vowel; two choices for the second vowel; and the intermediate places may be filled in 3! ways. Hence, there are (3)(2)(3!) or 36 such permutations since each such choice is independent of the preceding choices.

(c) The two even places may be filled in 2! ways while the three odd places may be filled in 3! ways. Since each choice is independent of the preceding choices there are (2!)(3!) or 12 such permutations.

(d) We observe that there is one way to choose *a* for the middle letter and 4! ways to fill in the remaining places to that there are (1)(4!) or 24 permutations with *a* as the middle letter. Since the total number of permutations is 120, there are 120 − 24 or 96 permutations without *a* as the middle letter.

> EXAMPLE 2. How many different signals can be made with three flags of different colors by displaying them one, two, or all at a time, with one above the other?
> Each distinguishable permutation of three objects taken r at a time will result in a distinguishable signal. Thus there are $P_1^3 + P_2^3 + P_3^3 = 3 + 6 + 6 = 15$ such signals.

EXERCISES

1. Use a tree to illustrate the permutations of the distinct letters a, b, c, d.

2. $P_r^n = n \cdot (n - 1) \cdots [n - (r - 1)]$ is expressed in this form as the product of how many factors? This is sometimes the easiest way to write an expression for P_r^n.

3. How many three-digit numerals are there (in base 10)?

4. Find the number of distinguishable permutations of the letters of the words "mathematics," "discipline," "onomatopoeia."

5. How many standard numerals denoting numbers less than 10,000 can be formed from the digits 1, 2, 3, 4, 5, 6, 7, without repetition? With repetition permitted?

6. A typesetter has to choose four type bars each consisting of $*$ or of $/$. How many of each should he choose to form a maximum number of different symbols?

7. How many ways can six pennies, four nickels, and three dimes be distributed among 13 children so that each may receive a coin?

8. In a certain village there are six streets running east and west and nine streets running north and south. How many ways can a person walk from the northwest corner to the southeast corner of the town, if he always takes the shortest path?

9. Find the sum of all numbers greater than 1000 whose standard numeral is formed from the digits 1, 2, 3, 4, without repeating any digit.

12.4. COMBINATIONS

Let A be a set consisting of n distinguishable objects and let B be a subset of A containing r elements. Then the elements of B are said to be a *combination* of the elements of A taken r at a time. The *number of combinations of n objects taken r at a time*, notation C_r^n, denotes the number of subsets of A which contain r elements.

Since changing the order in which the elements of a given set are listed does not change the set and since there are $r!$ arrangements of r objects, we see that $C_r^n = P_r^n/r!$ and hence

$$C_r^n = \frac{n(n - 1) \cdots [n - (r - 1)]}{r!} = \frac{n!}{r!\,(n - r)!}$$

Choosing any subset B with r elements automatically determines a subset of A

with $n - r$ elements, i.e., the set of elements of A which are not in B. Therefore $C_r^n = C_{n-r}^n$. Sometimes this relation simplifies computation.

EXAMPLE 1. A certain group of students contains seven boys and one girl. How many three-member committees can be selected that: (a) contain the girl as a member, (b) do not contain the girl as a member?

(a) The remaining two members of the committee can be selected from the seven boys in $C_2^7 = 21$ ways.

(b) The three members can be selected from the seven boys in $C_3^7 = 35$ ways. Note that every committee chosen from this particular group of students either contains the girl as a member or does not contain the girl as a member. Thus deduce that $C_3^8 = C_2^7 + C_3^7$.

EXAMPLE 2. How many distinguishable combinations of four letters can be selected from the letters of the word "Louisianian"?

We cannot mechanically use the formula for C_r^n since the letters involved $a, a, i, i, i, L, n, n, o, s, u$, are not all distinguishable. There are not four like letters and hence we may enumerate the logical possibilities as follows:

(1) Three like letters, the other different

(2) Two pairs of like letters

(3) Two like letters, the other two different

(4) Four different letters

An examination of our list of letters shows there is one set of three like letters. With the three i's we can take each of the remaining six distinguishable letters and thus there are six selections in case (1). There are three possibilities for case (2). We may select a pair of like letters in three ways and then select two of the remaining six distinct letters in C_2^6 ways, hence there are $3 \cdot C_2^6 = 45$ possibilities in case (3). There are $C_4^7 = 35$ possibilities in case (4). Thus the total number of possibilities is $6 + 3 + 45 + 35 = 89$.

EXAMPLE 3. How many distinguishable permutations of four letters can be arranged from letters of the word "Louisianian?"

The number of possible combinations in the various cases is given in the preceding example. We merely need to permute each of these in all possible ways. There are $6 \cdot \dfrac{4!}{3!} = 24$ permutations in case (1), $3 \cdot \dfrac{4!}{2!\,2!} = 18$ permutations in case (2), $45 \cdot \dfrac{4!}{2!} = 540$ permutations in case (3), and $35 \cdot 4! = 840$ permutations in case (4). Thus there are $24 + 18 + 540 + 840 = 1422$ permutations in all.

EXAMPLE 4. In how many ways may a dozen demitasse cups be distributed among three ladies so that each receives four cups?

We may select the cups for the first lady in C_4^{12} ways, for the second lady in C_4^8 ways, and for the third lady in C_4^4 ways. Since each choice is independent of the preceding choices there are $C_4^{12} \cdot C_4^8 \cdot C_4^4 = \dfrac{12!}{4!\,8!} \cdot \dfrac{8!}{4!\,4!} \cdot \dfrac{4!}{4!\,0!} = \dfrac{12!}{(4!)^3} = 34{,}650$ ways to distribute the cups.

Suppose the set $C = \{x, a_1, a_2, \ldots, a_n\}$. Then every subset of C which does not contain x is a subset of $\{a_1, a_2, \ldots, a_n\}$; while every subset of C which does contain x is a subset of $\{a_1, a_2, \ldots, a_n\}$ to which x has been adjoined. We see then that a set with $n + 1$ elements has twice as many subsets as a set with n elements. Now a set with one element has exactly two subsets, itself and the empty set, and $2 = 2^1$. Then a set with two elements will have $2 \cdot 2 = 2^2$ subsets, a set with three elements will have $2 \cdot 2^2 = 2^3$ subsets, and, in general, a set with n elements will have 2^n subsets or will have $2^n - 1$ nonempty subsets.

We observed in the first paragraph of this section that C_r^n denotes the number of subsets with r elements of a set with n elements. We extend this notation slightly and agree that $C_0^n = 1$, i.e., the number of subsets with 0 elements of a set with n elements is 1. (This subset, of course, is the vacuous set.) Then, as every subset of a set with n elements has either 0, 1, 2, $\ldots$, or n elements, we have $C_0^n + C_1^n + C_2^n + \cdots + C_n^n = 2^n$.

EXAMPLE 5. There are five novels on a shelf. In how many ways can a selection of one or more novels be made?

We have $C_1^5 + C_2^5 + C_3^5 + C_4^5 + C_5^5 = 2^5 - C_0^5 = 2^5 - 1 = 31$ ways.

EXERCISES

1. How many selections of fruit can be made from two apples, three bananas, and four oranges where at least one of each kind of fruit is selected?

2. In how many ways may five distinguishable objects be distributed to two persons so that each receives at least one object?

3. In how many ways may five distinguishable objects be distributed to two persons with no restrictions on the number each receives?

4. In how many ways may six (distinguishable) objects be put into three groups of two objects each?

5. Professor Doakes has ten students in his class, each of whom will

receive a grade of *A*, *B*, *C*, *D*, or *F*. How many possibilities are there for his grade list?

6. There are six different novels on a reading shelf with two copies of each novel, (a) In how many ways can one novel be selected? (b) In how many ways can one or more novels be selected?

12.5. PROBABILITY

The theory of probability has been greatly extended since its inception. Although early workers in this field were concerned primarily with relatively simple applications to games of chance, modern workers now deal with complex applications ranging from military and naval strategy, through quality control of manufacturing processes, to such problems as the location of Disneyland.

We will deal only with finite sets. We start with a universal set U whose elements form a set of all logical possibilities of the same type—usually the set of all possible outcomes of some experiment. We assume here, for the sake of simplicity, that each of these possible outcomes is equally likely to occur (although this assumption is not always valid). If a is any event with the property that for each possibility in U it can be determined whether or not a occurs, and if A is the subset of U consisting of those logical possibilities for which a does occur, then we define the *probability of the event* $a = c(A)/c(U)$.

For example, in rolling a die (a cube whose faces are numbered usually with the numerals

$$\circ, \; \overset{\circ}{\circ}, \; \overset{\circ}{\circ}\circ, \; \overset{\circ \; \circ}{\circ \; \circ}, \; \overset{\circ \; \circ}{\underset{\circ \; \circ}{\circ}}, \quad \text{and} \quad \overset{\circ\circ\circ}{\circ\circ\circ}$$

the plural of the word "die" is the more familiar "dice") the universal set U would consist of the six possible outcomes, i.e., the faces with 1, 2, 3, 4, 5, or 6 turned up. We have agreed that one face is as likely to come up as another. The event a that we roll an even number is one which occurs or fails to occur on each of our six logical possibilities. The set A, in this case, would consist of those times in which we roll a 2, 4, or 6. Then the probability of $a = c(A)/c(U) = 3/6 = 1/2$. Similarly the probability that we roll a seven is 0 while the probability we roll a number smaller than seven is 1. We note that the probability of an event will be 0, 1, or a number between 0 and 1. If b is the event that we roll a number >2, then, [for simplicity, let us denote the probability of b by $p(b)$] $p(b) = \frac{2}{3}$.

Let us denote by "ab" the event in which both events a and b occur and by "$a + b$" the event in which either event a or event b occurs. Then if A and B are the respective sets of possibilities for the events a and b, we see that $A \cap B$ is the set of possibilities for ab and $A \cup B$ is the set of possibilities for $a + b$.

If follows from our definition that

$$p(a + b) = \frac{c(A \cup B)}{c(U)} = \frac{c(A) + c(B) - c(A \cap B)}{c(U)}$$

$$= \frac{c(A)}{c(U)} + \frac{c(B)}{c(U)} - \frac{c(A \cap B)}{c(U)} = p(a) + p(b) - p(ab)$$

In the illustrative example above, ab would denote the event that we roll an even number greater than 2, so that $p(ab) = \frac{2}{6} = \frac{1}{3}$. Also $a + b$ would denote the event in which we either roll an even number or roll a number greater than 2 and $p(a + b) = \frac{5}{6}$. In this case we have verified the relation $p(a + b) = p(a) + p(b) - p(ab)$ since $\frac{5}{6} = \frac{1}{2} + \frac{2}{3} - \frac{1}{3}$.

EXAMPLE 1. An urn contains three red, four white, and five blue balls. If three balls are drawn (simultaneously) what is the probability all three are blue?
  In this case $c(U) = C_3^{12}$ and $c(A) = C_3^5$ where A is the set of possibilities in which all three balls are blue. Hence the probability is

$$\frac{C_3^5}{C_3^{12}} = \frac{1}{22}$$

EXAMPLE 2. What is the probability that if three dice are tossed simultaneously the total of the faces will be ten?
  There are $6 \cdot 6 \cdot 6 = 216$ logical possibilities. Not all of these look distinct if the dice are identical in appearance, but they are distinct possibilities (if we think of the three dice as consisting of one red die, one blue die, and one white die then all 216 possibilities would look distinct). The possibilities for a total of ten are 6, 3, 1; 6, 2, 2,; 5, 4, 1; 5, 3, 2; 4, 4, 2; and 4, 3, 3. Each of these can occur in 3! ways—the number of permutations of three objects. Hence there are 6(3!) = 36 ways to obtain a total of ten and so the probability is $\frac{36}{216} = \frac{1}{6}$.
  Would it make any difference in the probability of obtaining a total of ten in Example 2 if instead of tossing three dice simultaneously, three successive tosses of a single die were made?

EXERCISES

1. If two coins are flipped simultaneously what is the probability of obtaining: (a) two heads? (b) two tails? (c) one head and one tail?

2. What is the probability of throwing with two dice: (a) a total of seven? (b) a total of two? (c) a total of four?

3. What total is most likely to occur on one throw of two dice?

4. What is the probability that if three dice are tossed simultaneously the total of the faces will be seven?

5. What is the probability that two red balls and one white ball are drawn from the urn in Example 1?

6. If four cards are drawn from a standard deck of 52 cards, what is the probability that: (a) all four are aces? (b) exactly three are aces? (c) exactly two are aces? (d) exactly one is an ace? (e) at least one is an ace?

7. Mary states that a student will either pass or fail a course. Hence, she states, the probability of a student passing a course is $\frac{1}{2}$. Is she correct?

8. If two coins are tossed, what is the probability of having the same face up on both coins?

9. If two dice are tossed, what is the probability of having the same face up on both dice?

10. If three dice are tossed what is the probability that the total of the faces will be less than five?

11. In drawing two cards from a deck consisting of the 2, 3, 4, . . . , 10 of hearts what is the probability that: (a) the product of the numbers on the cards is even? (b) The product of the numbers is odd? Note that the sum of the answers to (a) and (b) must be 1.

12.6. CONDITIONAL PROBABILITY

Conditional probability is the probability that an event b will occur under the assumption that event a will occur; the notation is $p(b|a)$ (read "the probability of b given that a occurs"). If A is the set of possibilities for a and B the set of possibilities for b, then $A \cap B$ is the set of possibilities for the event ab. Thus $p(b|a) = c(A \cap B)/c(A)$ from the definition of probability, provided we assume $c(A) \neq 0$. But

$$\frac{c(A \cap B)}{c(A)} = \frac{c(A \cap B)/c(U)}{c(A)/c(U)} = \frac{p(ab)}{p(a)}$$

and so

(1) $p(b|a) \cdot p(a) = p(ab)$.

If a and b are unrelated then the occurrence or lack of occurrence of a will have no effect on the occurrence of b. The events a and b are called *independent* if $p(b|a) = p(b)$. In this case,

(2) $p(ab) = p(a) \cdot p(b)$, which is a very useful result.

EXAMPLE 1. A bag contains seven good and four bad light bulbs. Two bulbs are drawn successively (without replacement). What is the probability that both bulbs are good?

It is convenient to use a tree to illustrate the possibilities. (Fig. 12.3). Since there are seven good and four bad bulbs the probability of drawing a good bulb on the first draw is $\frac{7}{11}$ and of drawing a bad bulb is $\frac{4}{11}$. If a good bulb is drawn then there are six good and four bad bulbs remaining and so the probability of drawing a good bulb on the second draw is $\frac{6}{10}$ and of drawing a bad bulb is $\frac{4}{10}$. Similarly if a bad bulb is drawn first, then there are seven good and three bad bulbs remaining so that the probability of drawing a good bulb on the second draw is $\frac{7}{10}$ and of drawing a bad bulb is $\frac{3}{10}$.

Note that the sum of the probabilities of the branches emanating from each branch point is 1. Applying (1) shows that the probability of

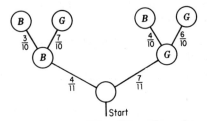

Figure 12.3

drawing two good bulbs would be $\frac{7}{11} \cdot \frac{6}{10} = \frac{21}{55}$. Similarly the probability of drawing two bad bulbs would be $\frac{4}{11} \cdot \frac{3}{10} = \frac{6}{55}$; the probability of drawing first a good and then a bad bulb would be $\frac{7}{11} \cdot \frac{4}{10} = \frac{14}{55}$; the probability of drawing first a bad and then a good bulb would be $\frac{4}{11} \cdot \frac{7}{10} = \frac{14}{55}$; and the probability of drawing one good and one bad bulb would be $\frac{14}{55} + \frac{14}{55} = \frac{28}{55}$.

This analysis of logical possibilities illustrates a case where there is *not* an equal probability for each of the possibilities. There are $11 \cdot 10 = 110$ ways in which we can choose first one bulb and then a second from a bag containing eleven bulbs. Each of these logical possibilities has an equal probability. There are $7 \cdot 6 = 42$ ways in which we can choose first one good bulb and then another. Thus the probability of drawing two good bulbs is $\frac{42}{110} = \frac{21}{55}$, which is in agreement with our previous result. However we must not assume that in every list of logical possibilities each possibility has an equal probability as we observed above.

EXAMPLE 2. Two cards are drawn successively from a deck without replacement. What is the probability that (i) both cards are red? (ii) The second card will be red?

Let a be the event that a red card is drawn on the first draw, b the event that a red card is drawn on the second draw, d the event that a black card is drawn on the first draw, and let A, B, and D be the respective sets of possibilities for these events.

(i) Then $p(ab) = p(a)p(b|a) = \frac{26}{52} \cdot \frac{25}{51} = \frac{25}{102}$.

(ii) The first card will be either black or red, but not both.

Hence $p(b) = p(ab + db) = p(ab) + p(db)$, since ab and db are mutually exclusive events. Now

$$p(db) = p(d) \cdot p(b|d) = \frac{26}{52} \cdot \frac{26}{51} = \frac{13}{51}$$

Hence

$$p(b) = \frac{25}{102} + \frac{13}{51} = \frac{1}{2}$$

How does the probability of drawing a red card on the second draw when the results of the first draw are not known (as in Example 2 (ii) above) compare with the probability of drawing a red card on the first draw?

EXERCISES

1. A die is thrown twice. What is the probability that the sum of the numbers on the upturned faces is greater than nine given that: (a) The first throw is a 5? (b) One of them is a 5?

2. A card is drawn from a deck of playing cards. What is the probability that it is an 8? Given that it is between 6 and 10, inclusive, what is the probability that it is an 8?

3. Miss Jones has 30 students in her class including 5 named Smith. She selects at random 2 students to go to the board. What is the probability that neither of these students is named Smith?

4. A card is drawn from a deck of playing cards.
   (a) What is the probability it is a queen?
   (b) What is the probability it is a heart?
   (c) What is the probability that both (a) and (b) occur?
   (d) Are events (a) and (b) independent?

5. A certain class contains 45 students, 13 color-blind students, 25 male students, and 4 color-blind female students. What is the probability that a male chosen at random is color-blind?

12.7. A SHORT DISCUSSION OF PROBABILITY

As we noted earlier, applications of probability occur in numerous places. Unfortunately the terms ordinarily used are often vague and sometimes even misused. We attempt here to clarify some misconceptions.

The study of probability was historically influenced by efforts to analyze various games of chance; these applications are very interesting (and sometimes rewarding). One may hear statements such as "the odds are six to five against making an 8 in a dice game." Let us examine what this statement means. First we have to define the term "odds." We say the odds of an event occurring are a to b (for a and b positive) if the probability of the occurrence of the event is $a/(a + b)$. In other words the odds that something will occur equals the number of possibilities of success divided by the number of possibilities of failure (assuming as usual that these are all equally likely), whereas probability is the number of possibilities of success divided by the total number of possibilities. Thus if a ball is chosen at random from an urn containing five white and three red balls the odds of choosing a white ball are five to three.

Now in the most common dice game played currently, if a player rolls an 8 (i.e., the total of the numbers appearing on the top faces of the dice is 8), he continues to roll until he either rolls another 8 (called "making his point") and wins, or rolls 7 and loses. Of the 36 different ways a pair of dice can land, five totals are eight (i.e., 6 and 2; 5 and 3; 4 and 4; 3 and 5; 2 and 6) while six totals are 7 (6 and 1; 5 and 2; 4 and 3; 3 and 4; 2 and 5; 1 and 6). Thus there are five ways of winning and six ways of losing (other totals which occur have no bearing and may be discarded). Thus the odds of 6 to 5 against making 8 are correct.

One also sees, in the newspaper perhaps, that Touchdown Teachers College is a 5 to 3 favorite to win a certain game. This should mean that Touchdown Teachers has about the same chance of winning as we had of drawing the white balls from the urn above. Actually it means that someone has estimated that these should be the odds (perhaps basing his judgment on how many people wish to bet on the respective teams) since the factors which influence the winning of football games are quite varied and impossible to assess properly.

Many times when one cannot make a mathematical determination of the probability of an event occurring, he resorts to an empirical or statistical determination. This means he examines what, he hopes, is a representative sample and asserts that the probability determined by the sample is a good approximation to the true probability.

For example, a seed grower who produces large quantities of seeds might select a representative sample of seeds by some random means and test them carefully, finding that 98 % of his test seeds germinate. He might then advertise that 98 % of his seeds will (probably) germinate. It is likely that he would omit the word "probably."

Another attempt, this time by insurance companies, to predict probabilities resulted in the American Experience Mortality Table. This table was prepared by taking 100,000 persons, 10 years old, and keeping a careful record of the deaths. Three of the original group lived to be 95 and none lived to be

96 years old. Thus one might say that the probability of a 10 year old living to be 95 years old is 3/100,000 and that the probability of a 10 year old living to be 96 years old is 0. Nonetheless, some persons do live to be 96 years old. This table also shows that 51,230 persons reached age 64 while 49,361 persons reached the age of 65 years. Thus one might say that the probability of a 10 year old reaching age 64 (or 65) is about $\frac{1}{2}$.

Predictions based on this table are actually too gloomy since it was prepared a number of years ago. Since then as our knowledge of nutrition, health, disease, and the like has grown, the average life span has lengthened. Thus, it became necessary to prepare more modern tables for use in those cases where one wanted actual outcomes to coincide rather closely with predicted outcomes.

Many times a baseball commentator will say something like "Line-drive Louie is a 300 hitter but he hasn't had a hit in his last eight times at bat so he's really due for a hit and will probably get one this time." To say Louie is a "300 hitter" means that his ratio of hits to times at bat is about $\frac{3}{10}$—or rather that it previously has been that. (Poor Louie may never get another hit.) But even if it were known that he is indeed a 300 hitter, his chances of getting a hit *at any time* are still 3 in 10.

The so-called "Law of Averages" is supposed to mean that if two results to an experiment are equally probable and the experiment is repeated a large number of times, then the ratio of the number of times one result occurs to the number of times the other occurs will be close to 1. It does not mean that number of times each occurs will be approximately the same.

Suppose we decide to toss a coin 2000 times. Before we start, we would expect to have about 1000 heads and 1000 tails in the 2000 tosses. We start tossing and 1000 tosses later, find that all tosses have been heads. We *do not* anticipate that the next 1000 tosses will be tails. Of the next 1000 tosses we expect 500 to be heads and 500 to be tails so that, at this stage, of the 2000 tosses we expect to have 1500 heads and 500 tails. Of course one should make sure that the coin is not a two-headed coin and that it is not weighted so that one side is more likely to be up than the other. But with a fair coin, our expectation for any future set of tosses will be about $\frac{1}{2}$ heads and $\frac{1}{2}$ tails.

We might point out that we defined probability as a ratio. We expect the ratio of the number of tosses on which heads come up to the total number of tosses to be about $\frac{1}{2}$. This does not necessarily mean that the number of times on which heads come up will be almost the same as the number of times on which tails come up. Observe that for any very large integer n, the ratio $(n + 1000)/2n$ is about $\frac{1}{2}$.

Thus in the example above, after n throws the ratio of the number of heads to the total number of tosses is about $\frac{1}{2}$. However at any stage there are about 1000 more tosses on which heads come up than there are tosses on which tails come up.

EXERCISES

1. If the probability that an event will occur is $\frac{2}{15}$, what are the odds that the event will occur?

2. If the odds of success are 8 to 5, what is the probability of failure?

3. What is the probability of throwing a 4 with a pair of dice before throwing a 7?

4. Name several examples where empirical methods are used to determine probabilities. Are they accurate?

13

13.1. INTRODUCTION

As is the case with many other words, the word "statistics" is used in several ways—a collection of numerical facts or data; data organized or tabulated in some manner; measurements made and conclusions drawn from certain data; techniques employed in collecting, organizing, and drawing conclusions about numerical data. At any rate statistics and its terminology permeate almost all aspects of our lives. When we are born, our birth is duly recorded along with various of our measurements. At least once every 10 years thereafter we (and some more measurements about us) are counted and tabulated again. In addition, we are asked which television program we are watching; we are asked whom we would vote for in the next election; we are inoculated with new vaccines for diseases, and later it is noted whether we contracted the diseases; temperatures and rainfalls are measured, recorded, and predicted; during the half-time intermission we are regaled with the statistics (where the word "statistics" is sometimes mispronounced) of the first half; and so on ad nauseum.

The science of statistics is profound and complicated and, as a result, is badly misunderstood by many people. It has been said that "you can prove anything by statistics"—this statement only means that it is possible to convince some people of erroneous conclusions by means of fallacious statistical arguments. In this very elementary introduction to statistics we would like to define and differentiate

statistics

237

between some of the terminology used as well as to give a general idea of some of the facets of the subject in an effort to eliminate some of the more common misconceptions.

The data one is given for a statistical analysis is usually referred to as a *distribution*. It consists of a set of numbers, each of which is a measurement. These numbers might be scores made by students on a certain test, or they might be ages, wages, blood pressures, etc. We wish to determine some *measure of central tendency*, i.e., some *average*. Types of averages that are considered in the succeeding sections are *arithmetic mean, geometric mean, median*, and *mode*. Further we would like to have some idea of how the measures are distributed with respect to the average—we would like a measure of the dispersion or deviation from the average. For this purpose we consider the *standard deviation* in a later section. For more advanced study we might also like to know whether there is a bunching of measures on one side of the average, whether the measures are exceptionally densely grouped at the average, or whether there are several places with exceptionally dense grouping. Such questions will not be considered in this book.

Sometimes one has two or more sets of data and wishes to determine whether there is a relationship existing between the two; i.e., one desires to measure the *correlation* between the given sets of data. For example, studies have been made of the scholastic attainments of high school students with cars and of those without cars. It has reputedly been concluded that there is a relationship and in particular that possession of a car is likely to adversely affect the grades of a high school student. We will not attempt to consider any of the various types of correlation measures.

The idea of a statistical inference is important. For example, suppose someone wanted to know the "average" height of college freshmen in the United States. If he selects and measures just one student from one school, he might measure an abnormally tall or short one. To minimize this possibility he selects several students at random (another term which needs careful definition), but again he might get a distorted sampling (e.g., the basketball team) or the students at this college might be different from those at other colleges in the country. His best test is to visit several campuses in different parts of the country, measure a number of students in each campus, and make his calculations from this data. His answer may still be inaccurate, but the larger the sampling he takes the greater the probability of accuracy. The size of the sample needed to give a certain probability of a certain accuracy is one of the problems of statistics. When the probability reaches some value, we may say we are statistically certain this is so or make a statistical inference that it is so.

Perhaps some remarks concerning our "gullibility quotient" are in order. Few of us would say that a paint brush painted a house; most of us would state that Mr. Jones painted his house with a brush. On the other hand, many of us seem to accept without question the statement that a giant electronic brain solved a problem. Yet, this machine can no more solve a problem than the paint brush can paint a house. The electronic brain does precisely what the programmer has directed—it is merely a faithful, mechanical robot. The reliability of the machine's results depends on the reliability of the men who solved and programmed the problem. Similarly, statistics alone are not very meaningful, but certain well-trained and intelligent persons can infer likelihoods from them. The probability of a statistical inference being valid might be high, but it is, nonetheless, merely a probability.

13.2. ARITHMETIC MEAN

The *arithmetic mean* of $x_1, x_2, \ldots, x_n$ is defined to be the sum of the numbers divided by n. We use the notation $\sum_{i=1}^{n} x_i$ to denote $x_1 + x_2 + \cdots + x_n$. Then $\sum_{i=1}^{n} x_i \Big/ n$ is the arithmetic mean of $x_1, \ldots, x_n$. (Sometimes positive numbers called "weights" and denoted by $f_1, \ldots, f_n$ are assigned to $x_1, \ldots, x_n$, respectively. Then the weighted arithmetic mean is $\sum_{i=1}^{n} f_i x_i \Big/ \sum_{i=1}^{n} f_i$. We will not consider weighted averages in this text.)

The definition of arithmetic mean gives a method of computing it.

EXAMPLE 1. On a certain mathematics test, scores of 95, 90, 85, 80, 78, 78, 78, 76, 76, 74, 72, 67, 67, 65, 60, 53, 36, and 30 were made. Find the arithmetic mean.

We usually would arrange the scores in order of magnitude, if they were not so arranged. If we let $x_1 = 95$, $x_2 = 90$, $\ldots$, $x_{18} = 30$, then

$$\sum_{i=1}^{18} x_i \Big/ 18 = 70.$$

An alternative procedure, which is preferable since it reduces the size of the numbers we deal with, is as follows. We estimate an average, then record the difference of each x_i from the average, and finally calculate a correction which applied to our estimated average gives the true average. We observe that 76 and 74 are the two middle terms and that the measures on the lower side seem to differ by more than the measures on the upper side. Hence, we decide to take a number which is a little smaller than 74, say 72. Then we record the differences $x_1 - 72 = 23$, $x_2 - 72 = 18$, $\ldots$, $x_{18} - 72 = -42$, and find that $\sum_{i=1}^{18} (x_i - 72) = -36$. Then $-36/18 = -2$ and applying the correction of -2 to 72 gives 70 as the average. This correction is valid because

$$72 + \frac{\sum_{i=1}^{18}(x_i - 72)}{18} = 72 + \frac{\sum_{i=1}^{18} x_i}{18} + \frac{18(-72)}{18}$$

$$= 72 + \frac{\sum_{i=1}^{18} x_i}{18} - 72 = \frac{\sum_{i=1}^{18} x_i}{18}$$

These results may be given in a table.

i	x_i	$x_i - a$	
1	95	23	
2	90	18	
3	85	13	
4	80	8	
5	78	6	
6	78	6	
7	78	6	
8	76	4	
9	76	4	
10	74	2	
11	72	0	$+90$
12	67	-5	
13	67	-5	
14	65	-7	
15	60	-12	
16	53	-19	
17	36	-36	
18	30	-42	-126
Total	1260		-36

An arbitrary choice of $a = 72$ is made. The end result will be the same regardless of the choice of a, but the closer a is to the true average, the smaller will be the numbers we deal with. Then

$$\frac{\sum_{i=1}^{18} x_i}{18} = \frac{1260}{18} = 70$$

for the first method. For the second method we see that

$$\frac{\sum_{i=1}^{18}(x_i - a)}{18} = \frac{-36}{18} = -2 \quad \text{and} \quad 72 + (-2) = 70.$$

Formerly, when work had to be done by hand or with the aid of only a desk calculator, it was customary to group the work in classes to simplify the computation. This introduced errors and hence made the results even less reliable. With the advent of the modern digital computer, such methods have become outmoded. A modern computer can easily compute the arithmetic mean, of say, 3678 such scores as we have been considering and give the result rounded correct to the nearest hundredth. If we use classes to "compute" the arithmetic mean, then our result might be incorrect by many units.

Let us illustrate this method by applying it to Example 1. One must first decide on the *length* of a *class interval* which, with test scores, will frequently be taken as 10; we will take as our class intervals 91–100, 81–90, etc. We then *tally* the results by making a tally mark in the appropriate class interval for each x_i in that class interval. The number of such tally marks in each class interval is called the *frequency*. The midpoint of the class interval is called the *class mark*. We tabulate the data as follows. Then we replace the given

class	tally	frequency	class mark
91–100	//	2	95.5
81–90	//	2	85.5
71–80	//// //	7	75.5
61–70	////	4	65.5
51–60	/	1	55.5
41–50		0	45.5
31–40	//	2	35.5

distribution by one with two scores of 95.5, two scores of 85.5, seven scores of 75.5, four scores of 65.5, one score of 55.5, and two scores of 35.5. The average of this new distribution we calculate as 70.5. One would use such a method as this only if his computations were too lengthy to be handled on a desk calculator and he did not have access to a computer. It is not intended that any of the exercises be worked by this method.

Terms such as average salary, average grade, average weight, and average height usually refer to the arithmetic mean.

EXERCISES

1. Find the arithmetic mean of the following distributions. In case the mean is not an integer, also obtain a decimal approximation rounded to the nearest hundredth.
    (a) 60, 66, 81, 58, 77, 73, 72, 61, 64, 88, 81, 52, 69, 75, 79, 78, 62, 64.
    (b) 35, 47, 52, 68, 68, 68, 69, 72, 75, 76, 76, 78, 92, 93, 95.
    (c) 35, 35, 35, 35, 48, 48, 48, 56, 56, 56, 56, 78, 78, 78, 78, 78.
    (d) 35.34, 47.34, 52.34, 65.34, 65.34, 72.34, 79.34, 80.34, 82.34, 83.34.

2. How does your answer in Exercise 1(a) compare with the answer to Example 1? Is the distribution in Exercise 1(a) similar to the distribution in Example 1? Why or why not?

3. Did you work Exercise 1(c) by a method slightly different from that you used on parts (a) and (b)? Why?

4. In Exercise 1(d) did you choose an estimated average such as 65.34 so as to make all of your differences integers?

13.3. MEDIAN, MODE, PERCENTILE, AND QUARTILE

A given distribution can be linearly ordered by arranging in order of magnitude. Then the middle term, if the number of measures is odd; or the arithmetic mean of the middle two terms, if the number of measures is even is defined as the *median* of the distribution. Thus the median of the distribution in Example 1 of the preceding paragraph is the arithmetic mean of 76 and 74, or 75. It isn't much of a task to linearly order the distributions in the exercises in this book but to linearly order a distribution of four or five thousand measures would be quite difficult. However, the modern digital computer can accomplish the task without much effort from us. A comparison of the median with the arithmetic mean gives some information on the dispersion of the distribution.

For our purposes we will define the *mode* (or *modes*) of a distribution with some values repeated as the value (or values) which occur a maximum number of times. If no values in the distribution are repeated then we say that the distribution has no mode. Thus 78 is the mode in the distribution of Example 1. The statement that the average American family has three children probably means that more families have three children than another number of children.

This definition of mode is satisfactory for the exercises in this book and will work well for such purposes as distribution of scores made on classroom tests. However, if one has a distribution of a large number of values which are quite close together, this definition might be useless. Thus one might have a distribution consisting of 4000 distinct measures each of which is expressed to four decimal places. Then by our definition there would be no mode. And yet there might be several values around which large numbers of values are densely clustered. Such values might be regarded as modes in more advanced work.

So far we have considered the arithmetic mean, the median, and the mode as averages. There are other types of averages which are used when the measures of central tendency we have considered so far prove to be unreliable. We are familiar with various indexes—a cost-of-living index, a wholesale price index, a food price index, etc. Some of these indexes are expressed as relative to a base year and some are expressed as relative to the preceding year. Consider the two tables below which represent the salary of a man.

	Table 1			Table 2	
Year	Index		Year	Index	
1961	2		1961	2	
1962	3		1962	3	
1963	4		1963	4	

The index in Table 1 is expressed relative to the base year 1960—i.e., the index for a given year is the ratio of the man's salary for that year to his salary in 1960. The arithmetic mean of the indexes is 3, and if he had received three times his base (i.e., 1960) salary for each of the years 1961, 1962, and 1963, then, his total salary for this period would have been exactly the same as he actually received.

The index in Table 2, is expressed as relative to the preceding year—i.e., the index for any given year is the ratio of his salary for that year to his salary for the preceding year. Since his salary for 1963 is 24 times his salary for 1960, the arithmetic mean is not a reliable average. If $x_1, x_2, \ldots, x_n$ are positive numbers, then their geometric mean is defined to be $\sqrt[n]{x_1 \cdot x_2 \cdots x_n}$, i.e., the nth root of their product. It can be shown that this gives a reasonable average for Table 2. We will not utilize the geometric mean; we merely mention it in passing (however, see Exercise 5).

Suppose we are given a distribution, say, $x_1, x_2, \ldots, x_n$. For any number y let j be the number of x_i such that $x_i < y$ and let k be the number of x_i such that $x_i > y$. Then y is called a 30 percentile if $j/n \leq \frac{30}{100}$ and $k/n \leq \frac{70}{100}$; it is called a 45 percentile if $j/n \leq \frac{45}{100}$ and $k/n \leq \frac{55}{100}$; etc.

For example, suppose we are given the distribution $x_1, \ldots, x_{20}$ where x_1 through $x_5 = 42$, x_6 through $x_8 = 48$, x_9 through $x_{14} = 64$, x_{15} through $x_{17} = 71$, $x_{18} = x_{19} = 81$, and $x_{20} = 95$. Then $y = 43$ is a 20 percentile since $j = 5$, $k = 15$, and $n = 20$. Note that 44, 45, 46, and 47 are also 20 percentiles.

If y is a 50 percentile then $j/n \leq \frac{50}{100}$ and $k/n \leq \frac{50}{100}$. If n is odd, then y must be the median. If n is even, then a 50 percentile is not unique, but the median is certainly a 50 percentile. One's percentile score on a test gives an accurate comparison of his results on the test compared with others who took the test—it tells him how many of the others he is above and how many he is below. Standardized tests are sometimes prepared by giving a test to a large number of students. Then percentiles are calculated—suppose a score of 42 is a 27 percentile. Then when Joe Doakes goes to enter college and is given this same test and makes a score of 42, his score is said to be a 27 percentile. This does not directly compare Joe with those who took the test with him, but rather it compares him with that group to which the test was given originally. It says, roughly speaking, that Joe scored higher than 27% of those who took the test and scored lower than 73% of those who took the test. The term *0 percentile* is sometimes used to denote the minimum possible score on a test and the term *100 percentile* to denote the maximum possible score.

In a similar fashion y is called the *first* (or *lower*) *quartile* if $j/n \leq \frac{1}{4}$ and $k/n \leq \frac{3}{4}$; and the *third* (or *upper*) *quartile* if $j/n \leq \frac{3}{4}$ and $k/n \leq \frac{1}{4}$. As before the *zero quartile* would usually denote the minimum possible score and the *fourth quartile*, the maximum possible score.

In a similar fashion *tertile*, *decile*, and, in fact, *m-tile* can be defined, and the interested reader should have little difficulty in defining these terms.

EXERCISES

1. Find, where possible, the median and the mode for each distribution in Exercise 1, Section 13.2.

2. Find 20, 40, 60, and 80 percentiles for each distribution in Exercise 1, Section 13.2.

3. Find the lower quartile, the median, and the upper quartile for each of the distributions in Exercise 1, Section 13.2.

4. Is a 25 percentile a lower quartile? Is a 75 percentile an upper quartile? Is there a percentile which can be used interchangeably with the second quartile (defined analogously with the first and third quartiles)?

5. (a) Find the arithmetic and geometric means of each of the following pairs of numbers (i) 9 and 4, (ii) 1 and 16, (iii) 9 and 11.
   (b) What do you conclude?
   (c) Can you prove your conclusion?

6. Joe states that the median is the value below which 50% of the measures lie and that it is, therefore, the 50 percentile.
   (a) If 75% of the measures lie below a certain value is it true that 50% of the measures lie below this value?
   (b) Are there distributions in which there exists a 50 percentile that is not the median?
   (c) Are there distributions in which the only 50 percentile is the median?
   (d) Are there distributions in which 50% of the measures do not lie below the median?

7. Mary states that a given percentile is the value which divides the range of a set of data into two parts such that a given percentage of the measures lies below this value. Is Mary correct?

I3.4. STANDARD DEVIATION

As indicated before it is desirable to have some idea of the scattering of a distribution with respect to the arithmetic mean. The two distributions, 5, 5, 5, 6, 6, 6, 6, 6, 6, 7, 7, 7, and 1, 1, 3, 3, 4, 6, 8, 9, 9, 11, 11, have the same arithmetic mean and yet the second distribution is more scattered than the first. We will give one such measure of dispersion in this section.

Although the sum of the differences from the arithmetic mean is 0 in each of the distributions above, the sum of the squares of the differences is not 0. The square root of the arithmetic mean of these squares is defined to be the *standard deviation* of the distribution and is denoted by σ. In other words, the standard deviation of $x_1, x_2, \ldots, x_n$ is

$$\sigma = \sqrt{\frac{\sum_{i=1}^{n}(x_i - \bar{x})^2}{n}}$$

where $\bar{x}$ is the arithmetic mean of $x_1, \ldots, x_n$.

We calculate the standard deviations for the distributions given above. Note that in each case the arithmetic mean $\bar{x}$ is 6, so we make the following tabulations.

x_i	$x_i - \bar{x}$	$(x_i - \bar{x})^2$	x_i	$x_i - \bar{x}$	$(x_i - \bar{x})^2$
5	−1	1	1	−5	25
5	−1	1	1	−5	25
5	−1	1	3	−3	9
6	0	0	3	−3	9
6	0	0	4	−2	4
6	0	0	6	0	0
6	0	0	8	2	4
6	0	0	9	3	9
7	1	1	9	3	9
7	1	1	11	5	25
7	1	1	11	5	25

For case I we have

$$\sigma = \sqrt{\frac{\Sigma(x_i - \bar{x})^2}{n}} = \sqrt{\frac{6}{11}} \approx \sqrt{.5454} \approx .74$$

For case II we have

$$\sigma = \sqrt{\frac{\Sigma(x_i - \bar{x})^2}{n}} = \sqrt{\frac{144}{11}} \approx \sqrt{13.09} \approx 3.60$$

We notice that in the second case the standard deviation is about five times the standard deviation in the first case. Thus the definition gives a means of calculating the standard deviation. Although this method is quite satisfactory to use with a computer, we will usually find it easier when working by hand to continue with the short cut utilized in computing the arithmetic mean. You will recall that to obtain the arithmetic mean $\bar{x}$ of the distribution $x_1, \ldots, x_n$, we estimated the arithmetic mean as, say, θ, and then calculated a correction δ with the property that $\bar{x} = \theta + \delta$. In fact

$$\delta = \frac{\displaystyle\sum_{i=1}^{n}(x_i - \theta)}{n} = \frac{\Sigma x_i}{n} - \frac{\Sigma \theta}{n} = \bar{x} - \theta$$

Now

$$(x_i - \bar{x})^2 = [(x_i - \theta) - \delta]^2 = (x_i - \theta)^2 - 2\delta(x_i - \theta) + \delta^2$$

so

$$\sigma^2 = \frac{\Sigma(x_i - \bar{x})^2}{n} = \frac{\Sigma[(x_i - \theta)^2 - 2\delta(x_i - \theta) + \delta^2]}{n}$$

$$= \frac{\Sigma(x_i - \theta)^2}{n} - 2\delta\frac{\Sigma(x_i - \theta)}{n} + \frac{\Sigma\delta^2}{n}$$

$$= \frac{\Sigma(x_i - \theta)^2}{n} - 2\delta^2 + \delta^2 = \frac{\Sigma(x_i - \theta)^2}{n} - \delta^2$$

Then

$$\sigma = \sqrt{\frac{\Sigma(x_i - \theta)^2}{n} - \delta^2}$$

Since we have already calculated the differences $(x_i - \theta)$ and the correction δ in computing $\bar{x}$, the additional labor to obtain the standard deviation σ, is not excessive for distributions such as are encountered in the exercises.

EXAMPLE 1. Approximate the standard deviation of the distribution 45, 52, 53, 68, 73, 75, 79, 84, 85, 90. It looks as though the mean will be about 70, so, we take $\theta = 70$. Then we prepare the following table.

x_i	$x_i - \theta$	$(x_i - \theta)^2$
45	-25	625
52	-18	324
53	-17	289
68	-2	4
	-62	
73	3	9
75	5	25
79	9	81
84	14	196
85	15	225
90	20	400
	66	2178

$$\Sigma(x_i - \theta) = 4 \qquad = \Sigma(x_i - \theta)^2$$
$$\sigma = \tfrac{4}{10} = .4$$

Take $\theta = 70$. Then

$$\delta = \frac{\Sigma(x_i - \theta)}{n} = .4 \quad \text{and} \quad \bar{x} = \theta + \delta = 70.4$$

Now

$$\frac{\Sigma(x_i - \theta)^2}{n} = \frac{2178}{10} = 217.8 \quad \text{and} \quad \delta^2 = .16$$

Hence

$$\sigma^2 = 217.8 - .16 = 217.64 \quad \text{and} \quad \sigma = \sqrt{217.64} \approx 14.75$$

Distributions that follow a certain pattern of dispersion are called *normal distributions* (we will not attempt to define these). In such distributions the median, mode, and arithmetic mean all coincide. Moreover nearly 68 % of the measures differ from the arithmetic mean by less than one standard deviation, nearly 96 % of the measures differ from the arithmetic mean by less than two standard deviations, and nearly 100 % of the measures differ from the arithmetic mean by less than three standard deviations.

Suppose a number of nails are placed on a panel (as in Fig. 13.1) so that a marble dropping through hits one nail after another. Then the marble must pass on one side or the other of each nail that it hits and presumably which side it goes on is a random choice. Thus if a large number of marbles are dropped one at a time at the place marked by an arrow through the array of nails and then collected in containers at the bottom of the panel, one might expect to find a normal distribution of marbles in the containers. This may be experimentally verified.

The assumption might be made that if the entire population of a country takes a test, then the distribution of grades should be a normal distribution (this assumption may or may not be reasonable). Since the sample in an elementary school is biased, e.g., all feeble-minded are excluded—one would expect the grades to run higher than in a normal distribution and so would have to make some allowances for this. Perhaps additional allowances would have to be made for a more highly selected group such as college students. Such assumptions can be made and then grades on tests can be determined by use of the standard deviation—this is what many students mean when they ask their professors if "they grade on a curve."

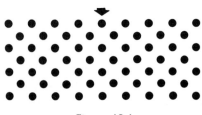

Figure 13.1

EXERCISES

1. Approximate the standard deviation for each of the distributions given in Section 13.2, Exercise 1.

2. Conduct some experiment to get a distribution of at least 20 entries. For example, you might throw some coins and count the number of "heads" that turn up each time—or give a test to some people and record their scores—or record the heights (weights or shoe size) of a number of your acquaintances, etc. Find the standard deviation of your distribution. If your distribution does not seem "normal," explain why.

14

14.1. COORDINATE SYSTEMS

A *one-dimensional coordinate system* means a coordinate system for a line. We have previously agreed that there is a 1–1 correspondence between the points on a line and the real numbers. Those 1–1 correspondences which preserve the natural order of the real numbers are called *coordinate systems*. We can think of placing a long ruler (one of the same length as the line) along a line. If every real number (in its natural order) is on the ruler and we match this real number with the point on the line it determines, then we have a one-dimensional coordinate system. For this reason some persons refer to the existence of these particular types of 1–1 correspondences between the real numbers and the points on a line as the "ruler axiom." It is clear that if we slide the ruler to one side or pick it up and place it down in the opposite direction that we will obtain other coordinate systems. In other words, we may choose any point as the point to match with 0 (this point is called the *origin*) and then choose either direction as the one to place our positive numbers (which we call the *positive direction*). The unique real number associated with a given point by any coordinate system is called the *coordinate* of the point.

In the chapter on Geometry we noted that it was possible to use distances to define coordinate systems or conversely to use coordinate systems to define distance. We adopt the latter alternative here and, accordingly, if the point P has coordinate x and the point Q has coordinate y then the

functions and graphs

distance from P to Q is defined as $|x - y|$. Now P and Q will have different coordinates in different systems but the distance from P to Q in any given system is the same as the distance from Q to P and this distance is positive whenever Q and P are distinct points. The distance between P and Q will sometimes change with the coordinate system. We can stretch or contract our ruler; if we do so in a uniform manner, we sometimes refer to this as a change of scale. If P and Q are distinct points then we may assign any real number x as the coordinate of P and any real number $y \neq x$ as the coordinate of Q, and then the coordinate of every other point on the line through P and Q is uniquely determined. We would usually accomplish this by assigning 0 to P and 1 to Q.

A *two-dimensional coordinate* system refers to a coordinate system for a plane. The type of two-dimensional coordinate system we will use is usually called a *Cartesian* coordinate system in honor of its inventor René Descartes,

Figure 14.1

the French mathematician. The system is obtained by starting with a pair of perpendicular lines in a plane and then putting a one-dimensional coordinate system on each of the lines so that the origin of each system is at the point of intersection of the lines and so that the same "ruler" may be used to give coordinates on both lines. We sometimes refer to this property by saying both lines have the same unit of length. Starting with a given pair of perpendicular lines (one horizontal and the other vertical) gives the four possibilities shown in Fig. 14.1. By a suitable rotation of the page together with looking either at the front or through the back of the sheet, any one of these can be made to appear the same as any other. Thus we can regard them as differing only by the orientation of the observer with respect to the plane and so we will not attempt to distinguish between them. We will ordinarily use the form of the first mentioned possibility.

If x is the coordinate of a point P on the horizontal axis and y is the coordinate of a point Q on the vertical axis, then a vertical line through P will intersect a horizontal line through Q in a unique point R of the plane. We will use as the coordinates of R the ordered pair of real numbers (x, y). The situation is shown in Fig. 14.2. Observe that the point with coordinates $(2, 3)$ is different from the point with coordinates $(3, 2)$ (see Fig. 14.3), which is why we refer to the coordinates as an "ordered" pair.

We assume that there is a 1–1 correspondence between points in the plane, and these ordered pairs of real numbers we have called the coordinates of the points.

As mentioned earlier the particular two-dimensional coordinate system given here is called a Cartesian coordinate system. By choosing different units of length for the horizontal and vertical lines or by choosing distinct intersecting lines which are not vertical we could, in a similar fashion, obtain a two-dimensional coordinate system which is not Cartesian. We will not consider such systems here.

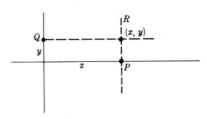

Figure 14.2

We can think of a two-dimensional coordinate system as being obtained by combining two one-dimensional coordinate systems. This topic will be pursued further in the next section.

In a right triangle the side which meets the interior of the right angle is called the *hypotenuse* of the right triangle, and the other two sides are called

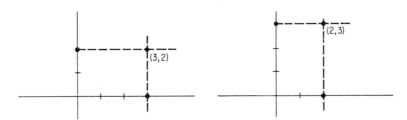

Figure 14.3

legs of the triangle. In Fig. 14.4 $\overline{AC}$ is the hypotenuse, and $\overline{AB}$ and $\overline{BC}$ are the legs. It can be shown that the square of the length of the hypotenuse is equal to the sum of the squares of the lengths of the legs. This result is perhaps the best known result of high school geometry and is known as the Pythagorean theorem. For an indication of a proof of this theorem see Exercise 14, page 253.

Now suppose P has coordinates (x_1, y_1) and Q has coordinates (x_2, y_2), and we wish to find the distance from P to Q which we denote by d. If we let T be the point with coordinates (x_1, y_2), then P, Q and T are vertices of a right triangle (Fig. 14.5). Since the distance from Q to T is $|x_1 - x_2|$ and the distance from T to P is $|y_1 - y_2|$, the Pythagorean theorem gives us $d^2 = (|x_1 - x_2|)^2 + (|y_1 - y_2|)^2 = (x_1 - x_2)^2 + (y_1 - y_2)^2$ or

$$d = \sqrt{(x_1 - x_2)^2 + (y_1 - y_2)^2}$$

Use of this formula will enable us to find the distance between two points whose coordinates are given. Sometimes, for brevity, one says "the point (a, d)" when he means "the point whose coordinates are (a, d)." We usually

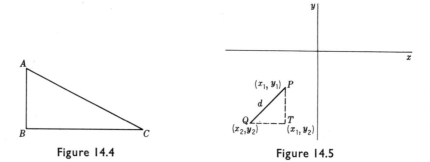

Figure 14.4   Figure 14.5

call the horizontal axis the *x-axis* and the vertical axis the *y-axis*. In accordance with this convention we have placed an "x" and a "y" on the respective axes.

EXERCISES

1. Set up a Cartesian coordinate system and plot (i.e., locate approximately by the intersection of a horizontal and a vertical line) the points whose coordinates are $(2, 3)$, $(3, 2)$, $(-1, 2)$, $(-1, -2)$, $(1, 2)$, $(0, 0)$, $(\frac{3}{2}, -\frac{1}{2})$, and (π, π).

2. Given the point P with coordinates $(2, 3)$ and the point Q with coordinates $(-2, 3)$. Find coordinates of points R and S such that P, Q, R, and S are vertices of a rectangle; of a square. Give the coordinate of a point T such that P, Q, and T are vertices of an isosceles triangle.

3. Discuss the degree of uniqueness of each of your answers to Exercise 2.

4. Given the point P with coordinates $(2, 3)$ and the point Q with coordinates $(1, 3)$. Find the coordinates of points R and S such that P, Q, R, and S are vertices of a rectangle; of a square.

5. Given the point P with coordinates $(2, 3)$ and the point Q with coordinates $(1, 3)$. Find the coordinates of a point R such that P, Q, and R are vertices of an isosceles triangle.

6. Discuss the degree of uniqueness of each of your answers to Exercise 5.

7. Find the distance from each point in Exercise 1 to each of the other points in the Exercise.

8. Consider the set composed of all points on a line parallel to the x-axis and two units above it. Describe the set composed of the coordinates of these points.

9. Consider the set composed of all points on a line parallel to the x-axis and two units below it. Describe the set composed of the coordinates of these points.

10. Describe the set of coordinates of the points on a line parallel to the y-axis and two units to the right of it.

11. Describe the set of coordinates of the points on a line parallel to the y-axis and two units to the left of it.

12. Describe the set of coordinates of the points to the left of the y-axis and below the x-axis.

13. Describe the set of coordinates of the points on the axes.

14. Given a right triangle whose sides have lengths of a, b, and c with c the length of the hypotenuse. Construct a square whose sides are $a + b$ in length. Insert copies of the triangle in the corners of this square as illustrated in Fig. 14.6. Show that the polygon formed by the four hypotenuses is a square; then use the fact that the area enclosed by the large square equals the sum of the areas enclosed by the triangles and the smaller square to deduce the Pythagorean theorem.

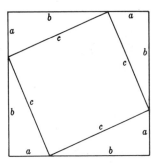

Figure 14.6

15. Describe the set of coordinates of the points which lie on a circle of radius 3 with center at the origin.

14.2. CARTESIAN PRODUCTS OF SETS; FUNCTIONS

If A and B are sets then by the *Cartesian product of A and B* (notation $A \times B$) we will mean the set of all ordered pairs (a, b) where $a \in A$ and $b \in B$. We refer to a as the *first element* of the ordered pair and to b as the *second element* of the ordered pair. For example, if M is the set of all men and W is the set of all women then $M \times W$ would consist of all possible couples that could be formed by pairing each man with each woman. Note that the elements of $M \times W$ are couples—a couple is an entity. Suppose that $A = \{\text{apple, pear}\}$ and $B = \{\text{banana, peach, orange}\}$. Then

$$A \times B = \{(\text{apple, banana}), (\text{apple, peach}), (\text{apple, orange}),$$
$$(\text{pear, banana}), (\text{pear, peach}), (\text{pear, orange})\}$$

We see that the elements of $A \times B$ can be arranged in a rectangular array where there are as many rows as there are elements in A, and there are as many columns as there are elements in B. We observe that no two ordered pairs in $A \times B$ will be the same. Hence it follows that $c(A \times B) = c(A) \cdot c(B)$, i.e., for finite sets A and B the cardinal number of $A \times B$ is the product of the cardinal number of A by the cardinal number of B. Consider the similarity between the rectangular array we obtained earlier, $\circ\,\circ \cdot {}^{\circ}_{\circ}{}^{}_{\circ} = {}^{\circ\circ\circ}_{\circ\circ\circ}$, and the rectangular array for $A \times B$ above. We could have defined multiplication of cardinal numbers in this fashion. However the concepts of finite sets, Cartesian products of sets, cardinal numbers of sets, and the fact we can replace any set by an equivalent set all combine to form a rather confusing muddle for the beginner. These difficulties do not present themselves at such an early stage with piles of stones and so we have utilized the "piles of stones" approach to counting numbers.

The sets A and B are termed *disjoint* if they have no element in common and *equivalent* (or *matching*) if they can be placed into 1–1 correspondence with each other.

Observe that if R is the set of real numbers then $R \times R$ is the set of coordinates of the points in a plane.

Most of us have a fairly good intuitive concept of the meaning of the word "function." We say that the rate of growth of crops is a function of the fertility of the soil and of the amount of rainfall; what we weigh is a function of the amount and the type of food we eat as well as the exercise we take, our metabolic rate, and other factors. We tend to think of one quantity as being a function of another quantity if it is dependent on this other quantity in some sense. But our intuitive concept of function is rather vague and difficult to make precise. At least it is only within the last century that a satisfactory definition of a function has been given. In the following paragraph we will define a function from set A onto set B.

Suppose we are given two sets, A and B, and a correspondence f between the elements of A and B with the properties that: (1) with every element $a \in A$, f associates a unique element of B [denoted by $f(a)$] and (2) every element of B is associated by f with at least one element of A. Then the totality of the set A, the set B, and the correspondence f, is called a *function* from A *onto* B.

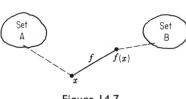

Figure 14.7

Moreover A is termed the *domain* of the function and B is termed the *range* of the function. We will sometimes say the function f is *defined* on A. If $B \subset C$ then we also say that f is a *function* from A *into* C.

We can think of set A as being in one bag, set B as being in another bag, and the correspondence f as strings connecting the elements of A with those of

B. Then if we remove an element, x, from the A bag (Fig. 14.7) a unique element, $f(x)$, will be pulled from the B bag by means of the string attached to the element, x, in A.

Suppose that A is the set of integers and f is the correspondence which associates with each integer the square of that integer. Then

$$2 \xrightarrow{f} f(2) = 4$$

$$3 \xrightarrow{f} f(3) = 9$$

$$-2 \xrightarrow{f} f(-2) = 4$$

$$0 \xrightarrow{f} f(0) = 0$$

$$x \xrightarrow{f} f(x) = x^2$$

We see that $B = \{0, 1, 4, 9, \ldots\}$ is the set consisting of all squares of integers. We note also that $f(2) = f(-2)$ in this case.

EXERCISES

1. If $A = \{1, 2\}$, $B = \{1, 2, 3\}$, and $C = \{3, 4, 5\}$ find $A \times B$ and $A \times C$. Is $A \times B$ equivalent to $A \times C$?

2. If A is equivalent to A' and B is equivalent to B' is $A \times B$ equivalent to $A' \times B'$?

3. If $A = \{1, 2\}$ and $B = \{3, 4, 5\}$ find six functions from A onto a subset of B (different functions might be onto different subsets of B).

4. Does there exist a function from $R \times R$ onto R where R is the set of real numbers?

5. If $A = \{$integers from 1 thru 10$\}$ and $B = \{$letters in the English alphabet$\}$, what is $A \times B$? What is $B \times A$? Can you find a 1–1 correspondence between them?

6. Can you find a function from A onto B (where A and B are as in Exercise 3 above)? From B onto A? How many?

7. Consider the function defined on the real numbers by $f(x)$ is the largest integer less than x. What is the range of this function? What is $f(2\frac{1}{2})$, $f(5.1), f(\frac{27}{8}), f(3), f(-1.2), f(-3), f(\pi)$?

8. For the function in Exercise 7 describe the set of all x such that $f(x) = 2$. Is $[f(\frac{3}{2})]^2 = f([\frac{3}{2}]^2)$?

9. Tell what is wrong with each of the following purported functions:
   (a) f is defined on R by $f(x)$ is the closest integer to x.
   (b) f is defined on the rationals by $f(a/b) = a$.
   (c) $f(x) = x + 2$.
   (d) f is defined from R onto R by $f(x) = x^2$.

14.3. GRAPHS

Let f be a function from A onto B. By the *graph* of f is meant the set of ordered pairs $(x, f(x))$ where x is in the domain A and $f(x)$ is the unique element in the range B associated with x by f. If A and B are each subsets of the set of real numbers, then the graph of f consists of a set of coordinates of points in the plane. If we can plot these points as in Section 14.1 then we will have a pictorial representation of the graph of the function or a sketch of the graph. Of course the picture of the graph is not the graph. Why? If one is told to draw George Washington he will understand he is supposed to draw a picture of George Washington and he realizes that the picture he draws is not George Washington. Similarly, if one is told to graph a certain function, he should realize he is supposed to draw a picture of the graph of the function and that the picture he draws of the graph is not the graph.

In this section we will only consider functions from A onto B where A and B are both subsets of the real numbers. We will, where possible, draw a picture of the graph of a function by plotting as accurately as is convenient the points of the graph. This might be a reasonable procedure for a graph which contains only a finite number of elements, but it would certainly be impossible for a graph with an infinite number of elements. In this case, one plots a few points and then connects them in a fashion which will be reasonable for the graph in question. How well the sketch conveys the concept of the graph depends on both the artistic and mathematical abilities of the person drawing the sketch. We will not attempt to sketch any very complicated graphs.

An element in the graph of a function is an ordered pair of real numbers $(x, f(x))$ where x is in the domain and $f(x)$ is in the range of the function. The coordinate of a point in the plane is an ordered pair of real numbers (x, y). Thus when we interpret the elements of the graph as coordinates of points in the plane we are implying $y = f(x)$. In the remainder of this section we will use y and $f(x)$ interchangeably.

Let us consider the function from $A = \{1, 2, 3, 4\}$ onto $B = \{1, 3, -4, 5\}$ with correspondence f such that $f(1) = 1, f(2) = 3, f(3) = -4$, and $f(4) = 5$.

EXAMPLE 1. Sketch the graph of the preceding function (see Fig. 14.8). The graph $= \{(1, 1), (2, 3), (3, -4), (4, 5)\}$, and the points which have these ordered pairs as coordinates are plotted on the Cartesian axes in Fig. 14.8.

Now let us consider the function from the reals onto the reals with correspondence f such that $f(x) = x$ (or $y = x$). Then the graph consists of all points (x, y) such that $y = x$.

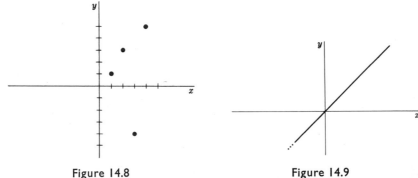

Figure 14.8   Figure 14.9

EXAMPLE 2. Sketch the graph of the preceding function. We wish to sketch the set of points whose coordinates are (x, y) where $x = y$. This states that, starting at the origin, we get to the point in question by traveling a horizontal distance x and then traveling the same vertical distance x. But these directions would always take us to a point on a line through the origin which determines an angle of measure 45° with the x-axis. On the other hand, every point on this line has a coordinate of the form (x, y) where $x = y$. Thus we would like to plot all points on this line, however, the line is too long to plot on our paper. Hence, we draw a line segment and utilize some dots to show that the sketch is incomplete (Fig. 14.9).

Sometimes it is understood that the domain is the set of all real numbers. Thus, for the example above, we might simply have been directed to sketch the graph of $y = x$. We would understand that the correspondence f is given by $f(x) = x$ and that the domain is the set of real numbers. The range is then uniquely determined whether or not we explicitly state it. We will follow this convention in the next set of exercises.

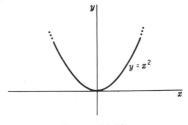

Figure 14.10

As an additional example let us consider the function from the reals onto the nonnegative reals with correspondence given by $f(x) = x^2$. A sketch of its graph, obtained by more advanced methods, is shown in Fig. 14.10. More generally, if $k \neq 0$ is a real number, then the graph of a function from the reals to the nonnegative reals if $k > 0$ or to the nonpositive reals if $k < 0$ with correspondence given by $f(x) = kx^2$ is called a *parabola*. Sketches of the graph for $k = \frac{1}{10}$ and $k = 10$ are shown in Fig. 14.11.

A body falling freely under the influence of the earth's gravitational attraction (and without any air resistance) will travel in a parabolic path.

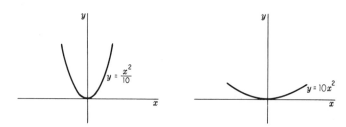

Figure 14.11

Parabolas appear in many places. For example, the uppermost cables on suspension bridges tend to be pulled into parabolic form by the load of the bridge. Flashlight reflectors, automobile headlight reflectors, and many radar antennas have a parabolic cross section.

EXERCISES

1. Plot the set of all points whose coordinates are of the form $(3, y)$ where y is a real number. Have you drawn a picture of the graph of a function?

2. Sketch the graph of $y = -x$.

3. Sketch the graph of $y = 3x$.

4. Sketch the graph of $y = -3x$.

5. Sketch the graph of $y = x$.

6. Sketch the graph of $y \le x$ (i.e., the set of all points with coordinates (x, y) for which it is true that $y \le x$).

7. Sketch the graph of $y \ge x$.

8. On the same coordinate system sketch the graphs of $y = x^2$, $y = 2x^2$, and $y = -x^2$.

9. On the same coordinate system sketch the graphs of $y = x$, $y = x^2$, $y = x^3$, and $y = x^4$.

10. For what value of k will the graph of $y = kx^2$ contain the point $(-2, 3)$?

15

15.1. INTRODUCTION

In comparatively recent times there has arisen a branch of mathematics called linear programming. It concerns itself with finding (in some sense) the "best" solutions to problems. The problems encountered arise in such fields as the military or industrial as well as in social sciences. The kinds of problems studied include such diversity as finding the best organization of machines and personnel on a farm or in some business, maximizing profits in blending gasolines with various octane ratings, and determining the best strategy in various games.

The methods we describe here will permit us to solve most of the usual problems, but may require somewhat more computation than more advanced techniques. The more advanced techniques are largely beyond the scope of this book. The interested reader, however, is referred to the book of Kemeny, Mirkil, Snell, and Thompson on *Finite Mathematical Structures* for an introduction to the subject.

15.2. LINEAR FORMS IN THE PLANE

An expression such as $c_1x + c_2y$ where at least one of $c_1, c_2 \neq 0$, is called a *linear form*. We consider here the problem of finding maximum values of a given linear form when x and y are restricted by the requirement that (x, y) be the coordinates of a point in a particular plane set called the *feasible set*. (Of course one or both of these maximum and minimum values may

linear programming

fail to exist.) The permissible values of x and y are called *feasible* values. The feasible values of x and y which yield a maximum or minimum value of the given form are called *optimal values*. Sometimes, instead of only determining maximum or minimum values of the form we wish to find all optimal values.

If $c_1 = 0$, then the form reduces to $c_2 y$ where $c_2 \neq 0$. Suppose that among the feasible values of x and y there is both a maximum and a minimum value of y. Then these values of y clearly determine the maximum and minimum values of the form. Which yields the maximum and which yields the minimum will depend on whether $c_2 > 0$ or $c_2 < 0$. If, e.g., $c_2 < 0$ and there is no maximum y, then the form does not attain a minimum value. Similar remarks pertain when $c_2 = 0$.

Hence let us suppose that $c_1 \neq 0$ and $c_2 \neq 0$ and set $c_1 x + c_2 y = k$. We observed in the preceding chapter that the (picture of the) graph of this function is a straight line—this accounts for the word "linear" in the title of this section. Distinct values of k yield distinct lines so that we may obtain infinitely many lines in this fashion. Our task is to select, from among the feasible values of x and y, the optimal values. These will then determine the maximum and minimum values of k. Note that the infinite family of lines we are considering has the property that any two lines in the set are parallel, and that the values of k increase as we move from line to line in one direction and decrease in the other direction. This observation gives us a method for solving our problem. We simply "slide" the line $c_1 x + c_2 y = k$ parallel to itself until it first "touches" the feasible set and then slide it more until it last touches the feasible set. The "first" and "last" feasible values are optimal values which give the maximum and minimum values of k (but not necessarily respectively).

EXAMPLE 1. Let the feasible set be the set of points on or inside the square with vertices $(1, 2)$, $(2, 1)$, $(3, 2)$, and $(2, 3)$. Let $c_1 = c_2 = 1$ so that the form is $x + y$ (see Fig. 15.1). We see that the coordinates of points along the segment from $(1, 2)$ to $(2, 1)$ yield optimal values of x, y which make $k = 3$. This is the minimum value attained by the form on the feasible set. The coordinates of points along the segment from $(2, 3)$ to $(3, 2)$ yield optimal values of x, y which make $k = 5$. This is the maximum value attained by the form on the feasible set.

If the feasible set is the interior of the square in the example above, then the given form (or any other one) would have neither a maximum nor a minimum value. This statement will be proved in the next section. A similar remark would apply to the interior of any set. Hence we normally take as feasible sets only sets which contain all their boundary points.

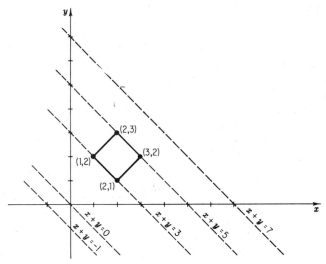

Figure 15.1

If the feasible set is the disk with center at $(1, 1)$ and radius 1, then the finding of optimal values would require more technique. We consider only feasible sets whose boundary is a union of lines, rays, or segments.

EXERCISES

1. Sketch the lines $3x - 2y = k$ for $k = 0, 1, 2, -1, -2$.

2. For the feasible set given in Example 1 find optimal values and maximum and minimum values of the given linear forms.

   (a) $-x - y$ (e) $2x - y$
   (b) $x - y$ (f) $-2x - y$
   (c) $-x + y$ (g) $-2x + y$
   (d) $2x + y$

3. If the feasible set is all points on, or interior to, the triangle with vertices $(0, 0)$, $(2, 0)$ and $(1, 1)$, find the optimal values of the given linear forms.

   (a) x (b) y (c) $x + y$ (d) $x - y$ (e) $2x - 3y$ (f) $5x + y$

4. The feasible set $= \{(x, y) \mid x \geq 1 \text{ and } y \geq 1\}$. Find the optimal values of the given linear forms

   (a) $2x + 3y$ (b) $2x - 3y$

15.3. POLYGONAL SETS

In this section we want to go a little deeper into some of the concepts introduced in the last section by providing more careful definitions and laying the foundations for an analytical approach to finding optimal values.

We need to define what is meant by a neighborhood of a point. As is often the case in mathematics, we take a word which in ordinary language has a sort of vague general meaning and we make it more precise. Let (x_0, y_0) be the coordinates of a point in the plane and let ϵ be a positive number. Consider the set of all points with coordinates (x, y) such that $|x - x_0| < \epsilon$ and $|y - y_0| < \epsilon$, i.e., the set of points whose x and y coordinates differ respectively from x_0 and y_0 by less than ϵ. This set of points is said to constitute a *neighborhood* of the point with coordinates (x_0, y_0). If a different ϵ is chosen, a different neighborhood of the point results. It is easily seen (Fig. 15.2) that the neighborhoods are the interiors of squares with the given point as center.

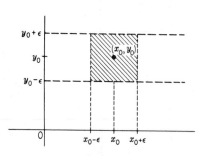

Figure 15.2

Now if F is some plane set and $b \in F$, then b is called an *interior point* of F if there is some neighborhood of b which is contained in F. A *boundary point* c of F is a point with the property that every neighborhood of c contains points of F and points not in F. A set F is called *closed* if every boundary point of F belongs to F. A set F is called *open* if every point in F is an interior point of F.

We would now like to prove the assertion that optimal values of a linear form cannot occur at interior points of the feasible set.

Suppose therefore we consider the linear form $c_1 x + c_2 y$, where at least one of c_1 and c_2 is different from zero, and let b be a point in the interior of the feasible set with coordinates (x_1, y_1). Since b is an interior point, there is some $\epsilon > 0$, such that if $|x - x_1| < \epsilon$ and $|y - y_1| < \epsilon$, then the point whose coordinates are (x, y) is in the feasible set. Suppose now that $c_1 \neq 0$, and, for definiteness, that $c_1 > 0$. If we let $x_2 = x_1 + (\epsilon/2)$ and $y_2 = y_1$, then (x_2, y_2) is in the feasible set and

$$c_1 x_2 + c_2 y_2 = c_1 \left(x_1 + \frac{\epsilon}{2} \right) + c_2 y_1$$

$$= (c_1 x_1 + c_2 y_1) + c_1 \frac{\epsilon}{2} > c_1 x_1 + c_2 y_1$$

Thus we see that the form is not maximal at (x_1, y_1). Similarly if we let $x_3 = x_1 - (\epsilon/2)$ and $y_3 = y_1$, then (x_3, y_3) is in the feasible set and

$$c_1 x_3 + c_2 y_3 < c_1 x_1 + c_2 y_1$$

therefore, the form is not minimal at $(x_1 y_1)$. If $c_1 < 0$

$$c_1 x_2 + c_2 y_2 < c_1 x_1 + c_2 y_1 < c_1 x_3 + c_2 y_3$$

so again (x_1, y_1) will not be optimal. Finally, if $c_1 = 0$, then $c_2 \neq 0$, and letting

$$(x_2, y_2) = \left(x_1, y_1 + \frac{\epsilon}{2} \right) \quad \text{and} \quad (x_3, y_3) = \left(x_1, y_1 - \frac{\epsilon}{2} \right)$$

will show (x_1, y_1) is not optimal. It follows that optimal values occur only at boundary points, and thus it is convenient to consider those feasible sets which contain their boundary points —in other words, we require that the feasible set be closed.

Another restriction which generally occurs in most applications and lends itself to easier analysis is convexity. A set is defined to be *convex* if, whenever two distinct points p and q belong to the set, the line segment with p and q as end points is contained in the set. It is easy to establish that the intersection of convex sets is convex (see Exercise 3).

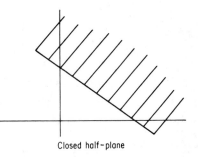

Closed half-plane

Figure 15.3

We have noted that the graph of an equation of the form $ax + by = d$ is a line. This line will separate the plane into two components. It can be shown that the coordinates of the points in one of these components will satisfy the inequality $ax + by < d$, whereas those of the points in the other component will satisfy the inequality $ax + by > d$ (see Exercise 10). Each of these components is called an *open half plane*. If the points on the line (which separates the plane) are included with those of one of the components, the resulting set is called a *closed half plane* (Fig. 15.3). The coordinates of a closed half plane satisfy an inequality of the form

$$ax + by \leq d \quad (\text{or } ax + by \geq d)$$

It can be shown that a half plane (open or closed), is convex, and, hence, that the intersections of half planes are convex. We will in general be interested in feasible sets which are the intersections of a finite number of closed half planes. Such sets are called *convex polygonal sets* and have the property that their boundaries are the union of a finite number of lines, rays, and line segments. A *vertex* of a convex polygonal set is a point that is the intersection of two of the rays or line segments which comprise the boundary. We note that a convex polygon (with interior) is a special case of a convex polygonal set.

A point in a convex polygonal set must be in all of the half planes whose intersection is the set; hence, the coordinates of such a point must satisfy all of the inequalities associated with the half planes. On the other hand it is clear that any point whose coordinates do satisfy each of the inequalities must be in each of the half planes and therefore in their intersection. In other words, we may describe a convex polygonal set as the graph of the simultaneous system

$$\begin{cases} a_1x + b_1y \le d_1 \\ a_2x + b_2y \le d_2 \\ \quad \cdot \\ \quad \cdot \\ \quad \cdot \\ a_kx + b_ky \le d_k \end{cases}$$

Moreover the interior of the set above could be described as the graph of the simultaneous system

$$\begin{cases} a_1x + b_1y < d_1 \\ a_2x + b_2y < d_2 \\ \quad \cdot \\ \quad \cdot \\ \quad \cdot \\ a_kx + b_ky < d_k \end{cases}$$

It is possible to add a further restriction to our feasible sets, namely boundedness. A set is called *bounded* if there is a neighborhood of the origin which contains the set. If a convex polygonal set is bounded, it becomes a convex polygon (with interior) and it can be shown that any form will have optimal values on such a feasible set. However in some applications the feasible sets are not bounded, and therefore we will not impose this restriction in general.

EXERCISES

1. Complete the proof that a form cannot achieve its optimal values at an interior point of the feasible set for the case $c_1 = 0$ but $c_2 \ne 0$.

2. Give three examples of convex sets, and three of nonconvex sets.

3. Prove that the intersection of convex sets is convex.

4. Is the union of convex sets convex?

5. Sketch the graph of the half plane $3x + 2y \leq 6$.

6. Can you write the inequality for the half plane in Exercise 5 in the form $ax + by \geq d$?

7. Sketch the graph of the system

$$\begin{cases} x + 2y < 3 \\ x - 3y < 4 \\ 2x + y < 5 \end{cases}$$

8. Write a simultaneous system whose graph is the first quadrant.

9. Can you find a nonempty set for which there are no boundary points? One with no interior points?

10. (a) From consideration of the graph show that the open half plane above the line $2x + 3y = 6$ satisfies the inequality $2x + 3y > 6$, whereas the open half plane below the line satisfies the inequality $2x + 3y < 6$.
(b) Show that the open half plane above the line $2x - 3y = 6$ satisfies the inequality $2x - 3y < 6$, whereas the open half plane below the line satisfies the inequality $2x - 3y > 6$.

15.4. LINEAR PROGRAMMING

We have noticed earlier that optimal points cannot occur in the interior of the feasible set. In general we can say even more about where the optimal points do occur. If the feasible set is bounded and, hence, a convex polygon with interior; it is intuitively clear that the "first" and "last" of the parallel lines to touch the feasible set ($c_1x + c_2y = j$ and $c_1x + c_2y = n$ in Fig. 15.4) normally do so at vertices of the set. (In case the "sliding" line is parallel to one of the edges of the feasible set, then, each point of that edge is an optimal point and the form is constant on that edge. However, it is still true that the vertices on that edge are optimal points.) Thus it is possible to find the optimal points by examining the values of the linear form at the vertices.

Before continuing we wish to give analytic arguments for the intuitive discussion above. Suppose $ax + by = d$ is the equation of any line; then, if $b \neq 0$ (i.e., the line is not vertical), we may rewrite the equation as $y = d/b - ax/b$. Now the value of the form $c_1x + c_2y$ at any point (x_1, y_1) on the given line is

$$c_1 x_1 + c_2 y_1 = c_1 x_1 + c_2 \left(\frac{d}{b} - \frac{a x_1}{b} \right)$$

$$= c_1 x_1 - \frac{c_2 a}{b} x_1 + \frac{c_2 d}{b}$$

$$= \left(c_1 - \frac{c_2 a}{b} \right) x_1 + \frac{c_2 d}{b}$$

If $(c_1 - c_2 a/b) > 0$, it follows that the larger x_1 is made the larger the value of the form will be. Thus if the entire line whose equation is $ax + by = d$ is

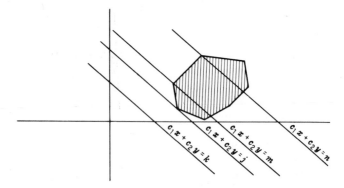

Figure 15.4

contained in the feasible set, there is no maximal value of the form. If $(c_1 - c_2 a/b) < 0$, we can make the form arbitrarily large by letting x_1 take on negative values large in absolute value. Since we can also get arbitrarily small values of the form (by reversing the procedures of choosing x_1 above), the only possible way to get optimal values, when the line $ax + by = d$ is contained in the feasible set, is to have $c_1 - c_2 a/b = 0$ or $c_1 = c_2 a/b$. But then

$$k = c_1 x + c_2 y = \left(\frac{c_2 a}{b} \right) x + c_2 y$$

$$\left(\frac{a}{b} \right) x + y = \frac{k}{c_2}$$

or

$$ax + by = \frac{bk}{c_2}$$

so that the graph of the form for any value k is parallel to the line in question.

Moreover, in this case, on the line $ax + by = d$,

$$c_1x_1 + c_2y_1 = \left(c_1 - \frac{c_2a}{b}\right)x_1 + \frac{c_2d}{b} = 0x_1 + \frac{c_2d}{b} = \frac{c_2d}{b}$$

a constant value.

Suppose now that we are looking for maximal values of the form $c_1x + c_2y$ on a feasible set which has part of the line $ax + by = d$ in its boundary. Then if, say $c_1 - c_2a/b > 0$, the largest value of the form on the line in the feasible set will occur at the largest value of x for which the point (x, y) is on the line and in the feasible set. In particular, if the part of the line in the boundary of the feasible set is a line segment, we see that the maximal value occurs at an end point of the line segment, i.e., a vertex. Since we know that maximal values (if any) occur on the boundary and maximal values on segments of the boundary occur at endpoints of those segments, we know that maximal values in the feasible set occur at vertices thereof. Similar arguments may be made about minimal points, and in case we are considering a vertical line or line segment ($b = 0$), we may modify the argument by "solving" for x and letting y vary.

We now look at some examples to illustrate and perhaps clarify some of the points made above.

EXAMPLE 1. Consider the feasible set defined by

$$\begin{cases} y \leq 2 \\ y \geq 1 \\ x \geq 1 \end{cases}$$

(a) Graph the feasible set.
(b) Find the optimal values to minimize the linear form $x + y$ and show that it has no maximum value.
(c) Find the optimal values to maximize the form $-x + y$ and show that it has no minimum value.
(d) Find the optimal values to minimize and also to maximize the form y.

(a) The graph of the feasible set is shown in Fig. 15.5.

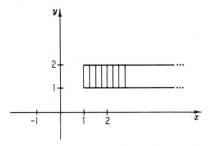

Figure 15.5

(b) Consideration of the family of lines $x + y = k$ shows that the "first" line to "touch" the feasible set is the line $x + y = 2$, which touches the feasible set at the optimal point $(1, 1)$ (see Fig. 15.6). Since $x + y \geq x + 1$, and x becomes arbitrarily large for points in the feasible set, it is clear that the form does not assume a maximum.

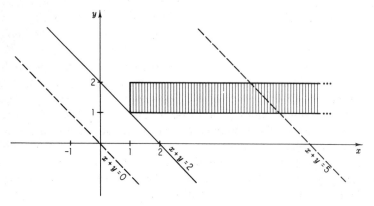

Figure 15.6

In this case we might have observed that y is a minimum along $y = 1$ while x is a minimum along $x = 1$ and so $x + y$ will be a minimum at their intersection which is the vertex $(1, 1)$.

(c) Consideration of the family of lines $-x + y = k$ shows that the "first" line to "touch" the feasible set is the line $-x + y = 1$ which touches the feasible set at the optimal point $(1, 2)$ (see Fig. 15.7). Since $-x + y \leq -x + 2$ and x becomes arbitrarily large for points

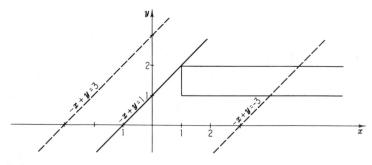

Figure 15.7

in the feasible set, it is clear that the form does not assume a minimum. On the other hand we might have observed that $-x$ is a maximum along $x = 1$ and y is a maximum along $y = 2$ so that $-x + y$ will be a maximum at their intersection which is the vertex $(1, 2)$.

(d) Consideration of the family of horizontal lines $y = k$ shows that $y = 1$ will be a minimum value and $y = 2$ will be a maximum value of the form. There are infinitely many optimal values. Note that although the feasible set contains rays, it does not contain any ray on which the form assumes at least two distinct values.

EXAMPLE 2. Find optimal points over the feasible set defined by

$$\begin{cases} y \leq 2 \\ y \geq 1 \\ x \leq 2 \\ x \geq 1 \end{cases}$$

of the form $2x - 3y$.

In this case the feasible set is bounded so that it is a polygon. Hence the given form (in fact, any form) has both maximum and minimum values which will occur at vertices. The lines $y = 2$, $y = 1$, $x = 2$, and $x = 1$ contain the boundary of the feasible set and their intersections give the vertices. Solving each pair of these equations simultaneously we see that there are four vertices, namely $(1, 1)$, $(1, 2)$, $(2, 1)$, and $(2, 2)$ (see Fig. 15.8), at which the given form assumes the respective values of -1, -4, 1,

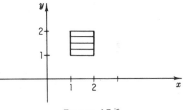

Figure 15.8

-2. Thus we see that $(1, 2)$ is an optimal point yielding a minimum value of -4 and that $(2, 1)$ is an optimal point yielding a maximum value of 1.

We observe that, as in the solution of Example 2 above, we may find the optimal points algebraically by finding the vertices by solving simultaneously pairs of the equations of the boundaries of the half planes whose intersection is the feasible set; then, we may find the maximum and minimum values on the vertices. It is necessary to check each such intersection to determine whether it is in the feasible set before evaluating the form at such a point—only those intersections which are in the feasible set are vertices.

This method indicates a way of extending our results. We may think of what we've been doing as being the two-dimensional case. The three-dimensional problem consists of optimizing forms like $c_1 x + c_2 y + c_3 z$ on feasible sets which are usually the intersection of a finite number of "half spaces," and may be interpreted as convex polyhedra with interiors. The points that satisfy the equation $c_1 x + c_2 y + c_3 z = k$ lie on a plane which we may think of sliding so that all of the resulting planes are parallel (see Fig. 15.9). The points of the feasible set where the plane "first" and "last" touches will, in general, be vertices as before and will be optimal points.

Algebraically we are given the feasible set as the simultaneous graph of inequalities of the following type.

$$\begin{cases} a_1 x + b_1 y + d_1 z \le e_1 \\ a_2 x + b_2 y + d_2 z \le e_2 \\ \quad . \\ \quad . \\ \quad . \\ a_n x + b_n y + d_n z \le e_n \end{cases}$$

A boundary of one of these half spaces is a plane satisfying the equation $a_i x + b_i y + d_i z = e_i$, and a vertex is the intersection of three such planes.

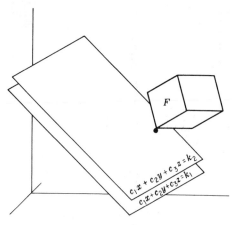

Figure 15.9

Thus we can find the vertices of the feasible set by solving simultaneously all possible combinations of three of these equations and then determining whether the solution is in the feasible set. Then as before we find the values of the form at each vertex and select the optimal values.

EXAMPLE 3. Find optimal points of the linear form $x - 2y + 3z$ over the feasible set defined by $x \ge 0$, $x \le 1$, $y \ge 0$, $y \le 1$, $z \ge 0$, $z \le 1$.

Although the intersection of two lines determines a vertex in the plane, as noted earlier, it takes the intersection of three planes to determine a vertex in three space. Solving $x = 0$, $y = 1$, $z = 0$ simultaneously yields the vertex $(0, 1, 0)$ at which the form assumes the value -2. In a similar fashion we find that the other vertices are $(0, 0, 0)$, $(1, 1, 0)$, $(1, 0, 0)$, $(0, 0, 1)$, $(0, 1, 1)$, $(1, 1, 1)$, and $(1, 0, 1)$ at which the form assumes the respective values 0, -1, 1, 3, 1, 2, and 4. Thus $(0, 1, 0)$ is an optimal point yielding the minimum value, -2, of the form, whereas $(1, 0, 1)$ is an optimal point yielding the maximum value, 4, of the form.

It is possible to extend these results to higher dimensions even though one can no longer draw pictures of the geometry; we can (in the n-dimensional case) solve n equations in n unknowns to find the "vertices," but we shall not do so here. We mention again that our methods are not the most expeditious for solving large numbers of, or very cumbersome, problems in linear programming, but that we have included the basic ideas involved in the subject.

EXERCISES

1. Work Example 1 by determining the vertices of the feasible set.

2. Find the optimal points of the following forms over the feasible set in Example 1.
   (a) $2x - 3y$ (c) $2x + 3y$
   (b) $3x - 2y$ (d) $-3x - 2y$

3. Find the optimal points of the following forms over the feasible set in Example 3.
   (a) $x + y + z$ (c) $-z$
   (b) $-x - 2y - 3z$ (d) $y + z$

4. Find the optimal values of the form y over the feasible set determined by $y \le 2$ and $y \ge 1$. Do these optimal values occur at vertices of the feasible set?

15.5. APPLICATIONS

Many problems can be interpreted as linear programming problems. In fact the current interest in linear programming arises primarily from the variety of applications that it possesses. We illustrate by means of examples, which may be over-simplified and may involve unrealistic numbers, but are nonetheless representative of applications of linear programming.

EXAMPLE 1. A baker makes oatmeal and sugar cookies which sell at a profit of 20¢ and 25¢ a box, respectively. A box of oatmeal cookies requires 3 min. for mixing, 2 min. for baking, and 1 min. for packaging, whereas a box of sugar cookies requires 2 min. for mixing, 3 min. for baking, and 1 min. for packaging. The mixing equipment is available for 18 hr per week, the baking ovens are available 20 hr per week, and the packaging machines are available for 7 hr per week. How many boxes of oatmeal and how many boxes of sugar cookies should the baker make per week in order to receive the maximum profit? (Assume he sells all his production.)

Let x = number of boxes of oatmeal cookies made per week, and y = number of boxes of sugar cookies made per week; therefore, $x \geq 0$ and $y \geq 0$. The time spent in mixing oatmeal cookies is $3x$ min., and the time spent mixing sugar cookies is $2y$ min. Since the total mixing time cannot exceed 1080 min., we have $3x + 2y \leq 1080$. Similarly the baking times $2x$ and $3y$ cannot total more than 1200 min.; therefore, $2x + 3y \leq 1200$—the sum of the packaging times, $x + y$, can't be greater than 420 min. We can now state our problem in the familiar form:

Find the optimal value which maximizes the linear form $.20x + .25y$ over the feasible set determined by

$$\begin{cases} x \geq 0 \\ y \geq 0 \\ 3x + 2y \leq 1080 \\ 2x + 3y \leq 1200 \\ x + y \leq 420 \end{cases}$$

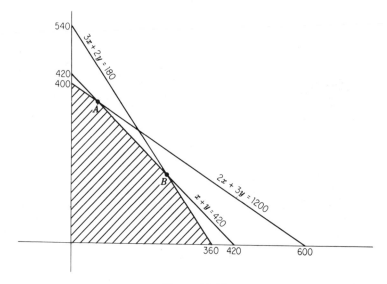

Figure 15.10

We sketch the feasible set shown shaded in Fig. 15.10. The vertices in the feasible set are seen to be $(0, 0)$; $(0, 400)$; $(60, 360)$—the point labeled A; $(240, 180)$—the point labeled B; and $(360, 0)$. Substituting the coordinates of the points in the form $.20x + .25y$ gives the values 0, 100, 102, 93, and 72, respectively. Hence a maximum profit of $102 results from making 60 boxes of oatmeal cookies and 360 boxes of sugar cookies.

Note that this solution uses the packaging equipment and baking ovens for all of the alloted time, but that it does not use 3 hr of allotted time on the mixing machines. This is sometimes referred to as *slack* in the solution.

EXAMPLE 2. A certain operator has two oil fields: one produces 5000 barrels of crude oil, 20,000 gal of brine, and 100,000 cu ft of natural gas daily at an operating cost of $1000 per day; the other produces 10,000 barrels of crude oil, 15,000 gal of brine, and 75,000 cu ft of natural gas daily at an operating cost of $1500 per day.

He has agreed to supply a refinery with 20,000 barrels of crude oil, 60,000 gal of brine, and 300,000 cu ft of natural gas per week. How many days per week should he operate each field so as to minimize his cost?

We let $x =$ the number of days per week the first field is operated and $y =$ the number of days per week the second field is operated. Then our problem is to minimize the form $1000x + 1500y$ over the feasible set determined by

$$\begin{cases} x \le 7 \\ y \le 7 \\ x \ge 0 \\ y \ge 0 \\ 5000x + 10000y \ge 20000 \\ 20000x + 15000y \ge 60000 \\ 100000x + 75000y \ge 300000 \end{cases}$$

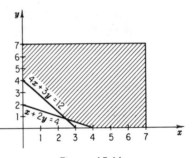

Figure 15.11

We graph the feasible set—the shaded region in Fig. 15.11. Observe that the given conditions are equivalent to the conditions

$$\begin{cases} x \ge 0 \\ y \ge 0 \\ y \le 7 \\ x \le 7 \\ x + 2y \ge 4 \\ 4x + 3y \ge 12 \\ 4x + 3y \ge 12 \end{cases}$$

The vertices are $(4, 0)$, $(0, 4)$, $(0, 7)$, $(7, 0)$, $(7, 7)$ and the intersection of the lines $x + 2y = 4$ and $4x + 3y = 12$ which we find to be $(\frac{12}{5}, \frac{4}{5})$. Testing in the form shows that the desired optimal values are $x = \frac{12}{5}$, $y = \frac{4}{5}$ which yield a minimum value of $3600.

Note that in this case all of the production is used. This is rather unusual for we normally have to over produce some items in order to meet all of the quotas.

However, if we suppose that the fields do not operate for fractional parts of a day, as is sometimes the case, then the preceding solution is not practical. In this case we demand that the optimal points have integer coordinates, i.e., that they be *lattice points*.

Some of our vertices, such as $(4, 0)$ and $(0, 4)$, are lattice points, whereas the vertex, $(\frac{12}{5}, \frac{4}{5})$, is not a lattice point. The closest lattice points to it in the feasible set are $(2, 2)$ and $(3, 1)$. Substitution of the coordinates of these lattice points into the form shows that the optimal values are $x = 4$ and $y = 0$ which yield a minimum value of $4000.

EXAMPLE 3. A tank truck with a capacity of 10,000 gal must carry at least 2000 gal of white gas, at least 5000 gal of diesel fuel, and not more than 1000 gal of mineral spirits. If the owner makes a profit of 3¢ per gal on white gas, 4¢ per gal on diesel fuel, and 5¢ per gal on mineral spirits, how much of each should he carry on each trip so as to make a maximum profit? (Assume that he can sell all he carries so that he leaves on each trip with a full tank.)

Let x, y, z denote the number of gallons of white gas, diesel fuel, and mineral spirits, respectively, to be carried on each trip. Then we wish to maximize the form $3x + 4y + 5z$ over the feasible set determined by

$$\begin{cases} x \geq 2000 \\ y \geq 5000 \\ z \leq 1000 \\ z \geq 0 \\ x + y + z = 10000 \end{cases}$$

At the vertices we must have $z = 0$ or $z = 1000$. Taking $z = 0$ and $x = 2000$ we find $y = 8000$ while by taking $y = 5000$ we obtain $x = 5000$, thus yielding the vertices $(2000, 8000, 0)$ and $(5000, 5000, 0)$. In a similar fashion, by taking $z = 1000$, we obtain the vertices $(2000, 7000, 1000)$ and $(4000, 5000, 1000)$. The desired optimal values are $x = 2000$, $y = 7000$, and $z = 1000$ which yield a profit of $390. Observe that we might have worked Example 3 as a two-dimensional problem by using

$$z = 10000 - x - y$$

(see Exercise 6).

EXAMPLE 4. A television station operates 15 hr per day and cannot spend more than $5000 per day. Each hour of network programs costs $500 and attracts 50,000 viewers. Each hour of local live programs costs $300 and attracts 25,000 viewers. Each hour of reruns costs $100 and attracts 12,000 viewers. If the station must carry at least 3 hr of network T.V. per day, and not more than 2 hr of reruns for each hour of local live T.V., how should the programs be arranged so that: (a) a maximum number of viewers is obtained and (b) the cost is minimum?

If we let x be the number of hours of local live T.V., and y be the number of hours of reruns, then $15 - x - y$ will be the number of hours of network programs. The feasible set is determined by the inequalities

$$
\begin{cases}
x \geq 0 \\
y \geq 0 \\
y \leq 2x \\
15 - x - y \geq 3 \text{ or } x + y \leq 12 \\
3x + y + 5(15 - x - y) \leq 50 \text{ or } 2x + 4y \geq 25
\end{cases}
$$

For (a) we wish to maximize $25{,}000x + 12{,}000y + 50{,}000(15 - x - y)$ or $750{,}000 - 25{,}000x - 38{,}000y$. We notice that we can do this by minimizing $25{,}000x + 38{,}000y$ (for then we will be subtracting the smallest number from $750{,}000$), and we also note that the values of x and y which make $25{,}000x + 38{,}000y$ smallest are precisely those which make $25x + 38y$ smallest. We therefore seek minimal values for $25x + 38y$. We sketch the graph of the feasible set in Fig. 15.12. The vertices of the feasible set are $(4, 8)$, $(2\frac{1}{2}, 5)$, and $(11\frac{1}{2}, \frac{1}{2})$. The values of the form $25x + 38y$ at these points are 404,

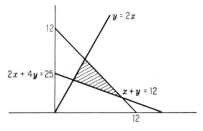

Figure 15.12

$252\frac{1}{2}$, and $306\frac{1}{2}$. Thus, the maximum number of viewers occurs for $2\frac{1}{2}$ hr of local live programs, 5 hr of reruns and $7\frac{1}{2}$ hr of network T.V. For (b) we wish to minimize

$$300x + 100y + 500(15 - x - y) = 7500 - 200x - 400y.$$

We can do this by maximizing $200x + 400y$ or more simply by maximizing $x + 2y$. This form, evaluated at the vertices previously established, yields 20, $12\frac{1}{2}$, and $12\frac{1}{2}$. Hence the lowest cost occurs for 4 hr of local live programs, 8 hr of reruns, and 3 hr of network shows.

EXERCISES

1. Work Example 1 under the assumption that the baking ovens are available 40 hr per week.

2. Work Example 3 under the assumption that the profits per gallon listed there are costs per gallon and that he wishes to minimize his cost.

3. In Example 1 we wished to maximize the form $.20x + .25y$. Now $.25 > .20$ and hence we should take y as large as possible. Is this reasoning correct? Why or why not?

4. Work Example 2 with the assumption that the operator has agreed to supply 30,000 barrels of oil, 80,000 gal of brine, and 400,000 cu ft of natural gas per week.

5. Find the optimal values which maximize the form in Example 2.

6. Work Example 3 as a two-dimensional problem.

7. Jess A. Playboy, a student at Ratrace Tech, awakes one day to find that final exams are imminent and that he has a 50 average in Math, English, and Advanced Diamond Cutting. He must get at least a 70 average in each of his courses and an 80 in English (in which he is on probation). For each hour spent studying his notes, he will raise his Math average one point, his English grade one point, and his Diamond Cutting grade three points. For each hour studying library materials his Math average will go up $\frac{1}{2}$ a point, his English average two points and his A.D.C. grade $\frac{1}{3}$ point. How many hours should he spend studying each way to get the required grades with the least study time?

8. According to the findings of the Witch Doctors Organization of Fuji (WOOF), the average islander needs 5 units of vitamin U, 10 of vitamin V, and 12 of vitamin W daily. The fruit of the Papaya tree contains 1 unit of U, 2 of V, and 2 of W while the fruit of the Mamaya contains 2 units of U, 3 of V, and 4 of W. What is the smallest number of each kind of fruit that should be eaten to get at least the minimum supply of vitamins?

16

One very interesting aspect of mathematics is its history. Many people find that retracing the evolution of the ideas of mathematics is fascinating, and there are many worthwhile books on the subject. In giving only a very cursory treatment of the subject, we will restrict ourselves to those topics in mathematics which have been discussed in previous chapters of this book.

Since mathematics goes back to prehistoric times, no one can say exactly where or when basic arithmetic evolved. Even after counting was developed, and mathematics (as well as other material) was recorded, only a few fragmentary specimens have survived or have been discovered. As a result many of our ideas of these early periods are obtained by assembling what few scraps of information we have and surmising the rest. Moreover there was much exchange of information among various countries, making it difficult to determine who conceived what concept or where this certain concept originated. To add further complications, apparently some concepts were discovered, forgotten, and rediscovered elsewhere.

It seems almost certain that many of the early number systems evolved out of 1–1 correspondences with fingers and/or toes. To bolster this conjecture is the fact that nearly all recorded systems are base 5, base 10, or base 20 (i.e., one hand, two hands, or hands and feet systems). One exception to this is the base 60 system used by the Babylonians. Vestiges of this system remain today in our using 60 seconds in a minute, 60 minutes in an hour, 360° in a circle, etc.

the history of mathematics

Early numerals probably included all the devices suggested in Chapter 1 of this text. In this connection it is interesting to note that the word "calculate" comes from the Greek word for stone or pebble. Many early calculations were performed on "dust boards" which evidently consisted of a board covered with fine sand in which the symbols could be traced and then easily "erased." These calculations were largely made for business purposes, including, at a surprisingly early date, such items as interest. As larger numbers were needed, positional notation was invented and the absence of a symbol for zero became a problem. Sometimes a blank space was used, sometimes it was hoped that one could tell from the context which number was meant, and sometimes the place value of a digit was indicated by other means.

The digit numerals (1, 2, 3, 4, 5, 6, 7, 8, 9) are usually called Hindu-Arabic numerals. It is evident that they were invented by the Hindus and carried to other countries by the Arabs. The original digits appear to have been the initial letters in the Hindu words for one through nine (which fortunately were all different). Many other peoples used letters from their alphabets as numerals (e.g., Roman numerals), but the Hindu numerals were particularly suited to base 10 positional notation, and have survived (with some modifications) as almost universal numerals today. It is difficult to determine when the numerals first came into use, but some recognizable digits appear in inscriptions believed to have been made in the third century B.C. It is interesting to note that the symbol for zero does not appear in India for perhaps another thousand years, although the Greeks may have used this symbol with Babylonian numerals somewhat earlier.

Most of our knowledge about the mathematics of this early period comes from Egyptian papyrus and Babylonian clay tablets which have been discovered and translated in comparatively recent times. It may well be that we attribute many discoveries to these peoples only because it is their records that we have found. In this connection there seems to be some evidence that the Chinese, in particular, had developed mathematics to a comparable state but little recorded information is available.

Various symbols to indicate the arithmetic operations were used before the ones in use today were standardized. In particular the plus sign "+" is said to have arisen from the Latin word "et" meaning "and." The origin of the minus sign is unclear, and the use of "×" for "times" only occurs fairly recently.

It should be mentioned that the ancients evidently based their arithmetic on empirical evidence, and, like many students of today, were not interested in proofs. It is to the Greeks that we look for the beginnings of mathematical proof. For the Greeks, if they did not invent this important phase of mathematics (which they may well have), at least undisputably were the first to recognize its value and to systematically endeavor to define mathematical entities and use the definitions and axioms to prove theorems. With the exception of geometry, for which the textbooks have remained virtually identical with Euclid's from about 300 B.C. on, the idea of a proof in an elementary textbook seems to have been abandoned for many centuries. In fact, most of the arithmetic textbooks of today consist of rules interspersed with routine problems for solution. Furthermore such items as the commutative, associative, and distributive laws are not usually explicitly formulated, although they are basic for many arithmetic processes.

The elementary results in number theory were known to the Greeks; in fact, in Euclid's *Elements* a logical and carefully formulated theory is presented. The Greek number theory is often developed by geometric methods, and the reliance on geometric methods (although often quite ingenious) points out the poor numerical and algebraic notation available at the time.

In our text we found it expedient to extend our number system to include the integers before introducing fractions. Historically, it happened conversely; can you explain why? Both the ancient Egyptians and Babylonians used fractions extensively in their trade and commerce as well as in calculating interest and measuring land. The base 60, used by the Babylonians, made it easy to express many of the common fractions—$\frac{1}{2}$ is thirty parts of 60, $\frac{1}{3}$ is twenty, $\frac{1}{4}$ is fifteen, etc. The Egyptians only had symbols for numerals equal to fractions with one in the numerator; so that, e.g., when they wanted to indicate $\frac{2}{5}$, they wrote the equivalent of $\frac{1}{3} + \frac{1}{15}$. During the middle ages the Hindus made notable advances in arithmetic and algebra. Arithmetic books have been found from this period which contain efficient methods of computation, including the grating method of multiplication. In these books fractions are indicated by writing one integer above another without a dividing line between them. The Hindus also used the technique of "casting out nines" to check the accuracy of their computations.

Negative numbers were developed comparatively late in the history of mathematics. Although the Hindus noted that negative numbers might be solutions to equations, they generally rejected them. While an occasional mention of negatives occurred from time to time, it was not until the 17th century that Descartes was able to use them systematically, and not until the middle of the 19th century that a complete logical development of negative numbers was generally available.

The fact that there is no rational number whose square is 2 was known to the Greeks about 500 B.C., at the time of Pythagoras. Since the Greeks were primarily geometricians, there was no question of the existence of $\sqrt{2}$—they simply called such numbers incommensurable. The paradoxes of the infinite also arose about this time (see Zeno's "Achilles and the Tortoise" problem). Eudoxus was a Greek mathematician who was able to incorporate the incommensurables into the mathematics of the day. Decimal numerals made their first appearance in the twelfth century although the Babylonians had used the same principle with their base 60 numerals. There were many different notations before the decimal point, as we know it, was more or less uniformly adopted (although the Germans still use a comma). The real numbers were not well defined until the work of Cantor and Dedekind in the nineteenth century.

Exponents are another example of mathematical symbols which were finally standardized after a long period of experimentation with various notations. The words "square" and "cube" for second power and third power are part of our heritage of the Greek thinking about algebraic operations geometrically. The radical sign "$\sqrt{}$" appears in a German text-book printed in 1525 and has survived to this day.

The use of mathematics in applications where very large (or very small) numbers are used—such as in astronomical work—leads inevitably to approximations and hence to errors. Thus approximations and errors have been with us since prehistoric times, but their mathematical treatment has been a comparatively recent development. The need for more careful analysis of the effects of approximation arose as mathematics, in the form of probability, was introduced into the physical sciences between the 19th and 20th centuries; this need became even more pronounced with the advent of electronic computers in the past few years.

On the other hand the idea of interest and its computation extends back as far as there are records. The Sumerians, who were absorbed by the Babylonians, have left clay tablets dating from about 2000 B.C., indicating that interest of 20 to 30% was charged for loans of various materials. Also, compound interest problems such as "how long would it take for a sum of money to double itself at 20% (compounded annually)," as well as tables of powers of numbers which could be used to solve such problems actually appear on various tablets.

The idea of sets, which has permeated into almost all branches of mathematics, was propounded by Cantor in 1895. Earlier, in 1638, Galileo had called attention to such matters as the fact that there is a 1–1 corre-spondence between the natural numbers and their squares. Some of the algebra of sets—unions and intersections—was exploited by Boole in 1854, although the symbolism we now use is much newer.

Probability was first studied in connection with games of chance. In the middle of the 17th century, two mathematicians, Fermat and Pascal, laid the ground work for probability theory. This theory together with the beginning of statistics was expanded in the 17th and 18th centuries by such men as DeMoivre, Huygens, and Bernoulli.

Geometry, as we have mentioned, is an ancient subject. Its beginnings undoubtedly occurred in the measurement of land. The first results were intuitive and sometimes were incorrect—e.g., the Bible indicates that the ratio of the circumference of a disk to its diameter is 3 (see I Kings 7: 23; II Chronicles 4: 2). The Greeks, as we have noted, are responsible for demonstrative geometry—i.e., giving definitions and postulates, and using these to prove theorems. Besides these geometric results we are indebted to the Greeks for the idea of deductive reasoning in mathematics. The geometry of Euclid was so well organized that it has persisted to recent times. The work of Descartes, published in 1637, gave rise to a branch of mathematics called analytic geometry. Analytic geometry utilizes the inter-relations between the picture of the graph of a function (as a geometric object), and the function, to enable us to do some geometric problems algebraically and vice versa.

Beginning about 1940, American and Russian mathematicians, working independently, studied a class of problems which are now classified under the general title of linear programming. The techniques they evolved are now being widely applied to a host of problems in varied fields of man's endeavor and are in many cases opening new vistas of efficiency.

In geometry, in linear programming, as well as in nearly all the other branches of mathematics we are now able to give more precise definitions and to point out more clearly the whys and wherefores because of the set notation, the idea of binary operations, 1-1 correspondences, and similar terms of the so-called "new mathematics." We hasten to emphasize that mathematics, in general, is quite old—only its presentation may be considered new.

As a final statement we wish to remind the reader that the material in this chapter is extremely superficial; we recommend, as highly worthwhile reading, some of the many books available both on the history of mathematics and the men who created mathematics.

selected additional readings

Many students will find their appetites whetted by the treatment of certain topics in the text and might desire to do some additional reading. For their convenience we list several references which do not demand excessive mathematical preparation on the part of the reader. It is obvious, of course, that the list is a mere sampling from among the many fine books available. Several of these references are available in inexpensive paperback editions.

A rather extensive list of texts, with remarks on each, is published by CUPM, and the experimental texts of the SMSG contain pertinent material.

CHAPTER 3

1. *Essays on Number Theory I.*
2. *Essays on Number Theory II*, School Mathematics Study Group.

CHAPTER 4

1. Christian, Robert R., *Introduction to Logic & Sets*. Boston: Ginn & Company, 1958.
2. Kemeny, John G., Hazelton Mirkil, James L. Snell, and Gerald L. Thompson, *Finite Mathematical Structures*. Englewood Cliffs, N.J.: Prentice-Hall, Inc., 1959.

CHAPTERS 5, 6, 7

1. Kelley, John L., *Introduction to Modern Algebra*. Princeton, N.J.: D. Van Nostrand Company, Inc., 1960.

CHAPTER 9

1. Heath, Sir Thomas L., *A Manual of Greek Mathematics*. New York: Dover Publications, Inc.
2. Moise, Edwin, *Elementary Geometry from an Advanced Standpoint*. London: Addison-Wesley Publishing Company, Inc., 1963 (portions of this book are at a more advanced level).

CHAPTER 11

1. Cassiday, Walter, and Carl C. Robusto, *Business Mathematics*. Englewood Cliffs, N.J.: Prentice-Hall, Inc., 1952.

CHAPTER 12

1. Levinson, Horace C., *Chance, Luck, and Statistics*. New York: Dover Publications, Inc., 1963.
2. Mosteller, Frederick, *et al.*, *Probability with Statistical Applications*. London: Addison-Wesley Publishing Company, Inc., 1961.

CHAPTER 13

1. *Probability with Statistical Applications*.

CHAPTER 14

1. *Finite Mathematical Structures*.

CHAPTER 15

1. Glicksman, Abraham M., *Linear Programming and the Theory of Games*. New York: John Wiley & Sons, Inc., 1963.
2. *Finite Mathematical Structures*.

CHAPTER 16

1. *A Manual of Greek Mathematics*.
2. Smith, David E., *History of Mathematics*. New York: Dover Publications, Inc.
3. Turnbull, Herbert W., *The Great Mathematicians*. New York: New York University Press, Inc., 1961.

$$S = (1 + i)^n$$

n	$\frac{1}{4}\%$	$\frac{7}{24}\%$	$\frac{1}{3}\%$	$\frac{5}{12}\%$	$\frac{1}{2}\%$
1	1.0025 0000	1.0029 1667	1.0033 3333	1.0041 6667	1.0050 0000
2	1.0050 0625	1.0058 4184	1.0066 7778	1.0083 5069	1.0100 2500
3	1.0075 1877	1.0087 7555	1.0100 3337	1.0125 5216	1.0150 7513
4	1.0100 3756	1.0117 1781	1.0134 0015	1.0167 7112	1.0201 5050
5	1.0125 6266	1.0146 6865	1.0167 7815	1.0210 0767	1.0252 5125
6	1.0150 9406	1.0176 2810	1.0201 6741	1.0252 6187	1.0303 7751
7	1.0176 3180	1.0205 9618	1.0235 6797	1.0295 3379	1.0355 2940
8	1.0201 7588	1.0235 7292	1.0269 7986	1.0338 2352	1.0407 0704
9	1.0227 2632	1.0265 5834	1.0304 0313	1.0381 3111	1.0459 1058
10	1.0252 8313	1.0295 5247	1.0338 3780	1.0424 5666	1.0511 4013
11	1.0278 4634	1.0325 5533	1.0372 8393	1.0468 0023	1.0563 9583
12	1.0304 1596	1.0355 6695	1.0407 4154	1.0511 6190	1.0616 7781
13	1.0329 9200	1.0385 8736	1.0442 1068	1.0555 4174	1.0669 8620
14	1.0355 7448	1.0416 1657	1.0476 9138	1.0599 3983	1.0723 2113
15	1.0381 6341	1.0446 5462	1.0511 8369	1.0643 5625	1.0776 8274
16	1.0407 5882	1.0477 0153	1.0546 8763	1.0687 9106	1.0830 7115
17	1.0433 6072	1.0507 5732	1.0582 0326	1.0732 4436	1.0884 8651
18	1.0459 6912	1.0538 2203	1.0617 3060	1.0777 1621	1.0939 2894
19	1.0485 8404	1.0568 9568	1.0652 6971	1.0822 0670	1.0993 9858
20	1.0512 0550	1.0599 7829	1.0688 2060	1.0867 1589	1.1048 9558
21	1.0538 3352	1.0630 6990	1.0723 8334	1.0912 4387	1.1104 2006
22	1.0564 6810	1.0661 7052	1.0759 5795	1.0957 9072	1.1159 7216
23	1.0591 0927	1.0692 8018	1.0795 4448	1.1003 5652	1.1215 5202
24	1.0617 5704	1.0723 9891	1.0831 4296	1.1049 4134	1.1271 5978
25	1.0644 1144	1.0755 2674	1.0867 5344	1.1095 4526	1.1327 9558
26	1.0670 7247	1.0786 6370	1.0903 7595	1.1141 6836	1.1384 5955
27	1.0697 4015	1.0818 0980	1.0940 1053	1.1188 1073	1.1441 5185
28	1.0724 1450	1.0849 6508	1.0976 5724	1.1234 7244	1.1498 7261
29	1.0750 9553	1.0881 2956	1.1013 1609	1.1281 5358	1.1556 2197
30	1.0777 8327	1.0913 0327	1.1049 8715	1.1328 5422	1.1614 0008
31	1.0804 7773	1.0944 8624	1.1086 7044	1.1375 7444	1.1672 0708
32	1.0831 7892	1.0976 7849	1.1123 6601	1.1423 1434	1.1730 4312
33	1.0858 8687	1.1008 8005	1.1160 7389	1.1470 7398	1.1789 0833
34	1.0886 0159	1.1040 9095	1.1197 9414	1.1518 5346	1.1848 0288
35	1.0913 2309	1.1073 1122	1.1235 2679	1.1566 5284	1.1907 2689
36	1.0940 5140	1.1105 4088	1.1272 7187	1.1614 7223	1.1966 8052
37	1.0967 8653	1.1137 7995	1.1310 2945	1.1663 1170	1.2026 6393
38	1.0995 2850	1.1170 2848	1.1347 9955	1.1711 7133	1.2086 7725
39	1.1022 7732	1.1202 8648	1.1385 8221	1.1760 5121	1.2147 2063
40	1.1050 3301	1.1235 5398	1.1423 7748	1.1809 5142	1.2207 9424
41	1.1077 9559	1.1268 3101	1.1461 8541	1.1858 7206	1.2268 9821
42	1.1105 6508	1.1301 1760	1.1500 0603	1.1908 1319	1.2330 3270
43	1.1133 4149	1.1334 1378	1.1538 3938	1.1957 7491	1.2391 9786
44	1.1161 2485	1.1367 1957	1.1576 8551	1.2007 5731	1.2453 9385
45	1.1189 1516	1.1400 3500	1.1615 4446	1.2057 6046	1.2516 2082
46	1.1217 1245	1.1433 6010	1.1654 1628	1.2107 8446	1.2578 7892
47	1.1245 1673	1.1466 9490	1.1693 0100	1.2158 2940	1.2641 6832
48	1.1273 2802	1.1500 3943	1.1731 9867	1.2208 9536	1.2704 8916
49	1.1301 4634	1.1533 9371	1.1771 0933	1.2259 8242	1.2768 4161
50	1.1329 7171	1.1567 5778	1.1810 3303	1.2310 9068	1.2832 2581

TABLE I.   AMOUNT OF 1 AT COMPOUND INTEREST   287

$$S = (1 + i)^n$$

n	$\frac{1}{4}\%$	$\frac{7}{24}\%$	$\frac{1}{3}\%$	$\frac{5}{12}\%$	$\frac{1}{2}\%$
51	1.1358 0414	1.1601 3165	1.1849 6981	1.2362 2022	1.2896 4194
52	1.1386 4365	1.1635 1537	1.1889 1971	1.2413 7114	1.2960 9015
53	1.1414 9026	1.1669 0896	1.1928 8277	1.2465 4352	1.3025 7060
54	1.1443 4398	1.1703 1244	1.1968 5905	1.2517 3745	1.3090 8346
55	1.1472 0484	1.1737 2585	1.2008 4858	1.2569 5302	1.3156 2887
56	1.1500 7285	1.1771 4922	1.2048 5141	1.2621 9033	1.3222 0702
57	1.1529 4804	1.1805 8257	1.2088 6758	1.2674 4946	1.3288 1805
58	1.1558 3041	1.1840 2594	1.2128 9714	1.2727 3050	1.3354 6214
59	1.1587 1998	1.1874 7935	1.2169 4013	1.2780 3354	1.3421 3946
60	1.1616 1678	1.1909 4283	1.2209 9659	1.2833 5868	1.3488 5015
61	1.1645 2082	1.1944 1641	1.2250 6658	1.2887 0601	1.3555 9440
62	1.1674 3213	1.1979 0013	1.2291 5014	1.2940 7561	1.3623 7238
63	1.1703 5071	1.2013 9400	1.2332 4730	1.2994 6760	1.3691 8424
64	1.1732 7658	1.2048 9807	1.2373 5813	1.3048 8204	1.3760 3016
65	1.1762 0977	1.2084 1235	1.2414 8266	1.3103 1905	1.3829 1031
66	1.1791 5030	1.2119 3689	1.2456 2093	1.3157 7872	1.3898 2486
67	1.1820 9817	1.2154 7171	1.2497 7300	1.3212 6113	1.3967 7399
68	1.1850 5342	1.2190 1683	1.2539 3891	1.3267 6638	1.4037 5785
69	1.1880 1605	1.2225 7230	1.2581 1871	1.3322 9458	1.4107 7664
70	1.1909 8609	1.2261 3813	1.2623 1244	1.3378 4580	1.4178 3053
71	1.1939 6356	1.2297 1437	1.2665 2015	1.3434 2016	1.4249 1968
72	1.1969 4847	1.2333 0104	1.2707 4188	1.3490 1774	1.4320 4428
73	1.1999 4084	1.2368 9816	1.2749 7769	1.3546 3865	1.4392 0450
74	1.2029 4069	1.2405 0578	1.2792 2761	1.3602 8298	1.4464 0052
75	1.2059 4804	1.2441 2393	1.2834 9170	1.3659 5082	1.4536 3252
76	1.2089 6291	1.2477 5262	1.2877 7001	1.3716 4229	1.4609 0069
77	1.2119 8532	1.2513 9190	1.2920 6258	1.3773 5746	1.4682 0519
78	1.2150 1528	1.2550 4179	1.2963 6945	1.3830 9645	1.4755 4622
79	1.2180 5282	1.2587 0233	1.3006 9068	1.3888 5935	1.4829 2395
80	1.2210 9795	1.2623 7355	1.3050 2632	1.3946 4627	1.4903 3857
81	1.2241 5070	1.2660 5547	1.3093 7641	1.4004 5729	1.4977 9026
82	1.2272 1108	1.2697 4813	1.3137 4099	1.4062 9253	1.5052 7921
83	1.2302 7910	1.2734 5156	1.3181 2013	1.4121 5209	1.5128 0561
84	1.2333 5480	1.2771 6580	1.3225 1386	1.4180 3605	1.5203 6964
85	1.2364 3819	1.2808 9086	1.3269 2224	1.4239 4454	1.5279 7148
86	1.2395 2928	1.2846 2680	1.3313 4532	1.4298 7764	1.5356 1134
87	1.2426 2811	1.2883 7362	1.3357 8314	1.4358 3546	1.5432 8940
88	1.2457 3468	1.2921 3138	1.3402 3575	1.4418 1811	1.5510 0585
89	1.2488 4901	1.2959 0010	1.3447 0320	1.4478 2568	1.5587 6087
90	1.2519 7114	1.2996 7980	1.3491 8554	1.4538 5829	1.5665 5468
91	1.2551 0106	1.3034 7054	1.3536 8283	1.4599 1603	1.5743 8745
92	1.2582 3882	1.3072 7233	1.3581 9510	1.4659 9902	1.5822 5939
93	1.2613 8441	1.3110 8520	1.3627 2242	1.4721 0735	1.5901 7069
94	1.2645 3787	1.3149 0920	1.3672 6483	1.4782 4113	1.5981 2154
95	1.2676 9922	1.3187 4435	1.3718 2238	1.4844 0047	1.6061 1215
96	1.2708 6847	1.3225 9069	1.3763 9512	1.4905 8547	1.6141 4271
97	1.2740 4564	1.3264 4825	1.3809 8310	1.4967 9624	1.6222 1342
98	1.2772 3075	1.3303 1706	1.3855 8638	1.5030 3289	1.6303 2449
99	1.2804 2383	1.3341 9715	1.3902 0500	1.5092 9553	1.6384 7611
100	1.2836 2489	1.3380 8856	1.3948 3902	1.5155 8426	1.6466 6849

$$S = (1 + i)^n$$

n	$\frac{7}{12}\%$	$\frac{2}{3}\%$	$\frac{3}{4}\%$	$\frac{7}{8}\%$	1%
1	1.0058 3333	1.0066 6667	1.0075 0000	1.0087 5000	1.0100 0000
2	1.0117 0069	1.0133 7778	1.0150 5625	1.0175 7656	1.0201 0000
3	1.0176 0228	1.0201 3363	1.0226 6917	1.0264 8036	1.0303 0100
4	1.0235 3830	1.0269 3452	1.0303 3919	1.0354 6206	1.0406 0401
5	1.0295 0894	1.0337 8075	1.0380 6673	1.0445 2235	1.0510 1005
6	1.0355 1440	1.0406 7262	1.0458 5224	1.0536 6192	1.0615 2015
7	1.0415 5490	1.0476 1044	1.0536 9613	1.0628 8147	1.0721 3535
8	1.0476 3064	1.0545 9451	1.0615 9885	1.0721 8168	1.0828 5671
9	1.0537 4182	1.0616 2514	1.0695 6084	1.0815 6327	1.0936 8527
10	1.0598 8865	1.0687 0264	1.0775 8255	1.0910 2695	1.1046 2213
11	1.0660 7133	1.0758 2732	1.0856 6441	1.1005 7343	1.1156 6835
12	1.0722 9008	1.0829 9951	1.0938 0690	1.1102 0345	1.1268 2503
13	1.0785 4511	1.0902 1950	1.1020 1045	1.1199 1773	1.1380 9328
14	1.0848 3662	1.0974 8763	1.1102 7553	1.1297 1701	1.1494 7421
15	1.0911 6483	1.1048 0422	1.1186 0259	1.1396 0203	1.1609 6896
16	1.0975 2996	1.1121 6958	1.1269 9211	1.1495 7355	1.1725 7864
17	1.1039 3222	1.1195 8404	1.1354 4455	1.1596 3232	1.1843 0443
18	1.1103 7182	1.1270 4794	1.1439 6039	1.1697 7910	1.1961 4748
19	1.1168 4899	1.1345 6159	1.1525 4009	1.1800 1467	1.2081 0895
20	1.1233 6395	1.1421 2533	1.1611 8414	1.1903 3980	1.2201 9004
21	1.1299 1690	1.1497 3950	1.1698 9302	1.2007 5527	1.2323 9194
22	1.1365 0808	1.1574 0443	1.1786 6722	1.2112 6188	1.2447 1586
23	1.1431 3771	1.1651 2046	1.1875 0723	1.2218 6042	1.2571 6302
24	1.1498 0602	1.1728 8793	1.1964 1353	1.2325 5170	1.2697 3465
25	1.1565 1322	1.1807 0718	1.2053 8663	1.2433 3653	1.2824 3200
26	1.1632 5955	1.1885 7857	1.2144 2703	1.2542 1572	1.2952 5631
27	1.1700 4523	1.1965 0242	1.2235 3523	1.2651 9011	1.3082 0888
28	1.1768 7049	1.2044 7911	1.2327 1175	1.2762 6052	1.3212 9097
29	1.1837 3557	1.2125 0897	1.2419 5709	1.2874 2780	1.3345 0388
30	1.1906 4069	1.2205 9236	1.2512 7176	1.2986 9280	1.3478 4892
31	1.1975 8610	1.2287 2964	1.2606 5630	1.3100 5636	1.3613 2740
32	1.2045 7202	1.2369 2117	1.2701 1122	1.3215 1935	1.3749 4068
33	1.2115 9869	1.2451 6731	1.2796 3706	1.3330 8265	1.3886 9009
34	1.2186 6634	1.2534 6843	1.2892 3434	1.3447 4712	1.4025 7699
35	1.2257 7523	1.2618 2489	1.2989 0359	1.3565 1366	1.4166 0276
36	1.2329 2559	1.2702 3705	1.3086 4537	1.3683 8315	1.4307 6878
37	1.2401 1765	1.2787 0530	1.3184 6021	1.3803 5650	1.4450 7647
38	1.2473 5167	1.2872 3000	1.3283 4866	1.3924 3462	1.4595 2724
39	1.2546 2789	1.2958 1153	1.3383 1128	1.4046 1843	1.4741 2251
40	1.2619 4655	1.3044 5028	1.3483 4861	1.4169 0884	1.4888 6373
41	1.2693 0791	1.3131 4661	1.3584 6123	1.4293 0679	1.5037 5237
42	1.2767 1220	1.3219 0092	1.3686 4969	1.4418 1322	1.5187 8989
43	1.2841 5969	1.3307 1360	1.3789 1456	1.4544 2909	1.5339 7779
44	1.2916 5062	1.3395 8502	1.3892 5642	1.4671 5534	1.5493 1757
45	1.2991 8525	1.3485 1559	1.3996 7584	1.4799 9295	1.5648 1075
46	1.3067 6383	1.3575 0569	1.4101 7341	1.4929 4289	1.5804 5885
47	1.3143 8662	1.3665 5573	1.4207 4971	1.5060 0614	1.5962 6344
48	1.3220 5388	1.3756 6610	1.4314 0533	1.5191 8370	1.6122 2608
49	1.3297 6586	1.3848 3721	1.4421 4087	1.5324 7655	1.6283 4834
50	1.3375 2283	1.3940 6946	1.4529 5693	1.5458 8572	1.6446 3182

TABLE I. AMOUNT OF 1 AT COMPOUND INTEREST 289

$$S = (1 + i)^n$$

n	$\frac{7}{12}\%$	$\frac{2}{3}\%$	$\frac{3}{4}\%$	$\frac{7}{8}\%$	1%
51	1.3453 2504	1.4033 6325	1.4638 5411	1.5594 1222	1.6610 7814
52	1.3531 7277	1.4127 1901	1.4748 3301	1.5730 5708	1.6776 8892
53	1.3610 6628	1.4221 3713	1.4858 9426	1.5868 2133	1.6944 6581
54	1.3690 0583	1.4316 1805	1.4970 3847	1.6007 0602	1.7114 1047
55	1.3769 9170	1.4411 6217	1.5082 6626	1.6147 1219	1.7285 2457
56	1.3850 2415	1.4507 6992	1.5195 7825	1.6288 4093	1.7458 0982
57	1.3931 0346	1.4604 4172	1.5309 7509	1.6430 9328	1.7632 6792
58	1.4012 2990	1.4701 7799	1.5424 5740	1.6574 7035	1.7809 0060
59	1.4094 0374	1.4799 7918	1.5540 2583	1.6719 7322	1.7987 0960
60	1.4176 2526	1.4898 4571	1.5656 8103	1.6866 0298	1.8166 9670
61	1.4258 9474	1.4997 7801	1.5774 2363	1.7013 6076	1.8348 6367
62	1.4342 1246	1.5097 7653	1.5892 5431	1.7162 4766	1.8532 1230
63	1.4425 7870	1.5198 4171	1.6011 7372	1.7312 6483	1.8717 4443
64	1.4509 9374	1.5299 7399	1.6131 8252	1.7464 1340	1.8904 6187
65	1.4594 5787	1.5401 7381	1.6252 8139	1.7616 9452	1.9093 6649
66	1.4679 7138	1.5504 4164	1.6374 7100	1.7771 0934	1.9284 6015
67	1.4765 3454	1.5607 7792	1.6497 5203	1.7926 5905	1.9477 4475
68	1.4851 4766	1.5711 8310	1.6621 2517	1.8083 4482	1.9672 2220
69	1.4938 1102	1.5816 5766	1.6745 9111	1.8241 6783	1.9868 9442
70	1.5025 2492	1.5922 0204	1.6871 5055	1.8401 2930	2.0067 6337
71	1.5112 8965	1.6028 1672	1.6998 0418	1.8562 3043	2.0268 3100
72	1.5201 0550	1.6135 0217	1.7125 5271	1.8724 7245	2.0470 9931
73	1.5289 7279	1.6242 5885	1.7253 9685	1.8888 5658	2.0675 7031
74	1.5378 9179	1.6350 8724	1.7383 3733	1.9053 8408	2.0882 4601
75	1.5468 6283	1.6459 8782	1.7513 7486	1.9220 5619	2.1091 2847
76	1.5558 8620	1.6569 6107	1.7645 1017	1.9388 7418	2.1302 1975
77	1.5649 6220	1.6680 0748	1.7777 4400	1.9558 3933	2.1515 2195
78	1.5740 9115	1.6791 2753	1.7910 7708	1.9729 5292	2.1730 3717
79	1.5832 7334	1.6903 2172	1.8045 1015	1.9902 1626	2.1947 6754
80	1.5925 0910	1.7015 9053	1.8180 4398	2.0076 3066	2.2167 1522
81	1.6017 9874	1.7129 3446	1.8316 7931	2.0251 9742	2.2388 8237
82	1.6111 4257	1.7243 5403	1.8454 1691	2.0429 1790	2.2612 7119
83	1.6205 4090	1.7358 4972	1.8592 5753	2.0607 9343	2.2838 8390
84	1.6299 9405	1.7474 2205	1.8732 0196	2.0788 2537	2.3067 2274
85	1.6395 0235	1.7590 7153	1.8872 5098	2.0970 1510	2.3297 8997
86	1.6490 6612	1.7707 9868	1.9014 0536	2.1153 6398	2.3530 8787
87	1.6586 8567	1.7826 0400	1.9156 6590	2.1338 7341	2.3766 1875
88	1.6683 6134	1.7944 8803	1.9300 3339	2.1525 4481	2.4003 8494
89	1.6780 9344	1.8064 5128	1.9445 0865	2.1713 7957	2.4243 8879
90	1.6878 8232	1.8184 9429	1.9590 9246	2.1903 7914	2.4486 3267
91	1.6977 2830	1.8306 1758	1.9737 8565	2.2095 4496	2.4731 1900
92	1.7076 3172	1.8428 2170	1.9885 8905	2.2288 7848	2.4978 5019
93	1.7175 9290	1.8551 0718	2.0035 0346	2.2483 8117	2.5228 2869
94	1.7276 1219	1.8674 7456	2.0185 2974	2.2680 5450	2.5480 5698
95	1.7376 8993	1.8799 2439	2.0336 6871	2.2878 9998	2.5735 3755
96	1.7478 2646	1.8924 5722	2.0489 2123	2.3079 1910	2.5992 7293
97	1.7580 2211	1.9050 7360	2.0642 8814	2.3281 1340	2.6252 6565
98	1.7682 7724	1.9177 7409	2.0797 7030	2.3484 8439	2.6515 1831
99	1.7785 9219	1.9305 5925	2.0953 6858	2.3690 3363	2.6780 3349
100	1.7889 6731	1.9434 2965	2.1110 8384	2.3897 6267	2.7048 1383

$$S = (1 + i)^n$$

n	$1\frac{1}{8}\%$	$1\frac{1}{4}\%$	$1\frac{3}{8}\%$	$1\frac{1}{2}\%$	$1\frac{3}{4}\%$
1	1.0112 5000	1.0125 0000	1.0137 5000	1.0150 0000	1.0175 0000
2	1.0226 2656	1.0251 5625	1.0276 8906	1.0302 2500	1.0353 0625
3	1.0341 3111	1.0379 7070	1.0418 1979	1.0456 7838	1.0534 2411
4	1.0457 6509	1.0509 4534	1.0561 4481	1.0613 6355	1.0718 5903
5	1.0575 2994	1.0640 8215	1.0706 6680	1.0772 8400	1.0906 1656
6	1.0694 2716	1.0773 8318	1.0853 8847	1.0934 4326	1.1097 0235
7	1.0814 5821	1.0908 5047	1.1003 1256	1.1098 4491	1.1291 2215
8	1.0936 2462	1.1044 8610	1.1154 4186	1.1264 9259	1.1488 8178
9	1.1059 2789	1.1182 9218	1.1307 7918	1.1433 8998	1.1689 8721
10	1.1183 6958	1.1322 7083	1.1463 2740	1.1605 4083	1.1894 4449
11	1.1309 5124	1.1464 2422	1.1620 8940	1.1779 4894	1.2102 5977
12	1.1436 7444	1.1607 5452	1.1780 6813	1.1956 1817	1.2314 3931
13	1.1565 4078	1.1752 6395	1.1942 6656	1.2155 5244	1.2529 8950
14	1.1695 5186	1.1899 5475	1.2106 8773	1.2317 5573	1.2749 1682
15	1.1827 0932	1.2048 2918	1.2273 3469	1.2502 3207	1.2972 2786
16	1.1960 1480	1.2198 8955	1.2442 1054	1.2689 8555	1.3199 2935
17	1.2094 6997	1.2351 3817	1.2613 1843	1.2880 2033	1.3430 2811
18	1.2230 7650	1.2505 7739	1.2786 6156	1.3073 4064	1.3665 3111
19	1.2368 3611	1.2662 0961	1.2962 4316	1.3269 5075	1.3904 4540
20	1.2507 5052	1.2820 3723	1.3140 6650	1.3468 5501	1.4147 7820
21	1.2648 2146	1.2980 6270	1.3321 3492	1.3670 5783	1.4395 3681
22	1.2790 5071	1.3142 8848	1.3504 5177	1.3875 6370	1.4647 2871
23	1.2934 4003	1.3307 1709	1.3690 2048	1.4083 7715	1.4903 6146
24	1.3079 9123	1.3473 5105	1.3878 4451	1.4295 0281	1.5164 4279
25	1.3227 0613	1.3641 9294	1.4069 2738	1.4509 4535	1.5429 8054
26	1.3375 8657	1.3812 4535	1.4262 7263	1.4727 0953	1.5699 8269
27	1.3526 3442	1.3985 1092	1.4458 8388	1.4948 0018	1.5974 5739
28	1.3678 5156	1.4159 9230	1.4657 6478	1.5172 2218	1.6254 1290
29	1.3832 3989	1.4336 9221	1.4859 1905	1.5399 8051	1.6538 5762
30	1.3988 0134	1.4516 1336	1.5063 5043	1.5630 8022	1.6828 0013
31	1.4145 3785	1.4697 5853	1.5270 6275	1.5865 2642	1.7122 4913
32	1.4304 5140	1.4881 3051	1.5480 5986	1.6103 2432	1.7422 1349
33	1.4465 4398	1.5067 3214	1.5693 4569	1.6344 7918	1.7727 0223
34	1.4628 1760	1.5255 6629	1.5909 2419	1.6589 9637	1.8037 2452
35	1.4792 7430	1.5446 3587	1.6127 9940	1.6838 8132	1.8352 8970
36	1.4959 1613	1.5639 4382	1.6349 7539	1.7091 3954	1.8674 0727
37	1.5127 4519	1.5834 9312	1.6574 5630	1.7347 7663	1.9000 8689
38	1.5297 6357	1.6032 8678	1.6802 4633	1.7607 9828	1.9333 3841
39	1.5469 7341	1.6233 2787	1.7033 4971	1.7872 1025	1.9671 7184
40	1.5643 7687	1.6436 1946	1.7267 7077	1.8140 1841	2.0015 9734
41	1.5819 7611	1.6641 6471	1.7505 1387	1.8412 2868	2.0366 2530
42	1.5997 7334	1.6849 6677	1.7745 8343	1.8688 4712	2.0722 6624
43	1.6177 7079	1.7060 2885	1.7989 8396	1.8968 7982	2.1085 3090
44	1.6359 7071	1.7273 5421	1.8237 1999	1.9253 3302	2.1454 3019
45	1.6543 7538	1.7489 4614	1.8487 9614	1.9542 1301	2.1829 7522
46	1.6729 8710	1.7708 0797	1.8742 1708	1.9835 2621	2.2211 7728
47	1.6918 0821	1.7929 4306	1.8999 8757	2.0132 7910	2.2600 4789
48	1.7108 4105	1.8153 5485	1.9261 1240	2.0434 7829	2.2995 9872
49	1.7300 8801	1.8380 4679	1.9525 9644	2.0741 3046	2.3398 4170
50	1.7495 5150	1.8610 2237	1.9794 4464	2.1052 4242	2.3807 8893

TABLE I. AMOUNT OF 1 AT COMPOUND INTEREST   291

$$S = (1 + i)^n$$

n	$1\frac{1}{8}\%$	$1\frac{1}{4}\%$	$1\frac{3}{8}\%$	$1\frac{1}{2}\%$	$1\frac{3}{4}\%$
51	1.7692 3395	1.8842 8515	2.0066 6201	2.1368 2106	2.4224 5274
52	1.7891 3784	1.9078 3872	2.0342 5361	2.1688 7337	2.4648 4566
53	1.8092 6564	1.9316 8670	2.0622 2460	2.2014 0647	2.5079 8046
54	1.8296 1988	1.9558 3279	2.0905 8019	2.2344 2757	2.5518 7012
55	1.8502 0310	1.9802 8070	2.1193 2566	2.2679 4398	2.5965 2785
56	1.8710 1788	2.0050 3420	2.1484 6639	2.3019 6314	2.6419 6708
57	1.8920 6684	2.0300 9713	2.1780 0780	2.3364 9259	2.6882 0151
58	1.9133 5259	2.0554 7335	2.2079 5541	2.3715 3998	2.7352 4503
59	1.9348 7780	2.0811 6676	2.2383 1480	2.4071 1308	2.7831 1182
60	1.9566 4518	2.1071 8135	2.2690 9163	2.4432 1978	2.8318 1628
61	1.9786 5744	2.1335 2111	2.3002 9164	2.4798 6807	2.8813 7306
62	2.0009 1733	2.1601 9013	2.3319 2065	2.5170 6609	2.9317 9709
63	2.0234 2765	2.1871 9250	2.3639 8456	2.5548 2208	2.9831 0354
64	2.0461 9121	2.2145 3241	2.3964 8934	2.5931 4442	3.0353 0785
65	2.0692 1087	2.2422 1407	2.4294 4107	2.6320 4158	3.0884 2574
66	2.0924 8949	2.2702 4174	2.4628 4589	2.6715 2221	3.1424 7319
67	2.1160 2999	2.2986 1976	2.4967 1002	2.7115 9504	3.1974 6647
68	2.1398 3533	2.3273 5251	2.5310 3978	2.7522 6896	3.2534 2213
69	2.1639 0848	2.3564 4442	2.5658 4158	2.7935 5300	3.3103 5702
70	2.1882 5245	2.3858 9997	2.6011 2190	2.8354 5629	3.3682 8827
71	2.2128 7029	2.4157 2372	2.6368 8732	2.8779 8814	3.4272 3331
72	2.2377 6508	2.4459 2027	2.6731 4453	2.9211 5796	3.4872 0990
73	2.2629 3994	2.4764 9427	2.7099 0026	2.9649 7533	3.5482 3607
74	2.2883 9801	2.5074 5045	2.7471 6139	3.0094 4996	3.6103 3020
75	2.3141 4249	2.5387 9358	2.7849 3486	3.0545 9171	3.6735 1098
76	2.3401 7659	2.5705 2850	2.8232 2771	3.1004 1059	3.7377 9742
77	2.3665 0358	2.6026 6011	2.8620 4710	3.1469 1674	3.8032 0888
78	2.3931 2675	2.6351 9336	2.9014 0024	3.1941 2050	3.8697 6503
79	2.4200 4942	2.6681 3327	2.9412 9450	3.2420 3230	3.9374 8592
80	2.4472 7498	2.7014 8494	2.9817 3730	3.2906 6279	4.0063 9192
81	2.4748 0682	2.7352 5350	3.0227 3618	3.3400 2273	4.0765 0378
82	2.5026 4840	2.7694 4417	3.0642 9881	3.3901 2307	4.1478 4260
83	2.5308 0319	2.8040 6222	3.1064 3291	3.4409 7492	4.2204 2984
84	2.5592 7473	2.8391 1300	3.1491 4637	3.4925 8954	4.2942 8737
85	2.5880 6657	2.8746 0191	3.1924 4713	3.5449 7838	4.3694 3740
86	2.6171 8232	2.9105 3444	3.2363 4328	3.5981 5306	4.4459 0255
87	2.6466 2562	2.9469 1612	3.2808 4300	3.6521 2535	4.5237 0584
88	2.6764 0016	2.9837 5257	3.3259 5459	3.7069 0723	4.6028 7070
89	2.7065 0966	3.0210 4948	3.3716 8646	3.7625 1084	4.6834 2093
90	2.7369 5789	3.0588 1260	3.4180 4715	3.8189 4851	4.7653 8080
91	2.7677 4867	3.0970 4775	3.4650 4530	3.8762 3273	4.8487 7496
92	2.7988 8584	3.1357 6085	3.5126 8967	3.9343 7622	4.9336 2853
93	2.8303 7331	3.1749 5786	3.5609 8916	3.9933 9187	5.0199 6703
94	2.8622 1501	3.2146 4483	3.6099 5276	4.0532 9275	5.1078 1645
95	2.8944 1492	3.2548 2789	3.6595 8961	4.1140 9214	5.1972 0324
96	2.9269 7709	3.2955 1324	3.7099 0897	4.1758 0352	5.2881 5429
97	2.9599 0559	3.3367 0716	3.7609 2021	4.2384 4057	5.3806 9699
98	2.9932 0452	3.3784 1600	3.8126 3287	4.3020 1718	5.4748 5919
99	3.0268 7807	3.4206 4620	3.8650 5657	4.3665 4744	5.5706 6923
100	3.0609 3045	3.4634 0427	3.9182 0110	4.4320 4565	5.6681 5594

$$S = (1 + i)^n$$

n	2 %	$2\frac{1}{4}$ %	$2\frac{1}{2}$ %	$2\frac{3}{4}$ %	3 %
1	1.0200 0000	1.0225 0000	1.0250 0000	1.0275 0000	1.0300 0000
2	1.0404 0000	1.0455 0625	1.0506 2500	1.0557 5625	1.0609 0000
3	1.0612 0800	1.0690 3014	1.0768 9063	1.0847 8955	1.0927 2700
4	1.0824 3216	1.0930 8332	1.1038 1289	1.1146 2126	1.1255 0881
5	1.1040 8080	1.1176 7769	1.1314 0821	1.1452 7334	1.1592 7407
6	1.1261 6242	1.1428 2544	1.1596 9342	1.1767 6836	1.1940 5230
7	1.1486 8567	1.1685 3901	1.1886 8575	1.2091 2949	1.2298 7387
8	1.1716 5938	1.1948 3114	1.2184 0290	1.2423 8055	1.2667 7008
9	1.1950 9257	1.2217 1484	1.2488 6297	1.2765 4602	1.3047 7318
10	1.2189 9442	1.2492 0343	1.2800 8454	1.3116 5103	1.3439 1638
11	1.2433 7431	1.2773 1050	1.3120 8666	1.3477 2144	1.3842 3387
12	1.2682 4179	1.3060 4999	1.3448 8882	1.3847 8378	1.4257 6089
13	1.2936 0663	1.3354 3611	1.3785 1104	1.4228 6533	1.4685 3371
14	1.3194 7876	1.3654 8343	1.4129 7382	1.4619 9413	1.5125 8972
15	1.3458 6834	1.3962 0680	1.4482 9817	1.5021 9896	1.5579 6742
16	1.3727 8571	1.4276 2146	1.4845 0562	1.5435 0944	1.6047 0644
17	1.4002 4142	1.4597 4294	1.5216 1826	1.5859 5595	1.6528 4763
18	1.4282 4625	1.4925 8716	1.5596 5872	1.6295 6973	1.7024 3306
19	1.4568 1117	1.5261 7037	1.5986 5019	1.6743 8290	1.7535 0605
20	1.4859 4740	1.5605 0920	1.6386 1644	1.7204 2843	1.8061 1123
21	1.5156 6634	1.5956 2066	1.6795 8185	1.7677 4021	1.8602 9457
22	1.5459 7967	1.6315 2212	1.7215 7140	1.8163 5307	1.9161 0341
23	1.5768 9926	1.6682 3137	1.7646 1068	1.8663 0278	1.9735 8651
24	1.6084 3725	1.7057 6658	1.8087 2595	1.9176 2610	2.0327 9411
25	1.6406 0599	1.7441 4632	1.8539 4410	1.9703 6082	2.0937 7793
26	1.6734 1811	1.7833 8962	1.9002 9270	2.0245 4575	2.1565 9127
27	1.7068 8648	1.8235 1588	1.9478 0002	2.0802 2075	2.2212 8901
28	1.7410 2421	1.8645 4499	1.9964 9502	2.1374 2682	2.2879 2768
29	1.7758 4469	1.9064 9725	2.0464 0739	2.1962 0606	2.3565 6551
30	1.8113 6158	1.9493 9344	2.0975 6758	2.2566 0173	2.4272 6247
31	1.8475 8882	1.9932 5479	2.1500 0677	2.3186 5828	2.5000 8035
32	1.8845 4059	2.0381 0303	2.2037 5694	2.3824 2138	2.5750 8276
33	1.9222 3140	2.0839 6034	2.2588 5086	2.4479 3797	2.6523 3524
34	1.9606 7603	2.1308 4945	2.3153 2213	2.5152 5626	2.7319 0530
35	1.9998 8955	2.1787 9356	2.3732 0519	2.5844 2581	2.8138 6245
36	2.0398 8734	2.2278 1642	2.4325 3532	2.6554 9752	2.8982 7833
37	2.0806 8509	2.2779 4229	2.4933 4870	2.7285 2370	2.9852 2668
38	2.1222 9879	2.3291 9599	2.5556 8242	2.8035 5810	3.0747 8348
39	2.1647 4477	2.3816 0290	2.6195 7448	2.8806 5595	3.1670 2698
40	2.2080 3966	2.4351 8897	2.6850 6384	2.9598 7399	3.2620 3779
41	2.2522 0046	2.4899 8072	2.7521 9043	3.0412 7052	3.3598 9893
42	2.2972 4447	2.5460 0528	2.8209 9520	3.1249 0546	3.4606 9589
43	2.3431 8936	2.6032 9040	2.8915 2008	3.2108 4036	3.5645 1677
44	2.3900 5314	2.6618 6444	2.9638 0808	3.2991 3847	3.6714 5227
45	2.4378 5421	2.7217 5639	3.0379 0328	3.3898 6478	3.7815 9584
46	2.4866 1129	2.7829 9590	3.1138 5086	3.4830 8606	3.8950 4372
47	2.5363 4351	2.8456 1331	3.1916 9713	3.5788 7093	4.0118 9503
48	2.5870 7039	2.9096 3961	3.2714 8956	3.6772 8988	4.1322 5188
49	2.6388 1179	2.9751 0650	3.3532 7680	3.7784 1535	4.2562 1944
50	2.6915 8803	3.0420 4640	3.4371 0872	3.8823 2177	4.3839 0602

TABLE I. AMOUNT OF 1 AT COMPOUND INTEREST   293

$$S = (1 + i)^n$$

n	2 %	$2\frac{1}{4}$ %	$2\frac{1}{2}$ %	$2\frac{3}{4}$ %	3 %
51	2.7454 1979	3.1104 9244	3.5230 3644	3.9890 8562	4.5154 2320
52	2.8003 2819	3.1804 7852	3.6111 1235	4.0987 8547	4.6508 8590
53	2.8563 3475	3.2520 3929	3.7013 9016	4.2115 0208	4.7904 1247
54	2.9134 6144	3.3252 1017	3.7939 2491	4.3273 1838	4.9341 2485
55	2.9717 3067	3.4000 2740	3.8887 7303	4.4463 1964	5.0821 4859
56	3.0311 6529	3.4765 2802	3.9859 9236	4.5685 9343	5.2346 1305
57	3.0917 8859	3.5547 4990	4.0856 4217	4.6942 2975	5.3916 5144
58	3.1536 2436	3.6347 3177	4.1877 8322	4.8233 2107	5.5534 0098
59	3.2166 9685	3.7165 1324	4.2924 7780	4.9559 6239	5.7200 0301
60	3.2810 3079	3.8001 3479	4.3997 8975	5.0922 5136	5.8916 0310
61	3.3466 5140	3.8856 3782	4.5097 8449	5.2322 8827	6.0683 5120
62	3.4135 8443	3.9730 6467	4.6225 2910	5.3761 7620	6.2504 0173
63	3.4818 5612	4.0624 5862	4.7380 9233	5.5240 2105	6.4379 1379
64	3.5514 9324	4.1538 6394	4.8565 4464	5.6759 3162	6.6310 5120
65	3.6225 2311	4.2473 2588	4.9779 5826	5.8320 1974	6.8299 8273
66	3.6949 7357	4.3428 9071	5.1024 0721	6.9924 0029	7.0348 8222
67	3.7688 7304	4.4406 0576	5.2299 6739	6.1571 9130	7.2459 2868
68	3.8442 5050	4.5405 1939	5.3607 1658	6.3265 1406	7.4633 0654
69	3.9211 3551	4.6426 8107	5.4947 3449	6.5004 9319	7.6872 0574
70	3.9995 5822	4.7471 4140	5.6321 0286	6.6792 5676	7.9178 2191
71	4.0795 4939	4.8539 5208	5.7729 0543	6.8629 3632	8.1553 5657
72	4.1611 4038	4.9631 6600	5.9172 2806	7.0516 6706	8.4000 1727
73	4.2443 6318	5.0748 3723	6.0651 5876	7.2455 8791	8.6520 1778
74	4.3292 5045	5.1890 2107	6.2167 8773	7.4448 4158	8.9115 7832
75	4.4158 3546	5.3057 7405	6.3722 0743	7.6495 7472	9.1789 2567
76	4.5041 5216	5.4251 5396	6.5315 1261	7.8599 3802	9.4542 9344
77	4.5942 3521	5.5472 1993	6.6948 0043	8.0760 8632	9.7379 2224
78	4.6861 1991	5.6720 3237	6.8621 7044	8.2981 7869	10.0300 5991
79	4.7798 4231	5.7996 5310	7.0337 2470	8.5263 7861	10.3309 6171
80	4.8754 3916	5.9301 4530	7.2095 6782	8.7608 5402	10.6408 9056
81	4.9729 4794	6.0635 7357	7.3898 0701	9.0017 7751	10.9601 1727
82	5.0724 0690	6.2000 0397	7.5745 5219	9.2493 2639	11.2889 2079
83	5.1738 5504	6.3395 0406	7.7639 1599	9.5036 8286	11.6275 8842
84	5.2773 3214	6.4821 4290	7.9580 1389	9.7650 3414	11.9764 1607
85	5.3828 7878	6.6279 9112	8.1569 6424	10.0335 7258	12.3357 0855
86	5.4905 3636	6.7771 2092	8.3608 8834	10.3094 9583	12.7057 7981
87	5.6003 4708	6.9296 0614	8.5699 1055	10.5930 0696	13.0869 5320
88	5.7123 5402	7.0855 2228	8.7841 5832	10.8843 1465	13.4795 6180
89	5.8266 0110	7.2449 4653	9.0037 6228	11.1836 3331	13.8839 4865
90	5.9431 3313	7.4079 5782	9.2288 5633	11.4911 8322	14.3004 6711
91	6.0619 9579	7.5746 3688	9.4595 7774	11.8071 9076	14.7294 8112
92	6.1832 3570	7.7450 6621	9.6960 6718	12.1318 8851	15.1713 6556
93	6.3069 0042	7.9193 3020	9.9384 6886	12.4655 1544	15.6265 0652
94	6.4330 3843	8.0975 1512	10.1869 3058	12.8083 1711	16.0953 0172
95	6.5616 9920	8.2797 0921	10.4416 0385	13.1605 4584	16.5781 6077
96	6.6929 3318	8.4660 0267	10.7026 4395	13.5224 6085	17.0755 0559
97	6.8267 9184	8.6564 8773	10.9702 1004	13.8943 2852	17.5877 7076
98	6.9633 2768	8.8512 5871	11.2444 6530	14.2764 2255	18.1154 0388
99	7.1025 9423	9.0504 1203	11.5255 7693	14.6690 2417	18.6588 6600
100	7.2446 4612	9.2540 4630	11.8137 1635	15.0724 2234	19.2186 3198

$$S = (1 + i)^n$$

n	$3\frac{1}{2}\%$	4%	$4\frac{1}{2}\%$	5%	$5\frac{1}{2}\%$
1	1.0350 0000	1.0400 0000	1.0450 0000	1.0500 0000	1.0550 0000
2	1.0712 2500	1.0816 0000	1.0920 2500	1.1025 0000	1.1130 2500
3	1.1087 1788	1.1248 6400	1.1411 6613	1.1576 2500	1.1742 4138
4	1.1475 2300	1.1698 5856	1.1925 1860	1.2155 0625	1.2388 2465
5	1.1876 8631	1.2166 5290	1.2461 8194	1.2762 8156	1.3069 6001
6	1.2292 5533	1.2653 1902	1.3022 6012	1.3400 9564	1.3788 4281
7	1.2722 7926	1.3159 3178	1.3608 6183	1.4071 0042	1.4546 7916
8	1.3168 0904	1.3685 6905	1.4221 0061	1.4774 5544	1.5346 8651
9	1.3628 9735	1.4233 1181	1.4860 9514	1.5513 2822	1.6190 9427
10	1.4105 9876	1.4802 4428	1.5529 6942	1.6288 9463	1.7081 4446
11	1.4599 6972	1.5394 5406	1.6228 5305	1.7103 3936	1.8020 9240
12	1.5110 6866	1.6010 3222	1.6958 8143	1.7958 5633	1.9012 0749
13	1.5639 5606	1.6650 7351	1.7721 9610	1.8856 4914	2.0057 7390
14	1.6186 9452	1.7316 7645	1.8519 4492	1.9799 3160	2.1160 9146
15	1.6753 4883	1.8009 4351	1.9352 8244	2.0789 2818	2.2324 7649
16	1.7339 8604	1.8729 8125	2.0223 7015	2.1828 7459	2.3552 6270
17	1.7946 7555	1.9479 0050	2.1133 7681	2.2920 1832	2.4848 0215
18	1.8574 8920	2.0258 1652	2.2084 7877	2.4066 1923	2.6214 6627
19	1.9225 0132	2.1068 4918	2.3078 6031	2.5269 5020	2.7656 4691
20	1.9897 8886	2.1911 2314	2.4117 1402	2.6532 9771	2.9177 5749
21	2.0594 3147	2.2787 6807	2.5202 4116	2.7859 6259	3.0782 3415
22	2.1315 1158	2.3699 1879	2.6336 5201	2.9252 6072	3.2475 3703
23	2.2061 1448	2.4647 1554	2.7521 6635	3.0715 2376	3.4261 5157
24	2.2833 2849	2.5633 0416	2.8760 1383	3.2250 9994	3.6145 8990
25	2.3632 4498	2.6658 3633	3.0054 3446	3.3863 5494	3.8133 9235
26	2.4459 5856	2.7724 6978	3.1406 7901	3.5556 7269	4.0231 2893
27	2.5315 6711	2.8833 6858	3.2820 0956	3.7334 5632	4.2444 0102
28	2.6201 7196	2.9987 0332	3.4296 9999	3.9201 2914	4.4778 4307
29	2.7118 7798	3.1186 5145	3.5840 3649	4.1161 3560	4.7241 2444
30	2.8067 9370	3.2433 9751	3.7453 1813	4.3219 4238	4.9839 5129
31	2.9050 3148	3.3731 3341	3.9138 5745	4.5380 3949	5.2580 6861
32	3.0067 0759	3.5080 5875	4.0899 8104	4.7649 4147	5.5472 6238
33	3.1119 4235	3.6483 8110	4.2740 3018	5.0031 8854	5.8523 6181
34	3.2208 6033	3.7943 1634	4.4663 6154	5.2533 4797	6.1742 4171
35	3.3335 9045	3.9460 8899	4.6673 4781	5.5160 1537	6.5138 2501
36	3.4502 6611	4.1039 3255	4.8773 7846	5.7918 1614	6.8720 8538
37	3.5710 2543	4.2680 8986	5.0968 6049	6.0814 0694	7.2500 5008
38	3.6960 1132	4.4388 1345	5.3262 1921	6.3854 7729	7.6488 0283
39	3.8253 7171	4.6163 6599	5.5658 9908	6.7047 5115	8.0694 8699
40	3.9592 5972	4.8010 2063	5.8163 6454	7.0399 8871	8.5133 0877
41	4.0978 3381	4.9930 6145	6.0781 0094	7.3919 8815	8.9815 4076
42	4.2412 5799	5.1927 8391	6.3516 1548	7.7615 8756	9.4755 2550
43	4.3897 0202	5.4004 9527	6.6374 3818	8.1496 6693	9.9966 7940
44	4.5433 4160	5.6165 1508	6.9361 2290	8.5571 5028	10.5464 9677
45	4.7023 5855	5.8411 7568	7.2482 4843	8.9850 0779	11.1265 5409
46	4.8669 4110	6.0748 2271	7.5744 1961	9.4342 5818	11.7385 1456
47	5.0372 8404	6.3178 1562	7.9152 6849	9.9059 7109	12.3841 3287
48	5.2135 8898	6.5705 2824	8.2714 5557	10.4012 6965	13.0652 6017
49	5.3960 6459	6.8333 4937	8.6436 7107	10.9213 3313	13.7838 4948
50	5.5849 2686	7.1066 8335	9.0326 3627	11.4673 9979	14.5419 6120

TABLE I. AMOUNT OF 1 AT COMPOUND INTEREST 295

$$S = (1 + i)^n$$

n	$3\frac{1}{2}\%$	4%	$4\frac{1}{2}\%$	5%	$5\frac{1}{2}\%$
51	5.7803 9930	7.3909 5068	9.4391 0490	12.0407 6978	15.3417 6907
52	5.9827 1327	7.6865 8871	9.8638 6463	12.6428 0826	16.1855 6637
53	6.1921 0824	7.9940 5226	10.3077 3853	13.2749 4868	17.0757 7252
54	6.4088 3202	8.3138 1435	10.7715 8677	13.9386 9611	18.0149 4001
55	6.6331 4114	8.6463 6692	11.2563 0817	14.6356 3092	19.0057 6171
56	6.8653 0108	8.9922 2160	11.7628 4204	15.3674 1246	20.0510 7860
57	7.1055 8662	9.3519 1046	12.2921 6993	16.1357 8309	21.1538 8793
58	7.3542 8215	9.7259 8688	12.8453 1758	16.9425 7224	22.3173 5176
59	7.6116 8203	10.1150 2635	13.4233 5687	17.7897 0085	23.5448 0611
60	7.8780 9090	10.5196 2741	14.0274 0793	18.6791 8589	24.8397 7045
61	8.1538 2408	10.9404 1250	14.6586 4129	19.6131 4519	26.2059 5782
62	8.4392 0793	11.3780 2900	15.3182 8014	20.5938 0245	27.6472 8550
63	8.7345 8020	11.8331 5016	16.0076 0275	21.6234 9257	29.1678 8620
64	9.0402 9051	12.3064 7617	16.7279 4487	22.7046 6720	30.7721 1994
65	9.3567 0068	12.7987 3522	17.4807 0239	23.8399 0056	32.4645 8654
66	9.6841 8520	13.3106 8463	18.2673 3400	25.0318 9559	34.2501 3880
67	10.0231 3168	13.8431 1201	19.0893 6403	26.2834 9037	36.1338 9643
68	10.3739 4129	14.3968 3649	19.9483 8541	27.5976 6488	38.1212 6074
69	10.7370 2924	14.9727 0995	20.8460 6276	28.9775 4813	40.2179 3008
70	11.1128 2526	15.5716 1835	21.7841 3558	30.4264 2554	42.4299 1623
71	11.5017 7414	16.1944 8308	22.7644 2168	31.9477 4681	44.7635 6163
72	11.9043 3624	16.8422 6241	23.7888 2066	33.5451 3415	47.2255 5751
73	12.3209 8801	17.5159 5290	24.8593 1759	35.2223 9086	49.8229 6318
74	12.7522 2259	18.2165 9102	25.9779 8688	36.9835 1040	52.5632 2615
75	13.1985 5038	18.9452 5466	27.1469 9629	38.8326 8592	55.4542 0359
76	13.6604 9964	19.7030 6485	28.3686 1112	40.7743 2022	58.5041 8479
77	14.1386 1713	20.4911 8744	29.6451 9862	42.8130 3623	61.7219 1495
78	14.6334 6873	21.3108 3494	30.9792 3256	44.9536 8804	65.1166 2027
79	15.1456 4013	22.1632 6834	32.3732 9802	47.2013 7244	68.6980 3439
80	15.6757 3754	23.0497 9907	33.8300 9643	49.5614 4107	72.4764 2628
81	16.2243 8835	23.9717 9103	35.3524 5077	52.0395 1312	76.4626 2973
82	16.7922 4195	24.9306 6267	36.9433 1106	54.6414 8878	80.6680 7436
83	17.3799 7041	25.9278 8918	38.6057 6006	57.3735 6322	85.1048 1845
84	17.9882 6938	26.9650 0475	40.3430 1926	60.2422 4138	89.7855 8347
85	18.6178 5881	28.0436 0494	42.1584 5513	63.2543 5344	94.7237 9056
86	19.2694 8387	29.1653 4914	44.0555 8561	66.4170 7112	99.9335 9904
87	19.9439 1580	30.3319 6310	46.0380 8696	69.7379 2467	105.4299 4698
88	20.6419 5285	31.5452 4163	48.1098 0087	73.2248 2091	111.2285 9407
89	21.3644 2120	32.8070 5129	50.2747 4191	76.8860 6195	117.3461 6674
90	22.1121 7595	34.1193 3334	52.5371 0530	80.7303 6505	123.8002 0591
91	22.8861 0210	35.4841 0668	54.9012 7503	84.7668 8330	130.6092 1724
92	23.6871 1568	36.9034 7094	57.3718 3241	89.0052 2747	137.7927 2419
93	24.5161 6473	38.3796 0978	59.9535 6487	93.4554 8884	145.3713 2402
94	25.3742 3049	39.9147 9417	62.6514 7529	98.1282 6328	153.3667 4684
95	26.2623 2856	41.5113 8594	65.4707 9168	103.0346 7645	161.8019 1791
96	27.1815 1006	43.1718 4138	68.4169 7730	108.1864 1027	170.7010 2340
97	28.1328 6291	44.8987 1503	71.4957 4128	113.5957 3078	180.0895 7969
98	29.1175 1311	46.6946 6363	74.7130 4964	119.2755 1732	189.9945 0657
99	30.1366 2607	48.5624 5018	78.0751 3687	125.2392 9319	200.4442 0443
100	31.1914 0798	50.5049 4818	81.5885 1803	131.5012 5785	211.4686 3567

$$S = (1 + i)^n$$

n	6 %	$6\frac{1}{2}$ %	7 %	$7\frac{1}{2}$ %	8 %
1	1.0600 0000	1.0650 0000	1.0700 0000	1.0750 0000	1.0800 0000
2	1.1236 0000	1.1342 2500	1.1449 0000	1.1556 2500	1.1664 0000
3	1.1910 1600	1.2079 4963	1.2250 4300	1.2422 9688	1.2597 1200
4	1.2624 7696	1.2864 6635	1.3107 9601	1.3354 6914	1.3604 8896
5	1.3382 2558	1.3700 8666	1.4025 5173	1.4356 2933	1.4693 2808
6	1.4185 1911	1.4591 4230	1.5007 3035	1.5433 0153	1.5868 7432
7	1.5036 3026	1.5539 8655	1.6057 8148	1.6590 4914	1.7138 2427
8	1.5938 4807	1.6549 9567	1.7181 8618	1.7834 7783	1.8509 3021
9	1.6894 7896	1.7625 7039	1.8384 5921	1.9172 3866	1.9990 0463
10	1.7908 4770	1.8771 3747	1.9671 5136	2.0610 3156	2.1589 2500
11	1.8982 9856	1.9991 5140	2.1048 5195	2.2156 0893	2.3316 3900
12	2.0121 9647	2.1290 9624	2.2521 9159	2.3817 7960	2.5181 7012
13	2.1329 2826	2.2674 8750	2.4098 4500	2.5604 1307	2.7196 2373
14	2.2609 0396	2.4148 7418	2.5785 3415	2.7524 4405	2.9371 9362
15	2.3965 5819	2.5718 4101	2.7590 3154	2.9588 7735	3.1721 6911
16	2.5403 5168	2.7390 1067	2.9521 6375	3.1807 9315	3.4259 4264
17	2.6927 7279	2.9170 4637	3.1588 1521	3.4193 5264	3.7000 1805
18	2.8543 3915	3.1066 5438	3.3799 3228	3.6758 0409	3.9960 1950
19	3.0255 9950	3.3085 8691	3.6165 2754	3.9514 8940	4.3157 0106
20	3.2071 3547	3.5236 4506	3.8696 8446	4.2478 5110	4.6609 5714
21	3.3995 6360	3.7526 8199	4.1405 6237	4.5664 3993	5.0338 3372
22	3.6035 3742	3.9966 0632	4.4304 0174	4.9089 2293	5.4365 4041
23	3.8197 4966	4.2563 8573	4.7405 2986	5.2770 9215	5.8714 6365
24	4.0489 3464	4.5330 5081	5.0723 6695	5.6728 7406	6.3411 8074
25	4.2918 7072	4.8276 9911	5.4274 3264	6.0983 3961	6.8484 7520
26	4.5493 8296	5.1414 9955	5.8073 5292	6.5557 1508	7.3963 5321
27	4.8223 4594	5.4756 9702	6.2138 6763	7.0473 9371	7.9880 6147
28	5.1116 8670	5.8316 1733	6.6488 3836	7.5759 4824	8.6271 0639
29	5.4183 8790	6.2106 7245	7.1142 5705	8.1441 4436	9.3172 7490
30	5.7434 9117	6.6143 6616	7.6122 5504	8.7549 5519	10.0626 5689
31	6.0881 0064	7.0442 9996	8.1451 1290	9.4115 7683	10.8676 6944
32	6.4533 8668	7.5021 7946	8.7152 7080	10.1174 4509	11.7370 8300
33	6.8405 8988	7.9898 2113	9.3253 3975	10.8762 5347	12.6760 4964
34	7.2510 2528	8.5091 5950	9.9781 1354	11.6919 7248	13.6901 3361
35	7.6860 8679	9.0622 5487	10.6765 8148	12.5688 7042	14.7853 4429
36	8.1472 5200	9.6513 0143	11.4239 4219	13.5115 3570	15.9681 7184
37	8.6360 8712	10.2786 3603	12.2236 1814	14.5249 0088	17.2456 2558
38	9.1542 5235	10.9467 4737	13.0792 7141	15.6142 6844	18.6252 7563
39	9.7035 0749	11.6582 8595	13.9948 2041	16.7853 3858	20.1152 9768
40	10.2857 1794	12.4160 7453	14.9744 5784	18.0442 3897	21.7245 2150
41	10.9028 6101	13.2231 1938	16.0226 6989	19.3975 5689	23.4624 8322
42	11.5570 3267	14.0826 2214	17.1442 5678	20.8523 7366	25.3394 8187
43	12.2504 5463	14.9979 9258	18.3443 5475	22.4163 0168	27.3666 4042
44	12.9854 8191	15.9728 6209	19.6284 5959	24.0975 2431	29.5559 7166
45	13.7646 1083	17.0110 9813	21.0024 5176	25.9048 3863	31.9204 4939
46	14.5904 8748	18.1168 1951	22.4726 2338	27.8477 0153	34.4740 8534
47	15.4659 1673	19.2944 1278	24.0457 0702	29.9362 7915	37.2320 1217
48	16.3938 7173	20.5485 4961	25.7289 0651	32.1815 0008	40.2105 7314
49	17.3775 0403	21.8842 0533	27.5299 2997	34.5951 1259	43.4274 1899
50	18.4201 5427	23.3066 7868	29.4570 2506	37.1897 4603	46.9016 1251

TABLE I.   AMOUNT OF 1 AT COMPOUND INTEREST   297

$$S = (1 + i)^n$$

n	6 %	$6\frac{1}{2}$ %	7 %	$7\frac{1}{2}$ %	8 %
51	19.5253 6353	24.8216 1279	31.5190 1682	39.9789 7698	50.6537 4151
52	20.6968 8534	26.4350 1762	33.7253 4799	42.9774 0026	54.7060 4084
53	21.9386 9846	28.1532 9377	36.0861 2235	46.2007 0528	59.0825 2410
54	23.2550 2037	29.9832 5786	38.6121 5092	49.6657 5817	63.8091 2603
55	24.6503 2159	31.9321 6963	41.3150 0148	53.3906 9004	68.9138 5611
56	26.1293 4089	34.0077 6065	44.2070 5159	57.3949 9179	74.4269 6460
57	27.6971 0134	36.2182 6509	47.3015 4520	61.6996 1617	80.3811 2177
58	29.3589 2742	38.5724 5233	50.6126 5336	66.3270 8739	86.8116 1151
59	31.1204 6307	41.0796 6173	54.1555 3910	71.3016 1894	93.7565 4043
60	32.9876 9085	43.7498 3974	57.9464 2683	76.6492 4036	101.2570 6367
61	34.9669 5230	46.5935 7932	62.0026 7671	82.3979 3339	109.3576 2876
62	37.0649 6944	49.6221 6198	66.3428 6408	88.5777 7839	118.1062 3906
63	39.2888 6761	52.8476 0251	70.9868 6457	95.2211 1177	127.5547 3819
64	41.6461 9967	56.2826 9667	75.9559 4509	102.3626 9515	137.7591 1724
65	44.1449 7165	59.9410 7195	81.2728 6124	110.0398 9729	148.7798 4662
66	46.7936 6994	63.8372 4163	86.9619 6153	118.2928 8959	160.6822 3435
67	49.6012 9014	67.9866 6234	93.0492 9884	127.1648 5631	173.5368 1310
68	52.5773 6755	72.4057 9539	99.5627 4976	136.7022 2053	187.4197 5815
69	55.7320 0960	77.1121 7209	106.5321 4224	146.9548 8707	202.4133 3880
70	59.0759 3018	82.1244 6327	113.9893 9220	157.9765 0360	218.6064 0590
71	62.6204 8599	87.4625 5339	121.9686 4965	169.8247 4137	236.0949 1837
72	66.3777 1515	93.1476 1936	130.5064 5513	182.5615 9697	254.9825 1184
73	70.3603 7806	99.2022 1461	139.6419 0699	196.2537 1675	275.3811 1279
74	74.5820 0074	105.6503 5856	149.4168 4047	210.9727 4550	297.4116 0181
75	79.0569 2079	112.5176 3187	159.8760 1931	226.7957 0141	321.2045 2996
76	83.8003 3603	119.8312 7794	171.0673 4066	243.8053 7902	346.9008 9236
77	88.8283 5620	127.6203 1101	183.0420 5451	262.0907 8245	374.6529 6374
78	94.1580 5757	135.9156 3122	195.8549 9832	281.7475 9113	404.6252 0084
79	99.8075 4102	144.7501 4725	209.5648 4820	302.8786 6046	436.9952 1691
80	105.7959 9348	154.1589 0683	224.2343 8758	325.5945 6000	471.9548 3426
81	112.1437 5309	164.1792 3577	239.9307 9471	350.0141 5200	509.7112 2101
82	118.8723 7828	174.8508 8609	256.7259 5034	376.2652 1340	550.4881 1869
83	126.0047 2097	186.2161 9369	274.6967 6686	404.4851 0440	594.5271 6818
84	133.5650 0423	198.3202 4628	293.9255 4054	434.8214 8723	642.0893 4164
85	141.5789 0449	211.2110 6229	314.5003 2838	467.4330 9878	693.4564 8897
86	150.0736 3875	224.9397 8134	336.5153 5137	502.4905 8119	748.9330 0808
87	159.0780 5708	239.5608 6712	360.0714 2596	540.1773 7477	808.8476 4873
88	168.6227 4050	255.1323 2349	385.2764 2578	580.6906 7788	873.5554 6063
89	178.7401 0493	271.7159 2451	412.2457 7558	624.2424 7872	943.4398 9748
90	189.4645 1123	289.3774 5961	441.1029 7988	671.0606 6463	1018.9150 8928
91	200.8323 8190	308.1869 9448	471.9801 8847	721.3902 1447	1100.4282 9642
92	212.8823 2482	328.2191 4912	505.0188 0166	775.4944 8056	1188.4625 6013
93	225.6552 6431	349.5533 9382	540.3701 1778	833.6565 6660	1283.5395 6494
94	239.1945 8017	372.2743 6441	578.1960 2602	896.1808 0910	1386.2227 3014
95	253.5462 5498	396.4721 9810	618.6697 4784	963.3943 6978	1497.1205 4855
96	268.7590 3028	422.2428 9098	661.9766 3019	1035.6489 4751	1616.8901 9244
97	284.8845 7209	449.6886 7889	708.3149 9430	1113.3226 1858	1746.2414 0783
98	301.9776 4642	478.9184 4302	757.8970 4390	1196.8218 1497	1885.9407 2046
99	320.0963 0520	510.0481 4181	810.9498 3698	1286.5834 5109	2036.8159 7809
100	339.3020 8351	543.2012 7103	867.7163 2557	1383.0772 0993	2199.7612 5634

$$P = (1 + i)^{-n}$$

n	$\frac{1}{4}\%$	$\frac{1}{3}\%$	$\frac{5}{12}\%$	$\frac{1}{2}\%$	$\frac{7}{12}\%$
1	0.9975 0623	0.9966 7774	0.9958 5062	0.9950 2488	0.9942 0050
2	0.9950 1869	0.9933 6652	0.9917 1846	0.9900 7450	0.9844 3463
3	0.9925 3734	0.9900 6630	0.9876 0345	0.9851 4876	0.9827 0220
4	0.9900 6219	0.9867 7704	0.9835 0551	0.9802 4752	0.9770 0302
5	0.9875 9321	0.9834 9871	0.9794 2457	0.9753 7067	0.9713 3688
6	0.9851 3038	0.9802 3127	0.9753 6057	0.9705 1808	0.9657 0361
7	0.9826 7370	0.9769 7469	0.9713 1343	0.9656 8963	0.9601 0301
8	0.9802 2314	0.9737 2893	0.9672 8308	0.9608 8520	0.9545 3489
9	0.9777 7869	0.9704 9395	0.9632 6946	0.9561 0468	0.9489 9907
10	0.9753 4034	0.9672 6972	0.9592 7249	0.9513 4794	0.9434 9534
11	0.9729 0807	0.9640 5620	0.9552 9211	0.9466 1489	0.9380 2354
12	0.9704 8187	0.9608 5335	0.9513 2824	0.9419 0534	0.9325 8347
13	0.9680 6171	0.9576 6115	0.9473 8082	0.9372 1924	0.9271 7495
14	0.9656 4759	0.9544 7955	0.9434 4978	0.9325 5646	0.9217 9780
15	0.9632 3949	0.9513 0852	0.9395 3505	0.9279 1688	0.9164 5183
16	0.9608 3740	0.9481 4803	0.9356 3656	0.9233 0037	0.9111 3686
17	0.9584 4130	0.9449 9803	0.9317 5425	0.9187 0684	0.9058 5272
18	0.9560 5117	0.9418 5851	0.9278 8805	0.9141 3616	0.9005 9923
19	0.9536 6700	0.9387 2941	0.9240 3789	0.9095 8822	0.8953 7620
20	0.9512 8878	0.9356 1071	0.9202 0371	0.9050 6290	0.8901 8346
21	0.9489 1649	0.9325 0236	0.9163 8544	0.9005 6010	0.8850 2084
22	0.9465 5011	0.9294 0435	0.9125 8301	0.8960 7971	0.8798 8816
23	0.9441 8964	0.9263 1663	0.9087 9636	0.8916 2160	0.8747 8525
24	0.9418 3505	0.9232 3916	0.9050 2542	0.8871 8567	0.8697 1193
25	0.9394 8634	0.9201 7192	0.9012 7012	0.8827 7181	0.8646 6803
26	0.9371 4348	0.9171 1487	0.8975 3041	0.8783 7991	0.8596 5339
27	0.9348 0646	0.9140 6798	0.8938 0622	0.8740 0986	0.8546 6782
28	0.9324 7527	0.9110 3121	0.8900 9748	0.8696 6155	0.8497 1118
29	0.9301 4990	0.9080 0453	0.8864 0413	0.8653 3488	0.8447 8327
30	0.9278 3032	0.9049 8790	0.8827 2610	0.8610 2973	0.8398 8395
31	0.9255 1653	0.9019 8130	0.8790 6334	0.8567 4600	0.8350 1304
32	0.9232 0851	0.8989 8468	0.8754 1577	0.8524 8358	0.8301 7038
33	0.9209 0624	0.8959 9802	0.8717 8334	0.8482 4237	0.8253 5581
34	0.9186 0972	0.8930 2128	0.8681 6599	0.8440 2226	0.8205 6915
35	0.9163 1892	0.8900 5444	0.8645 6364	0.8398 2314	0.8158 1026
36	0.9140 3384	0.8870 9745	0.8609 7624	0.8356 4492	0.8110 7897
37	0.9117 5445	0.8841 5028	0.8574 0372	0.8314 8748	0.8063 7511
38	0.9094 8075	0.8812 1290	0.8538 4603	0.8273 5073	0.8016 9854
39	0.9072 1272	0.8782 8528	0.8503 0310	0.8232 3455	0.7970 4908
40	0.9049 5034	0.8753 6739	0.8467 7487	0.8191 3886	0.7924 2660
41	0.9026 9361	0.8724 5920	0.8432 6128	0.8150 6354	0.7878 3092
42	0.9004 4250	0.8695 6066	0.8397 6227	0.8110 0850	0.7832 6189
43	0.8981 9701	0.8666 7175	0.8362 7778	0.8069 7363	0.7787 1936
44	0.8959 5712	0.8637 9245	0.8328 0775	0.8029 5884	0.7742 0317
45	0.8937 2281	0.8609 2270	0.8293 5211	0.7989 6402	0.7697 1318
46	0.8914 9407	0.8580 6249	0.8259 1082	0.7949 8907	0.7652 4923
47	0.8892 7090	0.8552 1179	0.8224 8380	0.7910 3390	0.7608 1116
48	0.8870 5326	0.8523 7055	0.8190 7100	0.7870 9841	0.7563 9884
49	0.8848 4116	0.8495 3876	0.8156 7237	0.7831 8250	0.7520 1210
50	0.8826 3457	0.8467 1637	0.8122 8784	0.7792 8607	0.7476 5080

TABLE II. PRESENT VALUE OF 1 AT COMPOUND INTEREST **299**

$$P = (1 + i)^{-n}$$

n	$\frac{1}{4}\%$	$\frac{1}{3}\%$	$\frac{5}{12}\%$	$\frac{1}{2}\%$	$\frac{7}{12}\%$
51	0.8804 3349	0.8439 0336	0.8089 1735	0.7754 0902	0.7433 1480
52	0.8782 3790	0.8410 9969	0.8055 6084	0.7715 5127	0.7390 0394
53	0.8760 4778	0.8383 0534	0.8022 1827	0.7677 1270	0.7347 1809
54	0.8738 6312	0.8355 2027	0.7988 8956	0.7638 9324	0.7304 5709
55	0.8716 8391	0.8327 4446	0.7955 7467	0.7600 9277	0.7262 2080
56	0.8695 1013	0.8299 7787	0.7922 7353	0.7563 1122	0.7220 0908
57	0.8673 4178	0.8272 2047	0.7889 8608	0.7525 4847	0.7178 2179
58	0.8651 7883	0.8244 7222	0.7857 1228	0.7488 0445	0.7136 5878
59	0.8630 2128	0.8217 3311	0.7824 5207	0.7450 7906	0.7095 1991
60	0.8608 6911	0.8190 0310	0.7792 0538	0.7413 7220	0.7054 0505
61	0.8587 2230	0.8162 8216	0.7759 7216	0.7376 8378	0.7013 1405
62	0.8565 8085	0.8135 7026	0.7727 5236	0.7340 1371	0.6972 4678
63	0.8544 4474	0.8108 6737	0.7695 4591	0.7303 6190	0.6932 0310
64	0.8523 1395	0.8081 7346	0.7663 5278	0.7267 2826	0.6891 8286
65	0.8501 8848	0.8054 8850	0.7631 7289	0.7231 1269	0.6851 8594
66	0.8480 6831	0.8028 1246	0.7600 0620	0.7195 1512	0.6812 1221
67	0.8459 5343	0.8001 4531	0.7568 5265	0.7159 3544	0.6772 6151
68	0.8438 4382	0.7974 8702	0.7537 1218	0.7123 7357	0.6733 3373
69	0.8417 3947	0.7948 3756	0.7505 8474	0.7088 2943	0.6694 2873
70	0.8396 4037	0.7921 9690	0.7474 7028	0.7053 0291	0.6655 4638
71	0.8375 4650	0.7895 6502	0.7443 6874	0.7017 9394	0.6616 8654
72	0.8354 5786	0.7869 4188	0.7412 8008	0.6983 0243	0.6578 4909
73	0.8333 7442	0.7843 2745	0.7382 0423	0.6948 2829	0.6540 3389
74	0.8312 9618	0.7817 2171	0.7351 4114	0.6913 7143	0.6502 4082
75	0.8292 2312	0.7791 2463	0.7320 9076	0.6879 3177	0.6464 6975
76	0.8271 5523	0.7765 3618	0.7290 5304	0.6845 0923	0.6427 2054
77	0.8250 9250	0.7739 5632	0.7260 2792	0.6811 0371	0.6389 9308
78	0.8230 3491	0.7713 8504	0.7230 1536	0.6777 1513	0.6352 8724
79	0.8209 8246	0.7688 2230	0.7200 1529	0.6743 4342	0.6316 0289
80	0.8189 3512	0.7662 6807	0.7170 2768	0.6709 8847	0.6279 3991
81	0.8168 9289	0.7637 2233	0.7140 5246	0.6676 5022	0.6242 9817
82	0.8148 5575	0.7611 8505	0.7110 8959	0.6643 2858	0.6206 7755
83	0.8128 2369	0.7586 5619	0.7081 3901	0.6610 2346	0.6170 7793
84	0.8107 9670	0.7561 3574	0.7052 0067	0.6577 3479	0.6134 9919
85	0.8087 7476	0.7536 2366	0.7022 7453	0.6544 6248	0.6099 4120
86	0.8067 5787	0.7511 1993	0.6993 6052	0.6512 0644	0.6064 0384
87	0.8047 4600	0.7486 2451	0.6964 5861	0.6479 6661	0.6028 8700
88	0.8027 3915	0.7461 3739	0.6935 6874	0.6447 4290	0.5993 9056
89	0.8007 3731	0.7436 5853	0.6906 9086	0.6415 3522	0.5959 1439
90	0.7987 4046	0.7411 8790	0.6878 2493	0.6383 4350	0.5924 5838
91	0.7967 4859	0.7387 2548	0.6849 7088	0.6351 6766	0.5890 2242
92	0.7947 6168	0.7362 7125	0.6821 2868	0.6320 0763	0.5856 0638
93	0.7927 7973	0.7338 2516	0.6792 9827	0.6288 6331	0.5822 1015
94	0.7908 0273	0.7313 8720	0.6764 7960	0.6257 3464	0.5788 3363
95	0.7888 3065	0.7289 5735	0.6736 7263	0.6226 2153	0.5754 7668
96	0.7868 6349	0.7265 3556	0.6708 7731	0.6195 2391	0.5721 3920
97	0.7849 0124	0.7241 2182	0.6680 9359	0.6164 4170	0.5688 2108
98	0.7829 4388	0.7217 1610	0.6653 2141	0.6133 7483	0.5655 2220
99	0.7809 9140	0.7193 1837	0.6625 6074	0.6103 2321	0.5622 4245
100	0.7790 4379	0.7169 2861	0.6598 1153	0.6072 8678	0.5589 8172

$$P = (1 + i)^{-n}$$

n	$\dfrac{7}{8}\%$	1%	$1\dfrac{1}{8}\%$	$1\dfrac{1}{4}\%$	$1\dfrac{3}{8}\%$
1	0.9913 2590	0.9900 9901	0.9888 7515	0.9876 5432	0.9864 3650
2	0.9827 2704	0.9802 9605	0.9778 7407	0.9754 6106	0.9730 5696
3	0.9742 0276	0.9705 9015	0.9669 9537	0.9634 1833	0.9598 5890
4	0.9657 5243	0.9609 8034	0.9562 3770	0.9515 2428	0.9468 3986
5	0.9573 7539	0.9514 6569	0.9455 9970	0.9397 7706	0.9339 9739
6	0.9490 7102	0.9420 4524	0.9350 8005	0.9281 7488	0.9213 2912
7	0.9408 3868	0.9327 1805	0.9246 7743	0.9167 1593	0.9088 3267
8	0.9326 7775	0.9234 8322	0.9143 9054	0.9053 9845	0.8965 0571
9	0.9245 8761	0.9143 3982	0.9042 1808	0.8942 2069	0.8843 4596
10	0.9165 6765	0.9052 8695	0.8941 5881	0.8831 8093	0.8723 5113
11	0.9086 1724	0.8963 2372	0.8842 1142	0.8722 7746	0.8605 1899
12	0.9007 3581	0.8874 4923	0.8743 7470	0.8615 0860	0.8488 4734
13	0.8929 2273	0.8786 6260	0.8646 4742	0.8508 7269	0.8373 3400
14	0.8851 7743	0.8699 6297	0.8550 2835	0.8403 6809	0.8259 7682
15	0.8774 9931	0.8613 4947	0.8455 1629	0.8299 9318	0.8147 7368
16	0.8698 8779	0.8528 2126	0.8361 1005	0.8197 4635	0.8037 2250
17	0.8623 4230	0.8443 7749	0.8268 0846	0.8096 2602	0.7928 2120
18	0.8548 6225	0.8360 1731	0.8176 1034	0.7996 3064	0.7820 6777
19	0.8474 4709	0.8277 3992	0.8085 1455	0.7897 5866	0.7714 6020
20	0.8400 9624	0.8195 4447	0.7995 1995	0.7800 0855	0.7609 9649
21	0.8328 0917	0.8114 3017	0.7906 2542	0.7703 7881	0.7506 7472
22	0.8255 8530	0.8033 9621	0.7818 2983	0.7608 6796	0.7404 9294
23	0.8184 2409	0.7954 4179	0.7731 3210	0.7514 7453	0.7304 4926
24	0.8113 2499	0.7875 6613	0.7645 3112	0.7421 9707	0.7205 4181
25	0.8042 8748	0.7797 6844	0.7560 2583	0.7330 3414	0.7107 6874
26	0.7973 1101	0.7720 4796	0.7476 1516	0.7239 8434	0.7011 2823
27	0.7903 9505	0.7644 0392	0.7392 9806	0.7150 4626	0.6916 1847
28	0.7835 3908	0.7568 3557	0.7310 7348	0.7062 1853	0.6822 3771
29	0.7767 4258	0.7493 4215	0.7229 4040	0.6974 9978	0.6729 8417
30	0.7700 0504	0.7419 2292	0.7148 9780	0.6888 8867	0.6638 5615
31	0.7633 2594	0.7345 7715	0.7069 4467	0.6803 8387	0.6548 5194
32	0.7567 0477	0.7273 0411	0.6990 8002	0.6719 8407	0.6459 6985
33	0.7501 4104	0.7201 0307	0.6913 0287	0.6636 8797	0.6372 0824
34	0.7436 3424	0.7129 7334	0.6836 1223	0.6554 9429	0.6285 6546
35	0.7371 8388	0.7059 1420	0.6760 0715	0.6474 0177	0.6200 3991
36	0.7307 8947	0.6989 2495	0.6684 8667	0.6394 0916	0.6116 3000
37	0.7244 5053	0.6920 0490	0.6610 4986	0.6315 1522	0.6033 3416
38	0.7181 6657	0.6851 5337	0.6536 9578	0.6237 1873	0.5951 5083
39	0.7119 3712	0.6783 6967	0.6464 2352	0.6160 1850	0.5870 7850
40	0.7057 6171	0.6716 5314	0.6392 3216	0.6084 1334	0.5791 1566
41	0.6996 3986	0.6650 0311	0.6321 2080	0.6009 0206	0.5712 6083
42	0.6935 7111	0.6584 1892	0.6250 8855	0.5934 8352	0.5635 1253
43	0.6875 5500	0.6518 9992	0.6181 3454	0.5861 5656	0.5558 6933
44	0.6815 9108	0.6454 4546	0.6112 5789	0.5789 2006	0.5483 2979
45	0.6756 7889	0.6390 5492	0.6044 5774	0.5717 7290	0.5408 9252
46	0.6698 1798	0.6327 2764	0.5977 3324	0.5647 1397	0.5335 5612
47	0.6640 0792	0.6264 6301	0.5910 8355	0.5577 4219	0.5263 1923
48	0.6582 4824	0.6202 6041	0.5845 0784	0.5508 5649	0.5191 8050
49	0.6525 3853	0.6141 1921	0.5780 0528	0.5440 5579	0.5121 3860
50	0.6468 7835	0.6080 3882	0.5715 7506	0.5373 3905	0.5051 9220

TABLE II.   PRESENT VALUE OF 1 AT COMPOUND INTEREST   301

$$P = (1 + i)^{-n}$$

n	$\frac{7}{8}\%$	1%	$1\frac{1}{8}\%$	$1\frac{1}{4}\%$	$1\frac{3}{8}\%$
51	0.6412 6726	0.6020 1864	0.5652 1637	0.5307 0524	0.4983 4003
52	0.6357 0484	0.5960 5806	0.5589 2843	0.5241 5332	0.4915 8079
53	0.6301 9067	0.5901 5649	0.5527 1044	0.5176 8229	0.4849 1323
54	0.6247 2433	0.5843 1336	0.5465 6162	0.5112 9115	0.4783 3611
55	0.6193 0541	0.5785 2808	0.5404 8120	0.5049 7892	0.4718 4820
56	0.6139 3349	0.5728 0008	0.5344 6843	0.4987 4461	0.4654 4829
57	0.6086 0817	0.5671 2879	0.5285 2256	0.4925 8727	0.4591 3518
58	0.6033 2904	0.5615 1365	0.5226 4282	0.4865 0594	0.4529 0770
59	0.5980 9571	0.5559 5411	0.5168 2850	0.4804 9970	0.4467 6468
60	0.5929 0776	0.5504 4962	0.5110 7887	0.4745 6760	0.4407 0499
61	0.5877 6482	0.5449 9962	0.5053 9319	0.4687 0874	0.4347 2749
62	0.5826 6649	0.5396 0358	0.4997 7077	0.4629 2222	0.4288 3106
63	0.5776 1238	0.5342 6097	0.4942 1090	0.4572 0713	0.4230 1461
64	0.5726 0211	0.5289 7126	0.4887 1288	0.4515 6259	0.4172 7705
65	0.5676 3530	0.5237 3392	0.4832 7602	0.4459 8775	0.4116 1731
66	0.5627 1158	0.5185 4844	0.4778 9965	0.4404 8173	0.4060 3434
67	0.5578 3056	0.5134 1429	0.4725 8309	0.4350 4368	0.4005 2709
68	0.5529 9188	0.5083 3099	0.4673 2568	0.4296 7277	0.3950 9454
69	0.5481 9517	0.5032 9801	0.4621 2675	0.4243 6817	0.3897 3568
70	0.5434 4007	0.4983 1486	0.4569 8566	0.4191 2905	0.3844 4949
71	0.5387 2622	0.4933 8105	0.4519 0177	0.4139 5462	0.3792 3501
72	0.5340 5325	0.4884 9609	0.4468 7443	0.4088 4407	0.3740 9126
73	0.5294 2082	0.4836 5949	0.4419 0302	0.4037 9661	0.3690 1727
74	0.5248 2857	0.4788 7078	0.4369 8692	0.3988 1147	0.3640 1210
75	0.5202 7615	0.4741 2949	0.4321 2551	0.3938 8787	0.3590 7483
76	0.5157 6322	0.4694 3514	0.4273 1818	0.3890 2506	0.3542 0451
77	0.5112 8944	0.4647 8726	0.4225 6433	0.3842 2228	0.3494 0026
78	0.5068 5447	0.4601 8541	0.4178 6337	0.3794 7879	0.3446 6117
79	0.5024 5796	0.4556 2912	0.4132 1470	0.3747 9387	0.3399 8636
80	0.4980 9959	0.4511 1794	0.4086 1775	0.3701 6679	0.3353 7495
81	0.4937 7902	0.4466 5142	0.4040 7194	0.3655 9683	0.3308 2609
82	0.4894 9593	0.4422 2913	0.3995 7670	0.3610 8329	0.3263 3893
83	0.4852 4999	0.4378 5063	0.3951 3148	0.3566 2547	0.3219 1263
84	0.4810 4089	0.4335 1547	0.3907 3570	0.3522 2268	0.3175 4637
85	0.4768 6829	0.4292 2324	0.3863 8882	0.3478 7426	0.3132 3933
86	0.4727 3188	0.4249 7350	0.3820 9031	0.3435 7951	0.3089 9071
87	0.4686 3136	0.4207 6585	0.3778 3961	0.3393 3779	0.3047 9971
88	0.4645 6640	0.4165 9985	0.3736 3621	0.3351 4843	0.3006 6556
89	0.4605 3671	0.4124 7510	0.3694 7956	0.3310 1080	0.2965 8748
90	0.4565 4197	0.4083 9119	0.3653 6916	0.3269 2425	0.2925 6472
91	0.4525 8187	0.4043 4771	0.3613 0448	0.3228 8814	0.2885 9652
92	0.4486 5613	0.4003 4427	0.3572 8503	0.3189 0187	0.2846 8214
93	0.4447 6444	0.3963 8046	0.3533 1029	0.3149 6481	0.2808 2085
94	0.4409 0651	0.3924 5590	0.3493 7976	0.3110 7636	0.2770 1194
95	0.4370 8204	0.3885 7020	0.3454 9297	0.3072 3591	0.2732 5468
96	0.4332 9075	0.3847 2297	0.3416 4941	0.3034 4257	0.2695 4839
97	0.4295 3234	0.3809 1383	0.3378 4861	0.2996 9666	0.2658 9237
98	0.4258 0654	0.3771 4241	0.3340 9010	0.2959 9670	0.2622 8594
99	0.4221 1305	0.3734 0832	0.3303 7340	0.2923 4242	0.2587 2843
100	0.4184 5159	0.3697 1121	0.3266 9805	0.2887 3326	0.2552 1916

$$P = (1 + i)^{-n}$$

n	$1\frac{1}{2}\%$	$1\frac{3}{4}\%$	2%	$2\frac{1}{4}\%$	$2\frac{1}{2}\%$
1	0.9852 2167	0.9828 0098	0.9803 9216	0.9779 9511	0.9756 0976
2	0.9706 6175	0.9658 9777	0.9611 6878	0.9564 7444	0.9518 1440
3	0.9563 1699	0.9492 8528	0.9423 2233	0.9354 2732	0.9285 9941
4	0.9421 8423	0.9329 5851	0.9238 4543	0.9148 4335	0.9059 5064
5	0.9282 6033	0.9169 1254	0.9057 3081	0.8947 1232	0.8838 5429
6	0.9145 4219	0.9011 4254	0.8879 7138	0.8750 2427	0.8622 9687
7	0.9010 2679	0.8856 4378	0.8705 6018	0.8557 6946	0.8412 6524
8	0.8877 1112	0.8704 1157	0.8534 9037	0.8369 3835	0.8207 4657
9	0.8745 9224	0.8554 4135	0.8367 5527	0.8185 2161	0.8007 2836
10	0.8616 6723	0.8407 2860	0.8203 4830	0.8005 1013	0.7811 9840
11	0.8489 3323	0.8262 6889	0.8042 6304	0.7828 9499	0.7621 4478
12	0.8363 8742	0.8120 5788	0.7884 9318	0.7656 6748	0.7435 5589
13	0.8240 2702	0.7980 9128	0.7730 3253	0.7488 1905	0.7254 2038
14	0.8118 4928	0.7843 6490	0.7578 7502	0.7323 4137	0.7077 2720
15	0.7998 5150	0.7708 7459	0.7430 1473	0.7162 2628	0.6904 6556
16	0.7880 3104	0.7576 1631	0.7284 4581	0.7004 6580	0.6736 2493
17	0.7763 8526	0.7445 8605	0.7141 6256	0.6850 5212	0.6571 9506
18	0.7649 1159	0.7317 7990	0.7001 5937	0.6699 7763	0.6411 6591
19	0.7536 0747	0.7191 9401	0.6864 3076	0.6552 3484	0.6255 2772
20	0.7424 7042	0.7068 2458	0.6729 7133	0.6408 1647	0.6102 7094
21	0.7314 9795	0.6946 6789	0.6597 7582	0.6267 1538	0.5953 8629
22	0.7206 8763	0.6827 2028	0.6468 3904	0.6129 2457	0.5808 6467
23	0.7100 3708	0.6709 7817	0.6341 5592	0.5994 3724	0.5666 9724
24	0.6995 4392	0.6594 3800	0.6217 2149	0.5862 4668	0.5528 7535
25	0.6892 0583	0.6480 9632	0.6095 3087	0.5733 4639	0.5393 9059
26	0.6790 2052	0.6369 4970	0.5975 7928	0.5607 2997	0.5262 3472
27	0.6689 8574	0.6259 9479	0.5858 6204	0.5483 9117	0.5133 9973
28	0.6590 9925	0.6152 2829	0.5743 7455	0.5363 2388	0.5008 7778
29	0.6493 5887	0.6046 4697	0.5631 1231	0.5245 2213	0.4886 6125
30	0.6397 6243	0.5942 4764	0.5520 7089	0.5129 8008	0.4767 4269
31	0.6303 0781	0.5840 2716	0.5412 4597	0.5016 9201	0.4651 1481
32	0.6209 9292	0.5739 8247	0.5306 3330	0.4906 5233	0.4537 7055
33	0.6118 1568	0.5641 1053	0.5202 2873	0.4798 5558	0.4427 0298
34	0.6027 7407	0.5544 0839	0.5100 2817	0.4692 9641	0.4319 0534
35	0.5938 6608	0.5448 7311	0.5000 2761	0.4589 6960	0.4213 7107
36	0.5850 8974	0.5355 0183	0.4902 2315	0.4488 7002	0.4110 9372
37	0.5764 4309	0.5262 9172	0.4806 1093	0.4389 9268	0.4010 6705
38	0.5679 2423	0.5172 4002	0.4711 8719	0.4293 3270	0.3912 8492
39	0.5595 3126	0.5083 4400	0.4619 4822	0.4198 8528	0.3817 4139
40	0.5512 6232	0.4996 0098	0.4528 9042	0.4106 4575	0.3724 3062
41	0.5431 1559	0.4910 0834	0.4440 1021	0.4016 0954	0.3633 4695
42	0.5350 8925	0.4825 6348	0.4353 0413	0.3927 7216	0.3544 8483
43	0.5271 8153	0.4742 6386	0.4267 6875	0.3841 2925	0.3458 3886
44	0.5193 9067	0.4661 0699	0.4184 0074	0.3756 7653	0.3374 0376
45	0.5117 1494	0.4580 9040	0.4101 9680	0.3674 0981	0.3291 7440
46	0.5041 5265	0.4502 1170	0.4021 5373	0.3593 2500	0.3211 4576
47	0.4967 0212	0.4424 6850	0.3942 6836	0.3514 1809	0.3133 1294
48	0.4893 6170	0.4348 5848	0.3865 3761	0.3436 8518	0.3056 7116
49	0.4821 2975	0.4273 7934	0.3789 5844	0.3361 2242	0.2982 1576
50	0.4750 0468	0.4200 2883	0.3715 2788	0.3287 2608	0.2909 4221

TABLE II. PRESENT VALUE OF 1 AT COMPOUND INTEREST 303

$$P = (1 + i)^{-n}$$

n	$1\frac{1}{2}\%$	$1\frac{3}{4}\%$	2%	$2\frac{1}{4}\%$	$2\frac{1}{2}\%$
51	0.4679 8491	0.4128 0475	0.3642 4302	0.3214 9250	0.2838 4606
52	0.4610 6887	0.4057 0492	0.3571 0100	0.3144 1810	0.2769 2298
53	0.4542 5505	0.3987 2719	0.3500 9902	0.3074 9936	0.2701 6876
54	0.4475 4192	0.3918 6947	0.3432 3433	0.3007 3287	0.2635 7928
55	0.4409 2800	0.3851 2970	0.3365 0425	0.2941 1528	0.2571 5052
56	0.4344 1182	0.3785 0585	0.3299 0613	0.2876 4330	0.2508 7855
57	0.4279 9194	0.3719 9592	0.3234 3738	0.2813 1374	0.2447 5956
58	0.4216 6694	0.3655 9796	0.3170 9547	0.2751 2347	0.2387 8982
59	0.4154 3541	0.3593 1003	0.3108 7791	0.2690 6940	0.2329 6568
60	0.4092 9597	0.3531 3025	0.3047 8227	0.2631 4856	0.2272 8359
61	0.4032 4726	0.3470 5676	0.2988 0614	0.2573 5801	0.2217 4009
62	0.3972 8794	0.3410 8772	0.2929 4720	0.2516 9487	0.2163 3179
63	0.3914 1669	0.3352 2135	0.2872 0314	0.2461 5635	0.2110 5541
64	0.3856 3221	0.3294 5587	0.2815 7170	0.2407 3971	0.2059 0771
65	0.3799 3321	0.3237 8956	0.2760 5069	0.2354 4226	0.2008 8557
66	0.3743 1843	0.3182 2069	0.2706 3793	0.2302 6138	0.1959 8593
67	0.3687 8663	0.3127 4761	0.2653 3130	0.2251 9450	0.1912 0578
68	0.3633 3658	0.3073 6866	0.2601 2873	0.2202 3912	0.1865 4223
69	0.3579 6708	0.3020 8222	0.2550 2817	0.2153 9278	0.1819 9241
70	0.3526 7692	0.2968 8670	0.2500 2761	0.2106 5309	0.1775 5358
71	0.3474 6495	0.2917 8054	0.2451 2511	0.2060 1769	0.1732 2300
72	0.3423 3000	0.2867 6221	0.2403 1874	0.2014 8429	0.1689 9805
73	0.3372 7093	0.2818 3018	0.2356 0661	0.1970 5065	0.1648 7615
74	0.3322 8663	0.2769 8298	0.2309 8687	0.1927 1458	0.1608 5478
75	0.3273 7599	0.2722 1914	0.2264 5771	0.1884 7391	0.1569 3149
76	0.3225 3793	0.2675 3724	0.2220 1737	0.1843 2657	0.1531 0389
77	0.3177 7136	0.2629 3586	0.2176 6408	0.1802 7048	0.1493 6965
78	0.3130 7523	0.2584 1362	0.2133 9616	0.1763 0365	0.1457 2649
79	0.3084 4850	0.2539 6916	0.2092 1192	0.1724 2411	0.1421 7218
80	0.3038 9015	0.2496 0114	0.2051 0973	0.1686 2993	0.1387 0457
81	0.2993 9916	0.2453 0825	0.2010 8797	0.1649 1925	0.1353 2153
82	0.2949 7454	0.2410 8919	0.1971 4507	0.1612 9022	0.1320 2101
83	0.2906 1531	0.2369 4269	0.1932 7948	0.1577 4105	0.1288 0098
84	0.2863 2050	0.2328 6751	0.1894 8968	0.1542 6997	0.1256 5949
85	0.2820 8917	0.2288 6242	0.1857 7420	0.1508 7528	0.1225 9463
86	0.2779 2036	0.2249 2621	0.1821 3157	0.1475 5528	0.1196 0452
87	0.2738 1316	0.2210 5770	0.1785 6036	0.1443 0835	0.1166 8733
88	0.2697 6666	0.2172 5572	0.1750 5918	0.1411 3286	0.1138 4130
89	0.2657 7997	0.2135 1914	0.1716 2665	0.1380 2724	0.1110 6468
90	0.2618 5218	0.2098 4682	0.1682 6142	0.1349 8997	0.1083 5579
91	0.2579 8245	0.2062 3766	0.1649 6217	0.1320 1953	0.1057 1296
92	0.2541 6990	0.2026 9057	0.1617 2762	0.1291 1445	0.1031 3460
93	0.2504 1369	0.1992 0450	0.1585 5649	0.1262 7331	0.1006 1912
94	0.2467 1300	0.1957 7837	0.1554 4754	0.1234 9468	0.0981 6500
95	0.2430 6699	0.1924 1118	0.1523 9955	0.1207 7719	0.0957 7073
96	0.2394 7487	0.1891 0190	0.1494 1132	0.1181 1950	0.0934 3486
97	0.2359 3583	0.1858 4953	0.1464 8169	0.1155 2029	0.0911 5596
98	0.2324 4909	0.1826 5310	0.1436 0950	0.1129 7828	0.0889 3264
99	0.2290 1389	0.1795 1165	0.1407 9363	0.1104 9221	0.0867 6355
100	0.2256 2944	0.1764 2422	0.1380 3297	0.1080 6084	0.0846 4737

$$P = (1 + i)^{-n}$$

n	$2\frac{3}{4}\%$	3%	$3\frac{1}{2}\%$	4%	$4\frac{1}{2}\%$
1	0.9732 3601	0.9708 7379	0.9661 8357	0.9615 3846	0.9569 3780
2	0.9471 8833	0.9425 9591	0.9335 1070	0.9245 5621	0.9157 2995
3	0.9218 3779	0.9151 4166	0.9019 4271	0.8889 9636	0.8762 9660
4	0.8971 6573	0.8884 8705	0.8714 4223	0.8548 0419	0.8385 6134
5	0.8731 5400	0.8626 0878	0.8419 7317	0.8219 2711	0.8024 5105
6	0.8497 8491	0.8374 8426	0.8135 0064	0.7903 1453	0.7678 9574
7	0.8270 4128	0.8130 9151	0.7859 9096	0.7599 1781	0.7348 2846
8	0.8049 0635	0.7894 0923	0.7594 1156	0.7306 9021	0.7031 8513
9	0.7833 6385	0.7664 1673	0.7337 3097	0.7025 8674	0.6729 0443
10	0.7623 9791	0.7440 9391	0.7089 1881	0.6755 6417	0.6439 2768
11	0.7419 9310	0.7224 2128	0.6849 4571	0.6495 8093	0.6161 9874
12	0.7221 3440	0.7013 7988	0.6617 8330	0.6245 9705	0.5896 6386
13	0.7028 0720	0.6809 5134	0.6394 0415	0.6005 7409	0.5642 7164
14	0.6839 9728	0.6611 1781	0.6177 8179	0.5774 7508	0.5399 7286
15	0.6656 9078	0.6418 6195	0.5968 9062	0.5552 6450	0.5167 2044
16	0.6478 7424	0.6231 6694	0.5767 0591	0.5339 0818	0.4944 6932
17	0.6305 3454	0.6050 1645	0.5572 0378	0.5133 7325	0.4731 7639
18	0.6136 5892	0.5873 9461	0.5383 6114	0.4936 2812	0.4528 0037
19	0.5972 3496	0.5702 8603	0.5201 5569	0.4746 4242	0.4333 0179
20	0.5812 5057	0.5536 7575	0.5025 6588	0.4563 8695	0.4146 4286
21	0.5656 9398	0.5375 4928	0.4855 7090	0.4388 3360	0.3967 8743
22	0.5505 5375	0.5218 9250	0.4691 5063	0.4219 5539	0.3797 0089
23	0.5358 1874	0.5066 9175	0.4532 8563	0.4057 2633	0.3633 5013
24	0.5214 7809	0.4919 3374	0.4379 5713	0.3901 2147	0.3477 0347
25	0.5075 2126	0.4776 0557	0.4231 4699	0.3751 1680	0.3327 3060
26	0.4939 3796	0.4636 9473	0.4088 3767	0.3606 8923	0.3184 0248
27	0.4807 1821	0.4501 8906	0.3950 1224	0.3468 1657	0.3046 9137
28	0.4678 5227	0.4370 7675	0.3816 5434	0.3334 7747	0.2915 7069
29	0.4553 3068	0.4243 4636	0.3687 4815	0.3206 5141	0.2790 1502
30	0.4431 4421	0.4119 8676	0.3562 7841	0.3083 1867	0.2670 0002
31	0.4312 8391	0.3999 8715	0.3442 3035	0.2964 6026	0.2555 0241
32	0.4197 4103	0.3883 3703	0.3325 8971	0.2850 5794	0.2444 9991
33	0.4085 0708	0.3770 2625	0.3213 4271	0.2740 9417	0.2339 7121
34	0.3975 7380	0.3660 4490	0.3104 7605	0.2635 5209	0.2238 9589
35	0.3869 3314	0.3553 8340	0.2999 7686	0.2534 1547	0.2142 5444
36	0.3765 7727	0.3450 3243	0.2898 3272	0.2436 6872	0.2050 2817
37	0.3664 9856	0.3349 8294	0.2800 3161	0.2342 9685	0.1961 9921
38	0.3566 8959	0.3252 2615	0.2705 6194	0.2252 8543	0.1877 5044
39	0.3471 4316	0.3157 5355	0.2614 1250	0.2166 2061	0.1796 6549
40	0.3378 5222	0.3065 5684	0.2525 7247	0.2082 8904	0.1719 2870
41	0.3288 0995	0.2976 2800	0.2440 3137	0.2002 7793	0.1645 2507
42	0.3200 0968	0.2889 5922	0.2357 7910	0.1925 7493	0.1574 4026
43	0.3114 4495	0.2805 4294	0.2278 0590	0.1851 6820	0.1506 6054
44	0.3031 0944	0.2723 7178	0.2201 0231	0.1780 4635	0.1441 7276
45	0.2949 9702	0.2644 3862	0.2126 5924	0.1711 9841	0.1379 6437
46	0.2871 0172	0.2567 3653	0.2054 6787	0.1646 1386	0.1320 2332
47	0.2794 1773	0.2492 5876	0.1985 1968	0.1582 8256	0.1263 3810
48	0.2719 3940	0.2419 0880	0.1918 0645	0.1521 9476	0.1208 9771
49	0.2646 6122	0.2349 5029	0.1853 2024	0.1463 4112	0.1156 9158
50	0.2575 7783	0.2281 0708	0.1790 5337	0.1407 1262	0.1107 0965

TABLE II.   PRESENT VALUE OF 1 AT COMPOUND INTEREST   305

$$P = (1 + i)^{-n}$$

n	$2\frac{3}{4}$ %	3 %	$3\frac{1}{2}$ %	4 %	$4\frac{1}{2}$ %
51	0.2506 8402	0.2214 6318	0.1729 9843	0.1353 0059	0.1059 4225
52	0.2439 7471	0.2150 1280	0.1671 4824	0.1300 9672	0.1013 8014
53	0.2374 4497	0.2087 5029	0.1614 9589	0.1250 9300	0.0970 1449
54	0.2310 9000	0.2026 7019	0.1560 3467	0.1202 8173	0.0928 3683
55	0.2249 0511	0.1967 6717	0.1507 5814	0.1156 5551	0.0888 3907
56	0.2188 8575	0.1910 3609	0.1456 6004	0.1112 0722	0.0850 1347
57	0.2130 2749	0.1854 7193	0.1407 3433	0.1069 3002	0.0813 5260
58	0.2073 2603	0.1800 6984	0.1359 7520	0.1028 1733	0.0778 4938
59	0.2017 7716	0.1748 2508	0.1313 7701	0.0988 6282	0.0744 9701
60	0.1963 7679	0.1697 3309	0.1269 3431	0.0950 6040	0.0712 8901
61	0.1911 2097	0.1647 8941	0.1226 4184	0.0914 0423	0.0682 1915
62	0.1860 0581	0.1599 8972	0.1184 9453	0.0878 8868	0.0652 8148
63	0.1810 2755	0.1553 2982	0.1144 8747	0.0845 0835	0.0624 7032
64	0.1761 8253	0.1508 0565	0.1106 1591	0.0812 5803	0.0597 8021
65	0.1714 6718	0.1464 1325	0.1068 7528	0.0781 3272	0.0572 0594
66	0.1668 7804	0.1421 4879	0.1032 6114	0.0751 2762	0.0547 4253
67	0.1624 1172	0.1380 0853	0.0997 6922	0.0722 3809	0.0523 8519
68	0.1580 6493	0.1339 8887	0.0963 9538	0.0694 5970	0.0501 2937
69	0.1538 3448	0.1300 8628	0.0931 3563	0.0667 8818	0.0479 7069
70	0.1497 1726	0.1262 9736	0.0899 8612	0.0642 1940	0.0459 0497
71	0.1457 1023	0.1226 1880	0.0869 4311	0.0617 4942	0.0439 2820
72	0.1418 1044	0.1190 4737	0.0840 0300	0.0593 7445	0.0420 3655
73	0.1380 1503	0.1155 7998	0.0811 6232	0.0570 9081	0.0402 2637
74	0.1343 2119	0.1122 1357	0.0784 1770	0.0548 9501	0.0384 9413
75	0.1307 2622	0.1089 4521	0.0757 6590	0.0527 8367	0.0368 3649
76	0.1272 2747	0.1057 7205	0.0732 0376	0.0507 5353	0.0352 5023
77	0.1238 2235	0.1026 9131	0.0707 2827	0.0488 0147	0.0337 3228
78	0.1205 0837	0.0997 0030	0.0683 3650	0.0469 2449	0.0322 7969
79	0.1172 8309	0.0967 9641	0.0660 2560	0.0451 1970	0.0308 8965
80	0.1141 4412	0.0939 7710	0.0637 9285	0.0433 8433	0.0295 5948
81	0.1110 8917	0.0912 3990	0.0616 3561	0.0417 1570	0.0282 8658
82	0.1081 1598	0.0885 8243	0.0595 5131	0.0401 1125	0.0270 6850
83	0.1052 2237	0.0860 0236	0.0575 3750	0.0385 6851	0.0259 0287
84	0.1024 0620	0.0834 9743	0.0555 9178	0.0370 8510	0.0247 8744
85	0.0996 6540	0.0810 6547	0.0537 1187	0.0356 5875	0.0237 2003
86	0.0969 9795	0.0787 0434	0.0518 9553	0.0342 8726	0.0226 9860
87	0.0944 0190	0.0764 1198	0.0501 4060	0.0329 6852	0.0217 2115
88	0.0918 7533	0.0741 8639	0.0484 4503	0.0317 0050	0.0207 8579
89	0.0894 1638	0.0720 2562	0.0468 0679	0.0304 8125	0.0198 9070
90	0.0870 2324	0.0699 2779	0.0452 2395	0.0293 0890	0.0190 3417
91	0.0846 9415	0.0678 9105	0.0436 9464	0.0281 8163	0.0182 1451
92	0.0824 2740	0.0659 1364	0.0422 1704	0.0270 9772	0.0174 3016
93	0.0802 2131	0.0639 9383	0.0407 8941	0.0260 5550	0.0166 7958
94	0.0780 7427	0.0621 2993	0.0394 1006	0.0250 5337	0.0159 6132
95	0.0759 8469	0.0603 2032	0.0380 7735	0.0240 8978	0.0152 7399
96	0.0739 5104	0.0585 6342	0.0367 8971	0.0231 6325	0.0146 1626
97	0.0719 7181	0.0568 5769	0.0355 4562	0.0222 7235	0.0139 8685
98	0.0700 4556	0.0552 0164	0.0343 4359	0.0214 1572	0.0133 8454
99	0.0681 7086	0.0535 9383	0.0331 8221	0.0205 9204	0.0128 0817
100	0.0663 4634	0.0520 3284	0.0320 6011	0.0198 0004	0.0122 5663

$$P = (1 + i)^{-n}$$

n	5 %	$5\frac{1}{2}$ %	6 %	7 %	8 %
1	0.9523 8095	0.9478 6730	0.9433 9623	0.9345 7944	0.9259 2593
2	0.9070 2948	0.8984 5242	0.8899 9644	0.8734 3873	0.8573 3882
3	0.8638 3760	0.8516 1366	0.8396 1928	0.8162 9788	0.7938 3224
4	0.8227 0247	0.8072 1674	0.7920 9366	0.7628 9521	0.7350 2985
5	0.7835 2617	0.7651 3435	0.7472 5817	0.7129 8618	0.6805 8320
6	0.7462 1540	0.7252 4583	0.7049 6054	0.6663 4222	0.6301 6963
7	0.7106 8133	0.6874 3681	0.6650 5711	0.6227 4974	0.5834 9040
8	0.6768 3936	0.6515 9887	0.6274 1237	0.5820 0910	0.5402 6888
9	0.6446 0892	0.6176 2926	0.5918 9846	0.5439 3374	0.5002 4897
10	0.6139 1325	0.5854 3058	0.5583 9478	0.5083 4929	0.4631 9349
11	0.5846 7929	0.5549 1050	0.5267 8753	0.4750 9280	0.4288 8286
12	0.5568 3742	0.5259 8152	0.4969 6936	0.4440 1196	0.3971 1376
13	0.5303 2135	0.4985 6068	0.4688 3902	0.4149 6445	0.3676 9792
14	0.5050 6795	0.4725 6937	0.4423 0096	0.3878 1724	0.3404 6104
15	0.4810 1710	0.4479 3305	0.4172 6506	0.3624 4602	0.3152 4170
16	0.4581 1152	0.4245 8109	0.3936 4628	0.3387 3460	0.2918 9047
17	0.4362 9669	0.4024 4653	0.3713 6442	0.3165 7439	0.2702 6895
18	0.4155 2065	0.3814 6590	0.3503 4379	0.2958 6392	0.2502 4903
19	0.3957 3396	0.3615 7906	0.3305 1301	0.2765 0832	0.2317 1206
20	0.3768 8948	0.3427 2896	0.3118 0473	0.2584 1900	0.2145 4821
21	0.3589 4236	0.3248 6158	0.2941 5540	0.2415 1309	0.1986 5575
22	0.3418 4987	0.3079 2567	0.2775 0510	0.2257 1317	0.1839 4051
23	0.3255 7131	0.2918 7267	0.2617 9726	0.2109 4688	0.1703 1528
24	0.3100 6791	0.2766 5656	0.2469 7855	0.1971 4662	0.1576 9934
25	0.2953 0277	0.2622 3370	0.2329 9863	0.1842 4918	0.1460 1790
26	0.2812 4073	0.2485 6275	0.2198 1003	0.1721 9549	0.1352 0176
27	0.2678 4832	0.2356 0450	0.2073 6795	0.1609 3037	0.1251 8682
28	0.2550 9364	0.2233 2181	0.1956 3014	0.1504 0221	0.1159 1372
29	0.2429 4632	0.2116 7944	0.1845 5674	0.1405 6282	0.1073 2752
30	0.2313 7745	0.2006 4402	0.1741 1013	0.1313 6712	0.0993 7733
31	0.2203 5947	0.1901 8390	0.1642 5484	0.1227 7301	0.0920 1605
32	0.2098 6617	0.1802 6910	0.1549 5740	0.1147 4113	0.0852 0005
33	0.1998 7254	0.1708 7119	0.1461 8622	0.1072 3470	0.0788 8893
34	0.1903 5480	0.1619 6321	0.1379 1153	0.1002 1934	0.0730 4531
35	0.1812 9029	0.1535 1963	0.1301 0522	0.0936 6294	0.0676 3454
36	0.1726 5741	0.1455 1624	0.1227 4077	0.0875 3546	0.0626 2458
37	0.1644 3563	0.1379 3008	0.1157 9318	0.0818 0884	0.0579 8572
38	0.1566 0536	0.1307 3941	0.1092 3885	0.0764 5686	0.0536 9048
39	0.1491 4797	0.1239 2362	0.1030 5552	0.0714 5501	0.0497 1341
40	0.1420 4568	0.1174 6314	0.0972 2219	0.0667 8038	0.0460 3093
41	0.1352 8160	0.1113 3947	0.0917 1905	0.0624 1157	0.0426 2123
42	0.1288 3962	0.1055 3504	0.0865 2740	0.0583 2857	0.0394 6411
43	0.1227 0440	0.1000 3322	0.0816 2962	0.0545 1268	0.0365 4084
44	0.1168 6133	0.0948 1822	0.0770 0908	0.0509 4643	0.0338 3411
45	0.1112 9651	0.0898 7509	0.0726 5007	0.0476 1349	0.0313 2788
46	0.1059 9668	0.0851 8965	0.0685 3781	0.0444 9859	0.0290 0730
47	0.1009 4921	0.0807 4849	0.0646 5831	0.0415 8747	0.0268 5861
48	0.0961 4211	0.0765 3885	0.0609 9840	0.0388 6679	0.0248 6908
49	0.0915 6391	0.0725 4867	0.0575 4566	0.0363 2410	0.0230 2693
50	0.0872 0373	0.0687 6652	0.0542 8836	0.0339 4776	0.0213 2123

TABLE II.   PRESENT VALUE OF 1 AT COMPOUND INTEREST   307

$$P = (1 + i)^{-n}$$

n	5 %	$5\frac{1}{2}$ %	6 %	7 %	8 %
51	0.0830 5117	0.0651 8153	0.0512 1544	0.0317 2688	0.0197 4188
52	0.0790 9635	0.0617 8344	0.0483 1645	0.0296 5129	0.0182 7952
53	0.0753 2986	0.0585 6250	0.0455 8156	0.0277 1148	0.0169 2548
54	0.0717 4272	0.0555 0948	0.0430 0147	0.0258 9858	0.0156 7174
55	0.0683 2640	0.0526 1562	0.0405 6742	0.0242 0428	0.0145 1087
56	0.0650 7276	0.0498 7263	0.0382 7115	0.0226 2083	0.0134 3599
57	0.0619 7406	0.0472 7263	0.0361 0486	0.0211 4096	0.0124 4073
58	0.0590 2291	0.0448 0818	0.0340 6119	0.0197 5791	0.0115 1920
59	0.0562 1230	0.0424 7221	0.0321 3320	0.0184 6533	0.0106 6592
60	0.0535 3552	0.0402 5802	0.0303 1434	0.0172 5732	0.0098 7585
61	0.0509 8621	0.0381 5926	0.0285 9843	0.0161 2834	0.0091 4431
62	0.0485 5830	0.0361 6992	0.0269 7965	0.0150 7321	0.0084 6695
63	0.0462 4600	0.0342 8428	0.0254 5250	0.0140 8711	0.0078 3977
64	0.0440 4381	0.0324 9695	0.0240 1179	0.0131 6553	0.0072 5905
65	0.0419 4648	0.0308 0279	0.0226 5264	0.0123 0423	0.0067 2134
66	0.0399 4903	0.0291 9696	0.0213 7041	0.0114 9928	0.0062 2346
67	0.0380 4670	0.0276 7485	0.0201 6077	0.0107 4699	0.0057 6247
68	0.0362 3495	0.0262 3208	0.0190 1959	0.0100 4392	0.0053 3562
69	0.0345 0948	0.0248 6453	0.0179 4301	0.0093 8684	0.0049 4039
70	0.0328 6617	0.0235 6828	0.0169 2737	0.0087 7275	0.0045 7443
71	0.0313 0111	0.0223 3960	0.0159 6921	0.0081 9883	0.0042 3558
72	0.0298 1058	0.0211 7498	0.0150 6530	0.0076 6246	0.0039 2184
73	0.0283 9103	0.0200 7107	0.0142 1254	0.0071 6117	0.0036 3133
74	0.0270 3908	0.0190 2471	0.0134 0806	0.0066 9269	0.0033 6234
75	0.0257 5150	0.0180 3290	0.0126 4911	0.0062 5485	0.0031 1328
76	0.0245 2524	0.0170 9279	0.0119 3313	0.0058 4565	0.0028 8267
77	0.0233 5737	0.0162 0170	0.0112 5767	0.0054 6323	0.0026 6914
78	0.0222 4512	0.0153 5706	0.0106 2044	0.0051 0582	0.0024 7142
79	0.0211 8582	0.0145 5646	0.0100 1928	0.0047 7179	0.0022 8835
80	0.0201 7698	0.0137 9759	0.0094 5215	0.0044 5962	0.0021 1885
81	0.0192 1617	0.0130 7828	0.0089 1713	0.0041 6787	0.0019 6190
82	0.0183 0111	0.0123 9648	0.0084 1238	0.0038 9520	0.0018 1657
83	0.0174 2963	0.0117 5022	0.0079 3621	0.0036 4038	0.0016 8201
84	0.0165 9965	0.0111 3765	0.0074 8699	0.0034 0222	0.0015 5742
85	0.0158 0919	0.0105 5701	0.0070 6320	0.0031 7965	0.0014 4205
86	0.0150 5637	0.0100 0664	0.0066 6340	0.0029 7163	0.0013 3523
87	0.0143 3940	0.0094 8497	0.0062 8622	0.0027 7723	0.0012 3633
88	0.0136 5657	0.0089 9049	0.0059 3040	0.0025 9554	0.0011 4475
89	0.0130 0626	0.0085 2180	0.0055 9472	0.0024 2574	0.0010 5995
90	0.0123 8691	0.0080 7753	0.0052 7803	0.0022 6704	0.0009 8144
91	0.0117 9706	0.0076 5643	0.0049 7928	0.0021 1873	0.0009 0874
92	0.0112 3530	0.0072 5728	0.0046 9743	0.0019 8012	0.0008 4142
93	0.0107 0028	0.0068 7894	0.0044 3154	0.0018 5058	0.0007 7910
94	0.0101 9074	0.0065 2032	0.0041 8070	0.0017 2952	0.0007 2138
95	0.0097 0547	0.0061 8040	0.0039 4405	0.0016 1637	0.0006 6795
96	0.0092 4331	0.0058 5820	0.0037 2081	0.0015 1063	0.0006 1847
97	0.0088 0315	0.0055 5279	0.0035 1019	0.0014 1180	0.0005 7266
98	0.0083 8395	0.0052 6331	0.0033 1150	0.0013 1944	0.0005 3024
99	0.0079 8471	0.0049 8892	0.0031 2406	0.0012 3312	0.0004 9096
100	0.0076 0449	0.0047 2883	0.0029 4723	0.0011 5245	0.0004 5459

TABLE III. AMOUNT OF ANNUITY OF 1 PER PERIOD

$$s_{\overline{n}|i} = \frac{(1+i)^n - 1}{i}$$

n	$\frac{1}{4}\%$	$\frac{1}{3}\%$	$\frac{5}{12}\%$	$\frac{1}{2}\%$	$\frac{7}{12}\%$
1	1.0000 0000	1.0000 0000	1.0000 0000	1.0000 0000	1.0000 0000
2	2.0025 0000	2.0033 3333	2.0041 6667	2.0050 0000	2.0058 3333
3	3.0075 0625	3.0100 1111	3.0125 1736	3.0150 2500	3.0175 3403
4	4.0150 2502	4.0200 4448	4.0250 6952	4.0301 0013	4.0351 3631
5	5.0250 6258	5.0334 4463	5.0418 4064	5.0502 5063	5.0586 7460
6	6.0376 2523	6.0502 2278	6.0628 4831	6.0755 0188	6.0881 8354
7	7.0527 1930	7.0703 9019	7.0881 1018	7.1058 7939	7.1236 9794
8	8.0703 5110	8.0939 5816	8.1176 4397	8.1414 0879	8.1652 5284
9	9.0905 2697	9.1209 3802	9.1514 6749	9.1821 1583	9.2128 8349
10	10.1132 5329	10.1513 4114	10.1895 9860	10.2280 2641	10.2666 2531
11	11.1385 3642	11.1851 7895	11.2320 5526	11.2791 6654	11.3265 1396
12	12.1663 8277	12.2224 6288	12.2788 5549	12.3355 6237	12.3925 8529
13	13.1967 9872	13.2632 0442	13.3300 1739	13.3972 4018	13.4648 7537
14	14.2297 9072	14.3074 1510	14.3855 5913	14.4642 2639	14.5434 2048
15	15.2653 6520	15.3551 0648	15.4454 9896	15.5365 4752	15.6282 5710
16	16.3035 2861	16.4062 9017	16.5098 5520	16.6142 3026	16.7194 2193
17	17.3442 8743	17.4609 7781	17.5786 4627	17.6973 0141	17.8169 5189
18	18.3876 4815	18.5191 8107	18.6518 9063	18.7857 8791	18.9208 8411
19	19.4336 1727	19.5809 1167	19.7296 0684	19.8797 1685	20.0312 5593
20	20.4822 0131	20.6461 8137	20.8118 1353	20.9791 1544	21.1481 0493
21	21.5334 0682	21.7150 0198	21.8985 2942	22.0840 1101	22.2714 6887
22	22.5872 4033	22.7873 8532	22.9697 7330	23.1944 3107	23.4013 8577
23	23.6437 0843	23.8633 4327	24.0855 6402	24.3104 0322	24.5378 9386
24	24.7028 1770	24.9428 8775	25.1859 2054	25.4319 5524	25.6810 3157
25	25.7645 7475	26.0260 3071	26.2908 6187	26.5591 1502	26.8308 3759
26	26.8289 8619	27.1127 8414	27.4004 0713	27.6919 1059	27.9873 5081
27	27.8960 5865	28.2031 6009	28.5145 7549	28.8303 7015	29.1506 1035
28	28.9657 9880	29.2971 7062	29.6333 8622	29.9745 2200	30.3206 5558
29	30.0382 1330	30.3948 2786	30.7568 5867	31.1243 9461	31.4975 2607
30	31.1133 0883	31.4961 4395	31.8850 1224	32.2800 1658	32.6812 6164
31	32.1910 9210	32.6011 3110	33.0178 6646	33.4414 1666	33.8719 0233
32	33.2715 6983	33.7098 0154	34.1554 4090	34.6086 2375	35.0694 8843
33	34.3547 4876	34.8221 6754	35.2977 5524	35.7816 6686	36.2740 6045
34	35.4406 3563	35.9382 4143	36.4448 2922	36.9605 7520	37.4856 5913
35	36.5292 3722	37.0580 3557	37.5966 8268	38.1453 7807	38.7043 2548
36	37.6205 6031	38.1815 6236	38.7533 3552	39.3361 0496	39.9301 0071
37	38.7146 1171	39.3088 3423	39.9148 0775	40.5327 8549	41.1630 2630
38	39.8113 9824	40.4398 6368	41.0811 1945	41.7354 4942	42.4031 4395
39	40.9109 2673	41.5746 6322	42.2522 9078	42.9441 2666	43.6504 9562
40	42.0132 0405	42.7132 4543	43.4283 4199	44.1588 4730	44.9051 2352
41	43.1182 3706	43.8556 2292	44.6092 9342	45.3796 4153	46.1670 7007
42	44.2260 3265	45.0018 0833	45.7951 6548	46.6065 3974	47.4363 7798
43	45.3365 9774	46.1518 1436	46.9859 7866	47.8395 7244	48.7130 9018
44	46.4499 3923	47.3056 5374	48.1817 5358	49.0787 7030	49.9972 4988
45	47.5660 6408	48.4633 3925	49.3825 1088	50.3241 6415	51.2889 0050
46	48.6849 7924	49.6248 8371	50.5882 7134	51.5757 8497	52.5880 8575
47	49.8066 9169	50.7902 9999	51.7990 5581	52.8336 6390	53.8948 4959
48	50.9312 0842	51.9596 0099	53.0148 8521	54.0978 3222	55.2092 3621
49	52.0585 3644	53.1327 9966	54.2357 8056	55.3683 2138	56.5312 9009
50	53.1886 8278	54.3099 0899	55.4617 6298	56.6451 6299	57.8610 5595

TABLE III.   AMOUNT OF ANNUITY OF 1 PER PERIOD   309

$$s_{\overline{n}|i} = \frac{(1+i)^n - 1}{i}$$

n	$\frac{1}{4}\%$	$\frac{1}{3}\%$	$\frac{5}{12}\%$	$\frac{1}{2}\%$	$\frac{7}{12}\%$
51	54.3216 5449	55.4904 4202	56.6928 5366	57.9283 8880	59.1985 7877
52	55.4574 5862	56.6759 1183	57.9290 7388	59.2180 3075	60.5439 0381
53	56.5961 0227	57.8648 3154	59.1704 4503	60.5141 2090	61.8970 7659
54	57.7375 9252	59.0577 1431	60.4169 8855	61.8166 9150	63.2581 4287
55	58.8819 3650	60.2545 7336	61.6687 2600	63.1257 7496	64.6271 4870
56	60.0291 4135	61.4554 2194	62.9256 7902	64.4414 0384	66.0041 4040
57	61.1792 1420	62.6602 7334	64.1878 6935	65.7636 1086	67.3891 6455
58	62.3321 6223	63.8691 4092	65.4553 1881	67.0924 2891	68.7822 6801
59	63.4879 9264	65.0820 3806	66.7280 4930	68.4278 9105	70.1834 9791
60	64.6467 1262	66.2989 7818	68.0060 8284	69.7700 3051	71.5929 0165
61	65.8083 2940	67.5199 7478	69.2894 4152	71.1188 8066	73.0105 2691
62	66.9728 5023	68.7450 4136	70.5781 4753	72.4744 7507	74.4364 2165
63	68.1402 8235	69.9741 9150	71.8722 2314	73.8368 4744	75.8706 3411
64	69.3106 3306	71.2074 3880	73.1716 9074	75.2060 3168	77.3132 1281
65	70.4839 0964	72.4447 9693	74.4765 7278	76.5820 6184	78.7642 0655
66	71.6601 1942	73.6862 7959	75.7868 9184	77.9649 7215	80.2236 6442
67	72.8392 6971	74.9319 0052	77.1026 7055	79.3547 9701	81.6916 3579
68	74.0213 6789	76.1816 7352	78.4239 3168	80.7515 7099	83.1681 7034
69	75.2064 2131	77.4356 1243	79.7506 9806	82.1553 2885	84.6533 1800
70	76.3944 3736	78.6937 3114	81.0829 9264	83.5661 0549	86.1471 2902
71	77.5854 2345	79.9560 4358	82.4208 3844	84.9839 3602	87.6496 5394
72	78.7793 8701	81.2225 6372	83.7642 5860	86.4088 5570	89.1609 4359
73	79.9763 3548	82.4933 0560	85.1132 7634	87.8408 9998	90.6810 4909
74	81.1762 7632	83.7682 8329	86.4679 1500	89.2801 0448	92.2100 2188
75	82.3792 1701	85.0475 1090	87.8281 9797	90.7265 0500	93.7479 1367
76	83.5851 6505	86.3310 0260	89.1941 4880	92.1801 3752	95.2947 7650
77	84.7941 2797	87.6187 7261	90.5657 9109	93.6410 3821	96.8506 6270
78	86.0061 1329	88.9108 3519	91.9431 4855	95.1092 4340	98.4156 2490
79	87.2211 2857	90.2072 0464	93.3262 4500	96.5847 8962	99.9897 1604
80	88.4391 8139	91.5078 9532	94.7151 0436	98.0677 1357	101.5729 8938
81	89.6602 7934	92.8129 2164	96.1097 5062	99.5580 5214	103.1654 9849
82	90.8844 3004	94.1222 9804	97.5102 0792	101.0558 4240	104.7672 9723
83	92.1116 4112	95.4360 3904	98.9165 0045	102.5611 2161	106.3784 3980
84	93.3419 2022	96.7541 5917	100.3286 5254	104.0739 2722	107.9989 8070
85	94.5752 7502	98.0766 7303	101.7466 8859	105.5942 9685	109.6289 7475
86	95.8117 1321	99.4035 9527	103.1706 3312	107.1222 6834	111.2684 7710
87	97.0512 4249	100.7349 4059	104.6005 1076	108.6578 7968	112.9175 4322
88	98.2938 7060	102.0707 2373	106.0363 4622	110.2011 6908	114.5762 2889
89	99.5396 0527	103.4109 5947	107.4781 6433	111.7521 7492	116.2445 9022
90	100.7884 5429	104.7556 6267	108.9259 9002	113.3109 3580	117.9226 8367
91	102.0404 2542	106.1048 4821	110.3798 4831	114.8774 9048	119.6105 6599
92	103.2955 2649	107.4585 3104	111.8397 6434	116.4518 7793	121.3082 9429
93	104.5537 6530	108.8167 2614	113.3057 6336	118.0341 3732	123.0159 2601
94	105.8151 4972	110.1794 4856	114.7778 7071	119.6243 0800	124.7335 1891
95	107.0796 8759	111.5467 1339	116.2561 1184	121.2224 2954	126.4611 3110
96	108.3473 8681	112.9185 3577	117.7405 1230	122.8285 4169	128.1988 2103
97	109.6182 5528	114.2949 3089	119.2310 9777	124.4426 8440	129.9466 4749
98	110.8923 0091	115.6759 1399	120.7278 9401	126.0648 9782	131.7046 6960
99	112.1695 3167	117.0615 0037	122.2309 2690	127.6952 2231	133.4729 4684
100	113.4499 5550	118.4517 0537	123.7402 2243	129.3336 9842	135.2515 3903

$$s_{\overline{n}|i} = \frac{(1+i)^n - 1}{i}$$

n	$\frac{7}{8}$ %	1 %	$1\frac{1}{8}$ %	$1\frac{1}{4}$ %	$1\frac{3}{8}$ %
1	1.0000 0000	1.0000 0000	1.0000 0000	1.0000 0000	1.0000 0000
2	2.0087 5000	2.0100 0000	2.0112 5000	2.0125 0000	2.0137 5000
3	3.0263 2656	3.0301 0000	3.0338 7656	3.0376 5625	3.0414 3906
4	4.0528 0692	4.0604 0100	4.0680 0767	4.0756 2695	4.0832 5885
5	5.0882 6898	5.1010 0501	5.1137 7276	5.1265 7229	5.1394 0366
6	6.1327 9133	6.1520 1506	6.1713 0270	6.1906 5444	6.2100 7046
7	7.1864 5326	7.2135 3521	7.2407 2986	7.2680 3762	7.2954 5893
8	8.2493 3472	8.2856 7056	8.3221 8807	8.3588 8809	8.3957 7149
9	9.3215 1640	9.3685 2727	9.4158 1269	9.4633 7420	9.5112 1335
10	10.4030 7967	10.4622 1254	10.5217 4058	10.5816 6637	10.6419 9253
11	11.4941 0662	11.5668 3467	11.6401 1016	11.7139 3720	11.7883 1993
12	12.5946 8005	12.6825 0301	12.7710 6140	12.8603 6142	12.9504 0933
13	13.7048 8350	13.8093 2804	13.9147 3584	14.0211 1594	14.1284 7745
14	14.8248 0123	14.9474 2132	15.0712 7662	15.1963 7988	15.3227 4402
15	15.9545 1824	16.0968 9554	16.2408 2848	16.3863 3463	16.5334 3175
16	17.0941 2028	17.2578 6449	17.4235 3780	17.5911 6382	17.7607 6644
17	18.2436 9383	18.4304 4314	18.6195 5260	18.8110 5336	19.0049 7697
18	19.4033 2615	19.6147 4757	19.8290 2257	20.0461 9153	20.2662 9541
19	20.5731 0526	20.8108 9504	21.0520 9907	21.2967 6893	21.5449 5697
20	21.7531 1993	22.0190 0399	22.2889 3519	22.5629 7854	22.8412 0013
21	22.9434 5973	23.2391 9403	23.5396 8571	23.8450 1577	24.1552 6663
22	24.1442 1500	24.4715 8598	24.8045 0717	25.1430 7847	25.4874 0155
23	25.3554 7688	25.7163 0183	26.0835 5788	26.4573 6695	26.8378 5332
24	26.5773 3730	26.9734 6485	27.3769 9790	27.7880 8403	28.2068 7380
25	27.8098 8900	28.2431 9950	28.6849 8913	29.1354 3508	29.5947 1832
26	29.0532 2553	29.5256 3150	30.0076 9526	30.4996 2802	31.0016 4569
27	30.3074 4126	30.8208 8781	31.3452 8183	31.8808 7337	32.4279 1832
28	31.5726 3137	32.1290 9669	32.6979 1625	33.2793 8429	33.8738 0220
29	32.8488 9189	33.4503 8766	34.0657 6781	34.6953 7659	35.3395 6698
30	34.1363 1970	34.7848 9153	35.4490 0769	36.1290 6880	36.8254 8602
31	35.4350 1249	36.1327 4045	36.8478 0903	37.5806 8216	38.3318 3646
32	36.7450 6885	37.4940 6785	38.2623 4688	39.0504 4069	39.8588 9921
33	38.0665 8820	38.8690 0853	39.6927 9829	40.5385 7120	41.4069 5907
34	39.3996 7085	40.2576 9862	41.1393 4227	42.0453 0334	42.9763 0476
35	40.7444 1797	41.6602 7560	42.6021 5987	43.5708 6963	44.5672 2895
36	42.1009 3163	43.0768 7836	44.0814 3417	45.1155 0550	46.1800 2835
37	43.4693 1478	44.5076 4714	45.5773 5030	46.6794 4932	47.8150 0374
38	44.8496 7128	45.9527 2361	47.0900 9549	48.2629 4243	49.4724 6004
39	46.2421 0591	47.4122 5085	48.6198 5906	49.8662 2921	51.1527 0636
40	47.6467 2433	48.8863 7336	50.1668 3248	51.4895 5708	52.8560 5608
41	49.0636 3317	50.3752 3709	51.7312 0934	53.1331 7654	54.5828 2685
42	50.4929 3996	51.8789 8946	53.3131 8545	54.7973 4125	56.3333 4072
43	51.9347 5319	53.3977 7936	54.9129 5879	56.4823 0801	58.1079 2415
44	53.3891 8228	54.9317 5715	56.5307 2957	58.1883 3687	59.9069 0811
45	54.8563 3762	56.4810 7472	58.1667 0028	59.9156 9108	61.7306 2810
46	56.3363 3058	58.0458 8547	59.8210 7566	61.6646 3721	63.5794 2423
47	57.8292 7347	59.6263 4432	61.4940 6276	63.4354 4518	65.4536 4131
48	59.3352 7961	61.2226 0777	63.1858 7097	65.2283 8824	67.3536 2888
49	60.8544 6331	62.8348 3385	64.8967 1201	67.0437 4310	69.2797 4128
50	62.3869 3986	64.4631 8218	66.6268 0002	68.8817 8989	71.2323 3772

TABLE III. AMOUNT OF ANNUITY OF 1 PER PERIOD   311

$$s_{\overline{n}|i} = \frac{(1+i)^n - 1}{i}$$

n	$\frac{7}{8}\%$	1%	$1\frac{1}{8}\%$	$1\frac{1}{4}\%$	$1\frac{3}{8}\%$
51	63.9328 2559	36.1078 1401	68.3763 5152	70.7428 1226	73.2117 8237
52	65.4922 3781	67.7688 9215	70.1455 8548	72.6270 9741	75.2184 4437
53	67.0652 9489	69.4465 8107	71.9347 2332	74.5349 3613	77.2526 9798
54	68.6521 1622	71.1410 4688	73.7439 8895	76.4666 2283	79.3149 2258
55	70.2528 2224	72.8524 5735	75.5736 0883	78.4224 5562	81.4055 0277
56	71.8675 3443	74.5809 8192	77.4238 1193	80.4027 3631	83.5248 2843
57	73.4963 7536	76.3267 9174	79.2948 2981	82.4077 7052	85.6732 9482
58	75.1394 6864	78.0900 5966	81.1868 9665	84.4378 6765	87.8513 0262
59	76.7969 3900	79.8709 6025	83.1002 4923	86.4933 4099	90.0592 5804
60	78.4689 1221	81.6696 6986	85.0351 2704	88.5745 0776	92.2975 7283
61	80.1555 1519	83.4863 6655	86.9917 7222	90.6816 8910	94.5666 6446
62	81.8568 7595	85.3212 3022	88.9704 2966	92.8152 1022	96.8669 5610
63	83.5731 2362	87.1774 4252	90.9713 4699	94.9754 0034	99.1988 7674
64	85.3043 8845	89.0461 8695	92.9947 7464	97.1625 9285	101.5628 6130
65	87.0508 0185	90.9366 4882	95.0409 6586	99.3771 2526	103.9593 5064
66	88.8124 9636	92.8460 1531	97.1101 7672	101.6193 3933	106.3887 9171
67	90.5896 0571	94.7744 7546	99.2026 6621	103.8895 8107	108.8516 3760
68	92.3822 6476	96.7222 2021	101.3186 9621	106.1882 0083	111.3483 4761
69	94.1906 0957	98.6894 4242	103.4585 3154	108.5155 5334	113.8793 8739
70	96.0147 7741	100.6763 3684	105.6224 4002	110.8719 9776	116.4452 2897
71	97.8549 0671	102.6831 0021	107.8106 9247	113.2578 9773	119.0463 5069
72	99.7111 3714	104.7099 3121	110.0235 6276	115.6736 2145	121.6832 3819
73	101.5836 0959	106.7570 3052	112.2613 2784	118.1195 4172	124.3563 8272
74	103.4724 6618	108.8246 0083	114.5242 6778	120.5960 3599	127.0662 8298
75	105.3778 5025	110.9128 4684	116.8126 6579	123.1034 8644	129.8134 4437
76	107.2999 0644	113.0219 7530	119.1268 0828	125.6422 8002	132.5983 7923
77	109.2387 8063	115.1521 9506	121.4669 8487	128.2128 0852	135.4216 0695
78	111.1946 1996	117.3037 1701	123.8334 8845	130.8154 6863	138.2836 5404
79	113.1675 7288	119.4767 5418	126.2266 1520	133.4506 6199	141.1850 5425
80	115.1577 8914	121.6715 2172	128.6466 6462	136.1187 9526	144.1263 4878
81	117.1654 1980	123.8882 3694	131.0939 3960	138.8202 8020	147.1080 8608
82	119.1906 1722	126.1271 1931	133.5687 4642	141.5555 3370	150.1308 2226
83	121.2335 3512	128.3883 9050	136.0713 9481	144.3249 7787	153.1951 2107
84	123.2943 2855	130.6722 7440	138.6021 9801	147.1290 4010	156.3015 5398
85	125.3731 5393	132.9789 9715	141.1614 7273	149.9681 5310	159.4507 0035
86	127.4701 6903	135.3087 8712	143.7495 3930	152.8427 5501	162.6431 4748
87	129.5855 3301	137.6618 7499	146.3667 2162	155.7532 8945	165.8794 9076
88	131.7194 0642	140.0384 9374	149.0133 4724	158.7002 0557	169.1603 3375
89	133.8719 5123	142.4388 7868	151.6897 4739	161.6839 5814	172.4862 8834
90	136.0433 3080	144.8632 6746	154.3962 5705	164.7050 0762	175.8579 7481
91	138.2337 0994	147.3119 0014	157.1332 1494	167.7638 2021	179.2760 2196
92	140.4432 5491	149.7850 1914	159.9009 6361	170.8608 6796	182.7410 6726
93	142.6721 3339	152.2828 6933	162.6998 4945	173.9966 2881	186.2537 5694
94	144.9205 1455	154.8056 9803	165.5302 2276	177.1715 8667	189.8147 4610
95	147.1885 6906	157.3537 5501	168.3924 3776	180.3862 3151	193.4246 9886
96	149.4764 6903	159.9272 9256	171.2868 5269	183.6410 5940	197.0842 8847
97	151.7843 8813	162.5265 6548	174.2138 2978	186.9365 7264	200.7941 9743
98	154.1125 0153	165.1518 3114	177.1737 3537	190.2732 7980	204.5551 1765
99	156.4609 8592	167.8033 4945	180.1669 3989	193.6516 9580	208.3677 5051
100	158.8300 1955	170.4813 8294	183.1938 1796	197.0723 4200	212.2328 0708

$$s_{\overline{n}|i} = \frac{(1 + i)^n - 1}{i}$$

n	$1\frac{1}{2}\%$	$1\frac{3}{4}\%$	2%	$2\frac{1}{4}\%$	$2\frac{1}{2}\%$
1	1.0000 0000	1.0000 0000	1.0000 0000	1.0000 0000	1.0000 0000
2	2.0150 0000	2.0175 0000	2.0200 0000	2.0225 0000	2.0250 0000
3	3.0452 2500	3.0528 0625	3.0604 0000	3.0680 0625	3.0756 2500
4	4.0909 0338	4.1062 3036	4.1216 0800	4.1370 3639	4.1525 1563
5	5.1522 6693	5.1780 8938	5.2040 4016	5.2301 1971	5.2563 2852
6	6.2295 5093	6.2687 0596	6.3081 2096	6.3477 9740	6.3877 3673
7	7.3229 9419	7.3784 0831	7.4342 8338	7.4906 2284	7.5474 3015
8	8.4328 3911	8.5075 3045	8.5829 6905	8.6591 6186	8.7361 1590
9	9.5593 3169	9.6564 1224	9.7546 2843	9.8539 9300	9.9545 1880
10	10.7027 2167	10.8253 9945	10.9497 2100	11.0757 0784	11.2033 8177
11	11.8632 6249	12.0148 4394	12.1687 1542	12.3249 1127	12.4834 6631
12	13.0412 1143	13.2251 0371	13.4120 8973	13.6022 2177	13.7955 5297
13	14.2368 2960	14.4565 4303	14.6803 3152	14.9082 7176	15.1404 4179
14	15.4503 8205	15.7095 3253	15.9739 3815	16.2437 0788	16.5189 5284
15	16.6821 3778	16.9844 4935	17.2934 1692	17.6091 9130	17.9319 2666
16	17.9323 6984	18.2816 7721	18.6392 8525	19.0053 9811	19.3802 2483
17	19.2013 5539	19.6016 0656	20.0120 7096	20.4330 1957	20.8647 3045
18	20.4893 7572	20.9446 3468	21.4123 1238	21.8927 6251	22.3863 4871
19	21.7967 1636	22.3111 6578	22.8405 5863	23.3853 4966	23.9460 0743
20	23.1236 6710	23.7016 1119	24.2973 6980	24.9115 2003	25.5446 5761
21	24.4705 2211	25.1163 8938	25.7833 1719	26.4720 2923	27.1832 7405
22	25.8375 7994	26.5559 2620	27.2989 8354	28.0676 4989	28.8628 5590
23	27.2251 4364	28.0206 5490	28.8449 6321	29.6991 7201	30.5844 2730
24	28.6335 2080	29.5110 1637	30.4218 6247	31.3674 0338	32.3490 3798
25	30.0630 2361	31.0274 5915	32.0302 9972	33.0731 6996	34.1577 6393
26	31.5139 6896	32.5704 3969	33.6709 0572	34.8173 1628	36.0117 0803
27	32.9866 7850	34.1404 2238	35.3443 2383	36.6007 0590	37.9120 0073
28	34.4814 7867	35.7378 7977	37.0512 1031	38.4242 2178	39.8598 0075
29	35.9987 0085	37.3632 9267	38.7922 3451	40.2887 6677	41.8562 9577
30	37.5386 8137	39.0171 5029	40.5680 7921	42.1952 6402	43.9027 0316
31	39.1017 6159	40.6999 5042	42.3794 4079	44.1446 5746	46.0002 7074
32	40.6882 8801	42.4121 9955	44.2270 2961	46.1379 1226	48.1502 7751
33	42.2986 1233	44.1544 1305	46.1115 7020	48.1760 1528	50.3540 3445
34	43.9330 9152	45.9271 1527	48.0338 0160	50.2599 7563	52.6128 8531
35	45.5920 8789	47.7308 3979	49.9944 7763	52.3908 2508	54.9282 0744
36	47.2759 6921	49.5661 2949	51.9943 6719	54.5696 1864	57.3014 1263
37	48.9851 0874	51.4335 3675	54.0342 5453	56.7974 3506	59.7339 4794
38	50.7198 8538	53.3336 2365	56.1149 3962	59.0753 7735	62.2272 9664
39	52.4806 8366	55.2669 6206	58.2372 3841	61.4045 7334	64.7829 7906
40	54.2678 9391	57.2341 3390	60.4019 8318	63.7861 7624	67.4025 5354
41	56.0819 1232	59.2357 3124	62.6100 2284	66.2213 6521	70.0876 1737
42	57.9231 4100	61.2723 5654	64.8622 2330	68.7113 4592	72.8398 0781
43	59.7919 8812	63.3446 2278	67.1594 6777	71.2573 5121	75.6608 0300
44	61.6888 6794	65.4531 5367	69.5026 5712	73.8606 4161	78.5523 2308
45	63.6142 0096	67.5985 8386	71.8927 1027	76.5225 0605	81.5161 3116
46	65.5684 1398	69.7815 5908	74.3305 6447	79.2442 6243	84.5540 3443
47	67.5519 4018	72.0027 3637	76.8171 7576	82.0272 5834	87.6678 8530
48	69.5652 1929	74.2627 8425	79.3535 1927	84.8728 7165	90.8595 8243
49	71.6086 9758	76.5623 8298	81.9405 8966	87.7825 1126	94.1310 7199
50	73.6828 2804	78.9022 2468	84.5794 0145	90.7576 1776	97.4843 4879

TABLE III.   AMOUNT OF ANNUITY OF 1 PER PERIOD   313

$$s_{\overline{n}|i} = \frac{(1+i)^n - 1}{i}$$

n	$1\frac{1}{2}\%$	$1\frac{3}{4}\%$	2%	$2\frac{1}{4}\%$	$2\frac{1}{2}\%$
51	75.7880 7046	81.2830 1361	87.2709 8948	93.7996 6416	100.9214 5751
52	77.9248 9152	83.7054 6635	90.0164 0927	96.9101 5661	104.4444 9395
53	80.0937 6489	86.1703 1201	92.8167 3746	100.0906 3513	108.0556 0629
54	82.2951 7136	88.6782 9247	95.6730 7221	103.3426 7442	111.7569 9645
55	84.5295 9893	91.2301 6259	98.5865 3365	106.6678 8460	115.5509 2136
56	86.7975 4292	93.8266 9043	101.5582 6432	110.0679 1200	119.4396 9440
57	89.0995 0606	96.4686 5752	104.5894 2961	113.5444 4002	123.4256 8676
58	91.4359 9865	99.1568 5902	107.6812 1820	117.0991 8992	127.5113 2893
59	93.8075 3863	101.8921 0405	110.8348 4257	120.7339 2169	131.6991 1215
60	96.2146 5171	104.6752 1588	114.0515 3942	124.4504 3493	135.9915 8995
61	98.6578 7149	107.5070 3215	117.3325 7021	128.2505 6972	140.3913 7970
62	101.1377 3956	110.3884 0522	120.6792 2161	132.1362 0754	144.9011 6419
63	103.6548 0565	113.3202 0231	124.0928 0604	136.1092 7221	149.5236 9330
64	106.2096 2774	116.3033 0585	127.5746 6216	140.1717 3083	154.2617 8563
65	108.8027 7215	119.3386 1370	131.1261 5541	144.3255 9477	159.1183 3027
66	111.4348 1374	122.4270 3944	134.7486 7852	148.5729 2066	164.0962 8853
67	114.1063 3594	125.5695 1263	138.4436 5209	152.9158 1137	169.1986 9574
68	116.8179 3098	128.7669 7910	142.2125 2513	157.3564 1713	174.4286 6314
69	119.5701 9995	132.0204 0124	146.0567 7563	161.8969 3651	179.7893 7971
70	122.3637 5295	135.3307 5826	149.9779 1114	166.5396 1758	185.2841 1421
71	125.1992 0924	138.6990 4653	153.9774 6937	171.2867 5898	190.9162 1706
72	128.0771 9738	142.1262 7984	158.0570 1875	176.1407 1106	196.6891 2249
73	130.9983 5534	145.6134 8974	162.2181 5913	181.1038 7705	202.6063 5055
74	133.9633 3067	149.1617 2581	166.4625 2231	186.1787 1429	208.6715 0931
75	136.9727 8063	152.7720 5601	170.7917 7276	191.3677 3536	214.8882 9705
76	140.0273 7234	156.4455 6699	175.2076 0821	196.6735 0941	221.2605 0447
77	143.1277 8292	160.1833 6441	179.7117 6038	202.0986 6337	227.7920 1709
78	146.2746 9967	163.9865 7329	184.3059 9558	207.6458 8329	234.4868 1751
79	149.4688 2016	167.8563 3832	188.9921 1549	213.3179 1567	241.3489 8795
80	152.7108 5247	171.7938 2424	193.7719 5780	219.1175 6877	248.3827 1265
81	156.0015 1525	175.8002 1617	198.6473 9696	225.0477 1407	255.5922 8047
82	159.3415 3798	179.8767 1995	203.6203 4490	231.1112 8763	262.9820 8748
83	162.7316 6105	184.0245 6255	208.6927 5180	237.3112 9160	270.5566 3966
84	166.1726 3597	188.2449 9239	213.8666 0683	243.6507 9567	278.3205 5566
85	169.6652 2551	192.5392 7976	219.1439 3897	250.1329 3857	286.2785 6955
86	173.2102 0389	196.9087 1716	224.5268 1775	256.7609 2969	294.4355 3379
87	176.8083 5695	201.3546 1971	230.0173 5411	263.5380 5060	302.7964 2213
88	180.4604 8230	205.8783 2555	235.6177 0119	270.4676 5674	311.3663 3268
89	184.1673 8954	210.4811 9625	241.3300 5521	277.5531 7902	320.1504 9100
90	187.9299 0038	215.1646 1718	247.1566 5632	284.7981 2555	329.1542 5328
91	191.7488 4889	219.9299 9798	253.0997 8944	292.2060 8337	338.3831 0961
92	195.6250 8162	224.7787 7295	259.1617 8523	299.7807 2025	347.8426 8735
93	199.5594 5784	229.7124 0148	265.3450 2094	307.5257 8645	357.5387 5455
94	203.5528 4971	234.7323 6850	271.6519 2135	315.4451 1665	367.4772 2339
95	207.6061 4246	239.8401 8495	278.0849 5978	323.5426 3177	377.6641 5398
96	211.7202 3459	245.0373 8819	284.6466 5598	331.8223 4099	388.1057 5783
97	215.8960 3811	250.3255 4248	291.3395 9216	340.2883 4366	398.8084 0177
98	220.1344 7868	255.7062 3947	298.1663 8400	348.9448 3139	409.7786 1182
99	224.4364 9586	261.1810 9866	305.1297 1168	357.7960 9010	421.0230 7711
100	228.8030 4330	266.7517 6789	312.2323 0591	366.8465 0213	432.5486 5404

$$s_{\overline{n}|i} = \frac{(1 + i)^n - 1}{i}$$

n	$2\frac{3}{4}$ %	3 %	$3\frac{1}{2}$ %	4 %	$4\frac{1}{2}$ %
1	1.0000 0000	1.0000 0000	1.0000 0000	1.0000 0000	1.0000 0000
2	2.0275 0000	2.0300 0000	2.0350 0000	2.0400 0000	2.0450 0000
3	3.0832 5625	3.0909 0000	3.1062 2500	3.1216 0000	3.1370 2500
4	4.1680 4580	4.1836 2700	4.2149 4288	4.2464 6400	4.2781 9113
5	5.2826 6706	5.3091 3581	5.3624 6588	5.4163 2256	5.4707 0973
6	6.4279 4040	6.4684 0988	6.5501 5218	6.6329 7546	6.7168 9166
7	7.6047 0876	7.6624 6218	7.7794 0751	7.8982 9448	8.0191 5179
8	8.8138 3825	8.8923 3605	9.0516 8677	9.2142 2626	9.3800 1362
9	10.0562 1880	10.1591 0613	10.3684 9581	10.5827 9531	10.8021 1423
10	11.3327 6482	11.4638 7931	11.7313 9316	12.0061 0712	12.2882 0937
11	12.6444 1585	12.8077 9569	13.1419 9192	13.4863 5141	13.8411 7879
12	13.9921 3729	14.1920 2956	14.6019 6164	15.0258 0546	15.4640 3184
13	15.3769 2107	15.6177 9045	16.1130 3030	16.6268 3768	17.1599 1327
14	16.7997 8639	17.0863 2416	17.6769 8636	18.2919 1119	18.9321 0937
15	18.2617 8052	18.5989 1389	19.2956 8088	20.0235 8764	20.7840 5429
16	19.7639 7948	20.1568 8130	20.9710 2971	21.8245 3114	22.7193 3673
17	21.3074 8892	21.7615 8774	22.7050 1575	23.6975 1239	24.7417 0689
18	22.8934 4487	23.4144 3537	24.4996 9130	25.6454 1288	26.8550 8370
19	24.5230 1460	25.1168 6844	26.3571 8050	27.6712 2940	29.0635 6246
20	26.1973 9750	26.8703 7449	28.2796 8181	29.7780 7858	31.3714 2277
21	27.9178 2593	28.6764 8572	30.2694 7068	31.9692 0172	33.7831 3680
22	29.6855 6615	30.5367 8030	32.3289 0215	34.2479 6979	36.3033 7795
23	31.5019 1921	32.4528 8370	34.4604 1373	36.6178 8858	38.9370 2996
24	33.3682 2199	34.4264 7022	36.6665 2821	39.0826 0412	41.6891 9631
25	35.2858 4810	36.4592 6432	38.9498 5669	41.6459 0829	44.5652 1015
26	37.2562 0892	38.5530 4225	41.3131 0168	44.3117 4462	47.5706 4460
27	39.2807 5467	40.7096 3352	43.7590 6024	47.0842 1440	50.7113 2361
28	41.3609 7542	42.9309 2252	46.2906 2734	49.9675 8298	53.9933 3317
29	43.4984 0224	45.2188 5020	48.9107 9930	52.9662 8630	57.4230 3316
30	45.6946 0830	47.5754 1571	51.6226 7728	56.0849 3775	61.0070 6966
31	47.9512 1003	50.0026 7818	54.4294 7098	59.3283 3526	64.7523 8779
32	50.2698 6831	52.5027 5852	57.3345 0247	62.7014 6867	68.6662 4524
33	52.6522 8969	55.0778 4128	60.3412 1005	66.2095 2742	72.7562 2628
34	55.1002 2765	57.7301 7652	63.4531 5240	69.8579 0851	77.0302 5646
35	57.6154 8391	60.4620 8181	66.6740 1274	73.6522 2486	81.4966 1800
36	60.1999 0972	63.2759 4427	70.0076 0318	77.5983 1385	86.1639 6581
37	62.8554 0724	66.1742 2259	73.4578 6930	81.7022 4640	91.0413 4427
38	65.5839 3094	69.1594 4927	77.0288 9472	85.9703 3626	96.1382 0476
39	68.3874 8904	72.2342 3275	80.7249 0604	90.4091 4971	101.4644 2398
40	71.2681 4499	75.4012 5973	84.5502 7775	95.0255 1570	107.0303 2306
41	74.2280 1898	78.6632 9753	88.5095 3747	99.8265 3633	112.8466 8760
42	77.2692 8950	82.0231 9645	92.6073 7128	104.8195 9778	118.9247 8854
43	80.3941 9496	85.4838 9234	96.8486 2928	110.0123 8169	125.2764 0402
44	83.6050 3532	89.0484 0911	101.2383 3130	115.4128 7696	131.9138 4220
45	86.9041 7379	92.7198 6139	105.7816 7290	121.0293 9204	138.8499 6510
46	90.2940 3857	96.5014 5723	110.4840 3145	126.8705 6772	146.0982 1353
47	93.7771 2463	100.3965 0095	115.3509 7255	132.9453 9043	153.6726 3314
48	97.3559 9556	104.4083 9598	120.3882 5659	139.2632 0604	161.5879 0163
49	101.0332 8544	108.5406 4785	125.6018 4557	145.8337 3429	169.8593 5720
50	104.8117 0079	112.7968 6729	130.9979 1016	152.6670 8366	178.5030 2828

TABLE III.   AMOUNT OF ANNUITY OF 1 PER PERIOD   315

$$s_{\overline{n}|i} = \frac{(1+i)^n - 1}{i}$$

n	$2\frac{3}{4}$ %	3 %	$3\frac{1}{2}$ %	4 %	$4\frac{1}{2}$ %
51	108.6940 2256	117.1807 7331	136.5828 3702	159.7737 6700	187.5356 6455
52	112.6831 0818	121.6961 9651	142.3632 3631	167.1647 1768	196.9747 6946
53	116.7818 9365	126.3470 8240	148.3459 4958	174.8513 0639	206.8386 3408
54	120.9933 9573	131.1374 9488	154.5380 5782	182.8453 5865	217.1463 7262
55	125.3207 1411	136.0716 1972	160.9468 8984	191.1591 7299	227.9179 5938
56	129.7670 3375	141.1537 6831	167.5800 3099	199.8055 3991	239.1742 6756
57	134.3356 2718	146.3883 8136	174.4453 3207	208.7977 6151	250.9371 0960
58	139.0298 5692	151.7800 3280	181.5509 1869	218.1496 7197	263.2292 7953
59	143.8531 7799	157.3334 3379	188.9052 0085	227.8756 5885	276.0745 9711
60	148.8091 4038	163.0534 3680	196.5168 8288	237.9906 8520	289.4979 5398
61	153.9013 9174	168.9450 3991	204.3949 7378	248.5103 1261	303.5253 6190
62	159.1336 8002	175.0133 9110	212.5487 9786	259.4507 2511	318.1840 0319
63	164.5098 5622	181.2637 9284	220.9880 0579	270.8287 5412	333.5022 8333
64	170.0338 7726	187.7017 0662	229.7225 8599	282.6619 0428	349.5098 8608
65	175.7098 0889	194.3327 5782	238.7628 7650	294.9683 8045	366.2378 3096
66	181.5418 2863	201.1627 4055	248.1195 7718	307.7671 1567	383.7185 3335
67	187.5342 2892	208.1976 2277	257.8037 6238	321.0778 0030	401.9858 6735
68	193.6914 2021	215.4435 5145	267.8268 9406	334.9209 1231	421.0752 3138
69	200.0179 3427	222.9068 5800	278.2008 3535	349.3177 4880	441.0236 1679
70	206.5184 2746	230.5940 6374	288.9378 6459	364.2904 5876	461.8696 7955
71	213.1976 8422	238.5118 8565	300.0506 8985	379.8620 7711	483.6538 1513
72	220.0606 2054	246.6672 4222	311.5524 6400	396.0565 6019	506.4182 3681
73	227.1122 8760	255.0672 5949	323.4568 0024	412.8988 2260	530.2070 5747
74	234.3578 7551	263.7192 7727	335.7777 8824	430.4147 7550	555.0663 7505
75	241.8027 1709	272.6308 5559	348.5300 1083	448.6313 6652	581.0443 6193
76	249.4522 9181	281.8097 8126	361.7285 6121	467.5766 2118	608.1913 5822
77	257.3122 2983	291.2640 7469	375.3890 6085	487.2796 8603	636.5599 6934
78	265.3883 1615	301.0019 9693	389.5276 7798	507.7708 7347	666.2015 6796
79	273.6864 9485	311.0320 5684	404.1611 4671	529.0817 0841	697.1844 0052
80	282.2128 7345	321.3630 1855	419.3067 8685	551.2449 7675	729.5576 9854
81	290.9737 2747	332.0039 0910	434.9825 2439	574.2947 7582	763.3877 9497
82	299.9755 0498	342.9640 2638	451.2069 1274	598.2665 6685	798.7402 4575
83	309.2248 3137	354.2529 4717	467.9991 5469	623.1972 2952	835.6835 5680
84	318.7285 1423	365.8805 3558	485.3791 2510	649.1251 1870	874.2893 1686
85	328.4935 4837	377.8569 5165	503.3673 9448	676.0901 2345	914.6323 3612
86	338.5271 2095	390.1926 6020	521.9852 5329	704.1337 2839	956.7907 9125
87	348.8366 1678	402.8984 4001	541.2547 3715	733.2990 7753	1000.8463 7685
88	359.4296 2374	415.9853 9321	561.1986 5295	763.6310 4063	1046.8844 6381
89	370.3139 3839	429.4649 5500	581.8406 0581	795.1762 8225	1094.9942 6468
90	381.4975 7170	443.3489 0365	603.2050 2701	827.9833 3354	1145.2690 0659
91	392.9887 5492	457.6493 7076	625.3172 0295	862.1026 6688	1197.8061 1189
92	404.7959 4568	472.3788 5189	648.2033 0506	897.5867 7356	1252.7073 8692
93	416.9278 3418	487.5502 1744	671.8904 2073	934.4902 4450	1310.0792 1933
94	429.3933 4962	503.1767 2397	696.4065 8546	972.8698 5428	1370.0327 8420
95	442.2016 6674	519.2720 2569	721.7808 1595	1012.7846 4845	1432.6842 5949
96	455.3622 1257	535.8501 8645	748.0431 4451	1054.2960 3439	1498.1550 5117
97	468.8846 7342	552.9256 9205	775.2246 5457	1097.4678 7577	1566.5720 2847
98	482.7790 0194	570.5134 6281	803.3575 1748	1142.3665 9080	1638.0677 6976
99	497.0554 2449	588.6288 6669	832.4750 3059	1189.0612 5443	1712.7808 1939
100	511.7244 4867	607.2877 3270	862.6116 5666	1237.6237 0461	1790.8559 5627

$$s_{\overline{n}|i} = \frac{(1 + i)^n - 1}{i}$$

n	5 %	$5\frac{1}{2}$ %	6 %	7 %	8 %
1	1.0000 0000	1.0000 0000	1.0000 0000	1.0000 0000	1.0000 0000
2	2.0500 0000	2.0550 0000	2.0600 0000	2.0700 0000	2.0800 0000
3	3.1525 0000	3.1680 2500	3.1836 0000	3.2149 0000	3.2464 0000
4	4.3101 2500	4.3422 6638	4.3746 1600	4.4399 4300	4.5061 1200
5	5.5256 3125	5.5810 9103	5.6370 9296	5.7507 3901	5.8666 0096
6	6.8019 1281	6.8880 5103	6.9753 1854	7.1532 9074	7.3359 2904
7	8.1420 0845	8.2668 9384	8.3938 3765	8.6540 2109	8.9228 0336
8	9.5491 0888	9.7215 7300	9.8974 6791	10.2598 0257	10.6366 2763
9	11.0265 6432	11.2562 5951	11.4913 1598	11.9779 8875	12.4875 5784
10	12.5778 9254	12.8753 5379	13.1807 9494	13.8164 4796	14.4865 6247
11	14.2067 8716	14.5834 9825	14.9716 4264	15.7835 9932	16.6454 8746
12	15.9171 2652	16.3855 9065	16.8699 4120	17.8884 5127	18.9771 2646
13	17.7129 8285	18.2867 9814	18.8821 3767	20.1406 4286	21.4952 9658
14	19.5986 3199	20.2925 7203	21.0150 6593	22.5504 8786	24.2149 2030
15	21.5785 6359	22.4086 6350	23.2759 6988	25.1290 2201	27.1521 1393
16	23.6574 9177	24.6411 3999	25.6725 2808	27.8880 5355	30.3242 8304
17	25.8403 6636	26.9964 0269	28.2128 7976	30.8402 1730	33.7502 2569
18	28.1323 8467	29.4812 0483	30.9056 5255	33.9990 3251	37.4502 4374
19	30.5390 0391	32.1026 7110	33.7599 9170	37.3789 6479	41.4462 6324
20	33.0659 5410	34.8683 1801	36.7855 9120	40.9954 9232	45.7619 6430
21	35.7192 5181	37.7860 7550	39.9927 2668	44.8651 7678	50.4229 2144
22	38.5052 1440	40.8643 0965	43.3922 9028	49.0057 3916	55.4567 5516
23	41.4304 7512	44.1118 4669	46.9958 2769	53.4361 4090	60.8932 9557
24	44.5019 9887	47.5379 9825	50.8155 7735	58.1766 7076	66.7647 5922
25	47.7270 9882	51.1525 8816	54.8645 1200	63.2490 3772	73.1059 3995
26	51.1134 5376	54.9659 8051	59.1563 8272	68.6764 7036	79.9544 1515
27	54.6691 2645	58.9891 0943	63.7057 6568	74.4838 2328	87.3507 6836
28	58.4025 8277	63.2335 1045	68.5281 1162	80.6976 9091	95.3388 2983
29	62.3227 1191	67.7113 5853	73.6397 9832	87.3465 2927	103.9659 3622
30	66.4388 4750	72.4354 7797	79.0581 8622	94.4607 8632	113.2832 1111
31	70.7607 8988	77.4194 2926	84.8016 7739	102.0730 4137	123.3458 6800
32	75.2988 2937	82.6774 9787	90.8897 7803	110.2181 5426	134.2135 3744
33	80.0637 7084	88.2247 6025	97.3431 6471	118.9334 2506	145.9506 2044
34	85.0669 5938	94.0771 2207	104.1837 5460	128.2587 6481	158.6266 7007
35	90.3203 0735	100.2513 6378	111.4347 7987	138.2368 7835	172.3168 0368
36	95.8363 2272	106.7651 8879	119.1208 6666	148.9134 5984	187.1021 4797
37	101.6281 3886	113.6372 7417	127.2681 1866	160.3374 0202	203.0703 1981
38	107.7095 4580	120.8873 2425	135.9042 0578	172.5610 2017	220.3159 4540
39	114.0950 2309	128.5361 2708	145.0584 5813	185.6402 9158	238.9412 2103
40	120.7997 7424	136.6056 1407	154.7619 6562	199.6351 1199	259.0565 1871
41	127.8397 6295	145.1189 2285	165.0476 8356	214.6095 6983	280.7810 4021
42	135.2317 5110	154.1004 6360	175.9505 4457	230.6322 3972	304.2435 2342
43	142.9933 3866	163.5759 8910	187.5075 7724	247.7764 9650	329.5830 0530
44	151.1430 0559	173.5726 6850	199.7580 3188	266.1208 5125	356.9496 4572
45	159.7001 5587	184.1191 6527	212.7435 1379	285.7493 1084	386.5056 1738
46	168.6851 6366	195.2457 1936	226.5081 2462	306 7517 6260	418.4260 6677
47	178.1194 2185	206.9842 3392	241.0986 1210	329.2243 8598	452.9001 5211
48	188.0253 9294	219.3683 6679	256.5645 2882	353.2700 9300	490.1321 6428
49	198.4266 6259	232.4336 2696	272.9584 0055	378.9989 9951	530.3427 3742
50	209.3479 9572	246.2174 7645	290.3359 0458	406.5289 2947	573.7701 5642

TABLE III. AMOUNT OF ANNUITY OF 1 PER PERIOD   317

$$s_{\overline{n}|i} = \frac{(1 + i)^n - 1}{i}$$

n	5 %	5½ %	6 %	7 %	8 %
51	220.8153 9550	260.7594 3765	308.7560 5886	435.9859 5454	620.6717 6893
52	232.8561 6528	276.1012 0672	328.2814 2239	467.5049 7135	671.3255 1044
53	245.4989 7354	292.2867 7309	348.9783 0773	501.2303 1935	726.0315 5128
54	258.7739 2222	309.3625 4561	370.9170 0620	537.3164 4170	785.1140 7538
55	272.7126 1833	327.3774 8562	394.1720 2657	575.9285 9262	848.9232 0141
56	287.3482 4924	346.3832 4733	418.8223 4816	617.2435 9410	917.8370 5752
57	302.7156 6171	366.4343 2593	444.9516 8905	661.4506 4569	992.2640 2213
58	318.8514 4479	387.5882 1386	472.6487 9040	708.7521 9089	1072.6451 4390
59	335.7940 1703	409.9055 6562	502.0077 1782	759.3648 4425	1159.4567 5541
60	353.5837 1788	433.4503 7173	533.1281 8089	813.5203 8335	1253.2132 9584
61	372.2629 0378	458.2901 4217	566.1158 7174	871.4668 1019	1354.4703 5951
62	391.8760 4897	484.4960 9999	601.0828 2405	933.4694 8690	1463.8279 8827
63	412.4698 5141	512.1433 8549	638.1477 9349	999.8123 5098	1581.9342 2733
64	434.0933 4398	541.3112 7170	677.4366 6110	1070.7992 1555	1709.4889 6552
65	456.7980 1118	572.0833 9164	719.0828 6076	1146.7551 6064	1847.2480 8276
66	480.6379 1174	604.5479 7818	763.2278 3241	1228.0280 2188	1996.0279 2938
67	505.6698 0733	638.7981 1698	810.0215 0236	1314.9899 8341	2156.7101 6373
68	531.9532 9770	674.9320 1341	859.6227 9250	1408.0392 8225	2330.2469 7683
69	559.5509 6258	713.0532 7415	912.2001 6005	1507.6020 3201	2517.6667 3497
70	588.5285 1071	753.2712 0423	967.9321 6965	1614.1341 7425	2720.0800 7377
71	618.9549 3625	795.7011 2046	1027.0080 9983	1728.1235 6645	2938.6864 7967
72	650.9026 8306	840.4646 8209	1089.6285 8582	1850.0922 1610	3174.7813 9805
73	684.4478 1721	887.6902 3960	1156.0063 0097	1980.5986 7123	3429.7639 0989
74	719.6702 0807	937.5132 0278	1226.3666 7903	2120.2405 7821	3705.1450 2268
75	756.6537 1848	990.0764 2893	1300.9486 7977	2269.6574 1869	4002.5566 2449
76	795.4864 0440	1045.5306 3252	1380.0056 0055	2429.5334 3800	4323.7611 5445
77	836.2607 2462	1104.0348 1731	1463.8059 3659	2600.6007 7866	4670.6620 4681
78	879.0737 6085	1165.7567 3226	1552.6342 9278	2783.6428 3316	5045.3150 1056
79	924.0274 4889	1230.8733 5254	1646.7923 5035	2979.4978 3148	5449.9402 1140
80	971.2288 2134	1299.5713 8693	1746.5998 9137	3189.0626 7969	5886.9354 2831
81	1020.7902 6240	1372.0478 1321	1852.3958 8485	3413.2970 6727	6358.8902 6258
82	1072.8297 7552	1448.5104 4294	1964.5396 3794	3653.2278 6198	6868.6014 8358
83	1127.4712 6430	1529.1785 1730	2083.4120 1622	3909.9538 1231	7419.0896 0227
84	1184.8448 2752	1614.2833 3575	2209.4167 3719	4184.6505 7918	8013.6167 7045
85	1245 0870 6889	1704.0689 1921	2342.9817 4142	4478.5761 1972	8655.7061 1209
86	1308.3414 2234	1798.7927 0977	2484.5606 4591	4793.0764 4810	9349.1626 0105
87	1374.7584 9345	1898.7263 0881	2634.6342 8466	5129.5917 9946	10098.0956 0914
88	1444.4964 1812	2004.1562 5579	2793.7123 4174	5489.6632 2543	10906.9432 5787
89	1517.7212 3903	2115.3848 4986	2962.3350 8225	5874.9396 5121	11780.4987 1850
90	1594.6073 0098	2232.7310 1660	3141.0751 8718	6287.1854 2679	12723.9386 1598
91	1675.3376 6603	2356.5312 2252	3330.5396 9841	6728.2884 0667	13742.8537 0526
92	1760.1045 4933	2487.1404 3976	3531.3720 8032	7200.2685 9513	14843.2820 0168
93	1849.1097 7680	2624.9331 6394	3744.2544 0514	7705.2873 9679	16031.7445 6181
94	1942.5652 6564	2770.3044 8796	3969.9096 6944	8245.6575 1457	17315.2841 2676
95	2040.6935 2892	2923.6712 3480	4209.1042 4961	8823.8535 4059	18701.5068 5690
96	2143.7282 0537	3085.4731 5271	4462.6505 0459	9442.5232 8843	20198.6274 0545
97	2251.9146 1564	3256.1741 7611	4731.4095 3486	10104.4999 1862	21815.5175 9788
98	2365.5103 4642	3436.2637 5580	5016.2941 0696	10812.8149 1292	23561.7590 0572
99	2484.7858 6374	3626.2582 6237	5318.2717 5337	11570.7119 5683	25447.6997 2617
100	2610.0251 5693	3826.7024 6680	5638.3680 5857	12381.6617 9381	27484.5157 0427

$$a_{\overline{n}|i} = \frac{1 - (1 + i)^{-n}}{i}$$

n	$\frac{1}{4}\%$	$\frac{1}{3}\%$	$\frac{5}{12}\%$	$\frac{1}{2}\%$	$\frac{7}{12}\%$
1	0.9975 0623	0.9966 7774	0.9958 5062	0.9950 2488	0.9942 0050
2	1.9925 2492	1.9900 4426	1.9875 6908	1.9850 9938	1.9826 3513
3	2.9850 6227	2.9801 1056	2.9751 7253	2.9702 4814	2.9653 3733
4	3.9751 2446	3.9668 8760	3.9586 7804	3.9504 9566	3.9423 4034
5	4.9627 1766	4.9503 8631	4.9381 0261	4.9258 6633	4.9136 7723
6	5.9478 4804	5.9306 1759	5.9134 6318	5.8963 8441	5.8793 8084
7	6.9305 2174	6.9075 9228	6.8847 7661	6.8620 7404	6.8394 8385
8	7.9107 4487	7.8813 2121	7.8520 5969	7.8229 5924	7.7940 1875
9	8.8885 2357	8.8518 1516	8.8153 2915	8.7790 6392	8.7430 1781
10	9.8638 6391	9.8190 8487	9.7746 0164	9.7304 1186	9.6865 1315
11	10.8367 7198	10.7831 4107	10.7298 9374	10.6770 2673	10.6245 3669
12	11.8072 5384	11.7439 9442	11.6812 2198	11.6189 3207	11.5571 2016
13	12.7753 1555	12.7016 5557	12.6286 0280	12.5561 5131	12.4842 9511
14	13.7409 6314	13.6561 3512	13.5720 5257	13.4887 0777	13.4060 9291
15	14.7042 0264	14.6074 4364	14.5115 8762	14.4166 2465	14.3225 4473
16	15.6650 4004	15.5555 9167	15.4472 2418	15.3399 2502	15.2336 8160
17	16.6234 8133	16.5005 8970	16.3789 7843	16.2586 3186	16.1395 3432
18	17.5795 3250	17.4424 4821	17.3068 6648	17.1727 6802	17.0401 3354
19	18.5331 9950	18.3811 7762	18.2309 0438	18.0823 5624	17.9355 0974
20	19.4844 8828	19.3167 8832	19.1511 0809	18.9874 1915	18.8256 9320
21	20.4334 0477	20.2492 9069	20.0674 9352	19.8879 7925	19.7107 1404
22	21.3799 5488	21.1786 9504	20.9800 7653	20.7840 5896	20.5906 0220
23	22.3241 4452	22.1050 1167	21.8888 7289	21.6756 8055	21.4653 8745
24	23.2659 7957	23.0282 5083	22.7938 9831	22.5628 6622	22.3350 9938
25	24.2054 6591	23.9484 2275	23.6951 6843	23.4456 3803	23.1997 6741
26	25.1426 0939	24.8655 3763	24.5926 9884	24.3240 1794	24.0594 2079
27	26.0774 1585	25.7796 0561	25.4865 0506	25.1980 2780	24.9140 8862
28	27.0098 9112	26.6906 3682	26.3766 0254	26.0676 8936	25.7637 9979
29	27.9400 4102	27.5986 4135	27.2630 0668	26.9330 2423	26.6085 8307
30	28.8678 7134	28.5036 2925	28.1457 3278	27.7940 5397	27.4484 6702
31	29.7933 8787	29.4056 1055	29.0247 9612	28.6507 9997	28.2834 8006
32	30.7165 9638	30.3045 9523	29.9002 1189	29.5032 8355	29.1136 5044
33	31.6375 0262	31.2005 9325	30.7719 9524	30.3515 2592	29.9390 0625
34	32.5561 1234	32.0936 1454	31.6401 6122	31.1955 4818	30.7595 7540
35	33.4724 3126	32.9836 6898	32.5047 2486	32.0353 7132	31.5753 8566
36	34.3864 6510	33.8707 6642	33.3657 0109	32.8710 1624	32.3864 6463
37	35.2982 1955	34.7549 1670	34.2231 0481	33.7025 0372	33.1928 3974
38	36.2077 0030	35.6361 2960	35.0769 5084	34.5298 5445	33.9945 3828
39	37.1149 1302	36.5144 1488	35.9272 5394	35.3530 8900	34.7915 8736
40	38.0198 6336	37.3897 8228	36.7740 2881	36.1722 2786	35.5840 1396
41	38.9225 5697	38.2622 4147	37.6172 9009	36.9872 9141	36.3718 4487
42	39.8229 9947	39.1318 0213	38.4570 5236	37.7982 9991	37.1551 0676
43	40.7211 9648	39.9984 7388	39.2933 3013	38.6052 7354	37.9338 2612
44	41.6171 5359	40.8622 6633	40.1261 3788	39.4082 3238	38.7080 2929
45	42.5108 7640	41.7231 8903	40.9554 8999	40.2071 9640	39.4777 4248
46	43.4023 7047	42.5812 5153	41.7814 0081	41.0021 8547	40.2429 9170
47	44.2916 4137	43.4364 6332	42.6038 8461	41.7932 1937	41.0038 0287
48	45.1786 9463	44.2888 3387	43.4229 5562	42.5803 1778	41.7602 0170
49	46.0635 3580	45.1383 7263	44.2386 2799	43.3635 0028	42.5122 1380
50	46.9461 7037	45.9850 8900	45.0509 1582	44.1427 8635	43.2598 6460

TABLE IV.   PRESENT VALUE OF ANNUITY OF 1 PER PERIOD   319

$$a_{\overline{n}|i} = \frac{1 - (1+i)^{-n}}{i}$$

n	$\frac{1}{4}\%$	$\frac{1}{3}\%$	$\frac{5}{12}\%$	$\frac{1}{2}\%$	$\frac{7}{12}\%$
51	47.8266 0386	46.8289 9236	45.8598 3317	44.9181 9537	44.0031 7940
52	48.7048 4176	47.6700 9205	46.6653 9401	45.6897 4664	44.7421 8335
53	49.5808 8953	48.5083 9739	47.4676 1228	46.4574 5934	45.4769 0144
54	50.4547 5265	49.3439 1767	48.2665 0184	47.2213 5258	46.2073 5853
55	51.3264 3656	50.1766 6213	49.0620 7651	47.9814 4535	46.9335 7933
56	52.1959 4669	51.0066 3999	49.8543 5003	48.7377 5657	47.6555 8841
57	53.0632 8847	51.8338 6046	50.6433 3612	49.4903 0505	48.3734 1020
58	53.9284 6730	52.6583 3268	51.4290 4840	50.2391 0950	49.0870 6898
59	54.7914 8858	53.4800 6580	52.2115 0046	50.9841 8855	49.7965 8889
60	55.6523 5769	54.2990 6890	52.9907 0584	51.7255 6075	50.5019 9394
61	56.5110 7999	55.1153 5106	53.7666 7800	52.4632 4453	51.2033 0800
62	57.3676 6083	55.9289 2133	54.5394 3035	53.1972 5824	51.9005 5478
63	58.2221 0557	56.7397 8870	55.3089 7627	53.9276 2014	52.5937 5787
64	59.0744 1952	57.5497 6216	56.0753 2905	54.6543 4839	53.2829 4073
65	59.9246 0800	58.3534 5065	56.8385 0194	55.3774 6109	53.9681 2668
66	60.7726 7631	59.1562 6311	57.5985 0814	56.0969 7621	54.6493 3888
67	61.6186 2974	59.9564 0842	58.3553 6078	56.8129 1165	55.3266 0040
68	62.4624 7355	60.7538 9543	59.1090 7296	57.5252 8522	55.9999 3413
69	63.3042 1302	61.5487 3299	59.8596 5770	58.2341 1465	56.6693 6287
70	64.1438 5339	62.3409 2989	60.6071 2798	58.9394 1756	57.3349 0925
71	64.9813 9989	63.1304 9490	61.3514 9672	59.6412 1151	57.9965 9579
72	65.8168 5774	63.9174 3678	62.0927 7680	60.3395 1394	58.6544 4488
73	66.6502 3216	64.7017 6423	62.8309 8103	61.0343 4222	59.3084 7877
74	67.4815 2834	65.4834 8595	63.5661 2216	61.7257 1366	59.9587 1959
75	68.3107 5146	66.2626 1058	64.2982 1292	62.4136 4543	60.6051 8934
76	69.1379 0670	67.0391 4676	65.0272 6596	63.0981 5466	61.2479 0988
77	69.9629 9920	67.8131 0308	65.7532 9388	63.7792 5836	61.8869 0297
78	70.7860 3411	68.5844 8812	66.4763 0924	64.4569 7350	62.5221 9021
79	71.6070 1657	69.3533 1042	67.1963 2453	65.1313 1691	63.1537 9310
80	72.4259 5169	70.1195 7849	67.9133 5221	65.8023 0538	63.7817 3301
81	73.2428 4458	70.8833 0082	68.6274 0467	66.4699 5561	64.4060 3118
82	74.0577 0033	71.6444 8587	69.3384 9426	67.1342 8419	65.0267 0874
83	74.8705 2402	72.4031 4206	70.0466 3326	67.7953 0765	65.6437 8667
84	75.6813 2072	73.1592 7780	70.7518 3393	68.4530 4244	66.2572 8585
85	76.4900 9548	73.9129 0146	71.4541 0846	69.1075 0491	66.8672 2705
86	77.2968 5335	74.6640 2139	72.1534 6898	69.7587 1135	67.4736 3089
87	78.1015 9935	75.4126 4591	72.8499 2759	70.4066 7796	68.0765 1789
88	78.9043 3850	76.1587 8329	73.5434 9633	71.0514 2086	68.6759 0845
89	79.7050 7581	76.9024 4182	74.2341 8720	71.6929 5608	69.2718 2283
90	80.5038 1627	77.6436 2972	74.9220 1212	72.3312 9958	69.8642 8121
91	81.3005 6486	78.3823 5520	75.6069 8300	72.9664 6725	70.4533 0363
92	82.0953 2654	79.1186 2645	76.2891 1168	73.5984 7487	71.0389 1001
93	82.8881 0628	79.8524 5161	76.9684 0995	74.2273 3818	71.6211 2017
94	83.6789 0900	80.5838 3882	77.6448 8955	74.8530 7282	72.1999 5379
95	84.4677 3966	81.3127 9616	78.3185 6218	75.4756 9434	72.7754 3047
96	85.2546 0315	82.0393 3172	78.9894 3950	76.0952 1825	73.3475 6967
97	86.0395 0439	82.7634 5354	79.6575 3308	76.7116 5995	73.9163 9075
98	86.8224 4827	83.4851 6964	80.3228 5450	77.3250 3478	74.4819 1294
99	87.6034 3967	84.2044 8802	80.9854 1524	77.9353 5799	75.0441 5539
100	88.3824 8346	84.9214 1663	81.6452 2677	78.5426 4477	75.6031 3712
∞	400.0000 0000	300.0000 0000	240.0000 0000	200.0000 0000	171.4285 7143

$$a_{\overline{n}|i} = \frac{1 - (1 + i)^{-n}}{i}$$

n	$\frac{7}{8}\%$	1%	$1\frac{1}{8}\%$	$1\frac{1}{4}\%$	$1\frac{3}{8}\%$
1	0.9913 2590	0.9900 9901	0.9888 7515	0.9876 5432	0.9864 3650
2	1.9740 5294	1.9703 9506	1.9667 4923	1.9631 1538	1.9594 9346
3	2.9482 5570	2.9409 8521	2.9337 4460	2.9265 3371	2.9193 5237
4	3.9140 0813	3.9019 6555	3.8899 8230	3.8780 5798	3.8661 9222
5	4.8713 8352	4.8534 3124	4.8355 8200	4.8178 3504	4.8001 8962
6	5.8204 5454	5.7954 7647	5.7706 6205	5.7460 0992	5.7215 1874
7	6.7612 9323	6.7281 9453	6.6953 3948	6.6627 2585	6.6303 5140
8	7.6939 7098	7.6516 7775	7.6097 3002	7.5681 2429	7.5268 5712
9	8.6185 5859	8.5660 1758	8.5139 4810	8.4623 4498	8.4112 0308
10	9.5351 2624	9.4713 0453	9.4081 0690	9.3455 2591	9.2835 5421
11	10.4437 4348	10.3676 2825	10.2923 1832	10.2178 0337	10.1440 7320
12	11.3444 7929	11.2550 7747	11.1666 9302	11.0793 1197	10.9929 2054
13	12.2374 0202	12.1337 4007	12.0313 3044	11.9301 8466	11.8302 5454
14	13.1225 7945	13.0037 0304	12.8863 6880	12.7705 5275	12.6562 3136
15	14.0000 7876	13.8650 5252	13.7318 8509	13.6005 4592	13.4710 0504
16	14.8699 6656	14.7178 7378	14.5679 9514	14.4202 9227	14.2747 2754
17	15.7323 0885	15.5622 5127	15.3948 0360	15.2299 1829	15.0675 4874
18	16.5871 7111	16.3982 6858	16.2124 1395	16.0295 4893	15.8496 1651
19	17.4346 1820	17.2260 0850	17.0209 2850	16.8193 0759	16.6210 7671
20	18.2747 1445	18.0455 5297	17.8204 4845	17.5993 1613	17.3820 7320
21	19.1075 2361	18.8569 8313	18.6110 7387	18.3696 9495	18.1327 4792
22	19.9331 0891	19.6603 7934	19.3929 0371	19.1305 6291	18.8732 4086
23	20.7515 3300	20.4558 2113	20.1660 3580	19.8820 3744	19.6036 9012
24	21.5628 5799	21.2433 8726	20.9305 6693	20.6242 3451	20.3242 3193
25	22.3671 4547	22.0231 5570	21.6865 9276	21.3572 6865	21.0350 0067
26	23.1644 5647	22.7952 0366	22.4342 0792	22.0812 5299	21.7361 2890
27	23.9548 5152	23.5596 0759	23.1735 0598	22.7962 9925	22.4277 4737
28	24.7383 9060	24.3164 4316	23.9045 7946	23.5025 1778	23.1099 8508
29	25.5151 3319	25.0657 8530	24.6275 1986	24.2000 1756	23.7829 6925
30	26.2851 3823	25.8077 0822	25.3424 1766	24.8889 0623	24.4468 2540
31	27.0484 6417	26.5422 8537	26.0493 6233	25.5692 9010	25.1016 7734
32	27.8051 6894	27.2695 8947	26.7484 4236	26.2412 7418	25.7476 4719
33	28.5553 0998	27.9896 9255	27.4397 4522	26.9049 6215	26.3848 5543
34	29.2989 4422	28.7026 6589	28.1233 5745	27.5604 5644	27.0134 2089
35	30.0361 2809	29.4085 8009	28.7993 6460	28.2078 5822	27.6334 6080
36	30.7669 1757	30.1075 0504	29.4678 5127	28.8472 6737	28.2450 9080
37	31.4913 6810	30.7995 0994	30.1289 0114	29.4787 8259	28.8484 2496
38	32.2095 3467	31.4846 6330	30.7825 9692	30.1025 0133	29.4435 7579
39	32.9214 7179	32.1630 3298	31.4290 2044	30.7185 1983	30.0306 5430
40	33.6272 3350	32.8346 8611	32.0682 5260	31.3269 3316	30.6097 6996
41	34.3268 7335	33.4996 8922	32.7003 7340	31.9278 3522	31.1810 3079
42	35.0204 4446	34.1581 0814	33.3254 6195	32.5213 1874	31.7445 4332
43	35.7079 9947	34.8100 0806	33.9435 9649	33.1074 7530	32.3004 1264
44	36.3895 9055	35.4554 5352	34.5548 5438	33.6863 9536	32.8487 4243
45	37.0652 6944	36.0945 0844	35.1593 1212	34.2581 6825	33.3896 3495
46	37.7350 8743	36.7272 3608	35.7570 4536	34.8228 8222	33.9231 9108
47	38.3990 9535	37.3536 9909	36.3481 2891	35.3806 2442	34.4495 1031
48	39.0573 4359	37.9739 5949	36.9326 3674	35.9314 8091	34.9686 9081
49	39.7098 8212	38.5880 7871	37.5106 4202	36.4755 3670	35.4808 2941
50	40.3567 6047	39.1961 1753	38.0822 1708	37.0128 7574	35.9860 2161

TABLE IV. PRESENT VALUE OF ANNUITY OF 1 PER PERIOD   321

$$a_{\overline{n}|i} = \frac{1 - (1+i)^{-n}}{i}$$

n	$\frac{7}{8}\%$	1 %	$1\frac{1}{8}\%$	$1\frac{1}{4}\%$	$1\frac{3}{8}\%$
51	40.9980 2772	39.7981 3617	38.6474 3345	37.5435 8099	36.4843 6164
52	41.6337 3256	40.3941 9423	39.2063 6188	38.0677 3431	36.9759 4243
53	42.2639 2324	40.9843 5072	39.7590 7232	38.5854 1660	37.4608 5566
54	42.8886 4757	41.5686 6408	40.3056 3394	39.0967 0776	37.9391 9178
55	43.5079 5298	42.1471 9216	40.8461 1514	39.6016 8667	38.4110 3998
56	44.1218 8647	42.7199 9224	41.3805 8358	40.1004 3128	38.8764 8826
57	44.7304 9465	43.2871 2102	41.9091 0613	40.5930 1855	39.3356 2344
58	45.3338 2369	43.8486 3468	42.4317 4896	41.0795 2449	39.7885 3114
59	45.9319 1939	44.4045 8879	42.9485 7746	41.5600 2419	40.2352 9582
60	46.5248 2716	44.9550 3841	43.4596 5633	42.0345 9179	40.6760 0081
61	47.1125 9198	45.5000 3803	43.9650 4952	42.5033 0054	41.1107 2829
62	47.6952 5847	46.0396 4161	44.4648 2029	42.9662 2275	41.5395 5935
63	48.2728 7085	46.5739 0258	44.9590 3119	43.4234 2988	41.9625 7396
64	48.8454 7296	47.1028 7385	45.4477 4407	43.8749 9247	42.3798 5101
65	49.4131 0826	47.6266 0777	45.9310 2009	44.3209 8022	42.7914 6832
66	49.9758 1984	48.1451 5621	46.4089 1975	44.7614 6195	43.1975 0266
67	50.5336 5040	48.6585 7050	46.8815 0284	45.1965 0563	43.5980 2975
68	51.0866 4228	49.1669 0149	47.3488 2852	45.6261 7840	43.9931 2429
69	51.6348 3745	49.6701 9949	47.8109 5527	46.0505 4656	44.3828 5997
70	52.1782 7752	50.1685 1435	48.2679 4094	46.4696 7562	44.7673 0946
71	52.7170 0374	50.6618 9539	48.7198 4270	46.8836 3024	45.1465 4448
72	53.2510 5699	51.1503 9148	49.1667 1714	47.2924 7431	45.5206 3573
73	53.7804 7781	51.6340 5097	49.6086 2016	47.6962 7093	45.8896 5300
74	54.3053 0638	52.1129 2175	50.0456 0708	48.0950 8240	46.2536 6511
75	54.8255 8253	52.5870 5124	50.4777 3259	48.4889 7027	46.6127 3994
76	55.3413 4575	53.0564 8637	50.9050 5077	48.8779 9533	46.9669 4445
77	55.8526 3520	53.5212 7364	51.3276 1510	49.2622 1761	47.3163 4471
78	56.3594 8966	53.9814 5905	51.7454 7847	49.6416 9640	47.6610 0588
79	56.8619 4762	54.4370 8817	52.1586 9317	50.0164 9027	48.0009 9224
80	57.3600 4721	54.8882 0611	52.5673 1092	50.3866 5706	48.3363 6719
81	57.8538 2623	55.3348 5753	52.9713 8286	50.7522 5389	48.6671 9328
82	58.3433 2216	55.7770 8666	53.3709 5957	51.1133 3717	48.9935 3221
83	58.8285 7215	56.2149 3729	53.7660 9104	51.4699 6264	49.3154 4484
84	59.3096 1304	56.6484 5276	54.1568 2674	51.8221 8532	49.6329 9122
85	59.7864 8133	57.0776 7600	54.5432 1557	52.1700 5958	49.9462 3055
86	60.2592 1321	57.5026 4951	54.9253 0588	52.5136 3909	50.2552 2125
87	60.7278 4457	57.9234 1535	55.3031 4549	52.8529 7688	50.5600 2096
88	61.1924 1097	58.3400 1520	55.6767 8169	53.1881 2531	50.8606 8653
89	61.6529 4768	58.7524 9030	56.0462 6126	53.5191 3611	51.1572 7401
90	62.1094 8965	59.1608 8148	56.4116 3041	53.8460 6035	51.4498 3873
91	62.5620 7152	59.5652 2919	56.7729 3490	54.1689 4850	51.7384 3524
92	63.0107 2765	59.9655 7346	57.1302 1992	54.4878 5037	52.0231 1738
93	63.4554 9210	60.3619 5392	57.4835 3021	54.8028 1518	52.3039 3823
94	63.8963 9861	60.7544 0982	57.8329 0997	55.1138 9154	52.5809 5016
95	64.3334 8065	61.1429 8002	58.1784 0294	55.4211 2744	52.8542 0484
96	64.7667 7140	61.5277 0299	58.5200 5235	55.7245 7031	53.1237 5324
97	65.1963 0375	61.9086 1682	58.8579 0096	56.0242 6698	53.3896 4561
98	65.6221 1028	62.2857 5923	59.1919 9106	56.3202 6368	53.6519 3155
99	66.0442 2333	62.6591 6755	59.5223 6446	56.6126 0610	53.9106 5998
100	66.4626 7492	63.0288 7877	59.8490 6251	56.9013 3936	54.1658 7914
∞	114.2857 1429	100.0000 0000	88.8888 8889	80.0000 0000	72.7272 7273

$$a_{\overline{n}|i} = \frac{1 - (1 + i)^{-n}}{i}$$

n	$1\frac{1}{2}\%$	$1\frac{3}{4}\%$	2%	$2\frac{1}{4}\%$	$2\frac{1}{2}\%$
1	0.9852 2167	0.9828 0098	0.9803 9216	0.9779 9511	0.9756 0976
2	1.9558 8342	1.9486 9875	1.9415 6094	1.9344 6955	1.9274 2415
3	2.9122 0042	2.8979 8403	2.8838 8327	2.8698 9687	2.8560 2356
4	3.8543 8465	3.8309 4254	3.8077 2870	3.7847 4021	3.7619 7421
5	4.7826 4497	4.7478 5508	4.7134 5951	4.6794 5253	4.6458 2850
6	5.6971 8717	5.6489 9762	5.6014 3089	5.5544 7680	5.5081 2536
7	6.5982 1396	6.5346 4139	6.4719 9107	6.4102 4626	6.3493 9060
8	7.4859 2508	7.4050 5297	7.3254 8144	7.2471 8461	7.1701 3717
9	8.3605 1732	8.2604 9432	8.1622 3671	8.0657 0622	7.9708 6553
10	9.2221 8455	9.1012 2291	8.9825 8501	8.8662 1635	8.7520 6393
11	10.0711 1779	9.9274 9181	9.7868 4805	9.6491 1134	9.5142 0871
12	10.9075 0521	10.7395 4969	10.5753 4122	10.4147 7882	10.2577 6460
13	11.7315 3222	11.5376 4097	11.3483 7375	11.1635 9787	10.9831 8497
14	12.5433 8150	12.3220 0587	12.1062 4877	11.8959 3924	11.6909 1217
15	13.3432 3301	13.0928 8046	12.8492 6350	12.6121 6551	12.3813 7773
16	14.1312 6405	13.8504 9677	13.5777 0931	13.3126 3131	13.0550 0266
17	14.9076 4931	14.5950 8282	14.2918 7188	13.9976 8343	13.7121 9772
18	15.6725 6089	15.3268 6272	14.9920 3125	14.6676 6106	14.3533 6363
19	16.4261 6837	16.0460 5673	15.6784 6201	15.3228 9590	14.9788 9134
20	17.1686 3879	16.7528 8130	16.3514 3334	15.9637 1237	15.5891 6229
21	17.9001 3673	17.4475 4919	17.0112 0916	16.5904 2775	16.1845 4857
22	18.6208 2437	18.1302 6948	17.6580 4820	17.2033 5232	16.7654 1324
23	19.3308 6145	18.8012 4764	18.2922 0412	17.8027 8955	17.3321 1048
24	20.0304 0537	19.4606 8565	18.9139 2560	18.3890 3624	17.8849 8583
25	20.7196 1120	20.1087 8196	19.5234 5647	18.9623 8263	18.4243 7642
26	21.3986 3172	20.7457 3166	20.1210 3576	19.5231 1260	18.9506 1114
27	22.0676 1746	21.3717 2644	20.7068 9780	20.0715 0376	19.4640 1087
28	22.7267 1671	21.9869 5474	21.2812 7236	20.6078 2764	19.9648 8866
29	23.3760 7558	22.5916 0171	21.8443 8466	21.1323 4977	20.4535 4991
30	24.0158 3801	23.1858 4934	22.3964 5555	21.6453 2985	20.9302 9259
31	24.6461 4582	23.7698 7650	22.9377 0152	22.1470 2186	21.3954 0741
32	25.2671 3874	24.3438 5897	23.4683 3482	22.6376 7419	21.8491 7796
33	25.8789 5442	24.9079 6951	23.9885 6355	23.1175 2977	22.2918 8094
34	26.4817 2849	25.4623 7789	24.4985 9172	23.5868 2618	22.7237 8628
35	27.0755 9458	26.0072 5100	24.9986 1933	24.0457 9577	23.1451 5734
36	27.6606 8431	26.5427 5283	25.4888 4248	24.4946 6579	23.5562 5107
37	28.2371 2740	27.0690 4455	25.9694 5341	24.9336 5848	23.9573 1812
38	28.8050 5163	27.5862 8457	26.4406 4060	25.3629 9118	24.3486 0304
39	29.3645 8288	28.0946 2857	26.9025 8883	25.7828 7646	24.7303 4443
40	29.9158 4520	28.5942 2955	27.3554 7924	26.1935 2221	25.1027 7505
41	30.4589 6079	29.0852 3789	27.7994 8945	26.5951 3174	25.4661 2200
42	30.9940 5004	29.5678 0135	28.2347 9358	26.9879 0390	25.8206 0683
43	31.5212 3157	30.0420 6522	28.6615 6233	27.3720 3316	26.1664 4569
44	32.0406 2223	30.5081 7221	29.0799 6307	27.7477 0969	26.5038 4945
45	32.5523 3718	30.9662 6261	29.4901 5987	28.1151 1950	26.8330 2386
46	33.0564 8983	31.4164 7431	29.8923 1360	28.4744 4450	27.1541 6962
47	33.5531 9195	31.8589 4281	30.2865 8196	28.8258 6259	27.4674 8255
48	34.0425 5365	32.2938 0129	30.6731 1957	29.1695 4777	27.7731 5371
49	34.5246 8339	32.7211 8063	31.0520 7801	29.5056 7019	28.0713 6947
50	34.9996 8807	33.1412 0946	31.4236 0589	29.8343 9627	28.3623 1168

TABLE IV.   PRESENT VALUE OF ANNUITY OF 1 PER PERIOD   323

$$a_{\overline{n}|i} = \frac{1 - (1 + i)^{-n}}{i}$$

n	$1\frac{1}{2}\%$	$1\frac{3}{4}\%$	2%	$2\frac{1}{4}\%$	$2\frac{1}{2}\%$
51	35.4676 7298	33.5540 1421	31.7878 4892	30.1558 8877	28.6461 5774
52	35.9287 4185	33.9597 1913	32.1449 4992	30.4703 0687	28.9230 8072
53	36.3829 9690	34.3584 4633	32.4950 4894	30.7778 0623	29.1932 4948
54	36.8305 3882	34.7503 1579	32.8382 8327	31.0785 3910	29.4568 2876
55	37.2714 6681	35.1354 4550	33.1747 8752	31.3726 5438	29.7139 7928
56	37.7058 7863	35.5139 5135	33.5046 9365	31.6602 9768	29.9648 5784
57	38.1338 7058	35.8859 4727	33.8281 3103	31.9416 1142	30.2096 1740
58	38.5555 3751	36.2515 4523	34.1452 2650	32.2167 3489	30.4484 0722
59	38.9709 7292	36.6108 5526	34.4561 0441	32.4858 0429	30.6813 7290
60	39.3802 6889	26.9639 8552	34.7608 8668	32.7489 5285	30.9086 5649
61	39.7835 1614	37.3110 4228	35.0596 9282	33.0063 1086	31.1303 9657
62	40.1808 0408	37.6521 3000	35.3526 4002	33.2580 0573	31.3467 2836
63	40.5722 2077	37.9873 5135	35.6398 4316	33.5041 6208	31.5577 8377
64	40.9578 5298	38.3168 0723	35.9214 1486	33.7449 0179	31.7636 9148
65	41.3377 8618	38.6405 9678	36.1974 6555	33.9803 4405	31.9645 7705
66	41.7121 0461	38.9588 1748	36.4681 0348	34.2106 0543	32.1605 6298
67	42.0808 9125	39.2715 6509	36.7334 3478	34.4357 9993	32.3517 6876
68	42.4442 2783	39.5789 3375	36.9935 6351	34.6560 3905	32.5383 1099
69	42.8021 9490	39.8810 1597	37.2485 9168	34.8714 3183	32.7203 0340
70	43.1548 7183	40.1779 0267	37.4986 1929	35.0820 8492	32.8978 5698
71	43.5023 3678	40.4696 8321	37.7437 4441	35.2881 0261	33.0710 7998
72	43.8446 6677	40.7564 4542	37.9840 6314	35.4895 8691	33.2400 7803
73	44.1819 3771	41.0382 7560	38.2196 6975	35.6866 3756	33.4049 5417
74	44.5142 2434	41.3152 5857	38.4506 5662	35.8793 5214	33.5658 0895
75	44.8416 0034	41.5874 7771	38.6771 1433	36.0678 2605	33.7227 4044
76	45.1641 3826	41.8550 1495	38.8991 3170	36.2521 5262	33.8758 4433
77	45.4819 0962	42.1179 5081	39.1167 9578	36.4324 2310	34.0252 1398
78	45.7949 8485	42.3763 6443	39.3301 9194	36.6087 2675	34.1709 4047
79	46.1034 3335	42.6303 3359	39.5394 0386	36.7811 5085	34.3131 1265
80	46.4073 2349	42.8799 3474	39.7445 1359	36.9497 8079	34.4518 1722
81	46.7067 2265	43.1252 4298	39.9456 0156	37.1147 0004	34.5871 3875
82	47.0016 9720	43.3663 3217	40.1427 4663	37.2759 9026	34.7191 5976
83	47.2923 1251	43.6032 7486	40.3360 2611	37.4337 3130	34.8479 6074
84	47.5786 3301	43.8361 4237	40.5255 1579	37.5880 0127	34.9736 2023
85	47.8607 2218	44.0650 0479	40.7112 8999	37.7388 7655	35.0962 1486
86	48.1386 4254	44.2899 3099	40.8934 2156	37.8864 3183	35.2158 1938
87	48.4124 5571	44.5109 8869	41.0719 8192	38.0307 4018	35.3325 0671
88	48.6822 2237	44.7282 4441	41.2470 4110	38.1718 7304	35.4463 4801
89	48.9480 0234	44.9417 6355	41.4186 6774	38.3099 0028	35.5574 1269
90	49.2098 5452	45.1516 1037	41.5869 2916	38.4448 9025	35.6657 6848
91	49.4678 3696	45.3578 4803	41.7518 9133	38.5769 0978	35.7714 8144
92	49.7220 0686	45.5605 3860	41.9136 1895	38.7060 2423	35.8746 1604
93	49.9724 2055	45.7597 4310	42.0721 7545	38.8322 9754	35.9752 4516
94	50.2191 3355	45.9555 2147	42.2276 2299	38.9557 9221	36.0734 0016
95	50.4622 0054	46.1479 3265	42.3800 2254	39.0765 6940	36.1691 7089
96	50.7016 7541	46.3370 3455	42.5294 3386	39.1946 8890	36.2626 0574
97	50.9376 1124	46.5228 8408	42.6759 1555	39.3102 0920	36.3537 6170
98	51.1700 6034	46.7055 3718	42.8195 2505	39.4231 8748	36.4426 9434
99	51.3990 7422	46.8850 4882	42.9603 1867	39.5336 7968	36.5294 5790
100	51.6247 0367	47.0614 7304	43.0983 5164	39.6417 4052	36.6141 0526
∞	66.6666 6667	57.1428 5714	50.0000 0000	44.4444 4444	40.0000 0000

$$a_{\overline{n}|i} = \frac{1 - (1 + i)^{-n}}{i}$$

n	$2\frac{3}{4}$ %	3 %	$3\frac{1}{2}$ %	4 %	$4\frac{1}{2}$ %
1	0.9732 3601	0.9708 7379	0.9661 8357	0.9615 3846	0.9569 3780
2	1.9204 2434	1.9134 6970	1.8996 9428	1.8860 9467	1.8726 6775
3	2.8422 6213	2.8286 1135	2.8016 3698	2.7750 9103	2.7489 6435
4	3.7394 2787	3.7170 9840	3.6730 7921	3.6298 9522	3.5875 2570
5	4.6125 8186	4.5797 0719	4.5150 5238	4.4518 2233	4.3899 7674
6	5.4623 6678	5.4171 9144	5.3285 5302	5.2421 3686	5.1578 7248
7	6.2894 0806	6.2302 8296	6.1145 4398	6.0020 5467	5.8927 0094
8	7.0943 1441	7.0196 9219	6.8739 5554	6.7327 4487	6.5958 8607
9	7.8776 7826	7.7861 0892	7.6076 8651	7.4353 3161	7.2687 9050
10	8.6400 7616	8.5302 0284	8.3166 0532	8.1108 9578	7.9127 1818
11	9.3820 6926	9.2526 2411	9.0015 5104	8.7604 7671	8.5289 1692
12	10.1042 0366	9.9540 0399	9.6633 3433	9.3850 7376	9.1185 8078
13	10.8070 1086	10.6349 5533	10.3027 3849	9.9856 4785	9.6828 5242
14	11.4910 0814	11.2960 7314	10.9205 2028	10.5631 2293	10.2228 2528
15	12.1566 9892	11.9379 3509	11.5174 1090	11.1183 8743	10.7395 4573
16	12.8045 7315	12.5611 0203	12.0941 1681	11.6522 9561	11.2340 1505
17	13.4351 0769	13.1661 1847	12.6513 2059	12.1656 6885	11.7071 9143
18	14.0487 6661	13.7535 1308	13.1896 8173	12.6592 9697	12.1599 9180
19	14.6460 0157	14.3237 9911	13.7098 3742	13.1339 3940	12.5932 9359
20	15.2272 5213	14.8774 7486	14.2124 0330	13.5903 2634	13.0079 3645
21	15.7929 4612	15.4150 2414	14.6979 7420	14.0291 5995	13.4047 2388
22	16.3434 9987	15.9369 1664	15.1671 2484	14.4511 1533	13.7844 2476
23	16.8793 1861	16.4436 0839	15.6204 1047	14.8568 4167	14.1477 7489
24	17.4007 9670	16.9355 4212	16.0583 6760	15.2469 6314	14.4954 7837
25	17.9083 1795	17.4131 4769	16.4815 1459	15.6220 7994	14.8282 0896
26	18.4022 5592	17.8768 4242	16.8903 5226	15.9827 6918	15.1466 1145
27	18.8829 7413	18.3270 3147	17.2853 6451	16.3295 8575	15.4513 0282
28	19.3508 2640	18.7641 0823	17.6670 1885	16.6630 6322	15.7428 7351
29	19.8061 5708	19.1884 5459	18.0357 6700	16.9837 1463	16.0218 8853
30	20.2493 0130	19.6004 4135	18.3920 4541	17.2920 3330	16.2888 8854
31	20.6805 8520	20.0004 2849	18.7362 7576	17.5884 9356	16.5443 9095
32	21.1003 2623	20.3887 6553	19.0688 6547	17.8735 5150	16.7888 9086
33	21.5088 3332	20.7657 9178	19.3902 0818	18.1476 4567	17.0228 6207
34	21.9064 0712	21.1318 3663	19.7006 8423	18.4111 9776	17.2467 5796
35	22.2933 4026	21.4872 2007	20.0006 6110	18.6646 1323	17.4610 1240
36	22.6699 1753	21.8322 5250	20.2904 9381	18.9082 8195	17.6660 4058
37	23.0364 1609	22.1672 3544	20.5705 2542	19.1425 7880	17.8622 3979
38	23.3931 0568	22.4924 6159	20.8410 8736	19.3678 6423	18.0499 0923
39	23.7402 4884	22.8082 1513	21.1024 9987	19.5844 8484	18.2296 5572
40	24.0781 0106	23.1147 7197	21.3550 7234	19.7927 7388	18.4015 8442
41	24.4069 1101	23.4123 9997	21.5991 0371	19.9930 5181	18.5661 0949
42	24.7269 2069	23.7013 5920	21.8348 8281	20.1856 2674	18.7235 4975
43	25.0383 6563	23.9819 0213	22.0626 8870	20.3707 9494	18.8742 1029
44	25.3414 7507	24.2542 7392	22.2827 9102	20.5488 4129	19.0183 8305
45	25.6364 7209	24.5187 1254	22.4954 5026	20.7200 3970	19.1563 4742
46	25.9235 7381	24.7754 4907	22.7009 1813	20.8846 5356	19.2883 7074
47	26.2029 9154	25.0247 0783	22.8994 3780	21.0429 3612	19.4147 0884
48	26.4749 3094	25.2667 0664	23.0912 4425	21.1951 3088	19.5356 0654
49	26.7395 9215	25.5016 5693	23.2765 6450	21.3414 7200	19.6512 9813
50	26.9971 6998	25.7297 6401	23.4556 1787	21.4821 8462	19.7620 0778

TABLE IV. PRESENT VALUE OF ANNUITY OF 1 PER PERIOD 325

$$a_{\overline{n}|i} = \frac{1 - (1 + i)^{-n}}{i}$$

n	$2\frac{3}{4}$ %	3 %	$3\frac{1}{2}$ %	4 %	$4\frac{1}{2}$ %
51	27.2478 5400	25.9512 2719	23.6286 1630	21.6174 8521	19.8679 5003
52	27.4918 2871	26.1662 3999	23.7957 6454	21.7475 8193	19.9693 3017
53	27.7292 7368	26.3749 9028	23.9572 6043	21.8726 7493	20.0663 4466
54	27.9603 6368	26.5776 6047	24.1132 9510	21.9929 5667	20.1591 8149
55	28.1852 6879	26.7744 2764	24.2640 5323	22.1086 1218	20.2480 2057
56	28.4041 5454	26.9654 6373	24.4097 1327	22.2198 1940	20.3330 3404
57	28.6171 8203	27.1509 3566	24.5504 4760	22.3267 4943	20.4143 8664
58	28.8245 0806	27.3310 0549	24.6864 2281	22.4295 6676	20.4922 3602
59	29.0262 8522	27.5058 3058	24.8177 9981	22.5284 2957	20.5667 3303
60	29.2226 6201	27.6755 6367	24.9447 3412	22.6234 8997	20.6380 2204
61	29.4137 8298	27.8403 5307	25.0673 7596	22.7148 9421	20.7062 4118
62	29.5997 8879	28.0003 4279	25.1858 7049	22.8027 8289	20.7715 2266
63	29.7808 1634	28.1556 7261	25.3003 5796	22.8872 9124	20.8339 9298
64	29.9569 9887	28.3064 7826	25.4109 7388	22.9685 4927	20.8937 7319
65	30.1284 6605	28.4528 9152	25.5178 4916	23.0466 8199	20.9509 7913
66	30.2953 4409	28.5950 4031	25.6211 1030	23.1218 0961	21.0057 2165
67	30.4577 5581	28.7330 4884	25.7208 7951	23.1940 4770	21.0581 0684
68	30.6158 2074	28.8670 3771	25.8172 7489	23.2635 0740	21.1082 3621
69	30.7696 5522	28.9971 2399	25.9104 1052	23.3302 9558	21.1562 0690
70	30.9193 7247	29.1234 2135	26.0003 9664	23.3945 1498	21.2021 1187
71	31.0650 8270	29.2460 4015	26.0873 3975	23.4562 6440	21.2460 4007
72	31.2068 9314	29.3650 8752	26.1713 4275	23.5156 3885	21.2880 7662
73	31.3449 0816	29.4806 6750	26.2525 0508	23.5727 2966	21.3283 0298
74	31.4792 2936	29.5928 8106	26.3309 2278	23.6276 2468	21.3667 9711
75	31.6099 5558	29.7018 2628	26.4066 8868	23.6804 0834	21.4036 3360
76	31.7371 8304	29.8075 9833	26.4798 9244	23.7311 6187	21.4388 8383
77	31.8610 0540	29.9102 8964	26.5506 2072	23.7799 6333	21.4726 1611
78	31.9815 1377	30.0099 8994	26.6189 5721	23.8268 8782	21.5048 9579
79	32.0987 9685	30.1067 8635	26.6849 8281	23.8720 0752	21.5357 8545
80	32.2129 4098	30.2007 6345	26.7487 7567	23.9153 9185	21.5653 4493
81	32.3240 3015	30.2920 0335	26.8104 1127	23.9571 0754	21.5936 3151
82	32.4321 4613	30.3805 8577	26.8699 6258	23.9972 1879	21.6207 0001
83	32.5373 6850	30.4665 8813	26.9275 0008	24.0357 8730	21.6466 0288
84	32.6397 7469	30.5500 8556	26.9830 9186	24.0728 7240	21.6713 9032
85	32.7394 4009	30.6311 5103	27.0368 0373	24.1085 3116	21.6951 1035
86	32.8364 3804	30.7098 5537	27.0886 9926	24.1428 1842	21.7178 0895
87	32.9308 3994	30.7863 6735	27.1388 3986	24.1757 8694	21.7395 3009
88	33.0227 1527	30.8604 5374	27.1872 8489	24.2074 8745	21.7603 1588
89	33.1121 3165	30.9324 7936	27.2340 9168	24.2379 6870	21.7802 0658
90	33.1991 5489	31.0024 0714	27.2793 1564	24.2672 7759	21.7992 4075
91	33.2838 4905	31.0702 9820	27.3230 1028	24.2954 5923	21.8174 5526
92	33.3662 7644	31.1362 1184	27.3652 2732	24.3225 5695	21.8348 8542
93	33.4464 9776	31.2002 0567	27.4060 1673	24.3486 1245	21.8515 6499
94	33.5245 7202	31.2623 3560	27.4454 2680	24.3736 6582	21.8675 2631
95	33.6005 5671	31.3226 5592	27.4835 0415	24.3977 5559	21.8828 0030
96	33.6745 0775	31.3812 1934	27.5202 9387	24.4209 1884	21.8974 1655
97	33.7464 7956	31.4380 7703	27.5558 3948	24.4431 9119	21.9114 0340
98	33.8165 2512	31.4932 7867	27.5901 8308	24.4646 0692	21.9247 8794
99	33.8846 9598	31.5468 7250	27.6233 6529	24.4851 9896	21.9375 9612
100	33.9510 4232	31.5989 0534	27.6554 2540	24.5049 9900	21.9498 5274
∞	36.3636 3636	33.3333 3333	28.5714 2857	25.0000 0000	22.2222 2222

$$a_{\overline{n}|i} = \frac{1 - (1 + i)^{-n}}{i}$$

n	5 %	$5\frac{1}{2}$ %	6 %	7 %	8 %
1	0.9523 8095	0.9478 6730	0.9433 9623	0.9345 7944	0.9259 2593
2	1.8594 1043	1.8463 1971	1.8333 9267	1.8080 1817	1.7832 6475
3	2.7232 4803	2.6979 3338	2.6730 1195	2.6243 1604	2.5770 9699
4	3.5459 5050	3.5051 5012	3.4651 0561	3.3872 1126	3.3121 2684
5	4.3294 7667	4.2702 8448	4.2123 6379	4.1001 9744	3.9927 1004
6	5.0756 9206	4.9955 3031	4.9173 2433	4.7665 3966	4.6228 7966
7	5.7863 7340	5.6829 6712	5.5823 8144	5.3892 8940	5.2063 7006
8	6.4632 1276	6.3345 6599	6.2097 9381	5.9712 9851	5.7466 3894
9	7.1078 2168	6.9521 9525	6.8016 9227	6.5152 3225	6.2468 8791
10	7.7217 3493	7.5376 2583	7.3600 8705	7.0235 8154	6.7100 8140
11	8.3064 1422	8.0925 3633	7.8868 7458	7.4986 7434	7.1389 6426
12	8.8632 5164	8.6185 1785	8.3838 4394	7.9426 8630	7.5360 7802
13	9.3935 7299	9.1170 7853	8.8526 8296	8.3576 5074	7.9037 7594
14	9.8986 4094	9.5896 4790	9.2949 8393	8.7454 6799	8.2442 3698
15	10.3796 5804	10.0375 8094	9.7122 4899	9.1079 1401	8.5594 7869
16	10.8377 6956	10.4621 6203	10.1058 9527	9.4466 4860	8.8513 6916
17	11.2740 6625	10.8646 0856	10.4772 5969	9.7632 2299	9.1216 3811
18	11.6895 8690	11.2460 7447	10.8276 0348	10.0590 8691	9.3718 8714
19	12.0853 2086	11.6076 5352	11.1581 1649	10.3355 9524	9.6035 9920
20	12.4622 1034	11.9503 8249	11.4699 2122	10.5940 1425	9.8181 4741
21	12.8211 5271	12.2752 4406	11.7640 7662	10.8355 2733	10.0168 0316
22	13.1630 0258	12.5831 6973	12.0415 8172	11.0612 4050	10.2007 4366
23	13.4885 7388	12.8750 4240	12.3033 7898	11.2721 8738	10.3710 5895
24	13.7986 4179	13.1516 9895	12.5503 5753	11.4693 3400	10.5287 5828
25	14.0939 4457	13.4139 3266	12.7833 5616	11.6535 8318	10.6747 7619
26	14.3751 8530	13.6624 9541	13.0031 6619	11.8257 7867	10.8099 7795
27	14.6430 3362	13.8980 9991	13.2105 3414	11.9867 0904	10.9351 6477
28	14.8981 2726	14.1214 2172	13.4061 6428	12.1371 1125	11.0510 7849
29	15.1410 7358	14.3331 0116	13.5907 2102	12.2776 7407	11.1584 0601
30	15.3724 5103	14.5337 4517	13.7648 3115	12.4090 4118	11.2577 8334
31	15.5928 1050	14.7239 2907	13.9290 8599	12.5318 1419	11.3497 9939
32	15.8026 7667	14.9041 9817	14.0840 4339	12.6465 5532	11.4349 9944
33	16.0025 4921	15.0750 6936	14.2302 2961	12.7537 9002	11.5138 8837
34	16.1929 0401	15.2370 3257	14.3681 4114	12.8540 0936	11.5869 3367
35	16.3741 9429	15.3905 5220	14.4982 4636	12.9476 7230	11.6545 6822
36	16.5468 5171	15.5360 6843	14.6209 8713	13.0352 0776	11.7171 9279
37	16.7112 8734	15.6739 9851	14.7367 8031	13.1170 1660	11.7751 7851
38	16.8678 9271	15.8047 3793	14.8460 1916	13.1934 7345	11.8288 6899
39	17.0170 4067	15.9286 6154	14.9490 7468	13.2649 2846	11.8785 8240
40	17.1590 8635	16.0461 2469	15.0462 9687	13.3317 0884	11.9246 1333
41	17.2943 6796	16.1574 6416	15.1380 1592	13.3941 2041	11.9672 3457
42	17.4232 0758	16.2629 9920	15.2245 4332	13.4524 4898	12.0066 9867
43	17.5459 1198	16.3630 3242	15.3061 7294	13.5069 6167	12.0432 3951
44	17.6627 7331	16.4578 5063	15.3831 8202	13.5579 0810	12.0770 7362
45	17.7740 6982	16.5477 2572	15.4558 3209	13.6055 2159	12.1084 0150
46	17.8800 6650	16.6329 1537	15.5243 6990	13.6500 2018	12.1374 0880
47	17.9810 1571	16.7136 6386	15.5890 2821	13.6916 0764	12.1642 6741
48	18.0771 5782	16.7902 0271	15.6500 2661	13.7304 7443	12.1891 3649
49	18.1687 2173	16.8627 5139	15.7075 7227	13.7667 9853	12.2121 6341
50	18.2559 2546	16.9315 1790	15.7618 6064	13.8007 4629	12.2334 8464

TABLE IV.   PRESENT VALUE OF ANNUITY OF 1 PER PERIOD   327

$$a_{\overline{n}|i} = \frac{1 - (1 + i)^{-n}}{i}$$

n	5 %	$5\frac{1}{2}$ %	6 %	7 %	8 %
51	18.3389 7663	16.9966 9943	15.8130 7607	13.8324 7317	12.2532 2652
52	18.4180 7298	17.0584 8287	15.8613 9252	13.8621 2446	12.2715 0604
53	18.4934 0284	17.1170 4538	15.9069 7408	13.8898 3594	12.2884 3152
54	18.5651 4556	17.1725 5486	15.9499 7554	13.9157 3453	12.3041 0326
55	18.6334 7196	17.2251 7048	15.9905 4297	13.9399 3881	12.3186 1413
56	18.6985 4473	17.2750 4311	16.0288 1412	13.9625 5964	12.3320 5012
57	18.7605 1879	17.3223 1575	16.0649 1898	13.9837 0059	12.3444 9085
58	18.8195 4170	17.3671 2393	16.0989 8017	14.0034 5850	12.3560 1005
59	18.8757 5400	17.4095 9614	16.1311 1337	14.0219 2383	12.3666 7597
60	18.9292 8952	17.4498 5416	16.1614 2771	14.0391 8115	12.3765 5182
61	18.9802 7574	17.4880 1343	16.1900 2614	14.0553 0949	12.3856 9613
62	19.0288 3404	17.5241 8334	16.2170 0579	14.0703 8270	12.3941 6309
63	19.0750 8003	17.5584 6762	16.2424 5829	14.0844 6981	12.4020 0286
64	19.1191 2384	17.5909 6457	16.2664 7009	14.0976 3534	12.4092 6190
65	19.1610 7033	17.6217 6737	16.2891 2272	14.1099 3957	12.4159 8324
66	19.2010 1936	17.6509 6433	16.3104 9314	14.1214 3885	12.4222 0671
67	19.2390 6606	17.6786 3917	16.3306 5390	14.1321 8584	12.4279 6917
68	19.2753 0101	17.7048 7125	16.3496 7349	14.1422 2976	12.4333 0479
69	19.3098 1048	17.7297 3579	16.3676 1650	14.1516 1660	12.4382 4518
70	19.3426 7665	17.7533 0406	16.3845 4387	14.1603 8934	12.4428 1961
71	19.3739 7776	17.7756 4366	16.4005 1308	14.1685 8817	12.4470 5519
72	19.4037 8834	17.7968 1864	16.4155 7838	14.1762 5063	12.4509 7703
73	19.4321 7937	17.8168 8970	16.4297 9093	14.1834 1180	12.4546 0836
74	19.4592 1845	17.8359 1441	16.4431 9899	14.1901 0449	12.4579 7071
75	19.4849 6995	17.8539 4731	16.4558 4810	14.1963 5933	12.4610 8399
76	19.5094 9519	17.8710 4010	16.4677 8123	14.2022 0498	12.4639 6665
77	19.5328 5257	17.8872 4180	16.4790 3889	14.2076 6821	12.4666 3579
78	19.5550 9768	17.9025 9887	16.4896 5933	14.2127 7403	12.4691 0721
79	19.5762 8351	17.9171 5532	16.4996 7862	14.2175 4582	12.4713 9557
80	19.5964 6048	17.9309 5291	16.5091 3077	14.2220 0544	12.4735 1441
81	19.6156 7665	17.9440 3120	16.5180 4790	14.2261 7331	12.4754 7631
82	19.6339 7776	17.9564 2768	16.5264 6028	14.2300 6851	12.4772 9288
83	19.6514 0739	17.9681 7789	16.5343 9649	14.2337 0889	12.4789 7489
84	19.6680 0704	17.9793 1554	16.5418 8348	14.2371 1111	12.4805 3230
85	19.6838 1623	17.9898 7255	16.5489 4668	14.2402 9076	12.4819 7436
86	19.6988 7260	17.9998 7919	16.5556 1008	14.2432 6239	12.4833 0959
87	19.7132 1200	18.0093 6416	16.5618 9630	14.2460 3962	12.4845 4592
88	19.7268 6857	18.0183 5466	16.5678 2670	14.2486 3516	12.4856 9066
89	19.7398 7483	18.0268 7645	16.5734 2141	14.2510 6089	12.4867 5061
90	19.7522 6174	18.0349 5398	16.5786 9944	14.2533 2794	12.4877 3205
91	19.7640 5880	18.0426 1041	16.5836 7872	14.2554 4667	12.4886 4079
92	19.7752 9410	18.0498 6769	16.5883 7615	14.2574 2680	12.4894 8221
93	19.7859 9438	18.0567 4662	16.5928 0769	14.2592 7738	12.4902 6131
94	19.7961 8512	18.0632 6694	16.5969 8839	14.2610 0690	12.4909 8269
95	19.8058 9059	18.0694 4734	16.6009 3244	14.2626 2327	12.4916 5064
96	19.8151 3390	18.0753 0553	16.6046 5325	14.2641 3390	12.4922 6911
97	19.8239 3705	18.0808 5833	16.6081 6344	14.2655 4570	12.4928 4177
98	19.8323 2100	18.0861 2164	16.6114 7494	14.2668 6514	12.4933 7201
99	19.8403 0571	18.0911 1055	16.6145 9900	14.2680 9826	12.4938 6297
100	19.8479 1020	18.0958 3939	16.6175 4623	14.2692 5071	12.4943 1757
∞	20.0000 0000	18.1818 1818	16.6666 6667	14.2857 1428	12.5000 0000

answers to the odd numbered exercises

CHAPTER I

1.2.

1. See whether there is a button in each button hole.
3. For instance, one can state that there is a 1–1 correspondence between the set of boys' and the set of girls' arms (where it is assumed, of course, that no girl has an arm missing).
5. The word "Joe" designates the individual named "Joe."
7. Is "fly" a verb or a noun?
9. Is "hide" a verb or a noun? What does "old" modify?

1.3.

3. Five others.

1.4.

1. Five.
3. See preceding text.

CHAPTER 2

2.1.

1. (a) ❘ ✶.
   (b) ⊥ ☐.
   (c) ✶ ⊥.
   (d) ⊐ ⊐.
✶. (b) ❘ ☐ ❘ ⊐.
   (c) ❘❘ ⊐ ☐ ⊥.

2.2.

1. See text.

✶. By answering the questions ❘❘ − ✶ = what and ✶ − ⊥ = what, we obtain the answer ❘✶. This could be denoted by encircling the filled in portion. Thus ❘❘ − ✶ = ⊗ and ✶ − ⊥ = Ⓘ.

(b) ⊥ − ⊥ = ⊡.
    ⊐ − ✶ = Ⓘ.
(c) ❘ ✶ − ⊐ = ⊟.
    ⊥ − ⊥ = ⊡.

329

1□. (a) ✳ ⊐ ⊥
    ⊥ ✳ ✳
    ‾‾‾‾‾
    |□ ⊐ .

✳ + (⊐) = | ⊥.
⊐ + (□) = ⊐.
⊥ + (|) = ✳.

(b) ✳ □ |
    | ⊥ ⊐
    ‾‾‾‾‾
    | ⊥ ⊥ .

⊐ + (⊥) = ||.
✳ + (⊥) = |□.
⊥ + (|) = ✳.

(c) ⊐ ⊥ ✳ |
    ⊐ ✳
    ‾‾‾‾‾‾
    ⊐ | ✳ ✳ .

✳ + (✳) = ||.
|□ + (✳) = |✳.
| + (|) = ⊥.
□ + (⊐) = ⊐.

2.3.

1. (a) |✳ ⊐ ⊐.
   (b) ⊥ □ □ ✳.
   (c) |✳ |⊐.
   (d) || □ ✳.

3. To find a numeral for the product of a given number by |□, simply annex a '□' at the right end of the standard numeral of the given number.

2.4.

1. *Hint:* Show first that $a \cdot a > a \cdot b$.
3. By definition.
5. *Hint:* Assume that A is a nonempty set which does not contain a first element. Then $1 \notin A$ for otherwise A would have a first element. Similarly $2 \notin A$, etc. Furthermore if $1, 2, \ldots, k \notin A$ then $k + 1 \notin A$. Then apply the principle of mathematical induction.

2.5.

1. Review definition of multiplication in terms of piles of stones and look at rectangular array above exercises.
3. If $a/0 = b$ then $a = 0 \cdot b = 0$ which is a contradiction unless $a = 0$. If $a = 0$ then $a = 0 \cdot b$ for every number b and so the quotient would not be unique. In the division algorithm if $b = 0$ then there exists no q unless $a = 0$ and in this case q is not unique.
5. Let $q = b + 1$ in Exercise 4. Then $aq \geq b + 1 > b$.

2.6.

1. (a) $q = 4$ and $r = 3$.
   (b) $q = 43$ and $r = 6$.
   (c) $q = 437$ and $r = 4$.
   (d) $q = 5$ and $r = 0$.

   (e) $q = 0$ and $r = 0$.
   (f) $q = 2$ and $r = 11$.
   (g) $q = 29$ and $r = 2$.
   (h) $q = 291$ and $r = 8$.

3. Begin with division by numbers whose standard numeral contains two digits and first restrict attention to those with units digit 0. Then the process is essentially the same as dividing by numbers whose standard numeral contains one digit. Then, when dividing by a number such as 47, one usually uses 40 as a trial divisor and if this results in too large a quotient it is modified accordingly. One extends the process similarly to numbers whose standard numeral contains three digits, etc.

2.7.

First Set of Exercises

1. (a)   847
         39
     ‾‾‾‾
   24000
    1200
     210
    7200
     360
      63
   ‾‾‾‾
   33033

(b)   2615
       934
  ‾‾‾‾‾‾
 1800000
  540000
    9000
    4500
   60000
   18000
     300
     150
    8000
    2400
      40
      20
  ‾‾‾‾‾‾
 2442410

3.

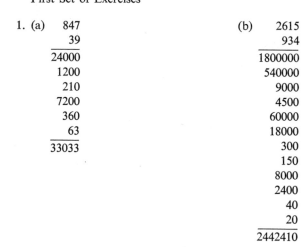

5. (a)   23
      32
    ‾‾‾
    736

(b)   67
     59
   ‾‾‾‾
   3953

7. (a) $21 = 1 \cdot 21$ Since
    $21 = 1 \cdot 21$ $19 = 16 + 2 + 1$
    $42 = 2 \cdot 21$ then
    $84 = 4 \cdot 21$ $19 \cdot 21 = 336 + 42 + 21 = 399$
    $168 = 8 \cdot 21$
    $336 = 16 \cdot 21$
    Similarly $53 \cdot 38 = 2014 = 38 \cdot 53$
    (b) Look at the last two parts of 7(a).

Second Set of Exercises

1. $q = 136$ and $r = 9$.
3. $q = 136$ and $r = 9$.

CHAPTER 3

3.1.

First Set of Exercises

3. All of them.
5. Theorem 1.
7. Even.

Second Set of Exercises

1. *Hint:* If $bc \leq 120$ and $b > 11$, then $c < 11$.
3. Sometimes.
5. 22.
7. (a) 11.
   (b) 73.

3.2.

1. *Hint:* If $b < c$ then $ab < ac$.

3.3.

First Set of Exercises

1. 13.
3. 10, 10, 1000, 10,000.
5. 27.
7. 3.

Second Set of Exercises

3. $(11123)_8$.
5. $(4211)_8$.
7. $(243546)_8$.
9. $(155)_6$.
11. $(14505)_6$.
13. $(5330T)_{12}$.

CHAPTER 4

4.1.

First Set of Exercises

1. (a) Exclusive.
   (b) Inclusive.
   (c) Inclusive.
   (d) Inclusive.
   (e) Inclusive.
3. (a) $A \cup B = B$.
   (b) $A \cap B = A$.
   (c) $\tilde{B} \subset \tilde{A}$.
5. $A \subset C$.
7. There are sixteen distinct subsets.

Second Set of Exercises

1. Some chickens understand French.
3. Yes.
5. No.
7. My gardener is very old.
9. All pawnbrokers are honest.

4.2.

1. Inconsistent.
3. Let P, N, Q be the sets of tosses on which the pennies, nickels, and quarters, respectively, turn up heads. Then $c(P \cup N) = c(P) + c(N) - c(P \cap N) = 70 + 50 - 31 = 89$. Hence $\overline{c(P \cup N)} = c(\tilde{P} \cap \tilde{N}) = 11$. Since the penny and the nickel are both tails on only 11 tosses, all three coins cannot be tails on more than 11 tosses.
   Also $c(N \cup Q) = 50 + 56 - 28 = 78$. Thus $\overline{c(P \cup N)} = c(\tilde{P} \cap \tilde{N}) = 11$ and $\overline{c(N \cup Q)} = c(\tilde{N} \cap \tilde{Q}) = 22$. Now $c(\tilde{P} \cup \tilde{Q} \cup \tilde{N}) = c(\tilde{P}) + c(\tilde{Q}) + c(\tilde{N}) - c(\tilde{P} \cap \tilde{Q}) - c(\tilde{P} \cap \tilde{N}) - c(\tilde{Q} \cap \tilde{N}) + c(\tilde{P} \cap \tilde{Q} \cap \tilde{N}) = 30 + 50 + 44 - c(\tilde{P} \cap \tilde{Q}) - 11 - 22 + c(\tilde{P} \cap \tilde{Q} \cap \tilde{N}) = 91 - c(\tilde{P} \cup \tilde{Q}) + c(\tilde{P} \cap \tilde{Q} \cap \tilde{N}) \leq 91$, since $c(\tilde{P} \cap \tilde{Q} \cap \tilde{N}) \leq c(\tilde{P} \cap \tilde{Q})$. Therefore $\overline{c(\tilde{P} \cup \tilde{Q} \cup \tilde{N})} = c(P \cap Q \cap N) \geq 9$.

CHAPTER 5

5.1.

1. Yes, No.
3. Yes, Yes.
5. (a) Yes.   (b) Yes.   (c) Yes.
7. (a) No.   (b) No.   (c) No.
9. (a) No.   (b) Yes.   (c) No.
11. (a) No.   (b) No.   (c) No.
13. (a) Yes.   (b) Yes.   (c) No.

5.2.

    5. No. When $a \geq b$.

    7. *Hint:* Add $a + b$ and $\bar{a} + \bar{b}$.

    9. No.

5.3.

    1. *Hint:* $a \cdot 0 = a \cdot (0 + 0)$.

    5. A1, A2, M1, M2, D1.

    7. Yes.

    9. A1, A2, A3, A5, M1, M2, M3, M5, D1, I1, I2.

5.4.

First Set of Exercises

    3. Refer to Example 4.

    5. $\frac{9}{10}$ by Example 6.

    7. *Hint:* Multiply each equation by a suitable factor.

    9. They are equal and different from zero.

Second Set of Exercises

    1. $c < 0$ implies $\bar{c} > 0$ so $a\bar{c} > b\bar{c}$, $a\bar{c} - b\bar{c} > 0$, $\overline{a\bar{c} - b\bar{c}} < 0$, $\overline{a\bar{c}} - \overline{b\bar{c}} < 0$, $ac - bc < 0$, $ac < bc$.

    3. *Hint:* Show $\bar{a} = \bar{1} \cdot a$ and apply Exercise 1.

    5. *Hint:* Compare $a \cdot a$ and $b \cdot b$ with $a \cdot b$.

CHAPTER 6

6.1.

    3. Subtraction is an operation on numbers and is independent of the numerals used to denote them.

    5. There is no solution.

    7. The solution set is $\{0\}$.

    9. $1 + x$.

6.2.

    1. $x = 4, y = 1$.

    3. For any rational number t; $x = t, y = 2t + 4$ is a solution.

    5. $x = 1, y = 2, z = -3$.

    7. $x = 2, y = 3, z = 1$.

    9. $x = 2, y = 0, z = 1, w = \frac{1}{2}$.

6.3.

    1. 13212.

    3. $\frac{21}{5}$ and $\frac{14}{5}$ ft.

    5. 20 nickels and 40 dimes.

    7. 56.

    9. 90 years old.

11. $5\frac{5}{11}$ min after $1:00$ o'clock.

13. 720.

15. $160.00.

17. 300 ft.

19. 4 pounds.

21. $1.05 and 5¢.

23. $111\frac{1}{9}$ yd.

25. 7¢ to the first and 1¢ to the second.

27. The mule was carrying 5 bales, the horse 7.

29. The man who bought the pawn ticket.

6.4.

1. 18 pounds of 20¢ and 6 pounds of 40¢ candy.

3. 24,000.

5. 10 hr.

7. $1\frac{3}{5}$ gal.

9. $7\frac{6}{7}\%$

11. $1\frac{34}{71}$ hr.

13. A should receive $2.24\frac{14}{39}$, B should receive $1.60\frac{10}{39}$, and C should receive $1.15\frac{15}{39}$.

15. 19 hr.

17. $180.

19. 675 men.

21. 49 days.

23. $\frac{1}{6}$ @ 9¢, $\frac{1}{6}$ @ 12¢, $\frac{1}{2}$ @ 15¢, $\frac{1}{6}$ @ 18¢, is one possibility.

25. For each $4 hog he sells, selling one for $6 and 3 hogs each for $10 is one possibility.

27. 3 hogs, 7 pigs, and 90 chickens.

29. $40 for A, $30 for B, $24 for C.

31. $30.

33. $1.44.

35. 65.

6.5.

1. $S = 2$, $T = 4$, and $O = 8$.

3. $O = 0$, $M = 1$, $Y = 2$, $E = 5$, $N = 6$, $D = 7$, $R = 8$, and $S = 9$.

5. $B = 2$, $A = 4$, $D = 5$, $E = 7$, and $C = 8$.

7. Solution 1: $R = 0$, $E = 1$, $O = 2$, $F = 4$, $I = 5$, $V = 7$, $N = 8$, and $U = 9$. Solution 2: $R = 0$, $E = 1$, $O = 2$, $F = 3$, $V = 4$, $I = 5$, $N = 6$, and $U = 8$.

9. In all cases $N = 1$, $T = 4$, $E = 7$, $H = 8$, and $S = 9$. Solution 1: $V = 0$, $R = 2$, and $O = 5$. Solution 2: $V = 2$, $R = 3$, and $O = 5$. Solution 3: $O = 2$, $V = 3$, and $R = 5$. Solution 4: $O = 2$, $V = 5$, and $R = 6$.

6.6.

3. The number of digits in the standard numeral of n written in base 3.

5. 2, 8, 4, respectively.

9. 4.

6.7.

1. We would have a magic square which totals 21.

3.

4	19	16
25	13	1
10	7	22

5. (a) Fill 5 quart can and pour into 3 quart can. Empty 3 quart can and pour remaining two quarts from 5 quart can into it. Then fill 5 quart can and use it to fill rest of 3 quart can.

(b) Fill 3 quart can and pour into 5 quart can. Fill 3 quart can and pour two quarts from it into 5 quart can. Empty 5 quart can. Pour remainder of 3 quart can into 5 quart can. Fill 3 quart can and then pour into 5 quart can.

7. Yes. Two cannibals cross and one returns. Two cannibals cross and one returns. Two missionaries cross and one missionary and one cannibal return. Two missionaries cross and the cannibal brings the boat back. Two cannibals cross and one returns. Two cannibals cross.

9. *Hint:* Note that both tribes will give the same answer to the question "What tribe are you from?"

11. His son's.

13. Fifth from the top.

15. Let us denote the couples by 1, 2, and 3, respectively, and suppose that Wife 3 is the one who can paddle.

Wife 3 takes Wives 1 and 2 over in two trips and brings the boat back. Then Husbands 1 and 2 go over and Couple 2 returns. Then Couple 3 goes over and Couple 1 returns. Then Husband's 1 and 2 go over and Wife 3 returns. Wife 3 brings over Wives 1 and 2 in two trips.

17. Denote the Manufacturers by $1, 2, \ldots, 10$. Take one coin from Manufacturer 1, two coins from Manufacturer 2, $\ldots$, on up to ten coins from Manufacturer 10, and weigh these on the calibrated scale. The coins should weigh 55 ounces. If the actual weight is off by $\frac{3}{10}$ of an ounce, then, Manufacturer 3 makes the defective coins, etc.

CHAPTER 7

7.1.

1. (a) Finite.
   (b) Infinite.
   (c) Infinite.
   (d) Finite.
   (e) Finite.
   (f) Cannot be determined.

(g) Either the existence of the earth will extend over an infinite number of years in which case the answer is indeterminate, or the earth will exist for only a finite number of years in which case the answer is finite.

3. *Hint:* Suppose the tortoise goes 1 yd per second and Achilles goes 10 yd per second, then you should be able to calculate how long it will take Achilles to catch the tortoise.

   To explain the paradox note that the time it takes Achilles to catch the tortoise has been broken up into an infinite number of pieces. This tends to make one think that the time is infinite because it has an infinite number of parts. Actually, as noted earlier in the text with the boy eating ice cream, the total remains the same no matter how it is subdivided.

7.2.

   1. No.

   3. (a) $\frac{2}{3}$.   (c) $\frac{1240}{99}$.

     (b) $\frac{7}{9}$.   (d) $\frac{653667}{99900}$.

   5. No.

   7. No.

   9. (a) 7.

     (b) 3.

  11. 9.

7.3.

   1. Irrational.

   7. No.

   9. No.

  11. Yes.

7.4.

   1. The empty set, a set of points whose coordinates form an open interval, an open ray.

   3. A closed interval or the union of two disjoint closed intervals.

   5. (a) $x < 3$, the labels of all points on the open ray to the left of the point whose label is 3.

     (b) $x < -\frac{7}{2}$, the labels of all points on the open ray to the left of the point whose label is $-\frac{7}{2}$.

     (c) $x \geq 1$, the labels of all points on the ray to the right of and including the point whose label is 1.

     (d) $x < 0$ or $x > \frac{1}{6}$, the labels of all points on the open ray to the left of the point whose label is 0 together with the labels of all points on the open ray to the right of the point whose label is $\frac{1}{6}$.

   7. All x such that $x < \frac{4}{3}$.

7.5.

   1. Yes. Pair $a \in A$ with $2a$ which is in B.

   3. Think of the paint as forming a 1 ft cube. Then it covers 1 sq. ft. Cut it in half and put the halves side by side and it will cover 2 sq ft, continuation of the process would theoretically cover an infinite number of square feet.

7.6.

1. (a) $\frac{1}{17}$ by $\frac{1}{595}$.
   (b) $\frac{3}{35}$ by $\frac{1}{420}$.
3. (a) $\frac{1423}{7140}$.
   (b) $\frac{1}{20}$.
5. (a) $10001.\dot{0}1\dot{1}$.
   (b) $122.\dot{1}0\dot{2}1\dot{2}$.
   (c) $23.3\dot{0}$.
7. $.\dot{2}$.
9. (a) $\frac{1}{2}$.
   (b) 1.
   (c) $\frac{5}{8}$.
11. $a = 85$ and $b = 139$.
13. 77, 91, 143, 169.

CHAPTER 8

8.1.

1. (a) $\frac{1}{16}$.   (d) 2.
   (b) -27.   (e) $\frac{6}{5}$.
   (c) 1.
3. (a) $ab^{-1} - b^{-2}$.
   (b) $1 - a^{-1}b^{-1}$.
   (c) $b^{-1} - a^{-1}b^{-2}$.
   (d) $a^{-1}b^{-3} - a^{-2}b^{-4}$.
   (e) $a^{-2}b^{-2} - c^{-2}$.
5. (a) 4.
   (b) $-\frac{1}{27}$.
   (c) $(a^2 + b^2)/(a + b)$.
   (d) x^2y^2.
   (e) $(xy)/(y - x)$.
7. Yes.
9. (a) $\frac{9031}{1961}$.
   (b) $\frac{37}{41}$.

8.2.

1. *Hint:* Consider cases (1) $a \leq 0$, $b > 0$ (2) $b \leq 0$ (3) $a > 0$.
3. *Hint* for first part: Show that the squares are the same and that both are positive. The desired numeral is $7\sqrt{2}$.
5. $\sqrt{x}$ if $x > 0$.
7. *Hint:* See hint in Exercise 3.

8.3.

1. *Hint:* If a is real then $a^2 \geq 0$.
3. For instance, $a = b = -1$.

CHAPTER 9

9.1.

1. P and Q are the same point. P and Q are distinct points. This is nonsense.
3. They are not the same. They may or may not be the same.
5. The empty set, a point, the given line segment.
7. A line is not a distance.

9.2.

1. The point C on the segment $\overline{AB}$ is the midpoint of segment $\overline{AB}$ if $d(A, C) = d(B, C)$.
3. 7.

9.3.

1. The empty set, a line, a plane.
3. It represents the intersection of two distinct planes.
5. Floor tiles, window panes, room dividers, linoleum patterns, wallpaper pattern, etc.
7. One possibility would be as shown in Fig. A.1.

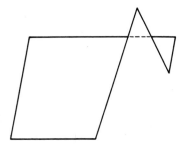

Figure A.I

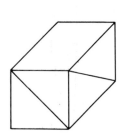

Figure A.2

9. 6.

9.4.

1. The edges of a table; the intersection of a wall and the ceiling; and the intersection of the same wall and the floor.
3. The diagonals on two adjacent faces of a box (see Fig. A.2).
5. Yes.
7. Yes.
9. No.

9.5.

3. (a) 15.
   (b) 9.
   (c) 20.
   (d) 14.

   (e) $\frac{5}{2} nr$
   (f) 36.
   (g) 48.
   (h) 42.

5. 52.
7. Yes. Yes.

9.6.

1. (a) 30.   (c) $\frac{10}{3}$.
   (b) 4320.   (d) $\frac{1}{929280}$.
3. (a) $\frac{50}{3}$¢
   (b) 50¢.
5. (a) 16.   (c) $\frac{1}{4}$.
   (b) 4096   (d) $\frac{1}{9}$.
7. The area of T is 3^2 times the area of S. Yes.

9.7.

1. The face of an orange slice, wheels, rings, etc.
5. Let P be the center of the circle and S and T points on the circle. Then $\overline{ST}$ is a diameter if $P \in \overline{ST}$. But then $d(S, T) = d(S, P) + d(P, T) = r + r = 2r$.

9.8.

First Set of Exercises.

1. The empty set, a point, a ray, a line segment.
3. No. No.
5. No, not according to our definition.

Second Set of Exercises

1. No. No. $0° <$ measure of an angle $< 360°$.
3. Draw a circle with center at A whose interior contains no other vertex of the polygon. Then any point which is in both the interior of the circle and the interior of the polygon will give the proper angle.
7. $360°$, $360°$, $360°$.

9.9.

1. Balls, blocks, pyramids, ice cream cones, etc.
3. A triangular region. A tetrahedron. A pyramid with a square base.
5. Yes (a triangular prism). Yes (an octogonal prism).

9.10.

1. (a) 6.   (c) $\frac{2}{9}$.
  (b) 10368.
3. The volume of $T = 27$ times the volume of S. Multiplying the lengths of the edges of a box by k, multiplies the volume by k^3.
5. It is multiplied by 8.
7. 80 cu ft.
9. 18.

9.11.

1. (a) 1.
  (b) 3.
  (c) 0.

CHAPTER 10

10.1.

1. (a) 5.
   (b) 7.
   (c) 0.
   (d) 4.
   (e) −4.
   (f) −5.
3. $2 < x < 4$.
5. $x \geq 3$.
7. "x if $x \geq 0$ or $-x$ if $x < 0$," e.g.
9. (a) Always.
   (b) Never.
   (c) Always.

10.2.

1. (a)   3.568.
   (b) 213.009.
   (c)   .600.
   (d)   .142.
   (e)   1.234.
   (f) 18.036.
3. $\frac{1}{300}$. $\frac{1}{99}$. $1\frac{1}{99}\%$.
5. The height of the building is between 394 and 406 ft.
7. No.

10.3.

1. (a) 17.3.
   (b) 5367.0.
3. No.
5. 0.

10.4.

1. 963.2875 sq ft is a lower bound and 969.5575 sq ft is an upper bound. 966.42 sq ft with error less than 3.2 sq ft.
3. If $|b - a| < e$ then $|3b - 3a| = 3|b - a| < 3e$.
5. $e_1 + e_2 + \cdots + e_n$.

10.5.

1. 100,000.
3. $16.
5. About $5\frac{1}{2}$ miles.

CHAPTER II

11.2.

1. $225.
3. 10%.
5. $2500 at 3% and $3500 at 5%.
7. 3%.

11.3.

1. $5\frac{5}{9}$%.
3. $8400.
5. 55.9%.
7. At discount one pays r% of S dollars while at simple interest one pays r% of P dollars and $P < S$.

11.4.

1. (a) $1120.
   (b) About $1123.60.
   (c) About $1125.51.
   (d) About $1126.49.
3. About $3423.30.

11.5.

1. (a) About $4116.29.
   (b) About $4015.28.
   (c) About $3374.31.
   (d) About $4219.84.

11.6.

1. (a) About $4888.64.
   (b) About $6377.50.
3. About $680.95.
5. About $385.63.
7. About $88.23.
9. About $3777.66.

11.7.

1. j is between 33% and 36%, converted monthly.
3. j is between 18% and 21%, converted monthly.
5. No.

CHAPTER 12

12.1.

1.

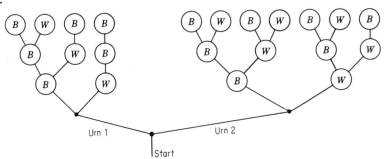

3. (a) 6.
   (b) 3.
   (c) 0.
   (d) 3.
   (e) 6.
   (f) 2.
5. Denote the novels by $N1, N2, \ldots, N5$; reads by R; does not read by D.

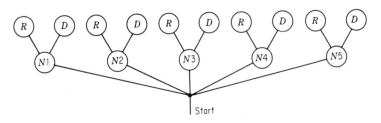

12.2.

First Set of Exercises

1. 720 weeks.
3. 6.
5. 840.

Second Set of Exercises

1. 960.
3. 34650.
5. 2177280.
7. 792.
9. 3115.
11. 10080.

12.3.

    1.

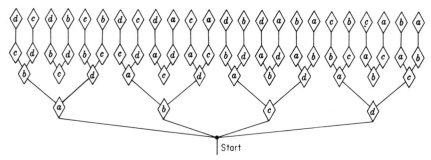

    3. 900.
    5. (a) 1099.
       (b) 2800.
    7. 60,060.
    9. 66,660.

12.4.

    1. 24.
    3. 32.
    5. 9,765,625.

12.5.

    1. (a) $\frac{1}{4}$.
       (b) $\frac{1}{4}$.
       (c) $\frac{1}{2}$.
    3. 7.
    5. $\frac{3}{55}$.
    7. No.
    9. $\frac{1}{6}$.
  11. (a) $\frac{5}{6}$.
      (b) $\frac{1}{6}$.

12.6.

    1. (a) $\frac{1}{3}$.
       (b) $\frac{3}{11}$.
    3. $\frac{20}{29}$.
    5. $\frac{9}{25}$.

12.7.

    1. 2 to 13.
    3. $\frac{1}{3}$.

CHAPTER 13

13.2.

1. (a) 70.
   (b) $70\frac{14}{15} \approx 70.93$.
   (c) $56\frac{1}{8} \approx 56.12$.
   (d) 66.34.

13.3.

1. (a) Median = 70.5, modes = 64 and 81.
   (b) Median = 72, mode = 68.
   (c) Median = 56, mode = 78.
   (d) Median = 68.84, mode = 65.34.
3. (a) 62 is a lower quartile, 70.5 is the median, and 78 is an upper quartile.
   (b) 68 is a lower quartile, 72 is the median, and 78 is an upper quartile.
   (c) 48 is a lower quartile, 56 is the median, and 78 is an upper quartile.
   (d) 52.34 is a lower quartile, 68.84 is the median, and 80.34 is an upper quartile.
5. (a) (i) 6.5 and 6.
         (ii) 8.5 and 4.
         (iii) 10 and $3\sqrt{11}$.
   (b) In each of these three cases the geometric mean is less than or equal to the arithmetic mean.
   (c) It can be proved in general for positive numbers.
7. No.

13.4.

1. (a) About 9.43.
   (b) About 16.08.
   (c) About 16.54 but answers could differ in second decimal place with varying procedures.
   (d) About 15.70.

CHAPTER 14

14.1.

3. The answers are not unique.
5. For example, $(\frac{3}{2}, \frac{5}{2})$.

7.

	$(2,3)$	$(3,2)$	$(-1,2)$	$(-1,-2)$	$(1,2)$	$(0,0)$	$(\frac{3}{2},-\frac{1}{2})$	(π,π)
$(2,3)$	$\cdots$	$\sqrt{2}$	$\sqrt{10}$	$\sqrt{34}$	$\sqrt{2}$	$\sqrt{13}$	$\frac{5}{2}\sqrt{2}$	$\sqrt{(\pi-2)^2+(\pi-3)^2}$
$(3,2)$	$\sqrt{2}$	$\cdots$	4	$4\sqrt{2}$	2	$\sqrt{13}$	$\frac{1}{2}\sqrt{34}$	$\sqrt{(\pi-3)^2+(\pi-2)^2}$
$(-1,2)$	$\sqrt{10}$	4	$\cdots$	4	2	$\sqrt{5}$	$\frac{5}{2}\sqrt{2}$	$\sqrt{(\pi+1)^2+(\pi-2)^2}$
$(-1,-2)$	$\sqrt{34}$	$4\sqrt{2}$	4	$\cdots$	$2\sqrt{5}$	$\sqrt{5}$	$\frac{1}{2}\sqrt{34}$	$\sqrt{(\pi+1)^2+(\pi+2)^2}$
$(1,2)$	$\sqrt{2}$	2	2	$2\sqrt{5}$	$\cdots$	$\sqrt{5}$	$\frac{1}{2}\sqrt{26}$	$\sqrt{(\pi-1)^2+(\pi-2)^2}$
$(0,0)$	$\sqrt{13}$	$\sqrt{13}$	$\sqrt{5}$	$\sqrt{5}$	$\sqrt{5}$	$\cdots$	$\frac{1}{2}\sqrt{10}$	$\pi\sqrt{2}$
$(\frac{3}{2},-\frac{1}{2})$	$\frac{5}{2}\sqrt{2}$	$\frac{1}{2}\sqrt{34}$	$\frac{5}{2}\sqrt{2}$	$\frac{1}{2}\sqrt{34}$	$\frac{1}{2}\sqrt{26}$	$\frac{1}{2}\sqrt{10}$	$\cdots$	$\sqrt{(\pi-\frac{3}{2})^2+(\pi+\frac{1}{2})^2}$
(π,π)	$\sqrt{(\pi-2)^2+(\pi-3)^2}$	$\sqrt{(\pi-3)^2+(\pi-2)^2}$	$\sqrt{(\pi+1)^2+(\pi-2)^2}$	$\sqrt{(\pi+1)^2+(\pi+2)^2}$	$\sqrt{(\pi-1)^2+(\pi-2)^2}$	$\pi\sqrt{2}$	$\sqrt{(\pi-\frac{3}{2})^2+(\pi+\frac{1}{2})^2}$	$\cdots$

9. The set of all ordered pairs $(a, -2)$ where a is a real number.

11. The set of all ordered pairs $(-2, a)$ where a is a real number.

13. The set of all ordered pairs (a, b) where $a = 0$ or $b = 0$.

15. The set of all ordered pairs (x, y) such that $\sqrt{x^2 + y^2} = 3$. (Since we have agreed that for nonnegative real numbers a, $\sqrt{a} \geq 0$, this equation is equivalent to the equation $x^2 + y^2 = 9$.)

14.2.

1. $A \times B = \{(1, 1), (1, 2), (1, 3), (2, 1), (2, 2), (2, 3)\}$ and $A \times C = \{(1, 3), (1, 4), (1, 5), (2, 3), (2, 4), (2, 5)\}$. Yes.

3. We give only the correspondence as the domain and range are clear. For example, $f_1(1) = 3$, $f_1(2) = 3$; $f_2(1) = 3$, $f_2(2) = 4$; $f_3(1) = 4$, $f_3(2) = 4$; $f_4(1) = 3$, $f_4(2) = 5$; $f_5(1) = 5$, $f_5(2) = 5$; $f_6(1) = 4$, $f_6(2) = 5$.

5. $A \times B$ is the set of ordered pairs (a, b) where a is 1, 10, or an integer between 1 and 10 and b is a letter in the English alphabet. $B \times A$ is the set of all ordered pairs (b, a) where b and a are defined as in the preceding sentence. Yes, e.g., match (a, b) with (b, a).

7. The set of integers. 2, 5, 3, 2, -2, -4, 3.

9. (a) For example, $f(\frac{1}{2})$ is not unique.
   (b) This is not a function on the rational numbers since the correspondence given depends on the numeral denoting the number.
   (c) The domain is not given.
   (d) The range does not include all the reals and so the function is *into*, not *onto*, *R*.

14.3.

1.   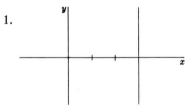   No. (Regarding y as a function of x.)

3.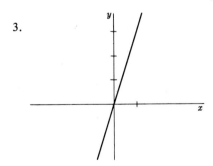

5.

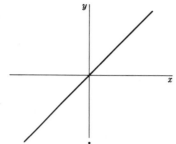

7.

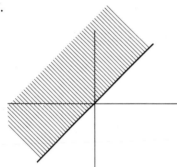

9.

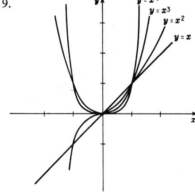

CHAPTER 15

15.2.

3. The coordinates of the points:
   (a) (0, 0) and (2, 0).
   (b) On the segment from (0, 0) to (2, 0), and (1, 1).
   (c) On the segment from (2, 0) to (1, 1), and (0, 0).

(d) On the segment from (0, 0) to (1, 1), and (2, 0).

(e) (1, 1) and (2, 0).

(f) (0, 0) and (2, 0).

15.3.

3. If points p and q are in the intersection of some sets, they are in each of those sets. Since those sets are convex, the segment from p to q is in each set, and, hence, in the intersection.

9. Yes, the whole plane. Yes, e.g., a line.

15.4.

1. The vertices are (1, 1) and (1, 2).

(b) Minimum at (1, 1).

(c) Maximum at (1, 2).

(d) Minimum at (1, 1), maximum at (1, 2).

3. (a) (0, 0, 0), (1, 1, 1).

(b) (0, 0, 0), (1, 1, 1).

(c) The points in the feasible set where $z = 0$. The points in the feasible set where $z = 1$.

(d) The points in the feasible set where y and $z = 0$. The points in the feasible set where y and $z = 1$.

15.5.

1. A maximum profit of $105 results from making no oatmeal cookies and 420 boxes of sugar cookies.

3. No. As y gets larger x might get smaller. Thus the largest value of $.20x + .25y$ might not occur at the largest value of y.

5. $x = 7, y = 7$.

7. 16 hr and 40 min on his notes and 6 hr and 40 min on his library materials.

index

351